LA ESTATUA DE PROMETEO

TEATRO DEL SIGLO DE ORO
Ediciones críticas 7

Dirigidas por KURT Y ROSWITHA REICHENBERGER
En colaboración con DON W. CRUICKSHANK / ALBERTO PORQUERAS

Consejo de Dirección:
DÁMASO ALONSO
CHARLES V. AUBRUN
JOSÉ MANUEL BLECUA
JEAN CANAVAGGIO
MANUEL CRIADO DE VAL
IGNACIO ELIZALDE
HANS FLASCHE
ALFREDO HERMENEGILDO
EVERETT W. HESSE
JOSÉ ANTONIO MARAVALL
FRANCO MEREGALLI
ALEXANDER A. PARKER
JUAN MANUEL ROZAS
FRANCISCO RUIZ RAMÓN
MANUEL SITO ALBA
ANGEL VALBUENA BRIONES

Pedro Calderón de la Barca

LA ESTATUA DE PROMETEO

A critical edition by
Margaret Rich Greer
With a Study of the Music by
Louise K. Stein

Kassel Edition Reichenberger 1986

Printed with the generous assistance of Princeton University

Figures 2–1 to 2–7 and 8–8 are reprinted courtesy of the Biblioteca Nacional, Madrid. The fotos were taken by Gerardo Kurtz, Madrid. Figure 7–1 is reprinted by kind permission of the Centre Nationale de la Recherche Scientifique, Paris. Our thanks are also due to the Biblioteca Municipal, Madrid, for the permission to reproduce figures 8–2 and 8–4 to 8–9 from the manuscript.

ISBN 3-923593-27-9

Lektorat und wissenschaftliche Betreuung: Eva Reichenberger
Satz und Druck: Druckhaus Thiele & Schwarz GmbH, 3500 Kassel-Waldau
Einbandgestaltung: Reiner Höfling, Kassel
Buchbinderische Verarbeitung: Großbuchbinderei Fleischmann, Fulda

TABLE OF CONTENTS

VI

PREFACE

Despite the towering stature of Pedro Calderón de la Barca in the drama of the Spanish Golden Age, an important segment of his work remains to date largely unexplored: the group of mythological dramas which he wrote for a court audience on various occasions of state. These works were part of an explosion of spectacular court entertainment that took place throughout Europe during the sixteenth and seventeenth centuries. In every court, the display was brilliant; yet rarely – if ever – did these entertainments find a playwright capable of giving them the dramatic coherence and depth of meaning that Calderón achieved in a number of his works. Calderón's mythological court plays earned great acclaim during his lifetime, but with the advent of the eighteenth century, the Bourbon dynasty and Neoclassicism, these dramas sank into an oblivion in which they remained for 250 years. In the years since World War II, however, critics in ever-increasing numbers have rediscovered that Calderón used mythology to create a dramatic world that is both original and profound.

La estatua de Prometeo, the last mythological court play which Calderón wrote, is by almost all readers' standards, a fitting climax to a unique genre. Many critics rank it as one of the finest works of Calderón's career, worthy of classification with such dramas as *La vida es sueño* and *La hija del aire.* Robert ter Horst, one of several recent writers on *La estatua de Prometeo,* considers the play an etiological work which provides an understanding of the nature of the conflict that occurs throughout Calderón's plays. Yet our knowledge of this important play is based on a very poor text, derived from its first publication in the pirated *Quinta Parte* of 1677, a volume roundly condemned by Calderón as completely unauthentic. That often garbled text has further suffered from the piling up of layers of editorial "correction", some inspired, but many completely arbitrary. Nevertheless, the *Quinta Parte* text has been our only source for *La estatua de Prometeo.*

The present edition is based on a manuscript copy of the play in the collection of the Biblioteca Municipal of Madrid. It is not an autograph copy, but it contains a much better text than that of the *Quinta Parte,* including a number of lines absent in the *princeps.* I have collated the manuscript text with those of the two 1677 editions of the *Quinta Parte* and with the text published in 1683 by Juan de Vera Tassis in the *Sexta Parte*. The resultant text will, I believe, bring the reader considerably closer to Calderón's original intentions in *La estatua de Prometeo*. The extensive introduction is also designed to bring the reader closer to the special world of this court theatre. Because of its spectacular nature and unique circumstances of presentation, the mythological court play must be treated not as a simple, written text, an aberrant form of the standard *comedia*, but as a total performance which derives its rich complexity of meaning from a diversity of codes in addition to the written or spoken word. Music, in particular, was a vital and integral part of the performance, and we have therefore included Louise Stein's explanation of the background and nature of the music in *La estatua de Prometeo* not in the appendix customary for such contributions, but as a major chapter in the introduction.

A great deal of credit is due to a number of people for their vital support in the completion of this project. I owe a special debt to A. A. Parker, not only for the general initiation into Golden Age literature which I was privileged to have as his student, but also for the suggestion of the Calderonian mythological plays as a fertile field of study. Parker also was instrumental in arranging for the assistance of D. W. Cruickshank, who has generously provided me with invaluable information and guidance based on his own incomparable knowledge of Calderonian textual criticism. Professor Stanislav Zimic merits many thanks for his thoughtful direction, enthusiastic support and careful reading of the doctoral dissertation which generated this edition. Kate Frost also provided vital guidance in the problems of editing and organization. Lee Fontanella, Juan López-Morillas and Douglass Parker have contributed general support and valuable assistance in their areas of expertise, for which I am grateful. Louise Stein deserves credit, not only for the section on music in the introduction of this edition, but also for providing me with other important information which she has gathered in her years of work in Spanish sources on music in Golden Age theatre. I am also indebted to the Fulbright Foundation, for providing the fellowship which made possible a year's study in the libraries and archives of Madrid. Finally, my special thanks to a number of friends and colleagues in Madrid, particularly to Vicenta Cortés, Jaime Moll und Mercedes Dexeus for the friendship and professional guidance which has made my work in Madrid both pleasant and profitable.

GENERAL INTRODUCTION

1 DEVELOPMENT OF THE MYTHOLOGICAL COURT PLAYS

1.1 Italian Roots

Calderón's mythological court plays, while on one hand a genre unique to Spain, were also part of an explosion of spectacular court entertainment throughout Europe in the sixteenth and seventeenth centuries. Such spectacles were, in a general sense, both a tool and an expression of the theory of absolutist rule. They focused attention, both within the state and in rival courts, on the importance of the prince because, as Roy Strong puts it:

> In a Europe dominated by the problem of rival religious creeds and the breakdown of the Universal Church, the monarch not only established himself as the arbiter in religious matters but gradually became adulated as the sole guarantor of peace and order within the State. Before the invention of the mechanical mass media of today, the creation of monarchs as an "image" to draw people's allegiance was the task of humanists, poets, writers and artists. During the sixteenth and seventeenth centuries the most profound alliance therefore occured between the new art forms of the Renaissance and the concept of the prince.[1]

The court entertainments, in a variety of styles, brought together music, dance, poetry, painting, architecture and mechanical engineering in the creation of spectacles that were at once an assertion and a legitimation of princely power.

The Renaissance spectacles, in their Italian origins, found a theoretical grounding in Aristotle's definition of the purpose of poetry as that of producing wonder in the mind of the spectator. At the same time, they reflected the philosophy that truth could best be presented in images. As Strong says,

---

1 Roy Strong, *Splendour at Court: Renaissance Spectacle and Illusion* (Boston: Houghton Mifflin Co., 1973), p. 19.

Fêtes speak to the visual sense in a lost vocabulary of strange attributes which we can no longer easily read but which, by the close of the sixteenth century, was a perfectly valid silent language within the make-up of the educated Roman mind.[2]

In these spectacles, meaning was conveyed not by reasoned discourse, but by a succession of allegorical images, generally of kings or gods bearing the attire or devices associated with ideal princely virtues. We can still find guides to the vocabulary of these devices in the emblems of Alciati, in the *imprese*, or personal devices symbolizing the royal houses, and in the mythological manuals which codified and interpreted classical myths for the educated Renaissance man.[3]

The spectacles served the interests not only of the Renaissance prince, but also of humanists interested in reviving the lost dramatic forms of classical antiquity. Inspired by reading the *De architectura* of the Roman architect-engineer Virtruvius on Greek stage scenery and machinery, they developed the proscenium arch, perspective stage scenery, and machinery for increasingly elaborate stage effects. The same humanistic preoccupation with ancient music and dance resulted in new forms of theatrical music and stage dancing which are the forebears of modern opera and ballet.[4]

The overwhelming choice for the subject matter of the spectacles, the figures and stories of classical mythology, satisfied at the same time the humanists' desire to revive a classical world, and the rulers' interest in the legitimizing power of association with divine forebears. The terrain for such association had long been prepared, particularly by the Sicilian writer Euhemerus of the third century B.C., whose theory of mythological interpretation was, essentially, that the gods were originally kings who had been idealized to the status of gods by their societies. Euhemerism reappeared in Renaissance mythographies, along with a variety of allegorical and analogical forms of mythological interpretation. While the creators of court entertainment may have used mythology allegorically, their purpose was not that of Christianizing or spiritualizing the myths, as Orgel has rightly pointed out:

> Modern historians of the subject regularly claim that Renaissance mythographers spiritualized and internalized their fables. In fact, the truth more often seems to me just the

---

2 Strong, *Spectacle*, p. 56.
3 Strong, *Spectacle*, pp. 56–58.
4 Strong, *Spectacle*, p. 21.

opposite. The pressure is not toward spiritualizing the physical, but toward embodying and sensualizing the moral and
abstract. The increasing tendency in the Renaissance to
illustrate mythographies, and to treat them as iconologies –
systems of images – is clear evidence of this.[5]

The use of mythological figures in court entertainment served on the
most obvious level as the embodiment of the idea of the divine right of
kings, and often as an expression of some immediate political goal of the
sovereign in question. Since the demise of the political systems that
supported them, these spectacles have often been disdained as nothing
more than fawning extravagances, fleeting assertions of a mirage of
power. Until recent years, Calderonian mythological plays had met with
the same condemnation. Yet as we will see subsequently, the great
Spanish dramatist succeeded in combining the standard elements of
court entertainment into a whole that was much more than the sum of its
parts. While continuing the praise of Hapsburg royalty in the framework
of his *fiestas*, Calderón retold the old stories in new ways within the
drama itself, employing the mythological figures to dramatize a complex
of political and moral issues having a depth and import which was as
enduring as the myth of power told by the spectacular shell was
evanescent.

The common elements of mythology, music, dance, elaborate scenery,
costumes and stage effects were combined into a variety of forms,
evolving in England into the court masque, in France the *ballet de cour*,
ancestor of classical ballet, and in Italy the *intermezzi* of Medici
Florence, which led to the development of opera.[6] Because of the close
political and cultural ties between Italy and Spain, it was the Italian
model which provided the most direct stimulus for the development of
the mythological court play in seventeenth-Century Spain.[7]

The development of the Italian *intermezzi* can be traced back to the end
of the fifteenth century, when a small group of short dramatic pieces
usually called "favole pastorali" were presented in the courts of Northern Italy, in Mantua, Ferrara and Milan. The plays have in common
pastoral elements, mythological themes, classical inspiration and music,

---

5 Stephen Orgel, "The Royal Theatre and the Role of the King", in *Patronage in the
Renaissance*, eds. Guy Fitch Lytle and Stephen Orgel (Princeton: Princeton University
Press, 1981), p. 264.

6 Strong, *Spectacle*, p. 49.

7 As Italian theatre and actors had earlier contributed significantly to the development of
popular Spanish theatre. See Othón Arróniz, *La influencia italiana en el nacimiento de
la comedia española* (Madrid: Editorial Gredos, 1969).

but Cynthia Pyle suggests that they would better be referred to as "favole mitologiche" because it is their mythological subject matter which binds them together.[8] Of the six "favole pastorali" extant today, the most famous are the *Favola d'Orfeo* by Angelo Poliziano, *Cefalo* by Niccolò da Correggio, *Pasithea* by Gaspare Visconti, and *Danae*, composed by Baldassare Taccone, with sets designed by Leonardo da Vinci.[9] These short pieces, written as distractions by the scholars and men of politics who composed them, were presented at gala occassions to members of the court, or sometimes to the residents of the city.[10] Poliziano's *Orfeo* was a kind of *intermezzo* or "entre-mets" apparently staged at a banquet given by the Cardinal Gonzaga in Mantua during Carnival of 1480.[11]

The mythological *intermezzi* which evolved from these first pieces were presented not between the courses at a banquet, but between the acts of court plays and other festivals for great occasions. Their greatest development took place in Florence, where the infant Medici dynasty employed art in general, and court spectaculars in particular, to legitimize its rule and to discourage any lingering republican instincts in its domain. A series of seven *intermezzi* written by Giovanbattista Strozzi, with music by Corteccia, produced by Pier Francesco Giamballari, were inserted into Antonio Landi's play *Il Commodo* on the occasion of the marriage of Cosimo de'Medici to Eleanor of Toledo in 1539. They were related to the play in theme, but unconnected with one another. As the century progressed, however, the *intermezzi* gained in unity of theme, while the stage effects took on ever more magnificent shape. The high point of the form was the series of *intermezzi* interspersed in Girolamo Bagagli's play *La Pellegrina* during the 1589 celebration of the marriage of Christina of Lorraine and Ferdinand de'Medici. The *intermezzi* were the product of the collaboration of a large number of artists, including Giovanni de Bardi, (under whose auspices the Camerata Fiorentina dei Bardi had pursued a program of humanistic musical reform, the fruits of which were incorporated in the *intermezzi*), rising young composers such as Emilio de'Cavalieri, Giulio Caccini and Jacopo Peri, and the architect Bernardo Buontalenti.[12]

---

8 Cynthia Munro Pyle, "Politian's *Orfeo* and other *favole mitologiche* in the Context of Late Quattrocento Northern Italy", Diss. Columbia University, 1976, p. 1. (A revised version of this dissertation will be published in book form in the near future.)

9 Pyle, "Favole mitologiche", pp. 1–3.

10 Pyle, "Favole mitologiche", p. 198.

11 Pyle, "Favole mitologiche", pp. 1, 53.

12 Strong, *Spectacle*, pp. 169–194.

The spectacular nature of these court entertainments lent great importance to the role of architects such as Buontalenti and his predecessor,
Vasari – to the extent that in Italy, France, and England, they often
overshadowed if not overruled the creative role played by the authors of
the pieces.[13]
It was through the importation of an Italian engineer that the new
theatrical style came to Spain in force. Although a variety of court
entertainments had been staged under previous Hapsburg kings, Carlos I
and Felipe II were not interested in theatre; royal patronage of the
theatre began under Felipe III, and quickly intensified on Felipe IV's
accession to the throne. Felipe IV's minister Olivares sent orders to the
Spanish ambassador to the papal court to bring back a *fontanero* – an
engineer specializing in the construction of fountains and garden water-
works.[14] The ambassador returned in 1626 with Cosme Lotti, a student
of Buontalenti who had already earned renown in Florence. He made an
immediate impression, as Shergold reports:

> Lope de Vega compares him to Hero of Alexandria in his skill
> in constructing mechanical figures, and on his arrival in Spain
> he is reported to have made a satyr's head which moved its
> eyes, ears, and hair, and opened its mouth to make such
> ferocious cries that it terrified all those who were not
> forewarned against it.[15]

With the arrival of Lotti, a new era began in court theatre in Spain. Lotti
worked in Spain for a number of years, and after his death, he was
succeeded by another Italian engineer, Baccio del Bianco, who designed
court plays until his death in 1657.[16]

1.2 Scenery and Stage Effects

Neither the use of illusionist stage scenery nor machine-produced stage
effects were new to Spain in the seventeenth century. Rather, it was the
sophistication and scale of their use which was novel. The discovery of
scientific perspective had been applied to painting since the mid-fifteenth

---

13 See Sebastian Neumeister, *Mythos und Repräsentation: Die mythologischen Festspiele
   Calderóns* (Munich: Wilhelm Fink Verlag, 1978), pp. 54–55.
14 Jonathan Brown and J. H. Elliott, *A Palace for a King: The Buen Retiro and the Court
   of Philip IV* (New Haven: Yale University Press, 1980), p. 47.
15 N. D. Shergold: *A History of the Spanish Stage from Medieval Times until the End of
   the Seventeenth Century* (Oxford: Clarendon Press, 1967), pp. 275–276.
16 Shergold, *Spanish Stage*, pp. 295, 304.

century,[17] and Spanish painters, fully cognizant of its use, applied it to
the creation of scenery for a court play as early as 1570, when an Amadís
representation in Burgos was said to have scenery "puesta en muy buena
perspectiua". This was probably a correct use of perspective on a two-
dimensional sheet of canvas, however. Lotti created a three-dimensional
perspective scene in 1629 for Lope de Vega's "opera" *La selva sin amor*,
with cut-out figures to heighten the effect, and he may have used
"lienços de prespetiuas" to create three-dimensional perspective for two
Calderonian plays in 1638.[18] Buontalenti had designed such perspective
scenery for the 1589 *intermezzi*, a crucial event in theatrical history,
because they set a norm for stage design which eventually came to
prevail throughout Europe for the next 300 years; that is, a stage framed
by a proscenium arch with ranks of side wings receding behind it to the
back of the stage where a back shutter closed off the view.[19] Lotti also
greatly extended the use of machinery to change scenes rapidly, so that
the stage could be quickly and repeatedly transformed from a sumptuous
palace to a humble village or fearsome cavern.[20] All the machinery
necessary for this *trompe l'oeil* theatre was incorporated in the Coliseo of
the Buen Retiro Palace, the new royal theatre inaugurated in 1640.

Mechanical devices were also being used to produce striking stage effects
before the arrival of Lotti, both in court entertainments and, to a more
limited extent, in the public theatres, but again, he multiplied their use in
a variety of complex ways. A system or pulleys and winches could make
actors, clouds, or even whole temples appear to descend rapidly from the
heavens, or to fly away on command. Through the use of trap doors,
mountains or palaces could be made to rise into view or sink suddenly
from sight as if destroyed. A mechanism called a "bofetón" either
rotated or sprang open to make characters seem to appear or disappear as
if by magic.[21] Sea scenes could be created, with sea monsters or ships
appearing or diasppearing, and fish moving up and down with the
illusionistic water, creating effects so realistic that on one occasion they
were reported to have caused sea-sickness among the ladies of the
court.[22] Many of the effects were heightened by the introduction of
artificial lighting, which made it possible to stage the spectacles at night.
The amount of wax alone required to light the stage and theatre for such

17 Strong, *Spectacle*, p. 73.
18 Shergold, *Spanish Stage*, p. 296.
19 Strong, *Spectacle*, p. 194.
20 Shergold, *Spanish Stage*, p. 296.
21 Shergold, *Spanish Stage*, pp. 222–223.
22 Shergold, *Spanish Stage*, p. 276.

productions was astounding. For the representation of Calderón's *Fortunas de Andrómeda y Perseo,* the royal waxworks had to supply 695 pounds of wax.[23]

Since there has survived no *memoria de apariencias* detailing the scene changes and special effects for any presentation of *La estatua de Prometeo,* we can only guess at the scenes and mechanisms used, based on the extant stage directions and indications in the text of the play itself. Judging from those sources, the use of scene changes and stage effects in *La estatua de Prometeo* seems very restrained, as compared with many other court plays. The printed editions show no scene changes,[24] only an opening indication of a boulder ("peñasco") that opens and from which Prometeo emerges. The Biblioteca Municipal (Madrid) manuscript, which has considerably more extensive stage directions, indicates only four scene changes, three of which occur in the last act. Both the first and second act are set in a scene of mountainous woods ("bosque sobre peñascos"); at the back of the stage there is a grotto of boulders with a door "capaz de vna persona", which opens for Prometeo's entrance. The entire grotto later opens to reveal the statue which Prometeo has constructed. The grotto was undoubtedly constructed in the "vestuario" or tiring room which was a standard feature at the back of the stage in both court and public theatres. Apparently the "grotto" could be transformed individually, separate from a total scene change, as Epimeteo later finds another grotto, more horrible than the first, with drums and trumpets resonating within; it opens, and from it emerges Palas. The third act opens with a forest scene, containing a boulder large enough to serve as a sacrificial pyre. The scene changes to a vista of the heavens for the debate between Apolo, Minerba and Palas and then to a forest scene, or, as an entry by a second scribal hand indicated, to a "selba florida". For the final scene, the setting apparently reverts to that which opened the third act, a forest with a boulder for a sacrificial pyre, and perhaps a grotto as well. The *vestuario* area in this act seems to have had two entrances, probably at either side of a backcloth; at one point, the actress playing Minerba/Pandora hides, and speaks behind the statue that is her double, and then goes to another part of the *vestuario,* from which she emerges to confuse Epimeteo and Merlín with her double presence.

---

23 N. D. Shergold and J. E. Varey, *Representaciones palaciegas: 1603–1699. Estudios y documentos* (London: Tamesis Books Ltd., 1983), pp. 18, 58.

24 This in itself is not particularly significant, as the text of those editions may derive from a performance in a public theatre; or scenic directions may have been contained in a separate memorandum.

The most impressive mechanical stage effect is the appearance of the chariot of the sun, which is pulled across the heavens from one side of the stage to the other. As it crosses, Minerba and Prometeo also appear on high, standing on, and partially hidden by a cloud. A number of characters also descend from heaven to the stage, or fly upward. Palas and Discordia are said to descend very rapidly, an effect that was a sure crowd-pleaser, since the audience was well aware of the danger this entailed for the actors involved.[25] Other special effects depend on lighting or sound effects: the theatre darkens ominously at one point, a blinding cloud of smoke appears as Pandora opens her urn, and Prometeo steals a lighted torch from Apollo's chariot and bears it down to earth and his statue. Sounds of thunder also threaten, and an earthquake takes place – perhaps only suggested by sound effects, but conceivably also reinforced by some shaking of the cloth wings and backdrop. There are a number of games of mistaken identity between Minerba, Pandora, and the statue, but these do not depend on any special devices other than the use of the *vestuario*.

A number of the effects used in *La estatua de Prometeo* were those mentioned by the Italian architect and painter Sebastian Serlio, in comments on the theoretical value of spectacle in his influential book *Arquitettura* published in 1545:

> Among all the things that may bee made by mens hands, thereby to yeeld admiration, pleasure to sight, and to content the fantasies of men; I think it is placing of a Scene, as it is shewed to your sight, where a man in a small place may see built by Carpinters or Masons, skilful in Perspective work, great Palaces, large Temples, and diverse Houses, both neere and farre off . . . In some other Scenes you may see the rising of the Sunne with his course about the world: and at the ending of the Comedie, you may see it goe downe most artificially, where at many beholders have been abasht. And when occasion serveth, you shall by Arte see a God descending downe from Heaven; you also see some Comets and Stars shoot in the skyes . . . which things, as occasion serveth, are so

---

25 The description of the performance and audience reaction to *Las fortunas de Andrómeda y Perseo* contained in the deluxe *suelta* edition now in the Houghton Library of Harvard University (MS Typ 258H) mentions the audience delight at a rapid descent. See the article describing the drawings and text by Phyllis Dearborn Massar, "Scenes for a Calderón Play by Baccio del Bianco", *Master Drawings* 15 (1977), 365–375.

pleasant to mens eyes, that a man could not see fairer with mens hands.[26]

Such effects were attainable only because of the staggering development in mechanics achieved in the sixteenth century. The pleasure they afforded was therefore double, residing not only in wonder and delight in the effects achieved, but also in the triumph of apparent total human control of the physical world. Federigo Zuccaro, a Roman mannerist painter, described his delight at these mechanical triumphs of human organization and engineering on seeing the backstage machinery in Mantua in 1608:

> It was delightful to see the windlasses mounted over the machines, the cables of optimum strength, the ropes and lines by which the machines were moved and guided, and the many stagehands who were needed to keep the apparatus in operation. Every man was at his station, and at a signal the machinery could be raised, lowered, moved, or held in a particular position. More than 300 workers were engaged and had to be directed, which required no less experience and skill than it did foresight and reason . . .[27]

The enthusiasm of sixteenth and seventeenth-century princes and lesser audiences for these spectacular effects usually worked to the detriment of the play as a dramatic text, for the power and glory afforded to the architect exceeded the control of the playwright. A primary reason for Calderón's success in achieving a unique level of dramatic integrity in his mythological court plays was precisely his refusal to surrender control of the production to the engineers, whether they be Cosme Lotti, Baccio del Bianco, or their Spanish successors. The history of Calderón's play on the Circe myth, *El mayor encanto amor,* gives us evidence of his insistence on the priority of dramatic coherence over spectacle. The original idea for the play was that of Cosme Lotti, who in a memorandum to Calderón, described a long list of devices which were to be included in the event. Calderón replied with a firm statement of rejection:

> Avnque esta trazada con mucho ynjenio, la traza de ella no es representable por mirar mas a la ynbencion de las tramoyas que al gusto de la representacion.[28]

---

26 Serlio, quoted in Strong, *Spectacle*, p. 192.
27 Cited in Strong, *Spectacle*, p. 193.
28 Calderón's letter was published by L. Rouanet, "Un Autographe inédit de Calderón", *Revue Hispanique* 6 (1899), 196–200.

He continued, saying that if he were to write the play, he could not follow Lotti's list, but that he was willing to select a number of the devices suggested. He did use a substantial number, and even introduced one or two new effects. As Shergold points out, Calderón used Lotti's memorandum much as he often used works of other playwrights – as an idea to be reworked for maximum dramatic effectiveness.[29] The resulting play is dramatically coherent, although somewhat shallow and less interesting – at least for a reader – than later Calderonian mythological plays. In a number of later plays, such as *Eco y Narciso*, the paired plays *Apolo y Climene* and *El hijo del sol, Faetón, Las fortunas de Andrómeda y Perseo, Ni amor se libra de amor*, and most of all in *La estatua de Prometeo*, Calderón created dramatic texts which were able to incorporate a whole range of spectacular effects, to the grater glory of both engineer and playwright.

1.3 Dance

To fully understand and appreciate Calderonian mythological plays requires a special imaginative effort on the part of present-day readers; all we have of the plays is black words on a white page, with here and there an artist's sketch or a few notes of music. Yet as we have seen above, the plays were conceived as total spectacles, a feast of many courses for the eyes and ears. Their effect depended not only on the poetry of the text, but also on music, dance, sumptuous costuming, elaborate perspective scenery and stunning stage effects. Of these vital ingredients, the only one which we can recreate in something approaching its original form for *La estatua de Prometeo* is its music, of which several fragments have been preserved and identified. Louise Stein places this music in the larger context of seventeenth-century Spanish theatre music in the following chapter.

Dance was also an integral part of the court spectacular, from the *loa* to the *fin de fiesta*, and within the work itself. Dance was, like music, traditionally associated with the theatre, although not with the approval of all observers: in 1616, the complaints against the scandalous nature of theatrical dancing brought the Council of Castile to forbid all dancing in the theatre. Predictably, the order was not long enforced.[30] Unfortunately, very little has been written on theatrical dance in Spain, but a few insights can perhaps be offered.

---

29 Shergold, *Spanish Stage*, pp. 280–283.

The dances which began and concluded the theatrical event, and filled in between acts, were sometimes completely sung, sometimes partly spoken. A distinction was made between two kinds of dance, that called "baile", and that called "danza". José Antonio González de Salas, writing in 1633, described the difference as follows:

> Las *danzas* son de movimientos más mesurados y graves, y en donde no se usa de los brazos sino de los pies solos: los *bailes* admiten gestos más libres de los brazos y de los pies juntamente.[31]

Cotarelo adds, however, that:

> ... esto de "más mesurados" no debe entenderse que sólo consistiesen en paseos, cadenas, cambios de puesto y otros sencillos que se observan en algunos bailes de sociedad modernos, pues tanto ó más violentos que los del baile eran los de ciertas danzas, como la *Gallarda*.[32]

The fullest description of seventeenth century theatrical court dance is the following given by Ivanova:

> Mention must also be made of the dances included in the comedies presented at the Buen Retiro Theatre: "Seguidillas de Eco," the jácara, canario, matachín, passacalla [sic], menuetto, and gallarda. All of them are figure dances and the danced interludes in these productions nearly always consisted of dances belonging to this group.[33]

Drawing from a manuscript by the Spanish dancing master, Juan Antonio Jaque, describing the construction of a number of dances apparently from the latter half of the seventeenth century, Ivanova concludes:

---

30 One of the few writers on Spanish dance, Ana Ivanova, claims that professional dancers were increasingly used in seventeenth-century Spanish theatre, with the result that the entire play sometimes became little more than a vehicle for the dance. See Ana Ivanova, *The Dancing Spaniards* (London: John Baker, 1970), p. 77. Ivanova's own involvement with dance probably led her to exaggerate its importance.

31 *Nueva idea de la tragedia antigua*, 1778 ed., p. 171, cited in Cotarelo, *Colección de entremeses*, p. clxv.

32 Cotarelo, *Colección de entremeses*, p. clxv.

33 Ivanova, *Dancing Spaniards*, p. 86.

> From this manuscript it will be seen that the Spaniards seemed to be very fond of figures that formed and reformed endlessly in various ways, half and full circles, danced clockwise or anticlockwise, with quarter turns giving the impression of charmingly original shapes of a petal or scallop design in the ground patterns. The descriptions refer in particular to the jácara, villano and folías, and give a very clear idea of the technical difficulty of the steps then demanded by the dancing masters. Once the simple peasant dances fell into their hands, they were simple no more. The turning steps alone would tax the technical prowess of any dancer today . . .[34]

We do not have any of the minor theatrical pieces that accompanied *La estatua de Prometeo*, and there are only two stage directions specifically mentioning dances within the work. The first is that accompanying Libia's song, "Venid, moradores", in Act I, 381, and the second at the beginning of Act III, which says that the company is to enter singing and dancing the same stanza that ended the second act; that is, "Al festejo, al festejo . . ." It seems probable that other sections not specifically mentioned were also danced, as no notation appears in the manuscript that dancing as well as song concluded the second act. Furthermore, Calderón's friend, Juan de Vera Tassis, who would certainly have seen this or similar plays, added the stage direction "cantando y baylando" to Act III, 68, where no such indications exists in the manuscript or the first two printed editions. The sections which are marked as having been danced are ideally suited for the sort of formal, intricate, circling dance which Ivanova describes.

---

34 Ivanova, *Dancing Spaniards*, p. 86.

2 LA PLÁTICA DE LOS DIOSES

Music and the Calderonian Court Play together with a transcription of the songs from *La estatua de Prometeo*

by Louise Kathrin Stein

In memory of James Harold Moore (1947–1984)

> La morte è dolce a chi la vita è amara;
> muoia ridendo chi piangendo nasce;
> rendiam queste atre fasce
> al Fato omai, ch'usura tanta esige,
> ch'avanza il capital con tante ambasce.
>
> Tommaso Campanella

2.1 Music and The *Comedia Nueva*

Music had been used in the Spanish theater before the seventeenth century, but with the codification of the *comedia* genre proposed in Lope de Vega's *Arte nuevo de hacer comedias* (1609), music and dancing were finally addressed as standard elements of theatrical performances.[1] Lope did not specifically define the role of music in the *comedia*, but the interest he expressed in his treatise did open the way for the development of music as an integral part of the genre. The theoretical basis for the inclusion of music was set out in the *Arte nuevo*, but the practical application and extension of these ideas in the Lopean *comedia* texts were the most important contribution toward the regular use of music in the theater of the early seventeenth century. Lope's use of music, demonstrated in the stage directions from his *comedia* texts, became the true model for the incorporation of music into the theater.

---

1 Lope Félix de Vega Carpio, *El arte nuevo de hacer comedias en este tiempo*, ed. Juana de José Prades (Madrid: CSIC, 1971), pp. 58–61, and pp. 152–156. Lope's idea that "cualquiera imitación poética/se hace de tres cosas que son: plática,/verso dulce, armonía o sea la música" (verses 54–56) is taken from Aristotle's *De Poetica*, see translation of Richard McKeon, *The Basic Works of Aristotle* (New York, 1941) pp. 1455–1456.

In the *comedias* of Lope and his contemporaries, both vocal and instrumental music had a variety of functions, as indicated by the stage directions. Vocal music (songs and sung dances) was used as a structural device as well as to create, enhance, or prolong the mood or emotional content of a scene.[2] Songs were indispensable as a vehicle for lyric poetry within the *comedia* text. This was the primary role of vocal music as described in the *Arte nuevo*.[3] Both vocal and instrumental music were employed to punctuate the action of the plot, to delineate sub-sections of a scene, to signal scene changes and, to announce stage entrances and exits. For example, the entrance of a royal personage or a band of soldiers was announced with the music of trumpets or drums.[4] The arrival of a group of carefree peasants was accompanied by a joyous song which included rustic instruments,[5] while a scene with Moorish characters often included a Moorish dance (perhaps a *morisca*) or singing accompanied by Moorish instruments.[6]

Both instrumental music and songs were an important resource for the creation of dramatic contrast. The sound of martial instruments, trumpets and drums, could be contrasted with the sound of a wedding dance or a love song. The music from a joyous peasant dance, heard as from afar, could interrupt a scene of profound reflection or tragedy, producing an immediately perceptible conflict of atmosphere.

Music in the plays of Lope de Vega and his contemporaries was, in one sense, used symbolically: for example, the music of shawms *(chirimías)* is often called for in *comedia* texts to accompany the appearance of holy or saintly figures onstage as well as the discovery of altars and other religious symbols.[7] But at the same time, it also reflected the realities of everyday life. That is, Lope's use of music clearly depended upon certain stylized associations.[8] The sounds of various instruments and of different types of songs and dances were used in connection with particular situations or kinds of characters, so that the music would

---

2 The dramatic function of songs in many of Lope's plays is discussed in Gustavo Umpierre, *Songs in the Plays of Lope de Vega* (London: Tamesis Books, Ltd., 1975).
3 *El arte nuevo* lines 54–56.
4 For example, in *La vida de San Pedro Nolasco*, I.
5 *San Isidro labrador de Madrid*, I, III, and *La burgalesa de Lerma*, III.
6 *El primer rey de Castilla*, I, and *El último godo*, I.
7 *La niñez de San Isidro*, I and II, and *Lo fingido verdadero*, III.
8 Music was used as a "symbolic prop;" see Ronald E. Surtz, *The Birth of a Theater: Dramatic Convention in the Spanish Theater from Juan del Encina to Lope de Vega* (Princeton and Madrid, 1979) pp. 181–185, for a discussion of the non-musical symbolic props.

immediately indicate a specific type of scene or the appearance of a certain character. Some of these associations developed from the everyday use of music in the actual life of the epoch. It seems fair to assume that shepherds and rural laborers did play the rustic instruments named in Lope's stage directions *(tamboril, flauta, gaita, pandero,* etc.), and we know from extant documentation that trumpets and drums were played to announce the *entrada* and *salida* of the nobility and of the royal family. Serenades were often sung to ladies from beneath their balconies in the deep of the night in sixteenth- and seventeenth-century Madrid, and after-dinner musical entertainments were common in the houses of the aristocracy and at court. Musical intervention in the theater of Lope's day was another means toward the all-important verisimilitude of the new *comedia* genre. Moreover, the musical sounds that were familiar to people of many walks of life also served as a link between the audience and the action of the stage, bringing the audience closer to the play.

The extant music from the theater of Lope's time differs substantially from the music that is preserved for the mythological plays of Calderón, and from the pieces for *La estatua de Prometeo* which are the focal point of this chapter. The few extant settings of early seventeenth-century theatrical song-texts are polyphonic and may be arrangements of well-known melodies. Since some of the song-texts were drawn from an existing body of folk or pseudo-popular texts,[9] it is likely that the musical tunes used in the polyphonic arrangements actually came from a pre-existent orally transmitted repertory of well-known songs, and that the extant settings of these tunes present, in each case, one of many versions of the basic melody, arranged by composers who were active at the court or in other circles of cultured Spanish life.[10] Thus, the settings that have survived to our day are many steps removed from the "original" models, and show us the work of trained composers and professional musicians. The songs are not (in their present-day form) specifically theatrical. Rather, the extant settings may be recomposed versions of songs that were performed in the theater.

The musical sources for the early repertoire are also quite different from the sources for the later, specifically theatrical songs. The repertoire of

---

9 Two fundamental contributions to the study of these poetic texts are: Margit Frenk Alatorre, *Estudios sobre lírica antigua* (Madrid: Editorial Castalia, 1978), and José María Alín, *El Cancionero Español de Tipo Tradicional* (Madrid: Taurus, 1978).

10 A detailed and documented study of the early theatrical songs and their concordances is included in my forthcoming doctoral dissertation *Music in the Seventeenth-Century Spanish Theater.*

well-known songs is preserved in several manuscript songbooks or *cancioneros*, anthologies of polyphonic songs dating from the first half of the seventeenth century.[11]

Many of the texts in this repertory, without their music, appear in the printed series of *cancioneros* and *romanceros* that were published in the first half of the seventeenth century.[12] Thus, there is a strong correspondence between the musical repertory preserved in manuscript musical sources and the widely disseminated poetic repertory of the printed poetic anthologies. This is further evidence for the idea that the songs from these collections were, indeed, part of a well-known and fairly popular corpus of tunes and texts. Since there are several very similar versions of many of these songs, it must be that the tunes were easily available, and that specific tunes and musical characteristics were closely identified with individual song-texts.[13]

2.2 Music and Court Theater to c.1650

During the reign of Philip III (1598–1621) and in the early years of the reign of Philip IV (d. 1665) there were three basic categories of theatrical performances at court: the *particulares* (privately staged *comedias* performed by professional acting companies), elaborately staged masques which were performed by members of the court, and a few spectacle plays which involved written dramatic texts, but which were nonetheless also performed by members of the royal family and courtiers.

The first type of theatrical court entertainment, the *particulares*, was always performed by one of the acting companies that was active in the public theaters or *corrales* of Madrid. The songs and instrumental music that were included in the *comedia* would have been performed by the

---

11 Songs from this repertory have been edited by Miguel Querol, see *Cancionero Musical de Góngora* (Barcelona, 1975), *Madrigales inéditos españoles del siglo XVII y Cancionero de la Casanatense* (Barcelona, 1981), *Música Barroca I: Polifonía Profana* (Barcelona, 1970), and *Romances y letras a tres voces* (Barcelona, 1956).

12 See Antonio Rodríguez Moñino, *Manual Bibliográfico de Cancioneros y Romanceros Impresos durante el siglo XVII* (2 vols.) (Madrid: Castalia, 1977–1978).

13 Similar conclusions about this musical repertory are suggested in John Baron, "Secular Spanish Solo Song in Non-Spanish Sources, 1599–1640", *Journal of the American Musicological Society* XXX (1977) pp. 20–42.

regular musicians who were part of the acting company. Although we might wonder if the royal chamber musicians were called in to bolster the musical parts of the *particulares*, there is no documentary evidence suggesting that this was actually so. The *particulares* allowed the King and the Queen to enjoy the *comedias* from the repertory of the public theaters, but did not contribute especially to the development of the musical court play.

The performances of large masques and pageants were usually staged to celebrate important events in the Spanish Hapsburg house, such as royal births and weddings. The theatrical entertainment was usually the high point in a series of festivities that could include triumphal processions, banquets, dances, equestrian games, and *particulares*. In these masques, the tableau was usually followed by a dance or *sarao* in which the King and the Queen both participated.

The best documented example of this type of festivity is the masque and ball that were celebrated in Valladolid on June 16, 1605 for the birth of Philip IV.[14] A special hall or *salón*, annexed to the palace in Valladolid, was built specifically to house this occasion, and was decorated with famous tapestries and elaborate artificial lighting. The seating plan for the audience and the performers was carefully drawn up in advance and strictly observed. The plan indicates that two choirs of singers from the royal chapel were seated in a raised gallery, facing each other in separate windows.[15] In the center of the hall, a temporary stage was constructed, containing a section of a temple with an elevated throne, overseen by the allegorical figure of Fame.

In addition to the two choirs of singers, there were instrumentalists playing stringed and wind instruments: violins, viols, recorders, sackbuts, cornettos, and shawms or crummhorns. Although it is difficult to determine from the sources just how these instruments performed in each of the musical parts of this masque, it is significant that, for the most part, the instruments were organized into homogeneous groups or families. This use of instrumental consorts in conjunction with pagean-

---

14 Sources for the 1605 festivities include: B.N.M. V.E. 56/94, *Relación de lo sucedido en la Ciudad de Valladolid, desde el felicissimo nacimiento del Príncipe* . . . (printed *relación*, n.d.); B.N.M. Ms. 18436, fol. 44–45 "Relación del Sarao"; B.N.M. Ms. 2807, fol. 240 "Relación de las fiestas que se hicieron en Valladolid . . . Recopilado por D. Gerónimo Gascón de Torquemada de la Cámara de los SSres. Príncipes de Saboya Por su Magestad."; Madrid, Real Academia de la Historia, Ms. 9/426 (Colección Salazar) "Sarao que sus magestades hicieron en palacio por el dichoso nacimiento del príncipe . . .".

15 Madrid, Archivo de Palacio, Sección administrativo leg. 671.

try places the 1605 Valladolid masque squarely within the Renaissance tradition.[16]

The sequence of events in the 1605 Valladolid masque is similar to that of many royal entertainments that had been celebrated in the sixteenth-century at courts in Spain and abroad.[17] The *máscara* opened with the allegorical figure of Fame sounding her trumpet (the mechanical device atop the temple accompanied by the sound of a real trumpet played within the temple structure). At this signal, the singers in the gallery sang verses praising the new-born prince in antiphonal style. According to one of the accounts, the choir sang in a three-part disposition of two trebles and tenor.[18] The last verse of the "hymn" was sung by both choirs together. At this point, the figure of Fame disappeared, and a triumphal carriage drawn by two ponies emerged from a door in the front of the hall. The carriage brought the Infanta, representing the enthroned figure of Virtue, into the area of the stage. As the Infanta reached the platform at the center of the room, another section of music commenced, played by the twelve *violones* and *violines* that entered by marching out from behind a curtain. The stringed-instrument players were followed closely by eight wind players (called *ministriles*), and they played together "*tañendo en mistura cierta sonada alegre y grave conpuesta para aquel efecto.*"[19] As the Infanta was led to her seat, the instrumentalists moved to a small platform located under the singers' gallery.

The central scene of the masque, an ornate throne adorned with allegorical and historical figures, was discovered as the choirs sang another text in alternation. When this hymn of praise was concluded, the figures of the masque (mythological characters, nymphs, and historical personages) danced to new music played by the *violones*. Shortly thereafter, the tableau was hidden from view by a curtain, and the dance that had been initiated by the figures from the stage was taken up by the members of the assembled audience. This was the beginning of the *sarao*,

---

16 The most detailed study of instrumentation in sixteenth-century entertainments is found in Howard Mayer Brown, *Sixteenth-Century Instrumentation: The Music for the Florentine Intermedii*, vol. 30 of Musicological Studies and Documents, American Institute of Musicology, 1973.

17 See, for example, Daniel Heartz, "A Spanish 'Masque of Cupid,'" *The Musical Quarterly* 49 (1963) and A. M. Nagler, *Theater Festivals of the Medici, 1539–1637* (Yale University Press, 1964).

18 "La capilla de su magestad repartida en dos choros el uno frontero del otro en las primeras ventanas y en la mitad de la sala, comenzó a cantar los versos siguientes a tres voces dos tiples y un tenor maravillosos." R.A.H. Ms. 9/426, fol. 21.

19 R.A.H. Ms. 9/426, fol. 22.

a sequence of figured dances (the *turdión*, the *madama de Orleans*, the *pavana*, the *gallarda*, and the *danza de la hacha*).

Unfortunately, the extant *relaciones* for the 1605 festivities do not name the composer or composers of the music for the *máscara* and *sarao*. We do know that the singers of the royal chapel performed, and we can assume that the instrumentalists who played were drawn from the ranks of the King's and Queen's musicians – that is, from the royal chamber players, the string players of the Queen's household, and the wind players associated with the chapel and *Casa de Castilla*.

There are two passing mentions of this entertainment in the accounts of the royal household. The choreography of the masque and the ball were created by Alonso Fernández, the *maestro de danzar* to both the King and the Queen, who also prepared the dancers. The music that was sung by the choirs during the masque was most probably composed by Juan de Namur, the then assistant chapel master *(teniente de capilla)*, as reported in an account of the chapel scribe in January of 1606.[20]

Large organized masques and pageants were also performed for the wedding celebration of Philip III and Margaret of Austria at Denia and Valencia in 1598, and in Madrid in 1601, 1602 and 1603. Like the Valladolid *máscara*, each of these entertainments displayed the elements of pageantry that were associated with royal celebrations throughout Europe and largely derived from the Renaissance fêtes tradition: the use of triumphal carriages and floats, the staging of non-dramatic spectacles arranged in *tableaux vivants*, the use of music as a background or nonparticipative force (the musicians are not in costume and do not take part in the staged activity), the use of dancing in conjunction with the tableaux, and the participation of members of the royal family in the masque and the dancing. These spectacles were not dramatic as such, because they had no dialogue and no plot. They did not need written out dramatic texts. The musical part of each spectacle was essential, but the characters in the scenes did not sing or play instruments as part of a story. These were the kinds of entertainments that also took place in France and Italy: they were not unique to the Spanish tradition.

The dramatic spectacle play, my third category of court entertainment, was clearly a precursor to the development of the Calderonian mytholo-

---

20 "De la mascara del Cerao que se hizo en las fiestas del Principe nuestro señor compuesta por Juan de Namur Teniente de la Capilla. 12 reales." From the "Cuenta de Claudio de la Sablonara Escriptor de la Capilla Real de Su Magd. del año 1605", countersigned January 10, 1606 by Mateo Romero. Madrid, Archivo de Palacio, Cuentas particulares, Leg. C-10.

gical plays and *zarzuelas*. This type of court play did depend on written dramatic texts by professional playwrights and used elaborate scenery and stage effects.[21] The actors were not professionals, but were members of the court and the royal family. After c.1611, these spectacle plays replaced the masques as the favorite entertainment when a select court audience celebrated important holidays. In general, these performances were given during the court's sojourns at country estates and palaces, such as Philip III's trips to Lerma in 1614 and 1618 and Philip IV's stay at Aranjuez in 1622. A brief chronological summary of these entertainments, with the titles of the works performed and the musical forces that were required, is presented in Table I. Unfortunately, as far as we know, none of the music for these spectacle plays has survived. Nonetheless, there are some extant descriptions of the performances, and from related documents we know that musicians from the royal household provided the vocal and instrumental music called for in the texts of the plays.

The first recorded spectacle play of the reign of Philip III was Lope de Vega's *El premio de la hermosura*, performed by the royal children and some of the ladies of the court during the court's visit to Lerma in November of 1614.[22] One of the extant *relaciones* mentions that "... *nunca se ha hecho en España fiesta con tantas circunstancias de grande por tantos respetos* ..."[23]

During the performance, three groups of musicians (a wind band, a violin band, and a vocal ensemble) played in a three-tiered gallery overlooking the stage: "*Estavan en un corredor de Teatro Los menistriles y avajo los biolines y en medio los musicos de voçes* ..."[24] Instrumental music accompanied the mechanical movement of clouds "*con toda la musica,*" and "*con la armonia de diferentes musicas.*"[25] Between the acts of the play some of the participants danced onstage; after Act I, the prince (Philip IV) danced the *galería de amor* with one of the court ladies, and the *españoleta* was danced after Act II.[26] In the final scene of

---

21 For information on the staging of court plays, see Shergold, pp. 244–297.

22 Shergold, pp. 252–255. Shergold, pp. 250–251, describes a few unnamed spectacle plays, including a play about Daphne and Apollo which was performed by courtiers, probably at Valencia during Carnival in 1599. In the documentation quoted by Shergold, musicians are mentioned: "En las barandillas que tiene esta pieza estavan algunos de la capilla de su Magestad que cantaron a ratos y otros se tañia con viguela de arco, clavicordio y corneta. Todos estavan sin verse."

23 B.N.M. Ms 18656/49 "D. Antonio de Mendoza. *Relación de la Comedia que en Lerma representaron la Reina de Francia y sus hermanos*", fol. 1.

24 *Ibid.*, fol. 3.

25 *Ibid.*, fol. 3v.

26 *Ibid.*, fol. 3v–4.

the play, Doña Catalina de Acuna, in the part of Leuridemo, sang an elegy accompanied with guitar.[27] The play was followed by a brief instrumental piece for the *violones* and a dance executed by twelve ladies of the court (the actresses of *El premio de la hermosura*) wearing masks and carrying torches.

These details of the 1614 performance of *El premio de la hermosura* illustrate the way that music was used in these early dramatic spectacle plays. Although they seem to have occasioned more music than the *comedias* for the public theaters, many of the techniques for incorporating music into the plays closely resemble the use of music in the *corrales*. This is not surprising, since the dramatists who provided the texts of the court plays (Lope de Vega, Luis Vélez de Guevara, Antonio Hurtado de Mendoza) were also writing *comedias* for the public theaters. However, the presence of professional musicians employed at court allowed these productions to exploit some of the musical techniques from the masques as well.

The descriptions of the 1617 performance of Luis Vélez's *El caballero del sol*[28] mention only shawms and trumpets and an ensemble of six singers. The latter began the performance by singing onstage ". . . *con destreza y musica grave un Romance de quexas amorosas . . .*"[29] The fact that the small vocal ensemble came onstage to open the performance with a sung ballad or *romance* is another example of the transference of techniques that had been tried and standardized in the Lopean *comedia*.

The 1622 performance of *La gloria de Niquea* represents, in some ways, a departure from the pervasive Spanish *comedia* tradition.[30] The author of the text, Juan de Tassis y Peralta, Count of Villamediana, was primarily a poet, and *La gloria de Niquea* was his only theatrical effort. Villamediana was an aristocrat who served the crown in Italy during the reign of Philip III. His years in Italy put him in contact with several

---

27 Both the manuscript account (B.N.M. Ms 18656/49) and the better-known printed account (*BAE* 234, pp. 405–413) indicate that the final elegy was sung by this lady in the part of Leuridemo, although the text, as we know it, indicates that a final sonnet was sung by Roselida. The guitar is mentioned in *BAE* 234, p. 412.

28 This play was performed during Philip III's stay in Lerma, on October 10, 1617, by servants of the Count of Saldaña. See Pedro de Herrera, *Translación del Santisimo Sacramento a la iglesia colegial de San Pedro en la villa de Lerma* (Madrid, 1618) fol. 29–33v. See also, Shergold, pp. 255–257.

29 Pedro de Herrera, fol. 31.

30 Juan Manuel Rozas, ed. *Obras* (Madrid: Castalia, 1969) pp. 7–15 and 48–52. See also Emilio Cotarelo y Mori, *El Conde de Villamediana* (Madrid, 1886).

influential Italian poets, and his aristocratic connections probably permitted him to experience Italian court entertainments.[31] *La gloria de Niquea*, commissioned by the Queen for the King's birthday celebration, was the first spectacle play performed in the reign of Philip IV. Villamediana's text was clearly inspired by his Italian experience,[32] and the scenery and machinery for the stage effects were designed by Giulio Cesare Fontana, "... *ingeniero mayor, y superintendente de las fortificaciones del Reyno de Nápoles* ..."[33] The play, performed by the Queen and ladies of the court, has virtually no plot development, but consists of a series of magnificent scenes on a chivalresque theme. The emphasis was on the visual spectacle, just as it had been in the earlier masques and pageants.[34] Antonio de Mendoza's printed *relación* of the performance indicates that *La gloria de Niquea* was intended as a special novelty for the court:

> ... Estas representaciones que no admiten el nombre vulgar de comedia, y se le dá de invencion, la decencia de Palacio (desprecio mas que imitacion de los espetaculos antiguos, de que aun oy Italia presume tanto de gentil) ...[35]

Hurtado de Mendoza refers to the genre (of the spectacle play) as an *invención* which need not heed the precepts of the true *comedia* since it is a royal entertainment and "... *se fabrica de variedad desatada* ..."[36] Villamediana's text is divided into two acts rather than the traditional three acts of the *comedia*, and the pause between the acts was devoted to a concert of instrumental music, instead of to an *entremés* or dancing.[37] The text was written to take advantage of the musical forces of the court: several choirs of singers were required, and the instruments included trumpets, drums, shawms, cornettos, sackbuts, flutes, viols, violins, lutes, guitars and theorbos. The musicians were seated in the upper galleries of the facade, divided into four choirs facing each other. It is

---

31 Biographical information in Emilio Cotarelo y Mori, *El Conde de Villamediana* (Madrid, 1886).
32 See the "Introducción" to Villamediana, *Obras*, ed. Juan Manuel Rozas (Madrid: Castalia, 1969).
33 B.N.M. R-15515. Antonio Hurtado de Mendoza, *Fiesta que se hizo en Aranjuez a los años del Rey Nuestro Señor D. Felipe IIII* (Madrid, 1623), fol. 5.
34 Shergold, pp. 268–270, discusses the staging of the play.
35 Hurtado de Mendoza, (R-15515) fol. 4.
36 Hurtado de Mendoza, (R-15515) fol. 13.
37 "... Acabó aqui la primera escena: tocaron los instrumentos apercibidos siempre en los intermedios, y la segunda empezo ansi." Hurtado de Mendoza, fol. 12v.

clear from the *relación* that instrumental music was especially important to the effect of the spectacle, for it announced each major change of scene, accompanied each of the discoveries, and each time a major character was lowered to the stage or lifted from the stage. Of course, music was a practical necessity, since it could disguise or cover the noise of the stage machines, hoists, and trap doors. This was as true for the spectacle plays as it was for the *comedias de tramoyas* and the *comedias de santos* that were popular in the public theaters. However, the court productions were endowed with a greater number and diversity of musicians, while the performances in the public theaters depended solely on the musical forces of the acting companies. According to Villamediana's text, instrumental music described as *"instrumentos músicos en diferentes coros"* accompanied the dance that opened the entertainment, executed by the Infanta and ladies wearing masks.[38] But, according to the *relación* by Hurtado de Mendoza, loud wind instruments (trumpets and shawms) opened the entertainment, and music played by *ministriles* (wind instrument players) gave way to that of *violones* (bowed string instruments) for the initial section of dancing.[39] Both of these sources indicate that, for the most part, instruments played in homogeneous groups or choirs. However, later in Mendoza's description mixed consorts seem to be indicated, although the specific groups that he suggests may be inaccurate:

> se dividian en quatro coros . . . con varios instrumentos, unos de guitarras, otros de flautas, y baxoncillos, otro de tiorbas, y otro de violones, y laudes.[40]

Comparing the text of the play with the *relación*, we find that the solo songs and songs for a small ensemble in this production were not particularly different from those called for in a play for the public stage. In the *loa*, four nymphs appear singing onstage. During Act I, *La Noche* (played by a negro Portuguese maidservant) comes onstage singing. At the opening of the second act, a nymph singing a sonnet offers the entertainment to the King. Solo songs in plays for the public theaters occur in situations similar to these, so Villamediana's text does not represent a major departure from the traditional *comedia* style in terms of the use and type of solo singing. The play did, however, take advantage of the greater number of singers available at court by using

---

38 Villamediana, *Obras*, ed. Rozas, pp. 361–362.
39 Hurtado de Mendoza (R-15515), fol. 6.
40 *Ibid.*, fol. 10.

multiple choirs that sang in antiphonal style. At several major points of division and at the end of the play, all of the choirs sang together with a *tutti* accompaniment of *"todos los instrumentos."*[41] As we have seen, the use of multiple choirs was a mainstay of both the spectacle plays and the earlier masques; hence this feature was not among the novelties of *La gloria de Niquea*.

During the court's stay at Aranjuez in the spring of 1622, two other spectacle plays were performed by the *meninas:* Antonio Hurtado de Mendoza's *Querer por solo querer* and Lope de Vega's *El vellocino de oro*.[42] *Querer por solo querer* was performed for the Queen's birthday celebration by the *meninas* under the direction of Doña María de Guzmán. Both of these spectacle plays used vocal and instrumental music in the standard ways. In addition, some of the associations of instruments with specific types of scenes from the *comedia* staging had been incorporated into the court spectacle plays, setting a precedent for Calderón's technique. For example, in *Querer por solo querer* trumpets and drums and a trumpet echo are used to suggest battle scenes and a warlike atmosphere. In Act I, the stage direction reads ". . . *Prosigue el ruido, suenen trompetas con mucha armonia, y estruendo de guerra . . ."*[43] In Act III, trumpets and drums sounding from offstage prompt Floranteo's response *"Suspende el aparato belicoso . . ."*[44]

Lope's play *El vellocino de oro*, like the other plays, began with a *loa*, and, like *La gloria de Niquea*, was divided into two acts, with a musical interlude between the acts. While there is no extant *relación* for this performance, the text of the play specifies that shawms, trumpets, and drums were used along with the traditional vocal music. In the *loa*, a voice responds in song from offstage, and *la música* (an unspecified group of voices and instruments) sings in praise of the King and Queen. The *torneo* is danced onstage in Act II, accompanied by instrumental music; significantly, the *torneo* was also used in Lope's *El premio de la hermosura*, and Hurtado de Mendoza's *Querer por solo querer*.

In 1648 the last spectacle play of the pre-Calderonian group was performed at court. This was Gabriel Bocángel y Unzueta's *El Nuevo Olimpo*, *"representación real y festiva máscara"* with which the court

---

41 *Ibid.*, fol. 8v, at the end of the prologue "diole las gracias la armonia de toda la musica, y la voz de todo el auditorio;" fol. 15, "Y con la mayor armonia de todos los instrumentos . . . acabando la representación."

42 The staging of these is described in Shergold, pp. 270–274.

43 B.N.M. R-12240, fol. 9v.

44 *Ibid.*, fol. 37.

celebrated the birthday of Philip IV's bride-to-be, Mariana de Austria.[45] This spectacle play, like *La gloria de Niquea*, attempted a revival of some strong elements from the earlier masques, although it also involved a written text. The play was performed by the ladies of the court with the musical participation of the Capilla Real.[46] In his advice to the reader in the printed edition of the play, Bocángel stressed the musical element:

> Espero que tendrá algun mérito en nuestra lengua, la novedad de introducir Coros de Música, que varian la representación, y la engrandecen. . . . En la composición desta, se notará tambien la novedad de averla conseguido cantada a todos los Coros y vozes que la Real Capilla consiente, aviendo trabajado en ajustar Clausulas Poeticas a todos sus tañidos, que muchos ni son versos ni caben en ellos. Ni tampoco se contenta la armonia de aquellos ayres con sencilleces de Prosa, cuya dificultad consiste, en haber precedido esta vez la Música a los Versos, o en aver obedecido estos las consonancias de aquella.[47]

First of all, Bocángel described the use of choirs with singers from the Royal Chapel as a novelty for the Spanish stage, when, of course, this had for some years been a normal feature of the spectacle plays and masques. Bocángel's claim in 1648 was no more justified than Villamediana's had been in 1622. However, *El Nuevo Olimpo* was exceptional because the music was written before the text, so that the poetic text had to be fitted to the music. Bocángel did not name the composer, and we do not know for certain whether the composer actually wrote new music for the spectacle or borrowed music from an existing repertory. In spite of the lacunae in Bocángel's description, there is evidence suggesting that new music was probably composed. In the accounts of the *violero* for the year 1648, there are two entries that in all probability refer to the preparations for *El Nuevo Olimpo*. Between October 24 and December 12 (1648), three guitars were brought to the house of the *maestro*, Carlos Patiño, in order to "try out" the songs for the entertainment.[48] Since

---

45 *Obras* de Don Gabriel Bocángel y Unzueta, ed. Rafael Benítez Claros (Madrid, 1946), II, pp. 142–217.

46 See Shergold, pp. 302–303.

47 *Obras*, p. 146.

48 B.N.M. Ms 14046/141, copy of Barbieri: "Mas se llevaron encordadas las guitarras a casa del maestro Carlos Patiño tres veces para probar los tonos de la comedia y mascara que hizo Su Alteza." (Original in Archivo de Palacio, Leg. 1117).

Bocángel stated that he wrote the text in less than a month, it seems plausible that the songs were ready for rehearsal by the beginning of December. Carlos Patiño, the *maestro de capilla*, may have been the composer, especially since the songs were "proven" at his house. The same set of accounts also includes the notice that the guitars were brought to the palace seven times for the rehearsals and the performance of the *fiesta*.[49] These entries must refer to *El Nuevo Olimpo*, since this was the only large performance in preparation at the time. Unfortunately, if indeed Patiño composed the music for this occasion, it is not known to be among his surviving works.

Up to this point, I have tried to present a general overview of the court plays that included significant musical participation and the ways that music was incorporated into these plays, without reviewing each and every one of the plays performed at court before 1650. I have presented the bulk of the documentation available on the music of these plays. Several patterns emerge from this sweeping survey. First of all, none of the plays in question can be seen as approaching the genre of opera. The uses for music and the performance of music in these early plays are clearly inherited from either the *comedia nueva* tradition or the Renaissance fêtes tradition. The use of large choirs and a variety of musical instruments, and the claims to novelty by the authors, do not make these plays any more "modern" or "operatic" than their predecessors. We do not find any concrete development or evolution in the direction of totally-sung theater. Putting the early seventeenth-century court plays into focus in the proper musical-historical context allows us to understand how and why the Calderonian court plays after 1650 (and the music that was composed for them) were, indeed, novel and more modern. Where Villamediana and Bocángel had failed to produce a new genre of lasting significance and appeal, Calderón succeeded.

Table 2–1: Early spectacle plays with music

date	place of performance	title/author	musical forces
1614	Lerma	*El premio de la hermosura* Lope de Vega	wind instruments violins solo singers vocal ensemble guitar

---

49 *Ibid.*: "Mas se llevaron a Palacio siete veces encordadas las guitarras para los ensayos y el dia de la ocasion de este fiesta de Su Alteza siempre con tres guitarras."

date	place of performance	title/author	musical forces
1617	Lerma	*El caballero del sol* Luis Vélez de Guevara	shawms trumpets ensemble of 6 singers
1622	Aranjuez	*Querer por solo querer* Hurtado de Mendoza	cornettos sackbuts viols
1622	Aranjuez	*La gloria de Niquea* Villamediana	trumpets shawms flutes and *bajoncillos* violins lutes and theorbos guitars ensemble of 3 female singers 4 choirs 2 solo songs
1622	Aranjuez	*El vellocino de oro* Lope de Vega	trumpets drums shawms ensemble of singers
1627	Madrid	*La selva sin amor* Lope de Vega "Egloga cantada" Opera in 7 scenes	7 solo voices ensemble of 3 voices 2 choirs orchestra of unspecified instruments
1635	Madrid	*El mayor encanto amor* Calderón	trumpet drums shawms vocal ensemble accompanied solo songs
1636	Madrid	*Los tres mayores prodigios* Calderón	trumpets and drums shawms vocal ensemble
1637	Madrid	*Auristela y Lisidante* Calderón	trumpets and drums vocal ensemble 3 soloists 2 choirs instrumental ensemble
1648	Madrid	*El nuevo Olimpo* Bocángel	trumpets shawms violin band 2 choirs

*The Calderón plays included traditional, pre-existent songs.

2.3 Calderón and the Creation of a Spanish Musical Theater

Calderón's mythological plays, created as dramatic spectacles for the Spanish Hapsburg Court, combine all of the fundamental elements that had become associated with the "court spectacle" before 1650. Calderón was the principal court dramatist from 1651 to his death in 1681. In this capacity, he seems to have been committed to a new form of court theater which could better exploit both the enhanced capabilities of the court stages and the musical resources of the court. Calderón drew on three principal types of theater in developing the new genre: the Lopean *comedia*, the earlier court masques and spectacle plays, and the new genre of Italian opera.

From the beginning of the seventeenth century, the simple *comedia nueva* had exploited vocal and instrumental music in a limited but functional way. In the Calderonian court plays, musical intervention takes on a new significance. In addition to being used as a structural device, musical content becomes more intimately associated with dramatic context. Songs and short choral refrains are still used to punctuate the fabric of the plot and to define scenes or sub-sections of scenes, but music assumed an expanded function in the court theaters and in the Baroque *teatro de representación*.[50] Calderón was traditional in the exploitation of pre-existent songs that would have been familiar to the audience. The presence of these songs alongside newly composed theatrical songs is highly significant: the traditional music of the Spanish *comedia* was retained in the larger form of the new court play.

Calderón knew and could draw upon the court spectacle as it had developed during his own lifetime: The heavily allegorical masques of the early seventeenth century, and the rudimentary dramatic spectacle plays by Lope de Vega, Vélez de Guevara, Hurtado de Mendoza, and the Conde de Villamediana. These plays, written for performance by amateur actors, simply did not contain the depth of meaning and complexity of the Calderonian plays, but from them Calderón might have developed some ideas about the symbolic use of music and the powerful nature of the musical contribution to the spectacle.

---

50 See Alicia Amadei-Pulice, "El stile rappresentativo en la comedia de teatro de Calderón," in *Approaches to the Theater of Calderón*, ed. Michael D. McGaha (University Press of America, Inc., 1982) pp. 215–229.

Calderón's third possible source of inspiration has been often mentioned but too-little explored. During the seventeenth century, a significant revolution in the history of music was taking place. Opera had been born and was fast spreading throughout Europe as a new musical genre and cultural phenomenon. Perhaps one feature of the early history of the operatic genre is that opera took on different characteristics of musical style, of subject matter, and of other performance-related qualities in different cities, and in different countries. Thus, although opera began in Florence, it soon spread to other cities in Italy, where it was adapted to the needs, tastes, and conditions of the host audience. For example, Italianate opera was also successful at the Hapsburg court in Vienna, yet the operatic style that developed at the Viennese court had some definite distinguishing features.

The revolution in musical thinking manifest in the development of the operatic genre in Italy also had a powerful effect on the other, nonoperatic genres of the European musical stage. In Spain, the court spectacle was codified by Calderón in a new genre called *zarzuela*, a hybrid form in which sung and spoken dialogue were combined.

When he began to write exclusively for the court in 1651, Calderón probably did not set out to develop the operatic genre in Spain, or to establish a totally Italian type of musical theater. However, Calderón was certainly inspired by his knowledge of the operatic experiments that had taken place in Italy. The two opera texts that Calderón wrote for the court in 1660 were deliberate attempts to introduce opera to the Spanish court: these are exceptions and should be carefully distinguished from the other works. In the *loa* to the first of these, *La púrpura de la rosa* (1659–1660), Calderón explicitly indicated his intention of introducing the Italian style of opera:

> que ha de ser
> Toda musica; que intenta
> Introducir este estilo,
> Porque otras naciones vean
> Competidos sus primores.

This quotation from the *loa* to *La púrpura de la rosa* has been frequently cited as evidence for the generalization that all of Calderón's court plays up to 1659 were "failed" or incomplete attempts to produce opera in Madrid. As this chapter will show, Calderón was probably not concerned with producing opera at the Court before 1659, although elements from the genre of Italian opera were of interest to him. The case for foreign influence has perhaps also been misunderstood, since foreign influence was not exclusively manifest in the production of totally sung drama. Non-Spanish techniques had been comfortably combined with traditional Spanish elements in court entertainments for some time. As we have seen, Franco-Italian pageantry was evident in the entertainments offered to the Spanish court in the early years of the seventeenth century; namely in the masques and pageants and then the dramatic spectacle plays.

However, the new current of Italian influence, the inescapable operatic wave, was even more powerful, and was most evident during the later years of the reign of Philip IV from c.1650 to 1665. The visual aspects of the productions were most strikingly modeled after the scenery and stage effects that had developed in the opera theaters of seventeenth-century Italy. Further, beginning in 1623, Italian designers and architects were brought to the Madrid court to supervise and direct the construction of stages and scenery. Calderón wrote the mythological court plays with the visual effects created by these artists at his disposal. Although there were strong similarities in the visual aspect of the productions and in the mythological or pastoral plots in both the Italian and the Spanish genres, there were some fundamental differences in the approach to the spectacle that prevented the operatic genre from really taking hold in Spain.

The Spanish theatrical tradition, with its strong emphasis on the importance of exaggerated histrionic expression, and its focus on the importance of proper declamation, could not easily accept completely sung drama. The practitioners of the histrionic art, the actors and actresses, seem to have had little desire to trade the glory of their emphatic spoken declamations for the complication and restriction of thoroughly sung roles.[51] In addition, the form and the structure of the *comedia nueva* were a potent cultural legacy that had already crossed into the territory of the court spectacle play of the 1620's and 1630's. Music had been assigned a function within the form, which defied radical changes. The Spanish theater of the Golden Age was the century's single-most forceful medium of cultural influence, of social criticism, and of political diffusion. From the first, the *comedia nueva* had been

---

51 See Jack Sage, "Texto y realización de *La estatua de Prometeo* y otros dramas musicales de Calderón," *Hacía Calderón. Coloquio Anglogermano Exeter 1969* (Berlin, 1970) pp. 37–45.

endowed with the dual social role of mirror and critic of society.[52] The theater was the central expressive medium for the cultural heritage of that society and was also a forum for contrasting views and artistic experimentation. Even the court spectacles were imbued with a strong sense of purpose, since from the first they were designed to praise the Spanish Hapsburg monarchy, and glorify that institution as the general leader and protector of the Catholic faith.

The text of the play was, traditionally, the principal means of dramatic expression and the most important element of the theatrical experience. Music was exploited as an expressive and structural resource, but music's power was controlled and only unleashed for certain calculated dramatic effects. The primacy of the text could not be usurped by music. This restriction on the use of music was an obvious impediment to the development of Spanish Baroque opera. Thus, although Calderón did write two opera texts (and these were successfully performed within his lifetime and even after his death), the creation of the *zarzuela* was his real attempt to solve the problem. In the mythological plays, Calderón developed a special meaning for music which grew from the very constraints of the genre and suited the tastes and prerequisites of the Spanish court audience. To create this multifaceted form, or *zarzuela*, Calderón drew on a number of traditions. Two fundamental musical types influenced the development of the genre: The music of the Calderonian *zarzuelas* can be best described as Spanish music with elements of the Italian operatic tradition.

The native musical tradition, the musical forms and techniques from the plays for the public theaters, were the primary source for the music of the Calderonian court plays. Popular dances and the rhythms of the early sung dances reappear in music for the *zarzuelas* and *fiestas cantadas*. The traditional strophic formula (*coplas* and *estribillo*) of the *romances* and *villancicos* resurfaces as a dominant formal characteristic of the airs or *tonadas*. The repertoire of the early musical *cancioneros* continues, in the guise of pre-existent songs, to coexist in the *zarzuelas* with the imported musical form of recitative. Calderón's baroque genre embraced the new and revolutionary imported musical forms, but also strongly maintained the characteristic elements of the native Spanish

---

52 In Covarrubias, *Tesoro de la Lengua Castellana* (Madrid, 1611) pp. 341–342, *"Comedia"*: "Es cierta especia de fábula, en la qual se nos representa como en un espejo, el trato y vida de la gente ciudadana y popular ... que con fingidos argumentos y marañas nos dibuxan el trato y condiciones de los hombres ... En fin un retrato de todo lo que passa en el mundo."

musical tradition. The *zarzuela* genre represents a fusion of speech and song, of tradition with innovation, and of two different musical aesthetics, one national and the other foreign.

However, in the hands of Calderón's musical collaborators even the recitatives and airs exhibit their own musical style, similar to, but distinct from, what we know to be Italian. In other words, while the formal aspects of recitatives and airs were inspired by foreign models, content and musical style show that the Spanish composers adapted the forms to a Spanish aesthetic. While the Italian composers who contributed to the development of the Baroque operatic style valued intellectual abstraction in an increasing relationship among musical form, affect, and dramatic expression, the Spanish composers were dedicated to clear and uncomplicated musical expression and to maintaining elements from a popular tradition.

One link between the Italian and the Spanish theater came in the person of the poet and librettist Giulio Rospigliosi, a major figure in the history of Roman opera, who was in Madrid as the papal legate from 1644 to 1653.[53] Rospigliosi may have had a key role in promoting Italian operatic ideas at the court of Philip IV, and, at the least, we may assume that he and Calderón would have had more than just a passing acquaintance during the lengthy stay in Madrid. While there is almost no information concerning Rospigliosi's literary activities in Spain, "the influence of Spanish drama is apparent" in the libretti written after his return to Rome in the spring of 1653.[54] I suspect that Rospigliosi's influence was important to Calderón's development of the new genre of Spanish court plays as well. Rospigliosi was at court for the preparation and performance of several court plays by Calderón between 1650 and 1653. In a letter from Madrid in July of 1652, Rospigliosi comments on the production of a large Spanish machine play in the Buen Retiro.[55] In the same year, Rospigliosi is said to have written a text for performance in Madrid, in support of efforts by the Italian contingent to introduce the recitative style to the Spanish court.[56] The fact remains that we know of no performance of Italian opera in Madrid during this period, and we do not know if the Spanish composers could have had any first-hand

---

53 Margaret Murata, *Operas for the Papal Court 1631–1668* (Ann Arbor: UMI Research Press, 1981) pp. 6–7.

54 *Ibid.*, pp. 49–50.

55 *Ibid.*, pp. 49 and 209.

56 Lorenzo Bianconi, *Storia della Musica*, IV: *Il Seicento* (Torino, 1982) p. 257. Quoted from an unnamed source.

knowledge of that genre. However, one tenuous musical connection can be suggested. An Italian singer associated with Roman opera was in Madrid during part of Rospigliosi's legation. In 1645 Rospigliosi sent for Lodovico Lenzi, a male soprano, to join him in Madrid.[57] This singer had at least one opportunity to display his abilities to Philip IV. In February of 1652 *"se llevo una guitarra a Palacio para oyr cantar Su Magestad al capon Italiano."*[58]

In the spring of 1652, several forces combined to bring about the enthusiastic production of Calderón's first mature spectacle play in the Coliseo theater of the Buen Retiro palace.[59] Although this play, *La fiera, el rayo, y la piedra* was not technically called a *zarzuela*, it was a prototypical effort in terms of the use of music.[60]

The most important musical innovation in the text of *La fiera, el rayo, y la piedra* is the introduction of recitative *(estilo recitativo)*[61] for the conversations of the gods, Cupid, Anteros, and Venus. The first extended section intended for recitative is Cupid's monologue in Act II beginning *"Si el orbe de la luna / esfera soberana . . ."* (*BAE* IX 496c), which, significantly, is written in seven- and eleven-syllable lines throughout.[62] The fact that this early example of recitative in a Calderonian text is written in the "Italian" meter heightens the importance of this passage and confirms that Calderón consciously imitated the Italian form. In this play, the seven- and eleven-syllable lines are also used for the sung dialogue between Cupid and Anteros in Act III (*BAE* IX, 505c–506a), which might suggest that these lines were

---

57 Murata, p. 7.
58 B.N.M. Ms 14046/145. Original document. Cuentas de Manuel de Vega, violero, 1652.
59 Staging of the play is discussed in Shergold, pp. 305–311.
60 In Calderón's earlier court plays (*El mayor encanto amor*, 1635; *Los tres mayores prodigios*, 1636; *Auristela y Lisidante*, 1637), music is used in the standard or traditional ways.
61 The stage directions differ in the three versions of the text of the play. The *editio princeps* (*Tercera parte de Comedias de Don Pedro Calderón de la Barca . . .* Madrid, 1664) offers very few specific stage directions with regard to music. The musical stage directions in the edition of Vera Tassis (*Tercera parte de comedias . . . Que nuevamente corregidas publica don Juan de Vera Tassis . . .* Madrid, 1687) are more specific, and the *BAE* edition generally follows Vera Tassis. The stage directions in the 1690 manuscript copy of the play (B.N.M. Ms 14614) do not contradict the Vera Tassis version insofar as musical participation is concerned. See also, Shergold, pp. 305–310.
62 The stage direction in the Vera Tassis (1687) edition reads: "cantando al estilo recitativo".

also sung as recitative. Both Cupid's recitative in Act II and the dialogue of Cupid and Anteros in Act III are punctuated by short choral statements; musicians from offstage in the first case, and by the two choirs *(coro de Cupido, coro de Anteros)* in the second.

Also in Act II, Anteros sings to Anajarte (a mortal), but neither the text meters nor the stage directions indicate that this strophic monologue with refrain was sung as a recitative. In fact, Anteros' sung monologue was probably a set piece or *tonada*, the equivalent of an aria.[63]

The text of the play calls for several vocal ensembles for the choral refrains or *estribillos* that punctuate the work. The "choir of Sirens" and the "choir of Tritons" from the opening scene are carefully indicated in the 1690 manuscript of the play. Four treble voices made up the choir of Sirens, and two tenors and two contralto singers sang the parts for the Tritons.[64]

Later in Act I, a grotto is discovered and the three Fates are seen singing from within *"en tono muy triste."* In a subsequent scene the repeated sung warnings of three Cyclopes are heard. This awesome trio is revealed hammering in their foundry as they sing the final repetition of their text. The songs of the Fates and the Cyclopes help to establish the element of mystery and the supernatural, and the repeated song of the Cyclopes is an audible link between the various sections of the scene.

The power of music – in this case the power of music to tame the "wild beast" *(la fiera)* – is the subject of an entire scene in the play. In Act I, Anajarte instructs her band of maidens to catch the *humana fiera* (Irifile) with the aid of the music of instruments and voices. The four maidens are posted at different corners of the stage, playing instruments and singing. Anajarte has instructed them to trade the musical instruments for weapons as soon as the *fiera* Irifile is within range, with the comment

---

63 There is an important textual concordance for this song-text from the end of Act II (*BAE* IX, 501a). The text of the "Tonada de Anteros en la Fiera, el Rayo, y la Piedra" is copied into Barcelona, Biblioteca del Instituto de Teatro, MS 82841 bis (fol. 36v–37), in the form of six coplas and estribillo. This would indicate that the six quattrains of text beginning "El correspondido amor/que rey en el orbe fui . ." were sung, in addition to the refrain "Ama al que ama Anaxarte . . .".

64 B.N.M. Ms 14614, *Fiesta de la Comedia Que mandó executar, en el Real Palacio de Valencia,* . . . fol. 4. Shergold, p. 308, interprets these musical stage directions as indicating that for the 1690 performance "the operatic element in this play is increased." However, a choir of eight voices would also have been possible and highly likely for the performances of this play in 1652, since similar choirs or vocal ensembles had already been widely used in connection with earlier court spectacle plays. Clearly, the use of choral music cannot be considered as exclusively "operatic."

that ". . . *No vienen a estar opuestas/Hoy dos tan opuestas cosas/Como instrumentos y flechas . . ."*
Unfortunately, the music for this play seems not to have survived, except for one pre-existent song *"Es verdad que yo la vi/En el campo entre las flores . . .,"* which is to be sung by *"músicos dentro"* in Act II.[65] The song is used in much the same way here as it would be in a *comedia* for the public stage. The song has little to do with the mythological and spectacular aspects of this play. Rather, the song directly highlights the various amorous problems of the mortals: the musicians (singing offstage) sing this well-known song, which prompts Anajarte to remark *"Bien sonora es, si no fuera/La letra de amor."* The musicians are Anajarte's musicians, singing at her request. Thus, Calderón has used the traditional *romance* as the music of the mortals; in this guise, traditional music is introduced into the new genre of the Calderonian spectacle play.
While the surviving texts of *La fiera, el rayo, y la piedra* illustrate some of Calderón's ideas for incorporating music into the new court spectacle play of the mid-century, we do not have enough documentation about the actual performances of this work to draw further conclusions.[66] However, we do have some important notices concerning the performance of a court play in the following year.
In the spring of 1653, the princess Maria Teresa organized festivities in the Buen Retiro to celebrate the return to good health of Queen Mariana. Calderón's *Fortunas de Andrómeda y Perseo* was probably performed on May 18 as the highpoint of the celebrations.[67] *Fortunas de Andrómeda y Perseo* deserves a separate chapter of its own,[68] but in this

---

65 A musical setting of "Es verdad que yo la vi . . .," with several variants in the song-text, is contained in the Cancionero de Olot (Olot, Biblioteca Pública, Ms. I–VIII, fol. 68). The song-text also appears in *Reinar despues de morir*, III by Luis Vélez de Guevara, and in the *Mogiganga de don Gayferos* by Suarez de Deza y Avila.

66 Only one oblique reference to the performance of 1652 appears in the accounts of the *violero*, Manuel de Vega, for that year: ". . . se aderezo el bajo de [Nicolas] Panela que se quebró en el Retiro en la Comedia grande." B.N.M. Ms. 14046/145.

67 Harvard University, Houghton Library, Ms Typ 258H. This presentation manuscript, which includes the text of the play, eleven drawings for the stage designs by Baccio del Bianco, and the music for the play, was first brought to public attention in Phyllis Dearborn Massar, "Scenes for a Calderón Play by Baccio del Bianco," *Master Drawings*, XV, 4 (1977) pp. 365–375. See also, John E. Varey, "Scenes, Machines and the Theatrical Experience in Seventeenth-Century Spain," *La Scenografia Barocca*, ed. Antoine Schnapper (Bologna: Editrice CLUEB, 1982), pp. 55–58.

68 See the forthcoming edition by John E. Varey and Jack Sage (based on the Harvard Ms.) to be published by Tamesis Books, Ltd., London. I am grateful to both Professors Varey and Sage for their generous assistance in leading me to the Harvard

essay only a few relevant points will be covered. The documentation for
Andrómeda y Perseo forms an important concentration of information
pertaining to a central work in the history of music in the Spanish
theater. Because the play was performed during the formative period for
theatrical music, any study of music in Spanish court theater must, at the
least include a brief summary of the documents: A presentation
manuscript of the play which includes the vocal music,[69] the seventeenth-century editions of the play,[70] and a letter of Baccio del Bianco
describing the staging of the play.[71]

The fundamental importance of the presentation manuscript cannot be
overestimated, for it shows that the seventeenth-century editions of the
text do not indicate exactly how much of the play was sung, nor do they
include precise stage directions for the instrumental music. The printed
texts of *Fortunas de Andrómeda y Perseo* are not unique in this regard;
for example, the printed text of the opera *Celos aun del aire matan* has
almost no indications for music.[72] The musical details of the performances must have been worked out among the dramatist, the composer, and
the musicians, or perhaps they were indicated on a separate memorandum but omitted in the subsequent publication of the play. We can
suppose that the actors and musicians did not rely solely on the printed
editions for later performances.

The presentation manuscript preserves several variant readings in the
text and several sections of text that are missing in the printed editions.
Most important, it includes a unique prologue to the play, which is
divided into two scenes or *mutaciones*. In the first *mutación*, the figures
of Poesía, Pintura and Música *"representavan cantando,"*[73] dedicating
the entertainment to the Queen. In the second scene of the prologue, the

---

source. A substantial section of my own forthcoming doctoral dissertation, *Music in
the Seventeenth-Century Spanish Theater* (The University of Chicago, Department of
Music) will also deal with *Fortunas de Andrómeda y Perseo*.

69 Harvard University, Houghton Library, Ms Typ 258H. According to Baccio's letter
of July 19, the manuscript was prepared "per mandare con la commedia e musiche
all'imperatore". See, P. Dearborn Massar, p. 367.

70 In *Parte veinte y una de Comedias nuevas, escogidas de los mejores Ingenios de España*
(Madrid: Joseph Fernandez de Buendia, 1663) pp. 47–96, and in *Sexta parte de
Comedias del celebre poeta español don Pedro Calderón de la Barca ...* que publica
don Juan de Vera Tassis y Villarroel (Madrid: Franciso Sanz, 1682).

71 Mina Bacci, "Lettere inedite di Baccio del Bianco", *Paragone* (Anno XIV, no. 157)
1963, pp. 71–72. Letter to Ferdinand II dated 19 July 1653.

72 See, for example, the *editio princeps* in *Parte XIX* of *Comedias nuevas escogidas de los
mejores ingenios de España* (Madrid: Melchor Sánchez, 1663).

73 Harvard, Ms Typ. 258H, fol. 6v.

giant Atlas (Atlante), probably an automaton,[74] sings in a "sonorous, grave, and low" voice[75] as he sustains the cloud bearing twelve ladies who represent the twelve stars that form the signs of the Zodiac. Atlante then lowers the twelve figures to the stage where they dance while carrying reflective shields and torches.[76]

The musical structure of the second scene of the prologue is virtually unique in Spanish theatrical music of the time. The entire scene is constructed from six short melodic fragments, that are arranged into an orderly closed structure with a basic pattern of repetitions. The fragments are first presented as the song of Atlante at the opening of the *mutación*, written in tenor clef as a unison, so that his melody and the bass line are one and the same. The four phrases of this melody/bass line become the initial four fragments of bass line that are used to generate the rest of the prologue. Each repetition of a fragment of the bass line carries with it a statement or repetition of a melodic fragment.[77]

While this rigid formulaic construction was uncommon in Spanish theatrical music, it was far from unusual in Italian opera of the time. However, although repeating bass patterns were a standard compositional and structural device in seventeenth-century music, these did not usually imply exact repetition of melodic fragments linked to the bass patterns. The musical structure of this scene of the prologue might suggest that Italianate formal structures were being experimented with by Calderón's musical collaborators in 1653, at the end of Rospigliosi's tenure in Madrid and just two years after the arrival of Baccio del Bianco.[78]

---

74 P. Dearborn Massar, pp. 369–370.

75 "... a la voz del Atlante: que sonora, profunda, y grabe prosiguio ...", Harvard Ms., fol. 9.

76 Both of these scenes from the Prologue have a strong thematic association with scenes from earlier Roman entertainments. The first scene for Poesía, Pintura, and Música recalls the *"Prologo"* to the opera *Il palazzo incantato* (libretto by Rospigliosi, music by Luigi Rossi) of 1642. The figure of Atlante is also present in this opera. See the facsimile edition ed. Howard Mayer Brown, *Italian Opera 1640–1770* (New York: Garland) vols. 2 and 58. The second scene from Calderón's prologue strongly suggests a connection to Ottavio Tronsarelli's *Ballo de' Segni Celesti* written for the Duke of Savoy in 1630. See Tronsarelli, *Drammi Musicali* (Rome: Corbelletti, 1631) pp. 317–326. The use of similar material in these scenes from the prologue to *Andrómeda y Perseo* and in the earlier Roman works is further evidence for Rospigliosi's influence.

77 Music for the second scene of the prologue, Harvard Ms., fols. 108–112v.

78 The composer of the music for *Fortunas de Andrómeda y Perseo* is not named in any of the documents known to this author. If the composer was Spanish (which seems more than likely), then Juan Hidalgo would be the obvious choice. However, the

However, the specific context of this scene explains the use of this overall structure. The song of Atlante, in the lower register, is the basis for the rest of the music of the scene, as if to reflect in musical terms the fact that the Atlante is sustaining the "weight of the globe" on his shoulders, or in the text itself: *"El que el globo sustenta/del orbe todo . . ."* When Atlante lowers the twelve stars to the stage, they take up his melody for their dance. The dance is described in the rubrics of the manuscript as *"un sarao: en que mudando metro y tono, remataron la loa con estas coplas dançadas, y bayladas."*[79] An organized set of musical phrases would have facilitated the choreographic display; the repetitive musical scheme would have been easy for the dancers to follow, and the *mudanzas* (sets of steps in the dance) were probably organized according to the simple musical structure.

It is clear from Baccio's letters that he was (as theatrical engineer or technical director) interested in bringing the Italian style of staging and production to Madrid. In his letter of July 19, 1653, which discusses but does not name *Fortunas de Andrómeda y Perseo*, Baccio expressed his annoyance with one of the traditional elements of Spanish theatrical music:

> Li accidenti seguiti in questa commedia non sono meno delli dell'anno passato, pero como ora hanno visto quella sono stati piu cattolici, pero non s'e potuto schifare che in una gloria di deita non vi fusse quattro guidoni vestiti di nero all'usanza con chitarre spagniole, cappa e spada, si come al calar del cielo i dodici segni dello zodiaco che erano 12 donne, usci dalla strada in confuso e i medesimi quattro a fare schiena al foro, uso di qua, che quando tratto di levare questa usanza poco meno che non mi crocifiggono, dicendo che e impossibile che ballino senza quelle chitarre di dietro; insomma la pulitezza delle scene, la puntualita delle strade, non usa qua ne e fatta per questi istrioni, anzi molti, detto che hanno i lor versi, se non si accenna che ritornino dentro, cor un voltar di schiena si intende essere dentro; abbattesi molte volte che il nemico, cercando l'altro, entra per una strada che riscontrandolo ad occhi veggenti del popolo, bada a ire come se non lo vedessi e mille altre improprieta, ne e possibile il porli in buona forma.[80]

---

compositional techniques that I describe for the Prologue were not used by Hidalgo in other extant pieces, bringing up the possibility that another composer, maybe an Italian, wrote the music for the prologue.

79 Harvard Ms., fol. 7.
80 M. Bacci, "Lettere inedite", p. 72.

The ever-present guitars were one traditional feature of music from the realm of the public theater that found its way into the court productions. Although Baccio del Bianco found them out of place in an elaborately decorated scene involving the dance of the twelve signs of the Zodiac, tradition had established that the guitars were allowed onstage for large danced scenes. The dancers for this scene were actresses who regularly worked in the public theaters as members of the acting companies. Of course, the same companies performed both in the *corrales* and at the court theaters, but the experience of performing a Calderonian spectacle play was still very new.

The guitars are the only instruments mentioned in Baccio's letter with reference to the performances of *Andrómeda y Perseo*. However, the rubrics written into the presentation manuscript of the play (prepared after the performances) do mention instrumental music. According to the rubric, the recitative dialogue of Palas and Mercurio in Act I was accompanied by the instrumental ensemble (*el coro de los instrumentos*), and later in Act I the fight between Palas and Discordia was accompanied by a *"batalla que tocavan los violones."* In Act III, *"cajas destempladas y sordinas roncas"* are mentioned in connection with the *"música lamentosa,"* which begins with the song *"La que nace para ser/ Estrago de la fortuna . . ."*[81] In contrast, the next scene, involving a dance of six sea-nymphs, required *"instrumentos y voces festivos dentro."* The instrumental ensemble was essential to the performance of the play, and in the above-mentioned rubrics we are given a glimpse of its function. Instrumental colors or timbres were associated with particular types of scenes. The word *"batalla,"* used in connection with the music played by the *violones* to accompany the conflict between Palas and Discordia, probably refers to a *concitato*, affective, agitated style of playing, and the affective significance of the association of *cajas destempladas* with *música lamentosa* is obvious.[82]

Fortunas de Andrómeda y Perseo is the first court play for which we have all of the vocal music. The musical score and the extant documentation

---

81 In *El mayor encanto amor*, III (*BAE* VII, p. 408) the stage direction reads "Tocan dentro cajas destempladas y una sordina". This is a common stage direction in Calderón's texts, and the sound of these instruments was used to emphasize pathos.

82 The terminology used in the manuscript for these instruments is problematic. The Spanish word *"violon"* (plural *violones*) was used to refer to a bass stringed instrument, but in Spain it could refer to any instrument of the violin family, as opposed to *vihuelas de arco* or viols. *Cajas destempladas y sordinas* probably describes drums that are tuned to two discordant pitches, and muted trumpets. The muted trumpets would sound one pitch higher than normal.

show that by 1653 the Calderonian court plays were already a strong mixture of Spanish and Italian elements, and the principal importation from the Italian musical world was the use of the recitative. The rubrics for Act I give us a delightful description of Spanish recitative as it was thought of in 1653:

> Y volviendo á enlaçar el argumento, . . . empeçaron su platica [Palas and Mercurio], a diferencia de los humanos, en un estilo recitatibo: que siendo un compuesto de representacion y musica; ni bien era musica, ni bien representacion; sino una entonada consonancia, á quien acompañava el coro de los instrumentos . . .[83]

With regard to dramatic propriety and verisimilitude, the use of sung dialogue in the form of recitative was justified, since recitative became the medium for the conversation of the gods. Also implicit in this description is the concept of *recitar cantando*,[84] the combination of declamation and song which resulted in an appropriately harmonious medium for the "language" or "diction" (*plática*) of the deities.[85] It is perhaps significant that in the final scene of Act I, in the struggle between Palas and Discordia, only Palas sings in recitative. Discordia, the *"mentida deidad,"* speaks *"sonando sin consonancia."*[86]

---

83 Harvard Ms., fol. 22v.

84 The description of recitative quoted from the Harvard Ms. is remarkably similar to Jacopo Peri's definition in his preface to *Euridice* (1601): he cites the need to "imitate speech in song" for dramatic poetry, and describes the style as "a harmony surpassing that of ordinary speech but falling so far below the melody of song as to take an intermediate form." Translated in Oliver Strunk, *Source Readings in Music History* (New York: W. W. Norton, 1950) p. 374. See the discussion of "recitar cantando" in Nino Pirrotta, "Early Opera and Aria," in *New Looks at Italian Opera* ed. William W. Austin (Ithaca: Cornell University Press, 1968) pp. 46–53. On Peri's technique for dramatic music, see Howard Mayer Brown, "How Opera Began: An Introduction to Jacopo Peri's *Euridice* (1600)," in *The Late Italian Renaissance, 1525–1630*, ed. Eric Cochrane (London, 1970), pp. 401–443. Peri's *Euridice* has also been published in a modern edition by Professor Howard Mayer Brown, as vols. XXXVI–XXXVII of *Recent Researches in the Music of the Baroque Era* (Madison: A–R Editions, Inc., 1981).

85 The word *plática* recalls a passage from Lope de Vega's *Arte nuevo de hacer comedias* (verses 54–56), in which music (harmony) is to be the vehicle for language, diction, and sweet verse. Calderón could easily have justified his acceptance of the recitative style for the "language" of the gods by referring to Lope's treatise and to the pertinent source passage in Aristotle's *Poetics* (McKeon translation pp. 1455–1456).

86 *BAE* IX, 238a. Palas describes Discordia thus: "Suspende la aleve lengua/Mentida deidad, pues basta/Que el acento de tu voz,/Sonando sin consonancia,/Diga quién eres, . . .".

Recitative had developed in the first place as a vehicle for the exposition of affect: a declamatory "speech-song" that was also closely linked to the *stile rappresentativo* (a theatrical concept and not a musical one). Recitative was the musical device in the service of the *stile rappresentativo* or, in Spanish, *representación*. The element of *representación* (in both the Calderonian court plays and in early seventeenth-century Italian operas) was achieved with the appropriate gestures, facial expressions, and movements of the actress, together with the expressive use of the voice in the recitative.[87]

While the Calderonian court plays were only partly sung, there is definitely an operatic quality to the use of music in these plays. There is a crucial difference between the use of song in earlier spectacle plays and masques and the "operatic" inspiration for the sung portions of these plays. The sophisticated Italianate visual effects of the earlier spectacle plays did not have a musical equivalent (witness the traditional use of music in *La gloria de Niquea* or *El nuevo Olimpo*). The songs and the way they functioned were not fundamentally different from songs in the *comedias* for the public theaters. However, the incorporation of recitative and the use of extended sections of sung dialogue beginning in the court plays from 1652 and 1653 did mean that, to some extent, Calderón had embraced the aesthetic and theoretical foundations of early opera.[88]

In purely musical terms, recitative is generally distinguished from other solo song by the characteristic duple meter (usually common time or 1/1), a slow harmonic rhythm and the use of sustained single notes in the bass line except at cadences and points of dramatic tension. The melodic style of the recitative developed in order to facilitate the declamation of the text, with combinations of smaller note values in a syllabic style. Spanish recitative approximates, but does not exactly imitate, the accepted paradigm of Italian recitative. In the extant music for Act I of *Fortunas de Andrómeda y Perseo*, for example, the recitative is notated in triple meter. The Spanish recitative style is much freer and less

---

87 The importance of expressive acting in connection with recitative and the "stile rappresentativo" was stressed by the creators of early opera. See, for example, the prefatory remarks or "A Lettori" to Emilio De' Cavalieri, *Rappresentatione di Anima, et di Corpo* (Rome, 1600), reprinted by Gregg Press, Ltd., 1967.

88 Giovanni Battista Doni (1595–1647), a Florentine theorist associated with early seventeenth-century opera, considered partly sung drama a viable alternative to opera. See Giovanni Battista Doni, *Trattato della Musica Scenica* (c. 1633–1635), Capitolo IV, "Che e molto meglio cantare parte delle azioni che tutte intere," extracted in Angelo Solerti, *Le Origini del Melodrama* (Torino, 1903) pp. 198–201.

declamatory with fewer repeated notes and a slightly faster harmonic rhythm.[89] It is entirely possible that the Spanish composers did not have first-hand knowledge of the Italian style. Further, since most of the dialogue in the Spanish court plays was spoken, a strict declamatory style in the sung dialogues may have been superfluous. In addition, the recitative settings of Spanish poetic texts show a marked attention to poetic structure as well as to the images in the text. Each line of text is set as a complete musical phrase, so that the tendency is toward a series of short balanced phrases with a regular pattern of frequent cadences. The cadential formulae tend to be more extended and embellished than those of Italian recitative.

The recitatives in *Andrómeda y Perseo* are of both the through-composed type and the strophic type. Some sections of recitative are punctuated by refrains or *estribillos* in triple meter in an arioso melodic style. These lyrical sections usually carry the return of a textual refrain and function in a way similar to the *ritornelli* of contemporary Italian opera. In *Fortunas de Andrómeda y Perseo*, as in Calderón's later court plays, textual refrains are also set as choral *estribillos*. Thus, the principle of the *ritornello* was present in the Spanish court play by 1653 and was used in conjunction with the already familiar dramatic device of the recurrent textual refrain. Of course, the formal device called *estribillo* had been used in Spanish music from the time of the earliest *villancicos*. The use of short refrains within a continuous recitative texture and the use of choral *estribillos* are other instances of the fusion of traditional Spanish techniques with elements of the newer, imported genre.

Aside from their use as refrains, the ariosos or airs from *Andrómeda y Perseo* also appear as independent strophic song settings, and some of them have the formal arrangement of songs with *coplas* and *estribillo*. In the strophic airs, slight variations in melody or rhythm sometimes occur in order to accomodate the verses of the song-text. However, the airs do not exhibit any use of the variation form or repetitive bass patterns.

In this prototype of the new Calderonian court play, closed-form songs or airs are generally used only in special dramatic situations, while through-composed recitative is used for most of the sung dialogue. As has been established, only the gods could sing in the new recitative style – a combination of speech and music – but whether the deities sing recitative or air depends on the dramatic situation. The airs are reserved

---

89 However, some of the recitative passages in *Fortunas de Andrómeda y Perseo* are closer to the strict recitative style than the later examples from, for example, *Celos aun del aire matan* and *La estatua de Prometeo*. For a closer analysis see the forthcoming edition by Varey and Sage, and my forthcoming doctoral dissertation.

for scenes in which the persuasive power of sensuous music is appropriate.[90] At the beginning of Act II of *Fortunas de Andrómeda y Perseo*, Morfeo's words to the sleeping mortal Perseo are set as arioso with refrain, perhaps to symbolize Morpheus' character, so that a gentle song is associated with the bringer of sleep. The *tonada* is the vehicle for the influence of the god over the powerless mortal, and, of course, the recitative speech of the gods could not be understood by mere mortals within Calderón's system.

Choral intervention had been an important part of the *comedias* in the public theaters and of the early court masques and amateur spectacle plays, and the theatrical chorus or *"cuatro escénico"* continued as part of the Calderonian court play. The definite formal structure of the polyphonic theatrical songs also originated in a native tradition, that of the polyphonic songs from the early seventeenth-century *cancioneros*. The choruses were normally written for four voice parts and a bass line, without notation for obligato instruments, although instruments may have doubled the vocal parts. A tri-partite structure was typical: the first section in strict homophony and homorhythm, the second section in a pseudo-contrapuntal style with imitative entries, and the third section showing a return to the homophony and homorhythm of the opening. In the four-part pieces from *Andrómeda y Perseo* the middle sections of the *cuatros* are very briefly stated. When the choral pieces take up a text that has been stated in the previous solo song or duo, the bass line of the solo or duo is used for the chorus as well, and the melody of the solo setting is preserved in the four-part setting.

The repertory of well-known contemporary songs was also drawn upon for the music of the court plays,[91] including *Andrómeda y Perseo*. In the appropriate scenes the mortal characters sing earthly songs just as the characters in a simple *comedia* do; another transference of practices that originated in the public theaters to the domain of the court stage. The surviving music for *Fortunas de Andrómeda y Perseo* includes a version

---

90 On the subject of Calderón's attitude toward music, see Jack Sage, "The function of music in the theater of Calderón," *Critical Studies of Calderón's Comedias*, ed. J. E. Varey (London, 1973) pp. 209–230, and "Texto y realización de *La estatua de Prometeo* y otros dramas musicales de Calderón," *Hacía Calderón. Coloquio Anglogermano Exeter 1969* (Berlin, 1970), pp. 37–52.

91 In plays by Calderón written both before and after *Andrómeda y Perseo*, traditional or pre-existent songs were used. See for example: *El mayor encanto amor, Auristela y Lisidante, Los tres mayores prodigios, La fiera, el rayo, y la piedra,* and *Fieras afemina amor*. See also, E. Wilson and Jack Sage, *Poesías líricas en las obras dramáticas de Calderón*, (London: Tamesis, 1964).

for solo voice and a four-part setting of the song *"Ya no les pienso pedir/ más lágrimas a mis ojos . . .,"* which we can compare with an earlier setting of the same text ascribed to Juan Blas in the Cancionero de Sablonara. Significantly, the settings from the Harvard Ms. (1653) and the Sablonara manuscript (c.1620–1625) are not identical, but they do share characteristic features of melody and rhythm. [See musical example 1] It seems then, that the composer or arranger of the 1653 version did not attempt to preserve exactly the earlier setting, but that the two versions of the same song were based on a common model, the well-known tune.[92]

In summary, the lavish court plays of 1652 and 1653 included music as one of the central elements of the spectacle, and by this date concepts and applications for music from the foreign genre of opera were integrated with techniques that had been developed in Spain in the preceeding half century. By 1653 Calderón's hybrid genre, in which spoken and sung dialogue were combined, was accepted as the standard for these entertainments.

It seems that Calderón's new genre was almost immediately accepted as the prototype for court plays by other dramatists. As early as the year 1656, the production of a little-known play by a minor dramatist demonstrates the rapid assimilation of musical techniques that had been pioneered in the Calderón plays produced in 1652 and 1653. During February of 1656, Luis de Ulloa y Pereyra's *Pico y Canente*[93] was first

---

92 Harvard, Houghton Library, Ms. Typ 258H, fols. 125–126. Munich, Bayerische Staatsbibliothek, Mus. Ms. E. (200), fol. 25. The song-text also appears in Calderón's *La desdicha de la voz*, III and in the *Bayle de las Estafas* by Vicente Suarez de Deza y Avila. The song-text was printed and reprinted in the many issues of the Segura, *Primavera* collection (Zaragoza, 1629), including the last edition of Madrid, 1659.

93 *Fiesta que la Serenissima Infanta Doña María Teresa de Austria mandó hazer, en celebracion de la salud de la Reyna nuestra Señora Doña Mariana de Austria. Executose en el Salon del Palacio de el Buen Retiro, y despues en su Coliseo.* (B.N.M. T-20695, undated *suelta*). According to Cayetano Alberto de la Barrera y Leirado, *Catálogo bibliográfico y biográfico del teatro antiguo español* (Madrid, 1860, reprinted by Tamesis Books Limited, London, 1968) p. 410, *Pico y Canente* was written by Luis de Ulloa Pereyra and Rodrigo Dávila Ponce de León. Don Antonio de Solís is credited with the *loa*, the two *entremeses*, and the *sainete* or *sarao* that followed Act III. The *loa* and the *sainete* were published posthumously in Antonio de Solís y Rivadeneira, *Varias poesías, sagradas y profanas* (Madrid: Antonio Román, 1692). The *Entremés de Juan Rana Poeta* is attributed to Solís in La Barrera, p. 628, and the *Entremés de los bolatines*, published in *Laurel de Entremeses varios* (Zaragoza, 1660), is assumed to be by Solís in María del Carmen Simón Palmer, *Manuscritos dramáticos del siglo de oro de la Biblioteca del Instituto del Teatro de Barcelona* (Madrid: C.S.I.C., 1977), p. 64. Of course, the *loa*, the two *entremeses*, and the final *sainete* were published in the the commemorative *suelta* edition with *Pico y Canente*.

Musical Example 1: Three settings of "Ya no les pienso pedir . . ."

1a

Opening of the setting by Juan Blas, Cancionero de Sablonara (c. 1620-1625)
[Munich, Bayerische Staatsbibliothek, Mus. Ms. E. (200), fol. 25]

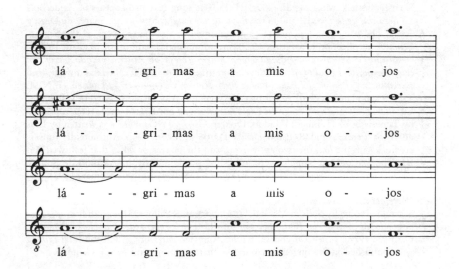

Musical Example 1b

"Ya no les pienso pedir . . ."

Opening of the four-part setting from *Fortunas de Andrómeda y Perseo*
(1653)
[Harvard University, Houghton Library, Ms. Typ 258H, fol. 125v-126]

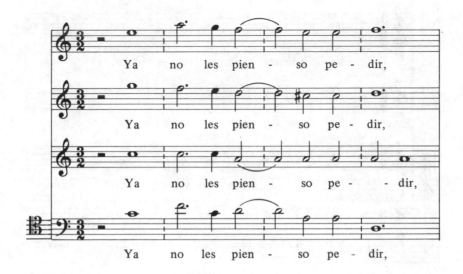

Musical Example 1c

"Ya no les pienso pedir . . ."

Opening of the solo setting from *Fortunas de Andrómeda y Perseo* (1653)
[Harvard University, Houghton Library, Ms. Typ 258H, fol. 125]

Ya   no   les   pien -   so   pe -   dir,

más lá   -   gri - mas   a   mis o -   -   jos

performed in the *Salón* of the Buen Retiro palace.[94] Due to its over-whelming success, the performances continued in the larger theater of the *Coliseo*, as indicated on the title page of the printed *suelta*. A descriptive account of the first performance is contained in a letter from the stage designer Baccio del Bianco to the Grand Duke of Tuscany dated March 3rd.[95]

---

94 Documents that probably relate to the production of *Pico y Canente* are included in Varey and Shergold, *Representaciones palaciegas: 1603–1699* (London: Tamesis, 1982), p. 59, and *Teatros y Comedias en Madrid: 1651–1665* (London: Tamesis, 1973), pp. 218–219.

95 Baccio del Bianco's letter dated "Madrid, 3 marzo 1656" (A.S.F., Mediceo f. 5409, c. 216) describes the performances of the play and the move to the Coliseo theater. See

The description of *Pico y Canente* given in Baccio del Bianco's letter includes a unique and fairly detailed mention of the musical instruments and musical organization of the performance. As the entertainment opened, the frontispiece curtain was displayed, covered with clouds and stars, while a *sinfonia* (an instrumental piece) was played by four guitars, a *violone*, and a violin.[96] Thus began the *loa*, which also ended with music in the form of a dance with castanets.[97] Another *sinfonia* accompanied the change of scenery that prepared Act I:

> Suonano le chitarre, il violone e il quarto di violino cor uno strumento di tasti, ciascuno quello che vuole e a suo gusto. Dopo questa sinfonia capona mutavasi il teatro del giardino in bosco . . .[98]

Baccio's account of this *sinfonia*, together with the words he used to describe the instrumental piece that began Act II – *"la solita mescolanza o sinfonia"* – indicate that the Spanish instrumental ensemble sounded undisciplined and chaotic to the Florentine designer. This poor evaluation of the court musicians provides us with the first evidence we have for the use of specific instruments in the court plays of the mid-century

---

Mina Bacci, "Lettere inedite" pp. 74–77. On the evidence of this date for the letter, I must abandon the assumption that the play was performed in 1653, included in my paper "Música existente para comedias de Calderón de la Barca", *Calderón: Actas del Congreso Internacional sobre Calderón y el Teatro Español del Siglo de Oro* (Madrid, 1983) tomo II, p. 1171. Emilio Cotarelo y Mori asserted that *Pico y Canente* was performed in 1651; see, *Actores famosos del siglo XVII* (Madrid, 1916), pp. 81–82.

96 "Il frontone della scena erano alcune colonne alli lati con festoni di frutte e sopra un padiglione tucto d'oro e cremisi raggruppato sopra le cornici; il fondo di questa rappresentava un cielo di notte tutto stelle e dopo una sinfonia di un violone, 4 chitarre e un mezzo violino cominciava . . .," ("Lettere inedite . . .," p. 75.). *Mezzo violino* is an uncommon term, which may refer to an "instrument of the middle," an alto or a tenor violin. See David D. Boyden, *The History of Violin Playing from its Origin to 1761* (London: Oxford University Press, 1965) pp. 42–45 and 115–119.

97 The text of the play does not indicate that instrumental music began the *loa*, nor does the text mention the dance at the end. "Lettere inedite," p. 75, ". . . risolve in un ballo con castagniette e nel mezzo Gian Rana con le sue buffonerie solite e così finì il prologo."

98 *Ibid.*, p. 75. Baccio's term "il quarto di violino" is problematic: it could be interpreted to mean that one of four violins was playing, or, loosely translated, it could mean that the group of four violins was playing. It is possible, but less likely, that Baccio refers to the violino piccolo, a small violin tuned higher than the ordinary treble violin. In any case, the instrument was of the violin family.

and the first mention of *sinfonias*.[99] The instrumental ensemble, continuo instruments and melody instruments, was peculiarly Spanish only because of the inclusion of guitars *(le chitarre)*; a keyboard instrument and a violin band would have been the mainstay in any opera orchestra of the time.[100]

In discussing *Pico y Canente*, Baccio del Bianco emphasizes only one of the sung portions of the play.[101] He points out the novelty of Canente's song "*Crédito es de mi decoro . . .*" from Act III, which the nymph sings while she is transformed into a cloud. According to Baccio's letter, he convinced the dramatist and the composer to write a *lamento* in the Italian style for Canente's sad transformation.

> Il poeta, dietro mia petizione distese un lamento mentre si convertiva in nube *et il musico compose alli mia consigli cosa assai italiana.* Fermavasi in piedi nel mezzo del tavolato e con gesti diceva sentirsi mancare i piedi e le forze al muoversi; veniva un fumo e la ricopriva tutta e dietro al fumo una nugoletta in forma di figura e a poco a poco salendo al cielo si mescolava con l'altre nugole. Faceva bella vista, *però dicevano che quel canto pareva semmana santa a maitines che voleva*

---

99 As we have seen, the *relaciones* for the spectacle plays of the reign of Philip III and of the early years of the reign of Philip IV do mention musical instruments and interludes, but the instrumental forces that Baccio describes represent a new type of ensemble. The 17th-century theater orchestra was composed mainly of continuo instruments and stringed instruments of the violin family. The loud wind instruments that figured prominently in the descriptions of the masques and early spectacle plays were not used for the later spectacle plays, which emphasized solo singing and were performed indoors.

100 The accounts of Mateo de Avila Salazar (the *organero* charged with the maintenance of the royal keyboard instruments) for February of 1656 contain the following references to the use of the harpsichord, probably for the performances of *Pico y Canente*: "En 9 de febrero por mandado del señor Marques deliche lleve el clavicinvalo al vuen retiro a los ensayos de las comedias gaste Doce Rs. con el asta que Su Magd. le vio," and [after Feb. 9] "Despues se me mando por su excelencia le bolví ese para que sirviese al pueblo ocho dias que se represento en que gaste cinquenta Reales . . . Y no me dió ninguna ayuda de costa aunque los arrendadores dieron ochocientos Rs. para los musicos que servimos en muchos dias, llevando se los quien dios save." B.N.M. Ms. 14021/154.

101 The printed *suelta* text (B.N.M. T-20695) indicates that several of the roles included songs. In the *loa*, Aurora, Flora, Apolo and the nymphs sing. In Act I, the musicians sing offstage and Canente sings a strophic solo song. In Act II, Canente sings a strophic solo song with refrain. In Act III, Canente sings two strophic solo songs, Celia and Manipes sing brief solos which are linked to brief choral interventions, Cupid sings a strophic song, and Canente sings to begin the *sarao*.

dire lamentaziones. Altri lo lodarono et come sempre chi loda
e chi no e chi biasima.[102]

There are several important points to be drawn from this brief quotation.
The first sentence is evidence that both the dramatist and the composer
were, to some degree, influenced by the Florentine's ideas: the Italian
scene designers were importers of the Italian style.[103] If we interpret this
quotation very literally, then we must assume that Baccio del Bianco was
looking over the composer's shoulder, trying to counsel him and
probably describing to the composer what a *lamento* was like. I suspect
that Juan Hidalgo, the Spanish composer for this play, had little if any
experience with contemporary Italian vocal music, and that he worked
from the non-technical advice of the Italian designer. In terms of
compositional technique, the piece in question does not evidence a direct
imitation of the *lamento*. Nevertheless, Baccio's remark that the
composer's *lamento* was *cosa assai italiana* or "Italian enough" suggests
that Hidalgo's lament in some way satisfied the Florentine designer.
Canente's lament has the same dramatic function as an Italian *lamento*,
and, while it does not evidence the specific compositional devices that we
associate with the *lamento* of the mid-seventeenth century, it does satisfy
other prerequisites of the form. In Italian operas of the first half of the
seventeenth century, the *lamento* was a highly expressive dramatic piece,
which often functioned as a self-contained scene that usually occurred
immediately prior to the final resolution of the plot.[104] Canente's lament
is certainly the dramatic highpoint of the plot, it forms a central part of a
scene (or could even be singled out as a separate scene), and it occurs just
before the final resolution, in which Archimidonte invokes Jupiter,
Saturn, Mars, Apollo, Mercury, Venus, the Moon, and Cupid to save
Canente and her Prince Pico from the powers of the evil Circe. Baccio's
description also indicates that Canente's lament satisfied another of the
characteristics of the *lamento*: the actress who played and sang the role
of Canente used gestures and postures to further the expressivity and
affective content of the scene.[105] As in the Italian genre, the affect

---

102 "Lettere inedite," p. 76.
103 The spread of opera from the earliest Italian centers to other European towns and
courts often occurred through just such direct and personal envoys. See the overview
in Michael Robinson, *Opera before Mozart* (London: 1966) pp. 24–25.
104 See Ellen Rosand, "Lamento", in *The New Grove Dictionary of Music and Musicians*,
ed. Stanley Sadie (1980), vol. 10, pp. 412–414.
105 The conceptual foundations of the *lamento* in seventeenth-century Italian opera are
discussed in Rosand, "Lamento".

(affetto) of the lament was conveyed through the combined expressive means of the music, the text, the movements, and even the facial gestures of the actress-singer.[106] Baccio had considerable praise for the actress who played and sang the role of Canente: *"Canente è una delle romere famosa nel cantare et è quella che per abilità del canto prima appresso di tutti."*[107] The actress that he refers to must have been one of the Romero sisters, Luisa and Mariana, who were active in the theatrical companies at this time.[108]

Fortunately, the music for Canente's lament has survived to our day, in the form of loose performing parts, and with an attribution to Juan Hidalgo. The musical parts have only the indication *"Solo de Juan Hidalgo de la muerte decanente."*[109] The transcription of Canente's lament illustrates that Hidalgo may only have worked with a superficial knowledge of the Italian genre. [See musical example 2] The piece does not sound like an Italian *lamento*, yet it is clearly written in an affective, dramatic recitative style. Furthermore, on the broadest conceptual level, the piece can be accepted as a lament:

> The lament is self-contained but it is not closed; it is not an aria. Its organization develops out of the internal exigencies of the text, and no superimposed formal structure determines its shape.[110]

Canente's lament conforms to this definition although it has none of the musical devices or "emblems" that have been associated with contemporary Italian laments.[111] The musical setting serves the text perfectly.

---

106 See Marco da Gagliano, "Ai Lettori" from *La Dafne* (Firenze: Christofano Marescotti, 1608), reprinted in Angelo Solerti, *Le Origini del Melodramma* (Torino, 1903), pp. 78–89, in addition to the prefatory comments from Cavaliere, *Rappresentatione*.

107 M. Bacci, "Lettere inedite," p. 76.

108 Luisa Romero also was assigned the role of Zéfalo in the opera *Celos aun del aire matan*, according to the printed cast list of the work included in the edition of the *Parte XIX* of *Comedias nuevas escogidas de los mejores ingenios de España* (Madrid, 1663). For information on the Romero sisters, see scattered references in: E. Cotarelo y Mori, *Actores famosos del siglo XVII* (Madrid, 1916); N. D. Shergold and J. E. Varey, *Los autos sacramentales en Madrid en la época de Calderón, 1637–1681* (Madrid, 1961); J. E. Varey and N. D. Shergold, *Teatros y Comedias en Madrid: 1651–1665* (London: Tamesis, 1973); and N. D. Shergold and J. E. Varey, *Representaciones palaciegas; 1603–1699* (London: Tamesis, 1982).

109 B.N.M. Ms M-3880/32 separate parts for soprano and for the unfigured bass line.

110 Ellen Rosand, "The Descending Tetrachord: An Emblem of Lament," *The Musical Quarterly*, LXV (1979), p. 348.

111 *Ibid.*, pp. 348–359.

Musical Example 2

From *Pico y Canente* (1656) B.N.M. Ms. M-3880/32
"Credito es de mi decoro" "Solo de Ju. hidalgo de la muerte decanente"

"Acomp.to a las coplas, son 5⁰"

2ª

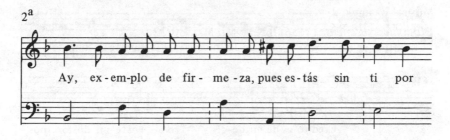

Ay, ex - em-plo de fir - me -za, pues es-tás sin ti por

mi, tam bién yo así im-i - tar -é tu fi -ne-za que -

-dan - do, que-dan - do sin ti por ti

3ª

Ay, el al-ma a ver - te su-be, ex-a -

-la - da   en tris - te   can - to,   por - que

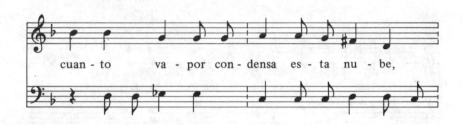

cuan - to   va - por con - densa es - ta nu - be,

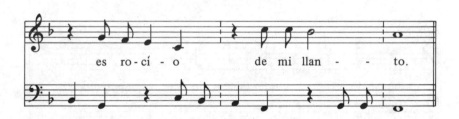

es ro - cí - o   de mi llan -   - to.

4ª

Ay,   la pos -   tre - ra   a - go - ní - a   se

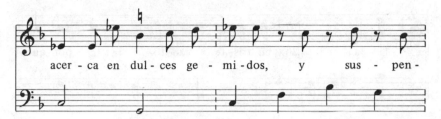

acer - ca en dul - ces ge - mi - dos,   y   sus - pen-

-di - dos,   an -he - lan   tu com-pañ-í - a mi

fe,   mi ser mis sen - ti - - dos.

5ª

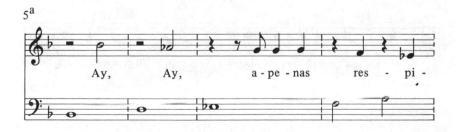

Ay,   Ay,   a - pe - nas   res - pi-

-ro,   que mi   voz   in - in - ter - ca -

in - ter - ca - den - te   su fin sien - te,

y   da   y   da el   úl - ti - mo   sus -

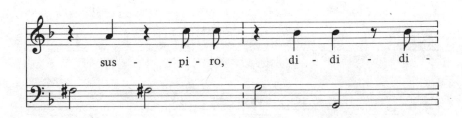

sus - -pi - ro,   di - di - di -

- cien-do   a - mor, y   Laur - en   y Laur   y Laur-

- ren   y Lau - - - ren - te.

The rhythmic organization of the piece is totally dependent on the text accents and the images in the text. The use of the *"Ay"* to begin each verse might be emblematic of a Spanish lament, in conjunction with the particularly vivid text painting at the words *"morir," "cantando," "muero."* Another obvious instance of text-painting occurs when the highest note of the piece is first touched upon at the word *"sube."* The musical setting is a graphic representation of the text and the action on the stage; as the lament progresses and the nymph becomes weaker, the melodic line and the bass line are punctuated by more and more frequent rests, illustrating Canente's gasps for air, especially in the last verse *"Ay, ay, apenas respiro . . .,"* when several words of the text are broken into syllables and repeated. Several musical gestures can be picked out of this piece as relating to the expression of lamentation, melancholy, and pathos. First of all, the opening figure of the leap of the descending fourth seems to have been associated with songs of complaint (compare with Minerva's lament from *La estatua de Prometeo,* see below, p. 67), and this figure recurs at the beginning of the fourth copla and on the word *"suspiro"* in the fifth copla. The effectiveness of the setting as a whole is increased by the use of unexpected harmonic shifts and chromaticism. Taken as a group, these details of the musical setting of the dramatic text reveal the composer's objective: the direct expression of the text through musical means in an open structure.[112]

This piece shows a remarkable freedom both in terms of the recitative style and overall structure. The dramatic Spanish recitative style is anything but strict, since short lyric harmonic and melodic sequences are freely inserted, the harmonic rhythm is never very slow and the bass line is flexible in its interplay with the vocal line. The formal organization of the text into strophes has been ignored by the composer, since the musical settings of the coplas are similar but not nearly exact repetitions: the musical setting is not really strophic. Perhaps the breakdown of the strophic formula could be effectively seen as the musical equivalent to Canente's dramatic situation. As she loses her corporeality and begins to disappear into a vaporific cloud, her singing (the nymph's main source of expression) in regular strophes would seem out of place. The breakdown of the form of her song is a realistic representation of her demise.

While this piece was clearly intended as a lament, it does not consistently exploit one of the principal musical characteristics associated with the Italian *lamento*: the descending tetrachord in the bass line.[113] The first stanza uses a descending tetrachord in the melody (from C-Bb-Ab-G-F # at the words *"morir ya con lo que lloro")* and so does the fifth stanza (Bb-Ab-G-F-Eb moving to D) at the words *"Ay, ay, apenas respiro,"* but the descending tetrachord is not in the bass line and can hardly be singled out as a primary generative force in the composition.

The last part of Baccio's description of this musical lament scene *(però dicevano che quel canto pareva semmana santa a maitines che voleva dire lamentaziones)* is somewhat enigmatic. On the one hand, it may refer to the audience's generalized reaction to the new vocal style. On the other hand, Baccio may be making a very fashionable private joke for the benefit of his reader, the Grand Duke of Tuscany. Baccio reports that the lament of Canente was compared to the lamentations sung during Holy Week, but we might wonder whether this comparison refers to the dull chanting of the long lamentation texts or the traditional pathos and expressivity of Spanish musical settings of the Holy Week lamentations.[114]

---

112 The broader category of the recitative soliloquy, proposed in Margaret Murata, "The Recitative Soliloquy", *Journal of the American Musicological Society* XXXII (1979), pp. 45–73, is also applicable to pieces in the Spanish repertory. Both of the "laments" that I discuss in this chapter fall within Margaret Murata's very useful definition.

113 Rosand, "The Descending Tetrachord," pp. 353–358.

114 A similar commentary was made concerning the first performance of Peri's *Euridice* in Florence: "[They say] that the music was tedious, that it sounded like the chanting of

This lament from *Pico y Canente* is among the earliest pieces of specifically theatrical music known,[115] and it is also among the first examples of Juan Hidalgo's theatrical style. If we believe Baccio's report of the audience reaction to the scene, then the newness of the musical style in 1656 and the formal freedom of this lament could have contributed to the novelty of the occasion, but it was probably the total pathetic effect of the scene that caused the public to associate the lament with the lamentations of Holy Week, since the latter were, traditionally, conspicuously chromatic and expressive of a deep spiritual sadness.

While *Pico y Canente* is not an outstanding literary product, it was a highly successful play in performance at court during the formative period for the newer court genre. The extant lament *"Crédito es de mi decoro . . ."* supports one of my main points: that Italian ideas concerning dramatic music and the use of recitative were particularly influential with regard to the court plays of the 1650's, but the Italian musical style did not replace the Spanish style. This is possibly due to the fact that the Spanish composers had little if any direct contact with the Italian music. The principal importers of the Italian theories were not musicians. The extant music for later court plays, including *La estatua de Prometeo*, shows that the Spanish style did not become increasingly "Italian" within the Calderonian genre.

In the intervening years between the productions of 1653–1656 and the first performance of Calderón's *La estatua de Prometeo* c.1670, the ways that music was used in the court plays did not change significantly, but more and more plays were written that included long sections of sung

---

the passion" (Emilio De' Cavalieri, in a letter of Nov. 1600). As Claude Palisca has noted, "Here someone coined a simile that was to enjoy much currency as a drawing-room cliché . . ." See, Claude V. Palisca, "Musical Asides in the Diplomatic Correspondence of Emilio De' Cavalieri," *Musical Quarterly* XLIX (1963), pp. 351–352. Baccio del Bianco's comment concerning Canente's lament could be another tongue-in-cheek appearance of this simile.

115 In addition to Canente's lament, there is an extant musical setting of the song-text "Esperando estan la Rosa/quantas contiene un vergel . . . ," which, in *Pico y Canente*, is sung by Aurora at the opening of the *loa*, and by Canente to begin the final *sainete* or *sarao*. The poetic text of this song has been ascribed to Góngora, and, whether or not the attribution is correct, the song-text probably predated the play. The song is found in an anonymous musical setting for three vocal parts, which probably represents one of many versions of the same basic song. See Miguel Querol, *Cancionero Musical de Góngora* (Barcelona, 1975), p. 29. The same song-text also appears in *El vaquero emperador*, I, by Matos Fragoso, Diamante, and Gil Enríquez; in Bances Candamo's *¿Cuál es el afecto mayor, lealtad, o sangre o amor?*, II; and later in *Los desagravios de Troya*, I (1712) by Martínez de la Roca and Escuder (B.N.M. R-9258, fol. 78–79).

text. The spectacle plays with music were called *fiestas* or *zarzuelas*, and the totally sung operas performed in 1660 were called *fiestas cantadas*.[116] The term *zarzuela* was first used in connection with *El laurel de Apolo* (1657), a two-act play with music written for performance at the palace of the Zarzuela, a royal hunting lodge located just outside of Madrid. In the *loa* to this play, the figure called *Zarzuela* enters accompanied by the music of *villanos ("rústicas canciones")* and traditional rustic instruments. Thus, the figure of the *Zarzuela*, described as *"rústicamente bella,"* has come to the Retiro palace to introduce her *fiesta*, which is not a *comedia*, but a *"fábula pequeña/en que, a imitación de Italia,/se canta y se representa."*[117] In essence, this passage states the nature of the new genre: the musical forms called for in Calderón's court plays show a mixture of traditional Spanish elements (*Zarzuela* and her rustic beauty) and of forms from the very young operatic genre that developed in Italy.[118]

The figure of *Zarzuela* reappears in a later work, the *loa* to the *"representación música"* or opera *La púrpura de la rosa*. In her conversation with the figure representing *el Vulgo* concerning the festivity that she is to bring to the court, the question of *afecto* (affect) arises. *Zarzuela* asks *"¿Dónde el afecto hallaré?"*, and *el Vulgo* replies *"En esas músicas bellas,/que Tristeza y Alegría/traen tras sí."* *Alegría* and *Tristeza* agree that music is the best vehicle for the affects: that the *músicas bellas* *"Voces de mi afecto son."*[119] The figure of *Música* then sings and dances, declaring that *"Y es verdad, que afectos/hacen milagros."* Thus, Calderón embraced not only the importance of "affect," but the idea that the affects – in this instance the extremes of sadness and happiness – were best expressed by music. The *loa* or prologue to Calderón's first opera text embodied one of the founding concepts for the creation of opera, and the concept that was the hallmark of opera in the Baroque era. Later in the *loa*, Calderón acknowledged that he was experimenting in an attempt to introduce the genre at court, but he carefully described *La púrpura de la rosa* as a *"pequeña*

---

116 While the term *zarzuela* was initially used to describe a two-act play with music, not all two-act plays with music are *zarzuelas* (c.f., the two-act spectacle plays from 1622), nor is the term necessarily inappropriate for the three-act plays with both spoken and sung dialogue.

117 *Loa* to *El Laurel de Apolo* (1657), available in *BAE* IX, 656c.

118 The close of Act III of *Fortunas de Andrómeda y Perseo* (Harvard Ms. fol. 97–99) contains a similar musical allegory with reference to the new genre: A "coro de dioses con instrumentos y vozes" appears in opposition to a group of musicians characterized by "flautas, y zampoñas rústicas," before the final celebration scene.

119 *BAE* IX, 675c.

representación," avoiding the notion of a totally sung *comedia*. As the *loa* closes, the concept of the power of the affects in music is tied to the problem of the operatic experiment:

> Advertid que afectos
> No son finezas.
> Bien podeis admitirlos,
> Dirá el aplauso,
> Si es verdad que afectos
> Hacen milagros.[120]

Although the *loas* from 1657 and 1660 contain essential statements of Calderón's intentions and of the conceptual foundation for the introduction of the Italianate forms into the Spanish court plays, the evidence of the 1652–1656 productions tells us that the form of the *zarzuela* was established by Calderón as early as 1652 with *La fiera, el rayo, y la piedra*.

The text of *La estatua de Prometeo* does not present any new and different usage for music when compared with the Calderonian court plays that I have already discussed. The mythological gods converse in recitative, and the music of the mortal characters is confined to festive songs and dances. The chorus participates anonymously as *"música dentro"* and as the voice of the collective gaiety of the shepherds.

Calderón's use of poetic meters in the song-texts attests to a highly developed attention to the associative significance of meter. In Act I, the festive song of the mortals (referred to in Timantes' speech as *pastores*) and Libia's solo are written in the hexasyllabic meter that is usually associated with traditional Spanish pastoral or pseudo-pastoral verse (at 381 and 388). In contrast, Minerva's first extended solo recitative is written in six strophes of *estancias*, in seven- and eleven-syllable lines: the Italianate meter which was particularly appropriate for recitative (at 500 and 588). When Palas appears *cantando* (645), *"De Júpiter y Latona . . .,"* the stage directions do not specify the recitative style, so that we cannot know precisely how this passage, in combination of 8-syllable romance and couplets of 12 syllables, was performed. However, the same metric scheme is used for Minerva's lines *"Ya que sobre el pedestal . . ."* (821–828 and 855–862), which have the indication *"rezitativo Minerva"* in the alternate text source for the play "BM." The same source contains a variant stage direction for Apollo indicating *"En tonada canta Apolo"* for his lines in *quintillas* (at 815).

---

120 *BAE* IX, 676c.

The predominant musical feature of Act II is the use of a repeated textual and musical refrain as an *estribillo*. This *estribillo* appears first as a chorus sung by *"música dentro"* (line 236), and reappears at lines 295, 384, 419, 446, 459, 488, and 496. In this section it is used for thematic unity, since the text of the refrain carries one of the central ideas of the play. Further, as a structural device, the *estribillo* punctuates and frames the long sections of spoken dialogue. At several points, Minerva and then Timantes sing the refrain with the chorus, so that they assume the point of view expressed in the *estribillo* text.

A new section of Act II is dominated by the long recitative dialogue of Palas and Discordia (beginning at line 499) in regular 8-syllable *romance* meter. An "intercalated estribillo" in the form of a chorus of *zagales* (*"Al festejo, al festejo, zagales..."*) interrupts the dialogue. The

Figure 2-1: Title Page, B.N.M. Ms M-3880/43

Figure 2-2: Three extant parts (from separate pages) B.N.M. Ms M-3880/43

complete song is stated to end Act II and to open Act III as a sung dance
(*"cantando y bailando"*). A repetition of this song is the vehicle for the
disguised Discordia's entry into Act III, and the song generates a scene
in which mortals (Libia and *villanas*) sing solo verses. Discordia,
disguised as a mortal, sings a short song in traditional *romance* meter
before she disappears from the stage (199–205); perhaps the song serves
as part of her disguise.

The central dialogue between Apolo and Palas is again cast in recitative
and ends with a refrain couplet (two eleven-syllable lines) sung as a duo.
The refrain is then taken up by Minerva with a slight variation in the
meaning of the text (366–367). Minerva converses with Apolo and Palas
(368–469) in song, which we may assume to have been recitative because

Figure 2–3: Title Page, B.N.M. Ms M–3880/55

of the length of the passage and the continuous heptasyllabic meter. The passage ends (470–471) as the three deities sing the refrain couplet (360–361).

Discordia's song *"En la ruda política . . ."* (at 944) is introduced with the justification *"sea carta de crehencia/la suabidad de mi acento,"* and rather than use the recitative style associated with godlike speech, Juan Hidalgo has set Discordia's text (944–979) as a strophic *"tono humano"* with nine quattrains or *coplas*. The song does not have a refrain, although it is linked to a brief four-voiced chorus. Both the song and the following choral piece exhibit a simple style and texture perhaps to sustain the notion of the *"suavidad"* that Discordia has mentioned. In the first line of the solo song the bass line and the melody are in parallel motion and in the same rhythm. In the chorus, the homorhythmic and homophonic style are maintained.

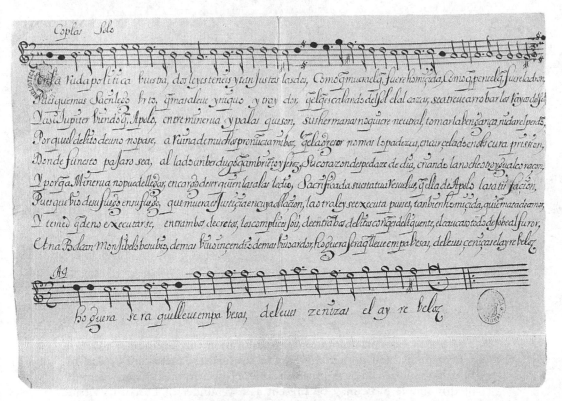

Figure 2–4: Solo and *tiple a 4*, B.N.M. Ms M–3880/55

Figure 2-5: Bass line and three parts, B.N.M. Ms M-3880/55

The use of hemiolas (notated with coloration in the original source), syncopations, and dotted rhythms in sesquialtera meter are typical of Hidalgo's music and of the Spanish style. However, the insistent hemiola of this simple piece may be present as a reminder of Discordia's true character as the *"mentida deidad."* The smooth, controlled texture of the song is only disturbed by the persistent use of hemiola, a rhythmic contradiction of the supposed sweetness of song that Discordia is trying to imitate. The hemiola of the opening is also used at the beginning of the second phrase and to begin the third phrase. This rhythmic figure is a characteristic and germinal element for this piece. The hemiola that dominates the bass line of the second section of the solo is retained in the bass line of the four-part piece, so that the solo and the chorus are unified by this rhythmic detail.

Discordia's song is typical of the Spanish style in its highly repetitive construction. While the strophic form is already based on simple reiteration of a rounded set of four musical phrases, this piece becomes even more dependent on repetition as a compositional device on the smaller scale. First of all, the score indicates that the last line of music (the third and fourth lines of the *copla*) was repeated in performance. More important, certain melodic and rhythmic figures are used several times, so that the song is constructed only by means of simple sequences and repetition. The brief choral section, while it is linked to the solo, is also used as a structural device, providing an audible backdrop for Discordia's flight from the stage and a rounded conclusion to the entire scene.

The musical centerpiece of the play was, perhaps, the solo *"Tonante Dios"* (1049) of Minerva, together with its continuation in the recitative argument of Minerva and Palas, which, in turn, leads directly into another strophic air for Discordia. Minerva's recitative *"Tonante Dios . . ."* is both a complaint and an invocation to Jupiter. In two of the sources for the text of the play, this song is referred to as a lament: *"Canta Minerva en voz de lamento,"* and *"Sale Minerva cantando como lamento."*[121] Minerva's song is another, later example of the Spanish *lamento*, and, not surprisingly, the musical style is similar to that of Canente's lament from 1656. The poetic text of this lament is written in strophic quattrains, yet the musical setting of Minerva's lament is a freely-composed expressive recitative, a precise setting of the text in terms of both text underlay (respect for the accents in the text) and the relationship between word and musical gesture. Each line of text is clearly set off either by rests, a melodic leap, a change of register, a change in harmony, or an abrupt change in rhythm or melodic movement. However, the musical setting is not strophic, so that again the composer (Juan Hidalgo) has ignored the form of the text. Dramatic

---

121 See below, the edition, verse 1048.

Figure 2-6: "*Solo Rezitativo Minerva*" B.N.M. Ms M-3880/22

musical expression of affect and attention to specific details in the text were clearly more important to the composer than the text form. Minerva's pleading tone is expressed in the figure of a descending leap of the interval of a fourth which occurs several times. Her characterization of Prometeo's crime as a relatively inconsequential matter at the words "*pequeño rayo al sol*" is stressed in that the word *pequeño* is set as a brief melisma in descending eighth-notes which spans a fourth. Minerva's final statement of indignation "*¿cómo que tenga más pena un robo que una traición?*" begins on the high A, the highest note reached thus far. The same pitch is reached again through ascending conjunct movement to the word "*solio*," the ascent representing the path that the invocation must take to reach the realm of Jupiter.

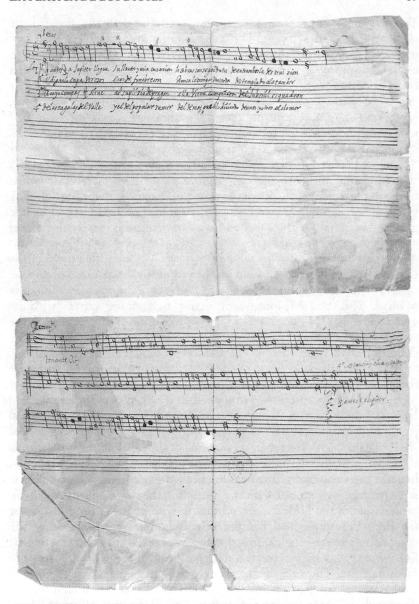

Figure 2–7: Parts for *Coplas* and *Acomp.*^{to} B.N.M. Ms M–3880/22

Text-painting is continued in the ensuing recitative dialogue, the struggle between Palas and Minerva. The combative nature of Palas is described musically by the use of insistent series of shorter note values (strict eighth notes) and a more varied melody which does not include recitation tones. In contrast, Minerva's reasonable character (*"Yo de las letras mortales . . ."*) is expressed with a more expansive setting, a lilting recitative/arioso, characterized by large leaps and a steady rhythm with regular alternation of longer and shorter notes, and with a graceful ascent by step to high G and a descent marked by strong regular dotted rhythms.

The closed-form air that follows the recitative is a simple, cheerful strophic setting of Discordia's text in four *coplas*. This piece shares some of the musical characteristics of the *tono* for Discordia that I have already discussed. Again, there is a central rhythmic figure that serves as the germinal material for the song, and again repetition is clearly the salient compositional technique.

The extant music for *La estatua de Prometeo* was identified for the first time by Jack Sage[122] and is found in a box of musical *cuadernos* or *papeles sueltos* with the siglum Mss. M-3880 of the Biblioteca Nacional in Madrid. This box of loose scores and performing parts (with its companion box M-3881) are arbitrary collections, that is, all of the scores do not necessarily proceed from the same place and date, and the collection may have entered the library as a mixed bundle of music. Similar arbitrary collections of loose scores and performing parts are found in the music archives of many Spanish cathedrals and in other libraries rich in seventeenth-century music. The physical appearance and layout of these sources is perhaps unique to Spanish music: each vocal part and instrumental part is written out separately on its own folded sheet of paper, with the *coplas* on one side of the fold and the *estribillo* on the other. Usually, all of the verses of the text for the *coplas* are underlaid beneath the vocal parts. The bass line, called *guión* or *acompañamiento*, is sometimes written out with the music for the *copla* and the *estribillo* on one side of the folded sheet, so that the other side is used as a cover for the whole piece and has the title and possibly the name of the composer. The songs, including the theatrical ones, are titled by the first line of text and may have the designation *"tono humano," "tonada humana,"* etc. The title of the play for which the song was written is almost never included in this type of musical source, although indications such as *"De la muerte de Canente,"* or *"Rezitativo Minerva."* have been useful in matching the songs to their respective plays.

---

122 Sage, "Texto y realización," Appendix.

Although the format of the musical sources indicates that they were probably used as performing parts, the music for *La estatua de Prometeo* is undated, so that we cannot know for certain how the sources relate to the three performances of the play (c. 1670, 1685, and 1693). The song-texts presented in the musical sources are, as expected, inaccurate renditions of the Calderonian text. However, certain details seem to link the reading of the text in these sources with the readings given in the BMM manuscript of *La estatua de Prometeo*, which was probably prepared for the 1685 performance. The archival documents that provide details about other aspects of the performances are of limited use in trying to connect the extant music with a specific production.[123] Five rehearsals are recorded for the performance in December of 1685, and two of these were dedicated exclusively to music. In connection with the performance that took place eight years later, only one general rehearsal is recorded. This might indicate that new music was not composed for the 1693 performance, but that the same pieces that were carefully rehearsed in 1685 were retained in the later production. Since the music was composed by Juan Hidalgo (d. March 31, 1685) before April of 1685, it is possible that the extant scores preserve the music that was used in the first production, and that the same pieces were also used in the later performances.

Although I have drawn conclusions at various stages throughout this essay, it seems appropriate to review briefly some of the major points. Music was introduced into the young genre of the *comedia nueva* at the beginning of the seventeenth century in anything but a haphazard fashion. The use of music was theoretically justified by Lope de Vega on the basis of a passage in Aristotle's *Poetics*, and the function of music in the comedia texts became standardized through Lope's practice.

The court productions before c.1650 did exploit music as an added element of spectacle and entertainment, but the actual use of music and the function of music did not differ substantially from the techniques that had already been standardized in the public theaters or in even earlier practices of Renaissance origin. The court plays before Calderón cannot be successfully compared to the early Italian operas. The use of music alone did not make the court plays more "operatic," and with the notable exception of *La Selva sin Amor* (1627), early Italian opera had little influence on the music of these early court spectacles.

---

123 See J. E. Varey and N. D. Shergold, *Teatros y Comedias en Madrid: 1666–1687* (London: Tamesis, 1975), p. 188; *Representaciones Palaciegas: 1603–1699* (London: Tamesis, 1982), pp. 168 and 249; and *Teatros y Comedias en Madrid: 1687–1699* (London: Tamesis, 1979), p. 293.

In the same vein, it is a mistake to think that the music for the Calderonian plays became increasingly operatic. Several court plays from the years 1652–1656 can be singled out as the earliest manifestations of operatic thinking, and of specifically Italian influence, but subsequent plays to c.1685 do not show a marked change of emphasis. They simply follow the example of the prototypes. This is as true for the extant music from these plays as it is for the techniques exhibited in the stage directions. We cannot find a true evolution during this period, and the two opera texts from 1659–1660 are clearly special cases, since subsequent court plays were not operas, but returned to the model established as early as 1652.

The question of Italian musical influence has also caused considerable controversy among scholars and Hispanists, but it has been approached with too much vague generalization. While it cannot be denied that Italian forms were assimilated into the Spanish theater, the notion that Spanish composers began to write in a purely Italian style is mistaken. As the musical illustrations included with this text will show, form did not dictate content in the Spanish theatrical songs. While the inspiration for the use of recitative was Italian, the Spanish composers adapted the form of recitative to their own needs with a peculiar musical style. The Spanish musical style was formulated within the aesthetic restrictions of the Spanish theatrical tradition, in which the literary text was to maintain supremacy over the musical setting. Text form was usually respected in settings of song-texts, but special exception was made in the case of dramatic laments.

The use of traditional songs (texts and tunes) insured, to some extent, the survival of the musical aspects of the traditional *comedia* alongside the newly imported Italian forms. In each of the spectacular court plays after 1650, traditional songs from the pre-existent repertory are present. This is evidence for a practice of borrowing and recomposition that certainly aided in the preservation of a Spanish musical style for theatrical music.

This edition of the music for *La estatua de Prometeo* is a contribution toward the re-evaluation of Calderón's mythological plays and their music. But these pieces are only a tiny fraction of the quantity of seventeenth-century secular vocal and theatrical music that is still available in the original sources.[124]

---

124 A list of and index to the extant music from the seventeenth-century Spanish theater is included as an appendix to my forthcoming doctoral dissertation, *Music in the Seventeenth-Century Spanish Theater*.

2.4 Transcriptions

Editorial Policy
The extant songs from *La estatua de Prometeo* are preserved in loose performing parts (B.N.M. Ms. M-3880/43, M-3880/55, and M-3880/22), so that they are not notated in score in the original sources. In these transcriptions, I have tried to preserve essential characteristics of the original sources. The characteristic Spanish seventeenth-century time signature that appears in the source as ₵₃ , has been rendered as $\frac{3}{2}$, and the note values have not been reduced. In the interest of clarity, regular dotted barlines have been introduced. Barlines that appear in the original sources are retained and rendered as solid barlines in the transcriptions. Accidentals in the manuscript source are retained, and editorial additions are enclosed in square brackets. The source M-3880/43 contains an incomplete set of parts, lacking the two treble parts for the four-part song and two solo *coplas*. I have added a possible conservative reconstruction of the missing parts to the transcriptions. The reconstruction of the solo *coplas* is based on the extant part for the bass line (*acomp°.*) and on the melody of the extant third treble part (*tiple 3°*). The reconstruction of the missing parts for the four-part vocal *estribillo* is based on other pieces by Juan Hidalgo that preserve similar musical characteristics.

N.B.: I wish to acknowledge, with gratitude, the help, advice and kind encouragement of Howard Mayer Brown and Gary P. Supanich.

B.N.M. Ms. M-3880/43 Tono humano Al festejo zagales. A 4 Juan Hidalgo
[incomplete set of parts; 2 treble parts missing] Act II, v. 619, 631
                                    Act III, v. 1, 31, etc.

[The two upper
treble parts repre-
sent a possible con-
servative reconstruc-
tion based on other
pieces by Juan
Hidalgo.]

A 4 tiple 3°

A 4

Al fes - te - jo al fes - te - jo za-

Acomp. to Estrivo. A 4

-ga - les, za - ga - les ve - nid, ve - nid al fes - te - jo

que a la nue - va dei -

que a la nue - va dei - dad des - tos mon-tes la o -

que a la nue - va dei - dad des - tos mon-tes la o -

que a la nue - va dei - dad des - tos mon-tes la o-

dad en fe de ser hi - - ja del fue -

fre -cen en fe de ser hi - - ja del fue -

fre - cen en fe de ser hi - - ja del fue -

fre - cen en fe de ser hi - - ja del fue -

go la tier - ra con flo - res el a - gua con

go la tier - ra con flo - res el a - gua con

go la tier - ra con flo - res el a - gua con

go la tier - ra con flo - res el a - gua con

per - las, el ay - re con plu - mas con sal - vas el e - co

per - las, el ay - re con plu - mas con sal - vas el e - co

per - las, el ay - re con plu - mas con sal - vas el e - co

per - las, el ay - re con plu - mas con sal - vas el e - co

[M-3880/43]

Act III, v. 41   Sung by Libia

[1ª Melody reconstructed from tiple 3]

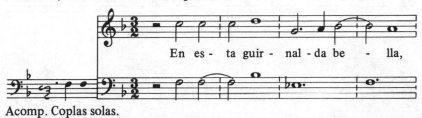

En es - ta guir - nal - da be - lla,

Acomp. Coplas solas.

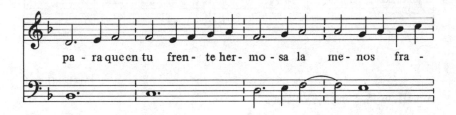

pa - ra que en tu fren - te her - mo - sa la me - nos fra -

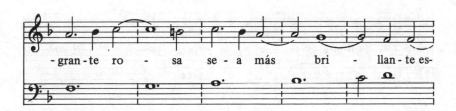

-gran - te ro - sa se - a más bri - llan - te es-

- tre - lla, te sir - ve, ci -

[M-3880/43]

Act III, v. 48 Sung by Villana 1ª

[2ª Melody reconstructed from tiple 3, bass line from Acomp.]

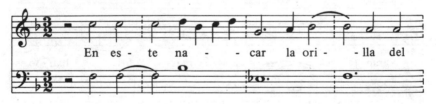

- mas que llo - - ra, los nec - - tos

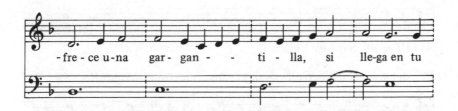

hi - los que bri - lla,   te o-

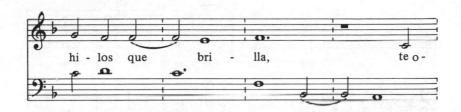

-fre - ce u-na gar-gan - - ti - lla, si lle-ga en tu

cue - llo a ver - - las. El a -gua con per- las.

[M-3880/43]

Act III, v. 55   Sung by Villana 2ª

Tiple 3°.   Coplas solo.

Si a plau - dió tus   he - chos gra -

[Bass line reconstructed from Acomp.]

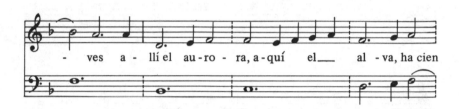

- ves   a - llí el au - ro - ra, a - quí   el___   al - va, ha cien

-do   a - tu   vis - ta sal - va,   la mú - si - ca___

___ de___ las a - - ves   y a -

-sí te sir - ven en sua - ves au - ras que go -

-zar pre- su - - - mas. El ay - re con plu-mas

[M-3880/43]

Act III, v. 62   Sung by Villana 3ª

Coplas solo. 4ª

To - do a tu her-mo_____

- sa dey - dad   se rin - de y se sa - cri - fi -

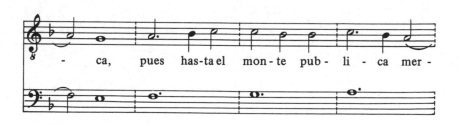

- ca,   pues has-ta el   mon - te   pub - li - ca mer -

- i - tos____ de tu____ bel - dad;

del   cla -   rín_____   la   sua - vi -

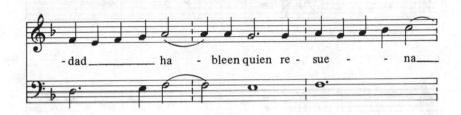

-dad_____   ha - bleen quien re - sue -   na___

___   gue - co,   con   sal - vas   el   e - co

B.N.M. Ms. M-3880/55. Tono humano. En la ruda politica buestra. Solo y A4
Juan Hidalgo.
Act III, v. 944

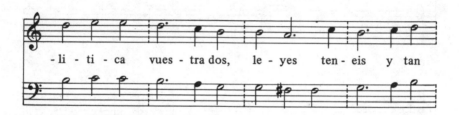

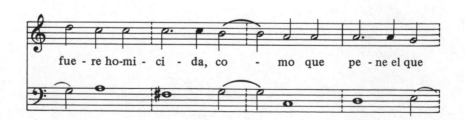

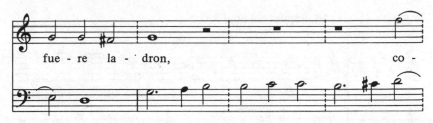

fue - re la - dron, co -

- mo que mue - ra el que fue - re ho-mi - ci - da co -

- mo que pe - ne el que fue - re la - dron

"Este pedazito es a 4 despues del Solo"

Ho - gue - ra se - ra que lle - ve en pa -

Ho - gue - ra se - ra que lle - ve en pa -

Ho - gue - ra se - ra que lle - ve en pa -

Ho - gue - ra se - ra que lle - ve en pa -

-ve - sas de le - ves ce - ni - zas el ay - re ve - loz

-ve - sas de le - ves ce - ni - zas el ay - re ve - loz

-ve - sas de le - ves ce - ni - zas el ay - re ve - loz

-ve - sas de le - ves ce - ni - zas el ay - re ve - loz

B.N.M. Ms. M-3880/22   Act III, v. 1048
Solo. Rezitativo de hidalgo. Tonante Dios.   [Juan Hidalgo]

Solo. Rezitativo Minerva.

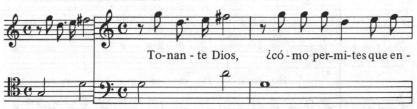

To-nan - te Dios,   ¿có - mo per-mi-tes que en -

-mien-de un - a   cul - pa   o - tra may - or?   ¿Es

me -nos de-li - to   que la Dis- cor-di-a hur-te tu voz, que el que

hur - te Pro - me - te - o   un pe - que - ño___ ra - yo al

sol? ¿Qué trai - ción   co - mo fal - se - ar   tus de -

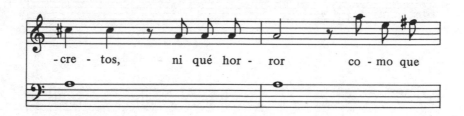

-cre - tos,   ni qué hor - ror   co - mo que

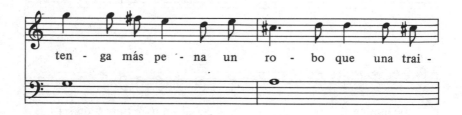

ten - ga más pe - na un   ro - bo que   una trai -

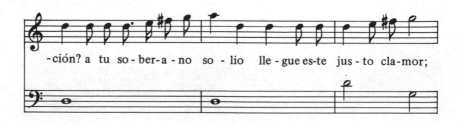

-ción? a tu so - ber-a - no so - lio   lle - gue es-te jus - to cla-mor;

mas ¿pa-ra qué, si pri-mer-o lle-gar yo pue-do? E-so no,

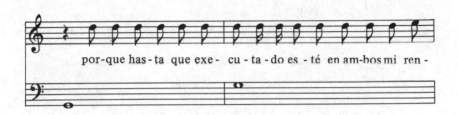

por-que has-ta que exe-cu-ta-do es-té en am-bos mi ren-

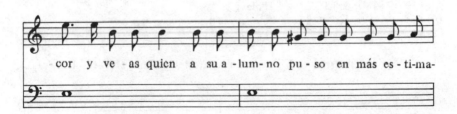

cor y ve-as quien a su a-lum-no pu-so en más es-ti-ma-

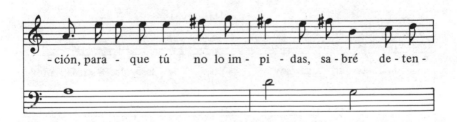

-ción, para-que tú no lo im-pi-das, sa-bré de-ten-

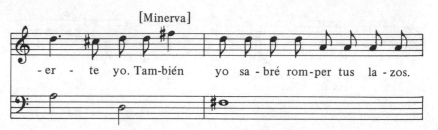

[Minerva]

-er - te yo. Tam-bién yo sa - bré rom-per tus la - zos.

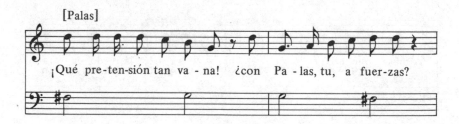

[Palas]

¡Qué pre-ten-sión tan va - na! ¿con Pa - las, tu, a fuer-zas?

[Minerva]   [Palas]

¿Pues, por-qué no? Por-que a par del mis-mo Mar- te, Dio - sa

[Minerva]

de las ar - mas soy. Yo de las le - tras; mor-

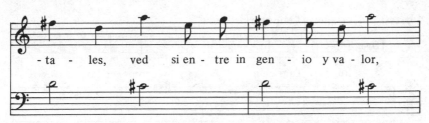

-ta - les, ved si en - tre in gen - io y va - lor,

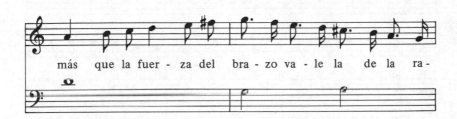

más que la fuer - za del bra - zo va - le la de la ra-

[Palas]

- zón: ¡suel - ta, ti - ra - na! No pu - de, ¡ay de mí! im-pe-dir-la.

[Discordia]

No a-que-so te des-con - fí - e por más que vue - le ve - loz,

4 bezes.   4. estancias tiene este pedazo.

[Discordia]   [4 coplas]

que an - tes que a Jú - pi - ter   lle - gue   su

llan - to y mi   a-cu - sa   -   zión   ha -

- bras   con -se - gui - do   tú   de en -

-tram - bos   la   des - truc -   ción

3 PERFORMANCES OF *LA ESTATUA DE PROMETEO*

The exact date of the opening performance of *La estatua de Prometeo* remains a puzzle, for extended investigation in the archives of Madrid has not yet yielded any documentation on that first performance. The scope of the puzzle can be somewhat reduced, however, by a process of elimination, using information on performances of other court plays.

On the basis of versification, Hilborn grouped *La estatua de Prometeo* with Calderón's late plays, and assigned it a date of 1669,[35] and Tyler and Elizondo have repeated that date.[36] Hilborn is certainly correct in his general classification, because the play is closely linked thematically and stylistically to several other plays and *autos* which date from 1668 to the mid-1670's. We can be quite certain that it was not written before 1669, because no court plays were produced from the death of Felipe IV (1665) until that year. The specific year of 1669 is not a possible date for *La estatua de Prometeo*, however; as the title pages of the printed editions of 1677 show, the play was produced for the annual celebration of the birthday of the queen mother, Mariana of Austria, on December 22.[37] The play scheduled for performance on December 22, 1669, (although postponed until January, 1670, as occurred with several such birthday celebrations), was another Calderonian mythological play, *Fieras afemina amor*. Since *La estatua de Prometeo* was printed in the *Quinta Parte* of Calderón's comedias, published in 1677, the latest possible date for the play is 1676.

Assuming that Calderón wrote the play shortly before its performance, we can safely assume, therefore, that it was written between 1670 and 1676. In his edition of the play, Aubrun suggests a date between 1670 and 1674, but he does not explain the reasons for his choice of those years.[38] We can definitely eliminate two years from that time span;

---

35 Harry W. Hilborn, *A Chronology of the Plays of D. Pedro Calderón de la Barca* (Toronto: The University of Toronto Press, 1938), pp. 70–72.

36 Richard W. Tyler and Sergio G. Elizondo, *The Characters, Plots and Settings of Calderón's Comedias* (Lincoln, Nebraska: Society of Spanish and Spanish-American Studies, 1981), p. 242.

37 The Biblioteca Municipal manuscript also calls it a "Fiesta de años" although it does not specify whose birthday it celebrated.

38 Aubrun, *Prometeo*, p. vii.

archival documents in Madrid show that the play produced for the queen mother's birthday in 1673 was *Los juegos bacanales,* of Agustín de Salazar y Torres.[39] Evidence accumulated by Varey and Shergold, particularly on the actors involved in the production, indicates that the 1672 work was *Los celos hacen estrellas,* by Juan Vélez de Guevara.[40] The French scholar Rosita Subirats, who has made an extensive study of several *legajos* in the Archivo del Palacio, reports that *La estatua de Prometeo* was staged in the Alcázar on August 2, 1675, by Antonio de Escamilla and Manuel Vallejo.[41] This was obviously not its first performance, for the lavish mythological plays were always presented first for an occasion of state – a royal birth, wedding or, most frequently, a royal birthday, as in the case of *La estatua de Prometeo.* They were often repeated subsequently in scaled-down versions, in the *corrales* or in private palace performances, such as this one, for which the two companies were paid a combined total of 600 *reales.* Since *La estatua de Prometeo* was presented on a reduced scale in August of 1675, we can be sure that it had seen a previous gala opening, and we can thus eliminate December 1675 and 1676 as possible opening dates. Having already eliminated the years 1669, 1672, and 1673, we are left with 1670, 1671, and 1674 as possible years of its gala first performance.

Of these four possible years, the most probable appears to be 1670, if we take into consideration information coming from the court theatre of Vienna. The Vienna court was closely linked to that in Madrid, culturally as well as politically, during that period, since the wife of the emperor Leopoldo I of Austria was Margarita María of Spain, daughter of Felipe IV. As soon as the young empress reached Vienna in late 1666, requests began returning to Madrid for copies of Spanish music and plays, and copies of operas and other court theatrical productions in Vienna were sent back to Madrid.[42] In celebration of Mariana's birthday, Leopoldo and Margarita offered a performance in 1669 of an opera entitled *Benche vinto, vince amore. ò Il Prometeo.*[43] The libretto was written in Spanish by an author who begs forgiveness for its faults,

---

39 See the introduction by Varey and Shergold to Juan Vélez de Guevara, *Los celos hacen estrellas* p. xlv.

40 Vélez de Guevara, *Celos,* pp. xlvii-liv.

41 Rosita Subirats, "Contribution à l'Établissement du Répertoire Théâtral à la cour de Philippe IV et de Charles II", *Bulletin Hispanique,* 79 (1977) 443.

42 See "Las relaciones literarias entre España y Austria, 1666–1673", in the Varey and Shergold introduction to Vélez de Guevara, *Celos,* pp. cv-cviii.

43 There is a copy in the Oesterreichische Nationalbibliothek in Vienna of a *suelta* edition of the three-act text, in Spanish, published by Mateo Cosmerovio, "Stampatore di Corte", and also a manuscript containing the music for the first two acts.

saying it is the first he has ever written.[44] The music is generally attributed to Antonio Draghi, an extremely prolific composer of operas, oratorios and other theatre music, who was one of the most prominent musicians in Vienna in the last third of the seventeenth century.[45]

In a letter of February 5, 1670, from Emperor Leopoldo I to the Austrian ambassador in Madrid, Count von Pötting, he says that he is sending nine copies of the opera presented for the queen mother's birthday, and requests that von Pötting give four to the queen mother and dispose of the other five as he pleases.[46] Most of the stories which Calderón used in his mythological court plays were drawn from Ovid's *Metamorphoses,* but the Prometheus story merits only a vague allusion in that work; furthermore, it did not figure among the mythological tales preferred by other artists in Golden Age Spain. It seems most conceivable that it was this Viennese opera, *Il Prometeo,* which suggested the Prometheus story as a subject for a Calderonian court play. Perhaps Mariana herself sent one of her copies along to Calderón, requesting that he consider recreating it.[47] If that was the case, it seems likely that Calderón wrote his play in the same year, for presentation on December 22, 1970.

Barring the discovery of some new archival source of information on the court plays, this dating can be only speculative, however. The newsletters of the Tuscan Embassy in Madrid, sent to the Grand Duke's Secretary of State in Florence, and preserved in the Archivio di Stato di Firenze, sometimes refer to performances celebrating the queen mother's birthday, but they mention only a *sarao* for December, 1670:

> Martedì della settimana passata giorno Natalizio della M[sta] della Regina . . . Ambasciatori, Grandi, et Sig[ri] della Corte in gala . . . Fu poi festeggiato il dopo pranzo con un Sarao, che fece il Re con i suoi Menini alla presenza della Regina, a che non intervennero però, che le solite Dame di S. M., no essendo stato permesso, che vi assistesse nè meno nessun Grande.[48]

---

44 Rudolf Schnitzler and Herbert Seifert identify this librettist as "Ximenes" in their article on Draghi in the *New Grove Dictionary of Music and Musicians,* 1980 edition.

45 That Draghi composed the music is less than certain. In the Grove Encyclopedia list of his works, "Aun vencido, vence amor (El Prometeo)" is listed as doubtful.

46 Privatbriefe Kaiser Leopold I an den Grafen F. E. Pötting, 1662–1673, in *Fontes Rerum Austriacarum* (Vienna: Kaiserlich-Königlichen Hof- und Staatsdruckerei, 1904), Vol. 57, p. 65.

47 Other than centering around Prometeo, the two works have few details in common. These will be examined in a subsequent section.

48 I am indebted to Prof. Shirley Whitaker for sending me this information from her yet-unpublished collection of transcriptions from this rich archival source. This comes from a letter dated 31 December 1670, Mediceo, *filza* 4980.

Mariana must have been pleased with Calderón's play, as it was presented again at the celebration of her birthday in 1685, by the companies of Manuel de Mosquera (owner of the Biblioteca Municipal manuscript) and Rosendo López. This is documented by a series of *baja* certificates in the archives of the Archivo Municipal, which are requests by the lessees of the public theatres for a discount in the rent for the days on which the acting companies were absent due to court performances. The certificate for December 19, 1685, is as follows:

> Yo Diego Alonsso de Vellar esc[no] de el Rey nuestro Senor, Residente en su Corte y prouincia doy fee que oy dia de la fecha siendo como a ora de entre nuebe y diez de la mañana vi esttar cerrado el Corral de la Cruz donde representta la Compania de Rossendo Lopez y tambien vi a esta dicha ora puesttos Carteles por Manuel de Mosquera que se Repressentta en el Corral de el Principe y a la ora de entre una y dos de la tarde vi que dichos carteles se hauian quitado y cerrado dicho corral y hauiendo passado a cassa de los susodichos Rosendo Lopes y Manuel de Mosquera y preguntadoles porque caussa no Representauan al pueblo cada uno en corral que le tocaua me respondieron que hauian tenido orden de el Excelentisimo Señor Condestable de Castilla para que ensaiassen la fiesta Intitulada la Estatua de Prometeo con loa, saynetes y fin de fiesta todo nuebo que se ha de hacer asus Magestades a la celebracion de los años de la Reyna madre nuestra Señora, y que por estta Caussa no podian Repressenttar al pueblo y para que constte de pedimiento de Antonio de Mendoza arrendedor de los corrales de Comedias de esta Corte doy el pressente en Madrid a diez y nuebe de Deziembre de mil y ss[os] y ochenta y cinco años, y lo signe – Antonio de Mendoza, Alonso de Vellar.[49]

There are similar documents for December 11, 14, 20 and 21, the last being the occasion of an "ensayo general". Documents in the Archivo del Palacio indicate that the performance was repeated on January 1 and 13 of 1686, with the companies receiving 192 *reales* for each performance. *La estatua de Prometeo* was again performed as a royal festival in the Coliseo of the Buen Retiro for the occasion of the birthday of Carlos II on November 6, 1693.

---

49 Archivo Municipal Legajo 2–456–3.

4 CRITICAL REJECTION AND REDISCOVERY OF CALDERÓN'S MYTHOLOGICAL PLAYS

Calderón's spectacular mythological plays retained their popularity to the end of the seventeenth century, even after the author's death in 1681. According to Neumeister, the mythological court *fiestas* were occasional pieces, so intimately tied to the particular circumstances of their creation and first production as to be virtually meaningless thereafter. The history of their production contradicts this theory, however; virtually all of the mythological plays were staged in subsequent years at court, and a number were performed in the public theatres as well. As noted previously, *La estatua de Prometeo* saw at least three productions after its opening in the early 1670's. With the demise of the Hapsburg monarchy, however, the mythological court festival gradually faded from view, unseated by two eighteenth-century opponents. On the one hand, Italian opera became the new vogue at court – and in the public theaters as well – under the first two Bourbon monarchs, Felipe V and Fernando VI.[50] An equally devastating enemy was the opposition of neoclassic critics, with their insistence on verisimilitude in the theatre. Even the relatively moderate Ignacio de Luzán, somewhat ambivalent in his rejection of Calderonian drama, totally condemned the mythogical plays, along with *comedias de santos* and other works involving the supernatural and marvelous.[51]

If in the eighteenth century, a neoclassisist esthetic imported from France worked to condemn to oblivion Calderonian drama in general, and his mythological works in particular, the opposing current of nineteenth-century German romanticism brought the first attempt to restore this Spanish dramatist to critical acclaim. In their search for liberation from rigid neoclassic rules, and for a conception of art that was both national and truly Christian, writers such as Ludwig Tieck, the Schlegel brothers, and Goethe found Calderón an ideal model. The mythological plays earned praise for precisely the apparent remove from

50 Shergold, *Spanish Stage*, p. 558; and Donald C. Buck, "Theatrical Productions in Madrid's Cruz and Príncipe Theaters during the Reign of Felipe V", Diss. University of Texas at Austin, 1980, pp. 23–24, 248–249.

51 Manuel Durán and Roberto González Echevarría, "Calderón y la crítica", in *Calderón y la crítica: Historia y antología* (Madrid: Editorial Gredos, 1976), p. 18.

mundane reality which neoclassicists had so condemned. August
Wilhelm Schlegel, who called himself the "ersten Missionar Calderóns in
Deutschland", as part of a larger projected translation project, translated
La devoción de la cruz, La banda y la flor and the mythological play *El
mayor encanto amor,* and sent them to Goethe. The latter, from his
practical experience as theatre director, picked the mythological play as
the one which should be produced first.[52] In a series of lectures on drama
in 1808, A.W. Schlegel bestowed high praise on the mythological pieces:

> Another class of his pieces is called by Calderón himself festal
> dramas *fiestas.* They were destined for representation at court
> on solemn occasions; and though they require the theatrical
> pomp of frequent change of decoration and visible wonders,
> and though music also is often introduced into them, still we
> may call them poetical operas, that is, dramas which, by the
> mere splendour of poetry, perform what in the opera can only
> be attained by the machinery, the music, and the dancing.
> Here the poet gives himself wholly up to the boldest flights of
> fancy, and his creations hardly seem to touch the earth.[53]

Calderonian mythological plays continued to receive critical attention in
Germany through the mid-1800's. In his 1845 *Geschichte der dramati-
schen Literatur und Kunst in Spanien,* Adolph F. von Schack briefly
described most of the plays, and praised their poetic and moral qualities,
but condemned the preponderance of spectacle in some:

> Por lo que hace á su mérito poético, han de estimarse algunas
> entre las mejores obras de Calderón, ofreciendo los mitos
> antiguos bajo un aspecto moral al estilo romántico; el
> elemento poético es siempre aquí lo principal, empleando sólo
> ese ornato externo y pomposo como una envoltura agradable.
> Al contrario, en otras fiestas se observa à menudo, por
> desgracia, que el poeta se amolda más al encargo que ha
> recibido, que á seguir sus propios naturales impulsos; el
> predominio de la pompa escénica, que ahoga alguna vez los
> arranques poéticos del autor, anuncia la decadencia del teatro,
> y al parecer arrastra en ella al poeta.[54]

---

52 Neumeister, *Mythos,* pp. 31, 35–36.
53 Augustus William Schlegel, *A Course of Lectures on Dramatic Art and Literature,*
   trans. John Black (London: Bell & Daldy, 1871), p. 503.
54 Adolfo Federico, Conde de Schack, *Historia de la literatura y del arte dramático en
   España,* trans. Eduardo de Mier (Madrid: Imprenta y Fundación de M. Tello, 1887), IV,
   408.

Von Schack's classification is rather eccentric, as he groups *La hija del aire* with the mythological plays, and *La estatua de Prometeo* with the religious plays, calling the latter a "trabajo profundo del mito de Prometeo, con arreglo á las ideas cristianas".[55] In 1856, Leopold Schmidt published the first article dedicated solely to Calderón's mythological plays, "Über Calderons Behandlung antiker Mythen". Schmidt treats Calderóns's possible sources, in Ovid and subsequent mythographers, describes eleven mythological plays, and praises Calderón's poetic handling of myth.[56] Schmidt defends Calderón against the charge by some critics that his plays show him to be ignorant of the classical myths:

> Natürlich ist das nicht Unkunde, sondern bewußte Vernach-
> lässigung einer für den poetischen Zweck gleichgültigen
> Genauigkeit, aber es zeigt immerhin, daß er die Überlieferung
> mit einem anderen Auge als mit dem des eigentlichen For-
> schers ansah; es war ein künstlerisches Auge, das in den oft
> zusammenhangslosen und verworrenen Notizen der ihm
> bekannten Mythologen lebensvolle Gestalten zu schauen
> vermochte.[57]

In the same year, the first article devoted exclusively to *La estatua de Prometeo* appeared, but in Spain, rather than Germany: that of Manuel Milá y Fontanals, "Dramas simbólicos de Calderón: *El Prometeo*". Milá y Fontanals classes the play with *La vida es sueño* as a symbolic drama which, while inferior to that play, is yet a work he describes as:

> . . . no poco notable . . . que ofrece la particularidad de tratar
> una fábula mitológica no tan sólo á guisa de espectáculo
> brillante y risueño sino con interpretación filosófica y pro-
> funda, y si bien con alteraciones debidas á la fantasía del poeta,
> con bastante fidelidad al conjunto de la narración clásica y en
> un estilo más acorde con el asunto de lo que pudiera
> esperarse.[58]

---

55 Von Schack, "Arte dramático", pp. 343–344.
56 David Norris Mackinnon, "The Mythological Dramas of Pedro Calderón de la Barca", Diss. University of Kentucky, 1977, pp. 18–19. The useful survey of the history of critical reactions to the mythological plays in this dissertation can be supplemented by Neumeister's overview, which concentrates on German critics.
57 Leopold Schmidt, "Ueber Calderons Behandlung antiker Mythen. Ein Beitrag zur Geschichte der Mythologie", *(Rheinisches) Museum für Philologie*, 10 (1856), p. 315; cited in Neumeister, *Mythos*, p. 37.
58 Manuel Milá y Fontanals, *Opúsculos literarios*, Vol. V of *Obras completas* (Barcelona: Librería de Álvaro Verdaguer, 1893), p. 85.

Milá y Fontanals' rather negatively-phrased praise is indicative of the
more general reaction to the mythological plays. Through the nineteenth
and into the twentieth centuries, they were either ignored or condemned
as a body unworthy of attention.[59] Hartzenbusch, in his edition of
Calderón's plays, dismisses the mythological plays as occasional pieces,
saying, "habrá quien le perdone como nosotros las comedias
mitológicas, en atencion á haber escrito las de capa y espada . . .[60]
Menéndez y Pelayo relegates the mythological plays to a subspecies of
the classification "géneros inferiores". His condemnation of them
summarizes most of the criticisms offered by other opponents, before
and since:

> En estas comedias mitológicas, como en toda especie de drama
> de espectáculo, el poeta queda siempre en grado y en categoría
> inferior al maquinista y al pintor escenógrafo. Eran obras que
> se destinaban al solaz de los Reyes y de la corte, ora en el
> Palacio, ora en el Buen Retiro, y en las cuales más se atendía al
> prestigio de los ojos que á la lucha de los afectos y los
> caracteres, ni á la verdad de la expresión.
> En vano sería buscar en estas obras nada del espíritu de la
> teogonía helénica, nada del carácter que los griegos pusieron
> en sus divinidades. Son unos dioses del Olimpo enteramente
> distintos de como estamos acostumbrados á imaginarlos. Son
> caballeros galantes y cortesanos, lo mismo que los héroes de
> las comedias de capa y espada.
> Calderón nunca acertó a ver más que el mundo de su tiempo, y
> áun éste no tal como era, sino de un modo algo ideal y
> fantástico.[61]

Even more damning is a later summary, in which Menéndez y Pelayo
says that posterity has justifiably condemned the mythological works to
oblivion. He continues:

> Hoy no tienen más interés que el histórico y el de algunos
> buenos versos acá y allá esparcidos y casi ahogados en un mar

---

59 The exceptions are two German works: Friedrich Wilhelm Valentin Schmidt
   described 108 of Calderón's works, including the mythological plays, in *Die
   Schauspiele Calderóns dargestellt und erläutert* (Elberfeld, 1857), and Engelbert
   Günthner, in his 800-pagebook *Calderón und seine Werke* (Freiburg, 1888), treated
   the mythological plays, including details of staging. See Neumeister, *Mythos*, p. 38.
60 BAE, Vol. VII, p. xi.
61 Marcelino Menéndez y Pelayo, *Calderón y su teatro*, 3rd. ed. (Madrid: Imprenta de A.
   Pérez Dubrull, 1884), pp. 365–366.

de enfática y culterana palabrería. Juzgar a Calderón por tales
dramas sería evidente injusticia. Buscar en ellos passión,
interés, caracteres y color de las respectivas épocas, fuera
necedad y desvarío.[62]

Pierre Paris treated the mythological plays in terms almost as negative, if
less vitriolic, in his 1925 article, "La Mythologie de Calderón".[63] This
piece, full of factual errors, centers on a description of *Apolo y Climene*
and *El hijo del sol, Faetón*, which he considers typical examples of these
works "d'ordre secondaire".

No voice was raised in defense of Calderón's mythological works until
the era of the Second World War. Writing in isolation during the war, the
German author Max Kommerell considered *Ni amor se libra de amor, El
mayor encanto amor, El monstruo de los jardines* and several mythological *autos* in his work on Calderón.[64] Kommerell's voice was little heeded
then, however. Credit for the development of a new appreciation of the
mythological plays goes instead to the critical insight of Angel Valbuena
Prat who, during the same period, wrote a full chapter on the
mythological plays in his book *Calderón: Su personalidad, su arte
dramático, su estilo y sus obras.* He finds them, in their resemblance to
modern scenic treatment and musical dramas, "uno de los géneros de
nuestra dramática del XVII más próximos a la sensibilidad y gusto
actuales", and says that their neglect and condemnation by nineteen-
century critics was unjust. Continues Valbuena Prat:

> La forma libre, anacrónica, esencial y no detallista, de tratar las
> fábulas de la antigüedad está mucho más cerca de la posición
> de un Gide (en *El Prometeo mal encadenado*) o de Cocteau (en
> el *Orfeo*) que de la sujeción al patrón clásico de las tragedias
> mitológicas de Racine. Racine era un genio que miraba al siglo
> clásico anterior, al XVI (como Poussin en la pintura); Calde-
> rón, el genio barroco del teatro, que en cierto modo puede
> hacernos pensar en la mitología subjetiva y grandiosa de los
> cuadros de Rubens.
>
> Calderón veía en los asuntos mitológicos más la idea capital
> que las incidencias. Concebía tales dramas tendiendo a inter-

---

62 Pedro Calderón de la Barca, *Teatro selecto* (Madrid: Libreria de Perlado, 1918), I, lxiii-
    lxiv; cited in Mackinnon, "Mythological Plays", p. 25.
63 In *Homenaje ofrecido a Menédez Pidal* (Madrid: Librería y Casa Editorial Hernando,
    S. A., 1925), I, 557–570.
64 Neumeister, *Mythos,* pp. 40–41.

pretar lo esencial poético y filosófico; la fábula como lírica y
como moralidad.[65]

Valbuena Prat pointed out that scenery, music, etc., did not vitiate the
poetic value of Calderóns creations, but rather heightened their power,
making these theatrical achievements an anticipation of Wagner's
synthesis of all the arts. He finds *Eco y Narciso* a truly lyrical drama,
containing pychological perceptions parallel to the discoveries of Adler
and Freud.[66] He describes *La estatua de Prometeo* in detail, as "una de
las obras más poéticas y profundas de Calderón" and after analyzing the
symbolism of the work concludes: "Así este Prometeo cristianizado en
espíritu, palpita de pensamiento, de poesía, de ricos elementos musicales
y de una escenografía refulgente."[67]

In 1954, W. G. Chapman followed Valbuena Prat's lead with "Las
comedias mitológicas de Calderón", a landmark article on this genre.
Chapman reviews the previous negative criticism, which he considers
most unjust, and the first positive valuations of Valbuena Prat and
Eugenio Frutos Cortés.[68] He describes the spectacular character of the
works, and recounts in considerable detail the nature of the mythological
heritage in seventeenth-century Europe, emphasizing the moral and
allegorical interpretations of myth by mythographers such as Pérez de
Moya and Vitoria. Chapman then summarizes a number of Calderonian
mythological plays, in relation to that mythological heritage. From that
survey, he concludes:

> Una visión de conjunto de los temas de las comedias
> mitológicas y de las interpretaciones de la mitología que éstos
> exhiben, indica que estas comedias no fueron pura y sim-
> plemente espectáculos. Calderón, en estas obras, se halla
> inserto en la tradición europea medieval de la interpretación
> moral de la mitología; estas obras son, bajo el lirismo, la
> música y lo espectacular, alegorías de la vida humana.[69]

To prove the seriousness of the mythological works, Chapman offers a
detailed and thoughtful analysis of *La estatua de Promoteo,* which he

---

65 Angel Valbuena Prat, *Calderón: Su personalidad, su arte dramático, su estilo y sus
   obras* (Barcelona: Editorial Juventud, 1941), pp. 169–170.
66 Valbuena Prat, *Calderón,* pp. 171–174.
67 Valbuena Prat, *Calderón,* pp. 177–183.
68 The latter in his book, *Calderón de la Barca* (Barcelona: Editorial Labor, S. A., 1949).
69 W. C. Chapman, "Las comedias mitológicas de Calderón", *Revista de Literatura,* 5
   (1954) 58.

considers "una obra de . . . extraordinaria intensidad y complejidad".[70] In his opinion, the play is no less significant than the versions of the Prometheus tale told by Aeschylus and Shelley, and merits ranking with Calderón's greatest works.[71]

Subsequent years have seen a steadily-increasing attention to the Calderonian mythological corpus, in a proliferation of articles on the individual plays. Charles Aubrun has contributed individual editions of *Eco y Narciso* and *La estatua de Prometeo,* as well as a brief survey of the genre as a whole.[72] M. Stroud has published an edition of *Celos aun del aire matan,* [73] and the critical edition of *Fieras afemina amor* begun by E. Wilson and completed by Cecilia Bainton has now appeared.[74] Shergold has made available invaluable information on the staging of the plays in his *History of the Spanish Stage,* [75] as have Varey and Shergold in various articles and their several books on the *Teatros y comedias de Madrid,* and particularly in their just-published volume, *Representaciones palaciegas, 1603-1699.*[76] Two recent books have been devoted exclusively to the mythological plays; that of Sebastian Neumeister, *Mythos und Repräsentation,*[77] a solid, if not totally satisfactory work; and that of Edwin Haverbeck, *El tema mitológico en el teatro de Calderón,*[78] an extremely superficial treatment.

The chorus of contemporary praise for the mythological works is not unanimous, however. In his singularly unsympathetic treatment of Calderón, James Maraniss recently dismissed the mythological plays with a disdain reminiscent of that of Menéndez y Pelayo:

> There is no better way for a reader to find out whether, in spite of everything, he really likes Calderón than for him to read a

---

70 Chapman, "Las comedias mitológicas", p. 59.

71 Chapman, "Las comedias mitológicas", p. 67.

72 The latter in an article "Estructura y significación de las comedias mitológicas de Calderón, in *Hacia Calderón,* Tercer coloquio anglogermano, Londres, 1973, (Berlin: Walter de Gruyter, 1976), pp. 148–155.

73 (San Antonio, Texas: Trinity University Press, 1981).

74 Kassel, Germany: Edition Reichenberger, 1984. Several other editions exist as unpublished Ph. D. theses: *Apolo y Climene,* edited by Lal Narinesingh, Cambridge, 1968; *El Jardin de la Falerina* by Robert Rudolf Bacalski, U. of New Mexico, 1972; and *El monstruo de los jardines* by Cecilia C. D. Bainton, Cambridge, 1977. A typescript edition of *El mayor encanto amor* edited by J. Alsina, was published in Paris in 1963 by the Institut hispanique D.E.S.

75 (Oxford: Oxford University Press, 1967).

76 (London: Tamesis Books Ltd., 1983).

77 (Munich: Fink Verlag, 1978).

78 (Valdivia, Chile: Universidad Austral de Chile, 1975).

few of the mythological plays, the *Fêtes galantes* Calderón composed for the entertainment of the royal family toward the end of his career and at the very end of Spain's century and a half of political presumption and literary greatness. These musical dramas are the merest and purest artifice; they elevate artifice itself into its own subject. Lacking any serious mimetic or intellectual substance, they have no religious, moral, political, social, or metaphysical content; they have only a style. To the person who dislikes this style, none of Calderón's work will finally mean very much; he who does like it will like it wherever he finds it, but perhaps he will like it most of all in those plays in which no important values are introduced or undermined.[79]

In contrast to Maraniss' opinion, it is my contention that Calderón took an essentially superficial genre, the spectacular mythological court play, and with his poetic genius and artistic control, made of it a profound exploration of human nature and human society. The following critical analysis of *La estatua de Prometeo* will, I hope, serve as a demonstration of his success.

---

79 James E. Maraniss, *On Calderón* (Columbia, Missouri: University of Missouri Press, 1978), p. 87.

5 THE STORY OF PROMETHEUS

Although the story of Prometheus as we know it derives from Greek mythology, it is but a part of a great cosmogonic myth which is both older and more widespread than Greek civilization, the story which attempts to explain the origin of our universe through the loving and warring of the personalized elemental forces of Sky, Earth, and Sea. Elements of it can be traced to Near Eastern mythology, with contributions from such distant sites as India and ancient Gaul.[80] Viewed with an even wider lens, as an etiological myth of the origin of fire, the tale is virtually universal, as all mythologies tend to attribute the conquest of this vital force to a legendary hero – perhaps first a brave animal, and subsequently a human figure with the courage to tame its mystery.[81] For fire contains in itself, in the material and symbolic possibilities it offers to man, the full range of potential meanings which successive interpretations have embodied in the story of Prometheus.

> Si tout ce qui change lentement s'explique par la vie, tout ce qui change vite s'explique par le feu. Le feu est l'ultra-vivant. Le feu est intime et il est universel. Il vit dans notre cœur, il vit dans le ciel. Il monte des profondeurs de la substance et latent, s'offre comme un amour. Il redescend dans la matière et se cache, contenu comme la haine et la vengeance. Parmi tous les phénomènes, il est vraiment le seul qui puisse recevoir aussi nettement les deux valorisations contraires: le bien et le mal. Il brille au Paradis. Il brûle à l'Enfer. Il est douceur et torture, il est cuisine et Apocalypse. Il est plaisir pour l'enfant assis sagement près du foyer; il punit cependant de toute désobéissance quand on veut jouer de trop près avec ses flammes. Il est bien-être et il est respect. C'est un dieu tutélaire et terrible, bon et mauvais. Il peut se contredire: il est un des principes d'explication universelle.[82]

---

80 Aeschylus, *Prometheus Bound*, trans. and ed., James Scully and C. J. Herington (London: Oxford University Press, 1975), p. 3.
81 Raymond Trousson, *Le Thème de Prométhée dans la littérature européenne* (Geneva: Librairie Droz, 1964), I, 5–7.
82 G. Bachelard, *La psychanalyse du feu*, pp. 21–22; cited in Trousson, *Prométhée*, p. 3.

As man's view of the organization of the universe has changed, so has his rendition and interpretation of the story of the fire-stealer whom we know as Prometheus.

Our oldest extant account of the Prometheus tale is that contained in two works of Hesiod, *Theogony*[83] and *Works and Days*, of the eighth century B.C. In the *Theogony*, verses 507-616, Hesiod says that the progeny of the Titan Japetus and "the neat ankled maid Clymene, daughter of Ocean",[84] were "stout-hearted . . . Atlas", whom Zeus assigned the task of supporting the heavens on his shoulders, "very glorious Menoetius", whom Zeus struck with a thunderbolt and sent down to Erebus for his presumption and pride, "clever Prometheus, full of various wiles", and "scatter-brained Epimetheus who from the first was a mischief to men who eat bread."[85] Prometheus first incurred the wrath of Zeus by dividing an ox, and tricking the sovereign god into accepting as his lot a pretty package of bones and white fat, while reserving for men all the meat. An irate Zeus hid the power of fire from men, but "the noble son of Iapetus" stole it from him in a fennel stalk. In revenge, Zeus (in the *Works and Days* account) vowed to "give men as the price for fire an evil thing in which they may all be glad of heart while they embrace their own destructions."[86] He therefore ordered Hephaestus to make a beautiful woman, whom the goddesses adorned to increase her beauty. "And he called this woman Pandora, because all they who dwelt on Olympus gave each a gift, a plague to men who eat bread."[87] Epimetheus accepted Pandora, forgetting Prometheus' warning never to accept a gift from Zeus, for fear it might be harmful to men. Pandora removed the lid from an urn containing the gifts of the gods, letting loose all sorts of miseries for man, as only Hope remained within the jar.

Prometheus, too, paid for his temerity, as Zeus ordered him bound with inextricable chains, with a shaft through his middle, while an eagle ate his immortal liver, devoured each day only to regenerate at night. In the *Theogony*, Hesiod adds that Hercules eventually slew the eagle and released Prometheus from his suffering, "not without the will of Olympian Zeus who reigns on high."[88]

---

83 Some critics question the attribution of this work to Hesiod. See Trousson, *Prométhée*, p. 9, n. 25.

84 Hesiod, *Theogony*, in *The Homeric Hymns and Homerica*, trans. Hugh G. Evelyn-White (New York: The Macmillan Co, 1914). All subsequent quotations from Hesiod are from the same volume.

85 Hesiod, *Theogony*, p. 117.

86 Hesiod, *Works and Days*, p. 7.

87 Hesiod, *Works and Days*, p. 9.

88 Hesiod, *Theogony*, p. 117.

In Hesiod's tale, Prometheus is not a dignified, heroic figure, but a daring "trickster" whose actions upset the balance between gods and men;[89] he is at best a dubious benefactor of mankind, as the net result is only an increase in man's sufferings. As Trousson states:

> Le poème est moins à la gloire du Voleur de Feu qu'à la louange d'un Zeus tout-puissant. Nous sommes encore fort loin du Titan libérateur: chez le poète d'Ascra, l'enterprise de Prométhée s'est soldée par un échec et l'auteur ne fait guère que définir la condition humaine dans l'optique pessimiste d'une lente décadence et de l'assujettissement à un Zeus impitoyable et même cruel.[90]

The overall message of the Hesiod story of Prometheus is, "You can't fool Zeus".

Aeschylus, who wrote the next major version of the Prometheus story in his tragedy *Prometheus Bound* in the fifth century, B.C., drew an even crueler Zeus within that play. The supreme god is depicted as a brutal tyrant, who rules without laws, seduces his female subjects, plans wholesale murder of his people, and trusts no one.[91] To dramatize his cruel injustice, Aeschylus introduces to the story Io, an innocent girl driven to madness by the combination of Zeus's lust for her and Hera's jealousy. Counterpoised to this innocent victim stands Prometheus, as a proud and knowing rebel against the tyranny of Zeus, whom he helped to bring to power.[92]

In contrast to the wily trickster of Hesiod's tale, and the semi-comic figure of other early portraits of Prometheus, Aeschylus makes of him a worthy opponent of Zeus, a true champion and willing martyr for mankind. Prometheus is here not an obscure cousin of Zeus, but his uncle, as Aeschylus makes him the son of Earth herself, from whom he draws his knowledge of future events.[93] As he stands chained to the rock, he tells the sympathizing chorus.

> Myself, I knew all this
> and knew it all along.
> Still,

89 Carlos García Gual, *Prometeo: Mito y tragedia* (Pamplona: Ediciones Peralta, 1979), p. 41.
90 Trousson, *Prométhée*, p. 14.
91 See Scully and Herington's introduction to Aeschylus, *Prometheus Bound*, pp. 11–12.
92 I do not pretend to present a balanced survey of this complex and fascinating play. In this and subsequent versions of the myth, I concentrate on those elements of the story which are germane to Calderón's rendition.
93 Scully and Herington, *Prometheus Bound*, pp. 4-8.

> I *meant* to be wrong.
> I knew what I was doing.
> Helping humankind
>   I helped myself to misery . . .[94]

But to mankind he brought with the stolen fire the birth of civilization. To childlike humans living unaware, as in a shapeless dream, and surviving like tiny ants in dark caves, he brought intelligence, "Made them masters of their own thought",[95] teaching them how to build houses, how to understand the cycles of day and night and of the seasons; he invented numbers, "wisdom above all others", and letters, "to be their memory of everything"; harnessed beasts of burden and invented ships; taught men how to use drugs against disease, the value of minerals in the earth, and the various forms of prophecy that enable them to understand and control their environment.[96] Summarizes Prometheus: "In a word: listen!/ All human culture comes from Prometheus."[97] Furthermore, Aeschylus leaves Pandora (and Epimetheus) out of the story, so no plague of sorrows comes to man to cancel the advances Prometheus bestowed on them; he is unquestionably their benefactor.

Aeschylus' Prometheus is not, however, a figure of blameless virtue set against a purely evil Zeus. His version of the story leaves a number of ambiguities in the drama, not the least of which is the fact that the *Prometheus Bound* was not an independent drama, but was followed by a sequel, *Prometheus Unbound*, which survives only in fragments.[98] From these bits, it appears that in the second play Prometheus, Io, and Herakles all moved from torment to release; that if the first play enacted the clash between brute force and unbending knowledge, then the second portrayed "the reconciliation of the almighty power of Zeus with the civilizing intelligence of Prometheus."[99] Scully and Herington caution, however, that:

> The long history of the interpretation of the *Prometheus Bound* is almost the history of a mirror. Romantics, liberals, and socialists, gazing into these disturbing depths, have found

---

94 *Prometheus Bound*, lines 402-408.
95 *Prometheus Bound*, lines 631-635.
96 *Prometheus Bound*, lines 640-734.
97 *Prometheus Bound*, lines 637-638.
98 This in turn may have been followed by a third play, the *Prometheus Pyrphoros* or "Fire-Carrier". See Scully and Herington, *Prometheus Bound, p. 16.*
99 Scully and Herington, *Prometheus Bound*, pp. 11, 17.

> there an Aeschylean justification of romanticism, liberalism, and socialism, respectively. Authoritarians on the contrary, from the medieval Byzantines onwards, have emphasized with approval the crushing punishment ultimately accorded to the rebel against the Supreme Authority. In a word: *Tell me what you are, and I will tell you what you think of the* Prometheus Bound . . .[100]

Trousson believes the play and its sequel to be both a celebration of the grandeur and progress of man. With time, the new ruler Zeus will learn that he, too, has limitations: he is subject to Necessity, and needs the knowledge of Prometheus.[101] Prometheus, who has been shown to possess some of the same faults as Zeus – stubbornness, anger, and rashness,[102] must also learn moderation.

> Le temps enseigne la sagesse et la modération et Prométhée lui-même, malgré la générosité de sa révolte, ne sera accepté que dans la mesure où il s'harmonisera, lui aussi, avec l'univers apaisé.[103]

Viewing the Prometheus plays in this optimistic light, one can certainly find a thematic kinship between the Greek tragedian and the Spanish dramatist writing two millenniums after him. Yet it is almost certain that Calderón drew the main ingredients of his story not from Aeschylus but from contemporary sources, as we will see presently. It is therefore doubly fascinating to find not only a certain correspondence between the two plays in the interpretations of the issues involved in the Prometheus story, but a number of striking parallels in dramatic presentation. Both were presented in a combination of spoken verse, chant or recitative, and song, according to the expressive intent of the passage involved. In both, a chorus sang and danced the popular response to the protagonists' sufferings. And the *Prometheus Bound*, like the court mythological plays, relied in part on machine-produced spectacular effects. The character Ocean, seated on a winged, four-legged monster, apparently "flew" in, thanks to some sort of mechanical crane, and the chorus may have been similarly airborne. The climax of the play saw Prometheus, rock and all, swallowed up in a great storm of thunder, blackness and quaking earth,[104] an effect exactly parallel to the scene of universal chaos

---

100 Scully and Herington, *Prometheus Bound*, p. 11.
101 Trousson, *Prométhée*, pp. 25, 36.
102 Scully and Herington, *Prometheus Bound*, p. 15.
103 Trousson, *Prométhée*, p. 35.
104 See Scully and Herington, *Prometheus Bound*, pp. 18–22.

that occurs in *La estatua de Prometeo* and a number of other Calderonian mythological plays. The genre of court spectaculars was born in the desire of Italian humanists to reproduce ancient drama in the modern world; in its maturity in Calderón's hands the result was not a reproduction, but certainly a creation that both in complexity of spirit and in "dramatic flesh" could claim kinship with its classical antecedent. All the basic elements of the Prometheus story derive from either Hesiod or Aeschylus. Over the centuries, however, certain features were dropped or added, some apparently coming from the oral, popular tradition in Greece,[105] others by contagion from parallel myths. From the fourth century B.C. on, Prometheus becomes not only the creator of man in the symbolic sense, as the initiator of civilization, but also in the material sense; he makes men of earth and water. At this point, the stolen fire becomes a symbol of the animating principle, the soul of the creature formed of clay. This new-formed being is usually without distinction of sex, although according to Menander's misogynistic account, Prometheus only made women.[106]

With the primitive era well past in which the myths could be told and accepted at face value as an explanation of the workings of a divine universe, contradictory theories evolved to render the familiar myths intelligible and acceptable. Seznec found them to be of three groups.

1. The historical school, associated with Euhemerus (third century B.C.), which sees the myths as more or less distorted histories of human heroes who have been elevated to the ranks of the gods;[107]
2. The physical tradition, which considers the myths stories of "the union or conflict of the elementary powers which constitute the universe, the gods then being cosmic symbols;"[108] and
3. The allegorical school, which treats them as fables expressing moral and philosophical ideas.

These theories, invented by the ancients themselves, enabled the myths to survive both the era of pagan non-belief in the old gods, and that of the Christian Middle Ages, up through and beyond the Renaissance, as Calderón's frequent allegorical use of myth attests.

---

105 Trousson, *Prométhée*, pp. 40–41.
106 Trousson, *Prométhée*, pp. 47–48; García Gual, *Prometeo*, pp. 59–60.
107 Jean Seznec, The Survival of the Pagan Gods: The Mythological Tradition and Its Place in Renaissance Humanism and Art, rev. ed., trans. Barbara F. Sessions (New York: Pantheon Books, 1953), pp. 4, 11–13.
108 Seznec, *Mythological Tradition*, p. 4.

Since Prometheus is not associated with any heavenly body, the second
of these two theories did not serve as a vehicle for his survival, but the
historical and allegorical approaches were both applied to the Prom-
etheus/Pandora story. Diodorus Siculus (first century B.C.) applied the
historical approach to Prometheus, identifying him as a governor of
Egypt, tormented by a river called "the Eagle" which continually
attacked his land, until Hercules contained the floods – i.e., "killed the
eagle".[109] Later historical interpretations made Prometheus an Egyptian
sage, a contemporary of Aesculapius and Lycurgus, and generally of
Moses as well.[110]

An early example of allegorical use is Plato's telling of the myth in the
dialogue *Protagoras*, apparently written about 390 B.C.[111] The purpose
of the version which Plato attributes to the Sophist philosopher is that of
providing an allegorical explanation of how men came to live in a
political society. In this dialogue, Prometheus shares the honor of
bringing civilization to men with Zeus, who has now become the
concerned caretaker of mankind. According to Plato's myth, the gods
molded mortal creatures from earth and fire, and charged Prometheus
and Epimetheus with equipping them with the necessary physical
faculties, food, and the like. Epimetheus took charge of the distribution
to all the beasts, but did it unwisely, so that nothing was left for mortal
men. Prometheus arrived to examine the distribution, and found man
"naked, unshod, unbedded, unarmed".[112] So he stole for them from
Hephaestus and Athena wisdom in the arts and fire, with which men
could provide for their daily needs, could learn to speak, and to worship
the gods. Prometheus, however, could not provide men with the civic
wisdom they needed to live together in peace and safety, since it was the
property of Zeus.

> So Zeus, fearing that our race was in danger of utter
> destruction, sent Hermes to bring respect and right among
> men, to the end that there should be regulation of cities and
> friendly ties to draw them together.[113]

If Plato used the Prometheus story allegorically to explain Athenian
political structure, Lucian used it parodically in the second century A.D.

---

109 Trousson, *Prométhée*, p. 49.
110 Trousson, *Prométhée*, p. 68.
111 García Gual, *Prometeo*, p. 53.
112 Plato, *Protagoras*, trans. W. R. M. Lamb (New York: G. P. Putnam's Sons, 1924),
     p. 131.
113 Plato, *Protagoras*, p. 135.

to belittle all the mythical figures involved. His dialogue *Prometheus* follows the general outline of Aeschylus' *Prometheus Bound*, although Lucian's Prometheus is the material creator of men, and in fact consumes most of the dialogue arguing that neither his creation of men nor his gift to them of the divine flame threatened the sphere of the gods. His argument in the case of fire is particularly interesting, as it contains the same points which Minerba uses in defending Prometeo before Apolo in Calderón's play, and I therefore quote it at length:

> and now, if you wish, I shall pass to fire and that reprehensible theft! In the name of the gods answer me this question without any hesitation; have we lost any fire since men have had it too? You can't say that we have. The nature of that possession is such, I suppose, that it is not diminished if anyone else takes some of it, for it does not go out when a light is procured from it. But surely it is downright stinginess to prevent things from being shared with those who need them when it does you no harm to share them. Inasmuch as you are gods, you ought to be kindly and "bestowers of blessings" and to stand aloof from all stinginess. In this case even if I had filched all your fire and taken it down to earth without leaving a bit of it behind, I should not be guilty of any great wrong-doing against you, for you yourselves have no need of it, as you do not get cold and do not cook your ambrosia and do not require artificial light. On the other hand, men are obliged to use fire, not only for other purposes but above all for the sacrifices . . .[114]

During the Middle Ages, the Prometheus story was of no particular importance, except as part of the general struggle of Christian thought against the persistent classical myths.[115] As Trousson points out, a modern "myth" has grown up, according to which the early church fathers saw in Prometheus' sympathy and suffering for man a pagan prefiguration of Christ, and commonly made some sort of philosophical assimilation of Prometheus to Christ. The idea can be traced back to the late seventeenth-century English commentator of Aeschylus, Thomas Stanley, but its diffusion and general acceptance occurred in the nineteenth and twentieth centuries. The only source cited by Stanley was Tertullian (2nd-3rd century A.D.), who makes two brief metaphorical comparisons between Prometheus and God (not Christ):

---

114 Lucian, *Protagoras*, trans. A. M. Harmon (Cambridge, Mass.: Harvard University Press, 1968), pp. 261–263.
115 Trousson, *Prométhée*, p. 59.

. . . omnia torpent, omnia rigent: nihil illic nisi feritas calet illa scilicet quae fabulas scenis dedit, de sacrificiis Taurorum et amoribus Colchorum, et crucibus Caucasorum. Sed nihil tam barbarum ac triste apud Pontum quem quod illic Marcion natus est, Scytha tetrior, Hamaxobio instabilior, Massageta inhumanior, Amazone audacior, nubilo obscurior, hieme frigidior, gelu fragilior, Istro fallacior, Caucasio abruptior. Quidni? penes quem verus Prometheus Deus omnipotens blasphemiis lancinatur.[116]

Viros enim justitia innocentia dignos deum nosse et ostendere a primordio in saeculum emisit spiritu divino inundatos, qui praedicarent deum unicum esse, qui universa condiderit, qui hominem de humo struxerit; hix enim est verus Prometheus . . .[117]

Trousson found no other evidence of such an assimilation and concluded that the Prometeus myth was simply indigestible for early Christianity:

"Il y a, dans la conception du personnage de Prométhée, mêlés aux sentiments angéliques (=sa pitié pour les hommes), des éléments lucifériens" (=sa haine de Zeus). Aussi la plupart des commentateurs suppriment-ils purement et simplement le symbole prométhéen, en faisant passer le mythe pour un récit grossier. Il est curieux d'observer que les innombrables similitudes découvertes entre Pandore et Prométhée d'une part, et des personnages de l'Ancien et du Nouveau Testament de l'autre, datent en réalité des temps modernes et qu'elles ne sont généralement que le produit d'imaginations avides de rapprochements aussi faciles qu'exaltants.[118]

Nor was the Prometheus story commonly cited in early works in the vernacular. The mythical stealer of fire does not figure among the many gods cited in the histories of Troy, or of Alexander, nor even in the *Roman de la Rose*. This relative neglect of Prometheus is probably due to the great diffusion of Ovid and Virgil, which contain only vague allusions to Prometheus.[119]

Even the Renaissance did not bring the myth of Prometheus burgeoning to new life. As Trousson puts it, "Si la Renaissance est un siècle

---

116 Tertullian, *Adversus Marcionem*, I, I, 247; cited in Trousson, *Prométhée*, p. 73.
117 *Apologeticus*, XVIII, 2; cited in Trousson, *Prométhée*, p. 77.
118 Trousson, *Prométhée*, pp. 63–64; quoting in part from A. Bonnard, *La révolte de Prométhée*, p. 436.
119 Trousson, *Prométhée*, pp. 79–81.

prométhéen, elle n'est pas le siècle de Prométhée".[120] Renaissance
knowledge of the tale did not come from a renewed reading of
Aeschylus, whose works were slow to earn new editions and translations. Hesiod's version was much earlier and more widely circulated. In
general, however, diffusion of the myth came from mythological
manuals rather than from direct contact with the classics.[121] One of the
first such manuals – and the most significant in the history of the
Prometheus myth – was the *De Genealogia deorum gentilium* which
Giovanni Boccaccio undertook in the mid-fourteenth century, and to
which he dedicated the last twenty-five years of his life. It circulated
widely, first in manuscript form, and after the invention of the printing
press, in multiple editions in Latin, Italian and Spanish. According to
Seznec, "It became, and remained for two centuries, the central storehouse
from which educated men drew their knowledge of the gods".[122]
Boccaccio dedicates a chapter to Prometheus – "De Prometheo Japeti
Filio, qui fecit Pandoram et genuit Ysidem et Deucalionem" (Book IV,
Chap. XLIV). Many of the details and interpretations he includes follow
the medieval euhemerist and allegorical tradition. For example, he cites
from the fifth-century mythographer Fulgentius the idea that Minerva,
entranced with Prometheus' statue, offered to lead him to Olympus,
from which he could bring back any useful gift; Prometheus saw and
stole the flame. Boccaccio interprets this as meaning that with wisdom as
his guide, Prometheus ascended toward heaven by reflection, and
received the flame of knowledge from God, the source of all wisdom. He
follows St. Augustine in saying that Prometheus was a man famous for
his learning, and quotes Eusebius, who made Prometheus a king of
Argos, and Lactantius, who named him as the inventor of statuary. Even
Boccaccio's first interpretation of Prometheus as the material creator of
man is clearly medieval, for he says that it was only a tale invented by
pagans in their ignorance of man's creation by the true God. However,
Boccaccio then adds the idea of a "second Prometheus", and in so doing,
opens the path for a new view of the fire-stealer. Drawing on the
mysterious Theodontius (whose work has been lost, but who appears to
have been a philosopher of Campanian origin who lived sometime in the
ninth to eleventh century),[123] Boccaccio reports that this second
Prometheus, a son of Japetus, left his family, went to Assyria, and after a

120 Trousson, *Prométhée*, p. 120.
121 Trousson, *Prométhée*, pp. 85–88.
122 Seznec, *Mythological Tradition*, pp. 220–224.
123 Seznec, *Mythological Tradition*, pp. 221–222.

long, voluntary exile in the Caucasus, descended to teach the Chaldeans
astrology, the origin of light and the customs of civilized men. Boccaccio
concludes that man is a double creation; he possesses a natural being,
created by God, with a reasonable soul and vegetative and sensitive
faculties. This natural being, however, fell into original sin and a debased
state of ignorance. Then the second Prometheus intervened, to give this
natural man his second, social being – to create civilized man:

> . . . secundus Prometheus insurgit, id est doctus homo, et eos
> tanquam lapideos suspiciens quasi de novo creat, docet et
> instruit, et demonstrationibus suis ex naturalibus hominibus
> civiles facit, moribus scientia et virtutibus insignes adeo ut
> liquido pateat alios produxisse naturam, et alios reformasse
> doctrinam.

He thus civilized men "qui a natura producti sunt, rudes et ignari
veniunt, imo ni instruantur, lutei agrestes et belve."[124]
Boccaccio's vision of this second Prometheus is a clear departure from a
medieval conception, in its view of the creation as a two-step process,
and in its glorification of human knowledge, or man as a being
potentially perfectible by his own efforts. Nevertheless, the principal
mythographers who followed Boccaccio in the sixteenth century –
Gyraldi, Natale Conti, and Vicenzo Cartari – did not follow Boccaccio's
innovative interpretation nor pay great attention to Prometheus.[125] His
idea does reappear, however – included amidst a wealth of traditional
historical and allegorical interpretations – in the mythography of Juan
Pérez de Moya, *Philosofia secreta*, which will be considered below, as a
probable source for Calderón's drama. Pérez de Moya's work was first
published in 1585. (Appropriate sections of this work have been
included as an appendix)
These mythological encyclopedias seemed to offer little inspiration to
poets to take up the Prometheus story. While other mythical figures,
drawn from poetic models in Ovid, Virgil and Horace, came in droves to
populate the poetry of the Renaissance, no important work was
dedicated to Prometheus, in Spain or elsewhere, until the end of the
seventeenth century. Poets did mention the myth somewhat more
frequently than in earlier times, but their usage was generally within the
medieval tradition. A few new elements were added to the tradition,
however. Ronsard, in his *Second livre des Hymnes. Hercule chrestien*,
drew the parallel between Prometheus and Christ that supposedly dated

---

124 Cited in Trousson, *Prométhée*, p. 89, n. 13.
125 Trousson, *Prométhée*, pp. 89–96.

from the church fathers. Under the double influence of Petrarchism and classical literature, other poets occasionally used the image of a suffering Prometheus as a metaphor for the lover's pain.[126] Although the image of a suffering Prometheus was used by Spanish poets – Fernando de Herrera, for example, refers to the mountain "do Prometeo gime i llora"[127] – the Petrarchist extension of his agony does not seem to have gained currency. A pessimistic view of contemporary society and a nostalgia for the mythical golden age sometimes found expression in reproaches against Prometheus for forming men or Pandora for releasing suffering on earth. Camoens, drawing inspiration from Horatian odes, voiced this pessimism.

> Trouxe o filho de Jàpteo do Céu
> O fogo que ajuntou ao peito humano
> Fogo que o mundo em armas ascendeu,
> Em mortes, em desonras (grande engano!)
> Quanto melhor nos fôra, Prometeu,
> E quanto pera o mundo menos dano,
> Que a tuà estàtua ilustre nâo tivera
> Fogo de altos desejos que a movera![128]

A few poets found in Prometheus a symbol of the creative artist. Paravicino compared lifelike portraiture to Prometheus' feat in a 1609 poem to El Greco: "Emulo de Prometeo en un retrato/ no afectes lumbre, el hurto vital deja."[129] Góngora alludes to the same comparison, in his 1620 poem "A un pintor flamenco, haciendo el retrato . . .":

> vanas cenizas temo al lino breve
> que émulo del barro le imagino,
> a quien (ya etéreo fuese, ya divino)
> vida le fio muda esplendor leve.[130]

Góngora alluded more explicitly to the Promethean robbery of fire in a 1619 poem, in which he compared it to the work of bees gathering from flowers the wax which made the candles burning in honor of Nuestra Señora de Atocha:

---

126 Trousson, *Prométhée*, pp. 120–130.
127 *Poesías* (Madrid: Ediciones de "La Lectura"', 1914), p. 175.
128 *Os Lusiadas*, canto IV, 103, ed. Frank Pierce (Oxford: Oxford University Press, 1981), p. 108.
129 quoted in Luis de Góngora, *Sonetos completos*, ed. Biruté Ciplijauskaité (Madrid: Clásicos Castalia, 1969), p. 100, n. 6.
130 *Sonetos completos*, p. 100.

> Esta de flores, cuando no divina,
>   industriosa unión, que ciento a ciento
>   las abejas, con rudo no argumento,
>   en ruda sí confunden oficina,
> cómplice Prometea en la rapiña
>   del voraz fue, del lúcido elemento,
>   a cuya luz süave es alimento,
>   cuya luz su recíproca es rüina.[131]

Lope de Vega applies this Promethean metaphor of creativity to the poetic gift, once in terms of the robbery of fire, once in terms of the resultant suffering. In his poem "Apolo", in which that god would disown all mediocre poets who claim him as their muse, Apolo asks, "¿Hurté la clara llama/ por quien atado al Cáucaso inhumano/ llora el gigante bárbaro, atrevido?"[132] In *La Arcadia*, he combines references to Dante and Prometheus in a floating emblem anchored to the prow of a ship, which he describes as follows:

> . . . un peñasco altísimo fabricado con maravilloso artificio, en la punta del cual se vía ligado con unas fuertes cadenas el ingenioso Danteo, a quien sacaba el corazón un águila, que como si viniera en el aire se movía . . . y la letra decía asi:
> Por tal saber tal penar,
>   por tal penar tal saber;
>   porque el bien se ha de tener
>   en lo que suele costar.[133]

In sum, Prometheus was a very minor mythological figure in Spanish poetry prior to Calderón's drama. One long, anonymous poem entitled *Eccos de la Musa Transmontana o Prometeo* does exist in manuscript form in the Biblioteca Nacional de Madrid, but it was almost certainly written after *La estatua de Prometeo*. The 100-octave poem opens and closes with a suffering and complaining Prometheus chained to a *peñasco* in the Caucasus, and thus may derive from a direct reading of Aeschylus by its author. Other details, such as the participation of Minerva in Prometheus' theft, and the idea of Prometheus as the inventor of statuary, could come from other classical sources, or mythological

---

131 *Sonetos completos*, p. 96.
132 Lope de Vega, *Lírica*, ed. José Manuel Blecua (Madrid: Clásicos Castalia, 1981), p. 148.
133 Lope de Vega, *La Arcadia*, ed. Edwin S. Morby (Madrid: Clásicos Castalia, 1975), p. 364.

dictionaries. One element in the poem, however, that a jealous Venus complaining to Zeus led Prometheus to his suffering, could not have had such sources, but seems to indicate that the poem was inspired by Calderón's play, in which a jealous Pallas plays just such a role. Cossío believes the poem to date from the end of the seventeenth century, and on fairly good external evidence, he tentatively attributes it to a Conde de San Juan, who during the last years of the reign of Carlos II, belonged to the group favoring the French claim to the Spanish throne.[134]

Prometheus did figure in several dramas during the sixteenth and seventeenth centuries, but none of them before that of Calderón possessed any lasting value. In Germany, Leonhard Culmann wrote *Pandora,* a five-act tragedy which Trousson dismisses, saying: "l'œuvre de Culmann n'est qu'une allegorie bourgeoise qui prêche la morale et l'obéissance filiale et met en garde contre les dangers du plaisir, représentés par Pandore".[135] In the *Lord's Masque* by Thomas Campion, a work containing a great number of mythological figures performed in 1613 for the marriage of the elector Palatine to the princess Elizabeth of England, Prometheus is called upon to bring the statuary to life to perform a ballet in honor of the newlyweds. His role, however, is minor in the piece.[136] Also performed in 1613, in Louvain, was the work of a Belgian, André Catulle, *Prometheus sive de origine scientiarum drama.* It had virtually no dramatic merit, but was a humanist exercise, full of extraneous erudition and local history. The only work that might have had certain significance as a predecessor to Calderón is an anonymous seventeenth-century manuscript entitled *Prometeo. Favola pastorale,* which originated in Bologna. A three-act pastoral drama in song and verse, the work was based on Lucian's version of the myth, with the addition of a number of characters, including Lico, a son of Prometheus, Cacus and Minor, and the two shepherds traditional in the genre. None of the additions are significant to the history of the myth, except perhaps inasmuch as the drama is a possible first attempt at a recreation of an Aeschylean trilogy of condemnation, punishment, and release.[137] Given its Italian origin and partly operatic nature, however, it is conceivable that this work was related to the Vienna opera *Il Prometeo* which may have inspired Calderón.

---

134 José María de Cossío, *Fábulas mitológicas en España* (Madrid: Espasa Calpe, S. A., 1952), pp. 494–499; Trousson, *Prométhée,* pp. 155–157.
135 Trousson, *Prométhée,* p. 136.
136 Trousson, *Prométhée,* pp. 136–138.
137 Trousson, *Prométhée,* pp. 161–165.

If the Prometheus story began to come to life again during the Renaissance, it was not thanks to the work of poets and dramatists, but of philosophers. A number of writers found new significance in the myth, beginning with the Florentine Filippo Villani in the fourteenth century, and continuing through Marsilio Ficino, Pietro Pomponazzi, Charles Bouelles, Francis Bacon and Giordano Bruno. With their writings, the focus of the myth changed:

> Après avoir démontré que Prométhée n'avait aucun attribut superhumain, la pensée médiévale se tenait pour quitte à l'égard du mythe en raisonnant de la manière suivante: les conquêtes de Prométhée ne sont possibles qu'à un dieu; or Prométhée n'est pas un dieu, donc ses conquêtes n'existent pas. Au contraire, le XVIme siècle accepte volontiers l'humanité du Titan, mais sans pour cela lui dénier ses bienfaits. Avec la Renaissance, Prométhée cesse pour toujours d'être un dieu, accepté ou non comme tel; il devient un homme et, se couvrant de la valeur du symbole, l'incarnation de la condition humaine. Prométhée est donc plus qu'un dieu et plus qu'un homme: il est l'Homme.[138]

In Ficino, he became the symbol of man as a reasoning being, whose tragedy is that of being halfway between the material and spiritual world, and who realizes his potential and rises toward happiness in his pursuit of knowledge, leaving behind the world of matter. Bouelles sees Prometheus rather as a more aristocratic version of Boccaccio's "second Prometheus", as the wise man who by the force of his spirit remakes the natural, earthly man, becoming by the force of his intellect his own creator and master, and ascending into a sphere where few can follow. In Bacon, the only thinker who dedicates considerable attention to a wide variety of details in the myth, Prometheus becomes the symbol of human nature and the human spirit, the discoverer of fire as a material fact essential to human industry, and the founder of the scientific method, whose goal is not that of escaping the material world into a rarified intellectualism, but of contributing to the advance of human society as a whole. Finally, with Bruno, Prometheus becomes a true rebel, a representative of man's search for truth and his revolt against dogma and spiritual restraint.[139]

Bruno's world view was far ahead of his time, however, and he paid for it by burning at the stake. Twentieth century readers are accustomed to the

---

138 Trousson, *Prométhée*, p. 118.
139 Trousson, *Prométhée*, pp. 100–120.

idea of Prometheus as a rebel against divine cruelty and injustice, as he is
recreated by Shelley and Goethe and their successors. If this defiance is
lacking in Calderón's Prometeo, we should not attribute this to some
inherent conservatism on Calderón's part, which would have caused him
to soften the story as he knew it, to downplay rebellion against the
established order. Calderón took the incoherent, contradictory, and
generally medieval account as he found it in the mythographers of his
time and made of it a powerful story of the human dilemma, unequalled
since the days of Aeschylus.

Que con cuydado se alcanza la ciencia.

Atado está Prometeo en alta roca
   Del Cáucaso, y el hígado comiendo
   Un águila le está, que entre la boca
   Quanto más come más le está crecien-
                                    [do.
   El su voluntad culpa, vana y loca,
   Crecerle su penar contino viendo,
   Qual crece el de los que saber pre-
                                    [sumen
   Las ciencias, que los ánimos consumen.

Figure 6-1: Alciati Emblem of Prometheus[140]

---

140 Alciato, *Emblemas*, Prologue by Manuel Montero Vallejo, (Madrid: Editora Nacio-
    nal, 1975), p. 81.

Given the relative unimportance of Prometheus in the European literary tradition prior to Calderón, what sources can we identify as providing possible inspiration for *La estatua de Prometeo*? The great majority of Calderonian mythological plays were based on stories drawn from the *Metamorphoses* of Ovid, which had been told and retold in Spanish poetry since the Renaissance, but Prometheus and Pandora do not figure among that number.

Prometheus was included in another book of substantial influence from the Renaissance to the eighteenth century – the *Emblematum Libellus* of Alciati. The 1549 edition of this book, published in Lyon, with Spanish translations of the epigrams by Bernardino Daza, contains a picture of Prometheus chained to a rocky landscape, with an eagle eating his liver, and is accompanied by a verse interpreting his suffering as that of those who presume to aspire to knowledge, which consumes the spirit. [See Figure 6-1] This medieval moral has little to do with Calderón's interpretation of the myth.

Another visual rendering of the Prometheus-Pandora story might, however, have been considerably more significant in the background of *La estatua de Prometeo*. Beginning in 1659, the ceiling of the Hall of Mirrors, the principal receiving salon of the Alcázar Palace in Madrid, was decorated by a series of frescos depicting the story of Pandora. Velázquez supervised the work, which was carried out by Agostino Mitelli and Angelo Colonna, two Bolognese fresco painters recruited by Velázquez on his second trip to Italy, and two Spanish painters, Francisco Carreño and Francisco Rizi (the latter the son of an Italian).[141] Velázquez apparently selected the Pandora myth as the subject, and drew up a plan that divided the ceiling into five different episodes.[142] The paintings were all destroyed in the 1734 fire which gutted the palace, but ten years before the fire, Antonio Palomino had published an extensive description of them.

---

141 Dora and Erwin Panofsky, *La caja de Pandora: Aspectos cambiantes de un símbolo mítico*, rev. ed. (Barcelona, Barral Editores, 1975), pp. 181–182; and Steven N. Orso, "In the Presence of the 'Planet King': Studies in Art and Decoration at the Court of Philip IV of Spain", Diss. Princeton University, 1978, p. 75.

142 Orso, "Art and Decoration", p. 75.

In the first scene, painted by Carreño, Vulcan showed the statue of Pandora to Jupiter, who had ordered him to make it, while the Cyclopes work in Vulcan's forge and shop in the background. The second scene, and principal picture, which occupied the center of the slightly concave ceiling, and was painted by Colonna, showed the various gods seated on thrones of clouds, bestowing their gifts on Pandora. The Panofskys believe this scene to have been derived from an engraving by Callot, either directly or through the related engraving of Cornelius Bloemaert.[143] [See figures 6-2 and 6-3.] In the third fresco, painted by Rizi, Jupiter gave Pandora a golden vase. In the fourth, also by Rizi, Prometheus rejected Pandora's advances while Hymen, the god of marriage, and a small Cupid left the scene in defeat. The fifth scene, begun by Carreño, finished by Rizi and later repainted in oil by Carreño after it suffered water damage, showed the marriage of Pandora and Epimetheus.[144] Interestingly, the sequence did not include the climactic

Figure 6-2: Engraving of Pandora by Callot

---

143 Panofsky, *Caja de Pandora*, p. 182.
144 Orso, "Art and Decoration", pp. 75–76.

Figure 6-3: Engraving of Pandora by Cornelius Bloemaert[145]

145 Panofsky, *Caja de Pandora*, p. 93.

episode of Pandora opening the urn and releasing the cloud of evils on
earth. The Panofskys offer a humorous speculation concerning its
absence: "¿Podemos presumir que Velázquez consideraba que la
humanidad ya estaba suficientemente castigada con las 'aflicciones y
desconsuelos' del matrimonio?"[146]
Orso's explanation of the series is more serious, but not quite convincing
either. After surveying all the paintings contained in the hall, an
assortment of regal portraits and pictures of both Biblical and mythological stories, Orso concludes that the plan for the hall was that of exalting
the Spanish kings from Carlos I to Felipe IV (Carlos II being added later)
as defenders of the Christian faith. Of the central Pandora fresco, he
says:

> The choice of the Pandora myth for the ceiling fresco also
> enhanced the presentation of the Spanish Hapsburgs as heroic
> proponents of Catholicism. According to legend, it was
> Pandora who released into the world all the evils that afflict
> mankind, and, as the Panofskys observed, the patristic tradi-
> tion equating her with Eve, who brought about the Fall of
> Man, had been revived in the sixteenth century. Because one of
> the subsidiary scenes from the fresco showed Prometheus
> wisely rejecting her advances, it is certain that she was meant
> to be seen in a negative light. The probable implication for the
> program was that the evils that Pandora/Eve released into the
> world were opposed by the Spanish Hapsburgs, Christian
> princes all.[147]

This was, says Orso, the intended "long-range" meaning of the
sequence. He proposes that it had a quite different "short-range"
message, that of celebrating the betrothal of Felipe IV's daughter María
Teresa to Louis XIV. The French had sought this union since 1653, but
lacking a male heir to the throne, Felipe IV had refused it for fear of
providing the French with an eventual claim to the throne. After the
birth of Felipe Próspero in November, 1657, however, the betrothal was
successfully negotiated as part of the peace of the Pyrenees in 1659, and
the marriage took place in 1660. Orso suggests that Velázquez antici-
pated that the marriage ceremony would be performed in the Hall of
Mirrors, since 1650 the salon where the king received distinguished
visitors. Therefore, the final scene of the Pandora sequence was omitted.

---

146 Panofsky, *Caja de Pandora*, p. 182.
147 Orso, "Art and Decoration", p. 128.

Instead, the dominant overhead image at the ceremony was the central oval in which the Olympian gods bestowed their gifts of beauty, grace and refinement upon Pandora. For that occasion the subject would have been interpreted as an allusion to the virtues of the bride-to-be, María Teresa, while the negative aspects of the myth were discreetly ignored.

Thereafter, says Orso, "the perceived significance of the fresco reverted to its more conventional meaning".[148]

Now there are several problems with this interpretation of the significance of the frescos. The most obvious is the sort of schizophrenic perception which it demands of seventeenth-century Spanish and French courtiers, who are required to read the same series of images as totally positive, or totally negative, as the occasion requires. It would also seem to be rather dangerous diplomatically: the Spanish court was to know the "true story" of Pandora and to perceive her as a danger to the Christian prince even in the absence of a picture of the final episode; yet those same Spaniards would be assuming that the French court was sufficiently innocent or ignorant of the full story to accept her as a bounteous gift.

Furthermore, while we may accept that some of the mythological paintings in the hall were chosen as warnings of the dangers to Christian princes, it seems doubtful that such a negative image would occupy the central ceiling position in the Hall, nor that such a position would be occupied by a story which reduced the allegorical equivalent of the king (Prometheus=Spanish King) to that of a secondary figure participating in only one of the five scenes.

Third – and perhaps most importantly – we cannot assume that seventeenth-century viewers would automatically perceive Pandora as a negative figure, as a pagan Eve. Trousson has demonstrated that the Prometheus/Christ parallel is a more modern phenomenon. The Panofskys, in mentioning the patristic Pandora/Eve association, complain that their source, H. Türck, "no es muy informativo acerca del origen del paralelo entre Pandora y Eva, que tiende a dar por evidente."[149] They do cite three sources for the association. The first, Tertullian, is anything but negative. In one place he says that Moses' description of Eve as the first woman proves that there was no Pandora. In another passage he refers to the Hesiodic Pandora as a verbal figure which denotes the perfect union of all things, thereby being applicable to the totality and perfection of

---

148 Orso, "Art and Decoration", p. 130.
149 Panofsky, *Caja de Pandora*, p. 24, n. 23.

Christ. This same Christological interpretation of Pandora also occurs in
Irenaeus.[150] The Panofskys give two examples of clearly negative
associations of Pandora with Eve, one in Gregory of Nazianzus, and the
other in Origen. Two negative associations do not a tradition make,
however. The Panofskys also describe another tradition in which
Pandora, the "all-gifted", represents a positive good for mankind. For
two scholars of the thirteenth and fourteenth centuries, Johannes
Tzetzes and Manuel Moscópulos, she represented human acquisition
(through the discovery of fire) of the arts, the skills and techniques
necessary for the development of a civilized style of life. This technologi-
cal interpretation was paralleled and interpenetrated by moralistic and
metaphysical interpretations of the Pandora myth. According to the
Panofsky summary of Plotinus,

> ... su formación por Prometeo y su posterior perfecciona-
> miento por todos los dioses, especialmente por Venus y las
> Gracias, significa que el universo visible, resplandeciente con
> las "luces" y "almas" a él otorgadas desde el exterior por la
> providencia divina ..., es aún más embellecido a base de
> ornamentos adicionales proporcionados por otras innumera-
> bles fuerzas espirituales (llamadas, en terminología plotiniana,
> "dioses" y "mentes"). El mito de Pandora, entonces, ilustra la
> afirmación básica del neoplatonismo de que el mundo material
> está infuso y, por así decirlo, iluminado por la belleza
> intelegible que emana de Dios, pero que en su descenso al
> mundo material es enriquecida y diversificada por agentes
> intermedios – pues, como expresa Ficino en su comentario del
> pasaje aquí debatido, "en las cosas naturales no sólo están
> inherentes fuerzas animales, sino además atribuciones inteligi-
> bles y divinas".[151]

The Panofskys have demonstrated that this conception of Pandora as the
encarnation of a Neoplatonic conception of beauty was fundamental to
Goethe's dramatic presentation of the myth.[152] Such a positive evaluation coordinates with Boccaccio's suggestion, repeated by Pérez de
Moya, of a second Prometheus whose creation of Pandora represents the
"re-creation" of man as a civilized being.
The beautiful Pandora surrounded by gods on the ceiling of the Hall of

---

150 Panofsky, *Caja de Pandora*, p. 24, n. 24.
151 Panofsky, *Caja de Pandora*, p. 156.
152 Panofsky, *Caja de Pandora*, pp. 156–160.

Mirrors probably was meant to represent – both in the long and short run, both to the Spaniards and French – not the first temptress, whose lures were to be shunned, but the "all-gifted" creature of beauty, the perfection of earthly civilization somehow associated with Spanish Hapsburg rule. The omission of the final episode of the story was not a sort of diplomatic ruse but a logical decision to ensure a favorable perception of the meaning of the story.

The same hall also contained pictures of a number of the other subjects of Calderonian mythological court plays, including one by Artemisia Gentileschi, *Hercules and Omphale,* which showed an enamoured Hercules meekly spinning thread among the women. Orso is disturbed by the presence in the hall of this non-heroic vision of Hercules, closely associated with Spain and the Spanish kings.[153] The story, another non-Ovidian tale, is the subject of *Fieras afemina amor,* which Calderón wrote for Mariana's birthday celebration in 1669, the first court spectacular since the death of Felipe IV. If *La estatua de Prometeo* was presented in 1670, it would have been the second lavish performance during this interregnum period, when Mariana possessed great power. We might speculate that the themes for the two plays, both less-than-common subjects of poetic and dramatic treatment in Spain, may have been suggested by Mariana, influenced to some extent by her familiarity with the painting and the frescos in the Hall of Mirrors. We know from Palomino's account that she and Felipe IV had followed the painting of the frescos with great interest:

> El Rey subía todos los días, y tal vez la Reina nuestra señora Doña María Ana de Austria, y las señoras infantas, a ver el estado, que llevaba esta obra; . . .[154]

Her familiarity with the frescos, depicting a woman's central role in human civilization, combined with the receipt of copies of the Vienna opera *Il Prometeo* in February, 1670, may have led her to suggest to Calderón the Prometheus-Pandora story as the subject of her birthday celebration for that year. Whether or not this speculative chain of events led to the writing of *La estatua de Prometeo,* the frescos certainly bear a relationship to the drama, for both communicate a favorable view of Pandora.

While the Vienna opera seems very likely to have played a role in the choice of the Prometheus theme, Calderón took little if any concrete

---

153 Orso, "Art and Decoration", pp. 55, 127.
154 Cited in Orso, "Art and Decoration", p. 76.

material from the work. One would hope that the opera justified its existence by the beauty of its music, for the libretto is little more than a mythological fruit salad. The basic story is of a competition between Jupiter, Prometeo and Peleo for the love of the goddess Tetis. Prometeo is rejected, and consoles himself by creating a beautiful statue, as in the Pygmalion story. The fire which Prometheus steals, with Minerva's aid, brings the statue to life, but "she" too rejects him, and is later struck dead by Mercury, whom Jupiter sends to chain Prometheus to the rock, while Pandora flies overhead, spreading evils for mankind. Hercules eventually frees him, and Prometheus marries the constant nymph Nisea, who has adored and pursued him throughout. The two ingredients of the opera which we may find reflected in *La estatua de Prometeo* are the blending of the story of Prometheus with that of Pygmalion (which Calderón had already included in *La fiera, el rayo y la piedra*), and possible links between two humorous passages. The first of these is a remark by the *gracioso* Satyro in Act II of *Il Prometeo* that he is so hungry "que me comiera (aunque son crudas) una dueña entera". Prometeo objects that they are not for eating, to which Satyro responds, "Pues ¿no? ¿No son cecina?" Although jokes about the appetite of the *gracioso* abound in Golden Age *comedias*, they are not usually carried to such cannibalistic lengths, and it therefore seems possible that this exchange suggested the remarks by Merlín in *La estatua de Prometeo* that the *"fiera"* took him off to be the main dish at her banquet, "porque el que crudo sabía / tanto, forçoso es que sepa / más, o cozido o asado". (Act I, lines 790-792). In another passage in the first act of *Il Prometeo*, when Prometheus says he will kiss Minerva's footprints, Satryo asks, "con tanta pata, ¿cuáles serán ellas?" which might conceivably have inspired Merlín's chivalrous statement to Pandora that he is "a sus patas puesto". (Act III, line 28). It is also conceivable that the opera might have suggested to him the division of Minerva into the twin goddesses Minerba and Palas. In the third act of the opera, Minerva and Arachne quarrel over which is the supreme weaver. Minerva rips Arachne's work, whereupon the latter comments, "Vences Minerva, por mirarte Palas".[155]

Whether or not Calderón drew upon direct contact with Aeschylus' *Prometheus Bound* is problematic. The parallels in dramatic presentation between the Greek tragedy and the Spanish play derive only very indirectly from the Greek model, inasmuch as the court spectaculars were the culmination of a Renaissance humanistic attempt to recreate

---

155 [Antonio Draghi?], *Benche vinto, vince amore. O Il Prometeo* (Vienna: Mateo Cosmerovio, Stampatore di Corte, [1669?]).

classical drama. While Calderón could have read Aeschylus in the Latin translation available since 1555, the works of the Greek tragedian did not capture the attention of many writers until the Romantic era.[156] That fact, combined with the very different plot structures, argues against any direct Calderonian usage of Aeschylus.

In contrast with Aeschylus, Lucian was very influential in Spanish literature;[157] Calderón almost certainly drew Minerba's defense of Prometeo from a direct reading of Lucian's version of the myth, since the mythological encyclopedias do not contain this version of his self-defense.

Although Calderón could also have read the Prometheus story in translations of Hesiod, or in a variety of earlier mythographers, his most likely source for the details of the story would have been the mythological encyclopedias of Juan Pérez de Moya or Fray Baltasar de Vitoria. Juan Pérez de Moya, a noted mathematician, published his work first in 1585, declaring his purpose in the title: *Philosofia secreta. Donde debaxo de historias fabulosas, se contiene mvcha doctrina, prouechosa a todos estudios. Con el origen de los Idolos, o Diosos de la Gentilidad.* Below this explicit title, he adds another declaration: "Es materia muy necesaria, para entender Poetas, y Historiadores". His work collects numerous, and often contradictory versions of the various mythological stories from a variety of sources, including heavy reliance on earlier mythographers, whom he often fails to acknowledge. True to his title, he dedicates extensive space to an exploration of the various possible historical, physical and allegorical interpretations of the stories.

Pérez de Moya devotes an entire chapter to Prometheus, in the fourth book of his work, entitled "Tratado de varones Heroycos, que dezian medio Dioses, con los sentidos Historicos, y Alegoricos de sus fabulas". He says that Prometheus was a son of Iapetus and the nymph Asia, or possibly Themis, and then recounts the basic story, minus the Hesiodian episode of dividing the ox into portions for the gods and for men. Prometheus, says Pérez de Moya, formed from earth and water an image of the gods; Minerva, pleased with its beauty and likeness to man, offered him anything he might need from the heavens. Prometheus answered that he did not know what they contained, and Minerva therefore raised him up to the heavens. Seeing that all the celestial bodies had "animas de fuego", and wishing to provide this spirit for his man,

---

156 M. R. Lida de Malkiel, *La tradición clásica en España* (Barcelona: Editorial Ariel, 1975), pp. 363–364.
157 Lida, *Tradición clásica*, p. 378.

Prometheus stole fire from Apollo's chariot and took it to earth, where it brought his clay man to life. The gods, angered by the theft, had Mercury chain him to a precipice in the Caucasus, and sent an eagle or vulture to eat his "entrañas y coraçon", which regenerated every night. They "pretend", says Pérez de Moya, that Hercules killed the eagle, and also that as penalty for the robbery, the gods sent to earth "enflaqueci-mientos, tristezas, enfermedades, y mugeres".

Pérez de Moya follows this account with an extended commentary on various "historical" and allegorical meanings of numerous details of the story. His chapter has been included in full as an appendix, not only as an example of the sorts of interpretation current in Calderón's time, but also because his ingenious, if often conflicting, explanations provide entertaining reading. He says that "los sabios Griegos" used this fable to explain the beginning of human life. Citing Lactancio, he credits Prometheus with creating robots: "fue el primero que hizo estatuas de hombre de barro, q̃ por si solas se mouiã, por tãto se le atribuye, como la fabula dize auer hecho el hõbre".

More significantly, he twice cites the concept of Prometheus as a second "creator" of man in his role of bringer of reason and civilization: He says that Prometheus, after studying astrology and "otras cosas de Philosofia natural" with the Chaldeans, returned to his semi-savage Assyrians, "a los quales trajo con leyes y costumbres a conuersacion ciuil. Por lo qual parece que de nueuo hizo a estos hombres, no siendo ellos antes hombres por su grosedad de entendimiento". Later he says that Minerva's raising of Prometheus to the heavens signifies the understanding of truth and "orden para el gouierno de la vida politica" which results from contemplation. He continues, "Por las quales cosas lo que primero era de barro, quiere dezir los ignorantes comēçaron a ser hombres. esto es a saber vsar đ razõ". This concept of Prometeo as the potential civilizer of human society is central to *La estatua de Prometeo*. Calderón probably also drew from Pérez de Moya the suggestion that Prometeo, in his quest for understanding, had gone to study with the Chaldeans. The other wealth of interpretations in the *Philosophia secreta* chapter do not seem to have provided Calderón with any significant material.

Pérez de Moya also includes a curious chapter on Epimetheus in his book six, "en que se ponen fabulas pertenecientes a transmutaciones". Citing Leoncio, he says that Epimetheus was, along with his brother Prometheus, the first to make a statue of man from clay; on the authority of Theodontius, he says that for this act, an angered Jupiter changed him into a monkey, and exiled him to the "Isla Pitagusa". One

of the interpretations which Pérez de Moya then offers is that
Epimetheus signifies the sensual appetite which acts on its desires.
Epimeteo is such a character in *La estatua de Prometeo,* but Calderón
had previously created several pairs of contrasting brothers, and would
not have needed Pérez de Moya to suggest that characterization to him.
Pérez de Moya's work was published in four more editions in the
sixteenth and seventeenth centuries – in 1599, 1611, 1628, and 1673.[158]
Even more popular, however, was the two-volume encyclopedia com-
piled by Fray Baltasar de Vitoria, the *Teatro de los dioses de la gentilidad,*
the first volume appearing in 1620, the second in 1623.[159] Lope de Vega
wrote the *aprobación* for this work, and expressed in it the contemporary justification for devoting attention to pagan mythology:

> . . . en cuya historia mitológica no hallo cosa que repugne a
> nuestra Santa Fe, ni a las buenas costumbres, antes bien una
> lección importantíssima a la inteligencia de muchos libros,
> cuya moralidad emboluió la antigua filosofía en tantas fábulas
> para exornación y hermosura de la Poesía, Pintura y Astrolo-
> gía, y en cuyo ornamento los teólogos de la gentilidad, desde
> Mercurio Trimegisto, hasta el diuino Platón hallaron por
> símbolos y geroglíficos la explicación de la naturaleza de las
> cosas, como conste del Pimandro y del Timeo, que los
> Egypcios por cosas sagradas tanto escondieron del vulgo.
> Muestra el Autor en este libro suma lección y erudición y
> faltaua verdaderamente en nuestra lengua, como le tienen las
> de Italia y Francia por varios autores . . .[160]

Despite this moralistic justification, Vitoria devotes little attention to
allegorical interpretations. His basic account of the Prometheus story is
drawn from Hesiod, and he incorporates into it additional details told by
a wide variety of sources, from classical poets through the sixteenth-
century mythographer Conti, and carefully cites the sources in marginal
notes. He does not add any significant details to the traditional accounts,
and the only specific link that can be made between his account and
Calderón's play is the aphorism which both include, and which Vitoria
attributes to Aristotle, that "the sun and man generate men".[161] If

---

158 Seznec, *Mythological Tradition,* p. 318.
159 A third volume was added in 1688 by Fray Juan Bautista Aguilar.
160 Quoted in John Richard LeVan, "From Tradition to Masterpiece: Circe and
    Calderón", Diss. University of Texas at Austin, 1981, pp. 34–35.
161 Baltasar de Vitoria, *Primera parte del Teatro de los dioses de la gentilidad* (Madrid:
    Juan de Ariztia, 1738), pp. 444–445.

Calderón did indeed look to a mythological encyclopedia for the Prometheus story, that of Pérez de Moya seems to have offered him richer material.

Whatever inspiration Calderón may have drawn from the Pandora frescos, from the Vienna opera, from Lucian and Pérez de Moya, the original shape and dramatic power of *La estatua de Prometeo* derive not from any previous renderings of the myth, but from Calderón's unique dramatic genuis.

7 Myths and Texts in the Courtly Fiesta

A common element in most critical discussions of Calderonian mythological plays and *autos* is a commentary on how Calderón "changes the
myth". This is a misleading approach, for it implies that "the myth"
exists or existed as a unitary, unvarying text, and that Calderón was
unusual in his freehanded alteration of the story to his own ends. If
myths can be read in such form, it is only in the mythological
dictionaries which have served as handy sources of instant erudition
from the days of Boccacio to the twentieth century. In reality, myths
become static only when men no longer find them relevant to
contemporary experience; while their meaning lives, they change, and
every artistic rendering of the myth molds a new form. As Reuben
Brower stated,

> Although we commonly speak of "the Oedipus myth" or "the
> Hercules myth", and though anthropologists refer to mythical
> "archetypes" or "structures", it can be said that there are no
> myths, only versions. To put it another way, there are only
> texts for interpretation, whether the text is written or oral, a
> piece of behavior – a dance or a cockfight – a drawing or a
> painting, a sculptured stone, or a terracotta pot... My
> primary concerns in exploring each text will be how the
> "same" myth – the universalizing "the" seems unavoidable –
> is transformed when rendered in word or in line and color and
> what parallels and contrasts can be observed.[162]

Like every great artist, from Hesiod and Aeschylus to Goethe and
Shelley, Calderón made the Prometheus story his own, reshaping it to
suit his own perceptions of the structure and tensions of the universe he
inhabited.

Because Calderón's translation of the story is both verbal and visual (to
borrow from Brower's title), and extends beyond the limits of the stage
to include the whole court of Spain in its field of vision, to incorporate
its context into its text, the rich complexity of meaning which it conveys
cannot be perceived in a simple reading of the play as a self-contained
literary work.

---

162 Reuben A. Brower, "Visual and Verbal Translation of Myth: Neptune in Virgil,
Rubens, Dryden", *Daedalus* 101 (1972), p. 155.

Critics who read the mythological plays as closed units have generally described and interpreted them as variant forms either of the standard *comedia* or the *auto*. In his extremely superficial treatment, Erwin Haverbeck classifies the mythological plays, on the basis of characters, plot structure and standard motifs, as a subset of what he calls the *comedias de enredo*.[163] Most critics, however, have looked beyond these surface similarities and, perceiving in the works a more profound investigation of the human condition, have interpreted them as fundamentally religious plays. Charles Aubrun said:

> Calderón fit de cette classe d'opéras à grand spectacle le support de quelques thèmes théologiques. De plus cette sorte de comédie musicale devint le cadre de ses réflexions sur l'homme dans le monde, sur l'étique.[164]

Wilson and Moir lead students in this same direction, saying that Calderón's mythological plays contain "more or less allegorical hints in their action and in single scenes. They are a kind of secular *autos*, which hint at philosophical or religious truths without specifically declaring them".[165] This statement, tentative and carefully qualified as it is in speaking of "allegorical hints" and "philosophical *or* religious truths", is misleading only in calling the plays "a kind of secular *autos.*" A number of less cautious subsequent critics have treated the mythological plays as if they were intended as specifically religious allegories. The most thorough-going example of this class of interpretation is that of *La estatua de Prometeo* by Paul Mooney:

> I find the presentation of religious dogma to be the principal concern of Calderón throughout the work. The play is an explication of Catholicism in regard to three theological concerns: the role of destiny in the life of man; the moral import of good and evil in human actions; and the role of the prophet in the introduction of religion into a primitive society.[166]

---

163 Erwin Haverbeck O., *El tema mitológico en el teatro de Calderón,* Colección de Anejos de Estudios Filológicos, No. 6, (Valdivia, Chile: Universidad Austral de Chile, 1975), p. 77.

164 Charles V. Aubrun, Introduction, *La estatua de Prometeo,* by Pedro Calderón de la Barca (Paris: Centre de Recherches de l'Institut d'Etudes Hispaniques, [1965], p. ix.

165 Edward M. Wilson and Duncan Moir, *Golden Age Drama, 1492–1700,* (New York: Barnes & Noble, Inc., 1971), pp. 113–114.

166 Paul Arthur Mooney, "A Reevaluation of Past and Current Critical Opinion on the *comedias mitológicas* of Pedro Calderón de la Barca", Unpub. Ph. D. dissertation, Pennsylvania State University, 1973, p. 175.

The fact that so many critical readings of the mythological plays have centered on religious concepts may be due to the widely held – and widely criticized – view that myth is a precursor to religion.[167] This is the view espoused by Ernst Cassirer, who has stated:

> In the development of human culture we cannot fix a point where myth ends or religion begins. In the whole course of its history religion remains indissolubly connected and penetrated with mythical elements. On the other hand myth, even in its crudest and most rudimentary form, contains some motives that in a sense anticipate the higher and later religious ideals. Myth is from its very beginning potential religion.

The justification for retelling pagan mythological stories in the Christian era was indeed this concept – that they contained pre-Christian intuitions of the true God. Safeguarded by that theological justification, however, artists from the Renaissance forward used mythical tales for totally "areligious" if not irreligious purposes. Calderón was, of course, a profoundly Catholic writer, and the ethical issues central to his mythological plays reflect that faith. His use of mythology to explicate or celebrate the Christian faith is, however, limited to the mythological *autos*. In the mythological court plays, on the contrary, the mythical tales serve Calderón as artistically and politically convenient material on which to base an exploration of the secular basis of human society.

If the mythological court plays are to be fully appreciated as a unique dramatic corpus, they must be approached as such, with an eye to the special intermesh of text and context which their performance represented. In performance, in their courtly setting, the plays conveyed not one, but three intertwined texts, which we may for convenience label a "myth of royal power", a "universal myth", and a "political myth".

7.1 The Myth of Royal Power

That one function of the court plays was the telling of a myth of power is immediately obvious. As we have seen, they originated in the *intermezzi* which the Medicis developed as an artistic demonstration of their dominion in Florence; they and other forms of court spectaculars were

---

167 Levi-Strauss's theory of myth as a "logical model capable of overcoming a contradiction" is an equally if not more valid explanation of its use in Calderón's mythological plays. Claude Levi-Strauss, *Structural Anthropology*, p. 229, cited in G. S. Kirk, *Myth, Its Meaning and Functions in Ancient and Other Cultures*, (Berkeley: U. of California Press, 1970), p. 48.

intimately linked with the interests of absolutist power. For this, they were roundly condemned by nineteenth-century critics, as nothing more than extravagant flattery of the royal family that commissioned them. In Maravall's more complex and convincing theory, spectacular theatrical productions are a kind of propaganda, a display of power and wealth working to dazzle into submission any centers of internal or external opposition to the power of the Hapsburg kings.[168] The total theatrical event, from the entrance of the audience to the last formal curtsy and exit of the royalty, provided a model of a universe under control, a universe whose tensions could be explored and resolved under the watchful eyes of the monarchy. To a courtly society founded on the theory of the absolute power of kingship, and dedicated to the maintenance of the Catholic Hapsburg empire, yet faced with the realities of insurmountable domestic problems and external opposition, the retelling of this myth of power must have afforded considerable psychic comfort. It also achieved some measure of success as propaganda for the Spanish royalty, as a number of enthusiastic descriptions by Spanish and foreign observers attest.

The message was conveyed in two ways, the first of which was the physical disposition of the theatre itself. Wherever the plays were presented, in the Coliseo of the Buen Retiro, the Salón Dorado of the Alcázar, or in open air, the arrangement of the viewing area seems to have been such that the royal family constituted the first element or pole of the spectacle, with the performance on stage being the second pole, focused carefully toward the regal viewers. Other members of the audience were placed in such a manner that they could maintain both poles of the spectacle within their field of vision. The royalty were either placed on a raised platform or in some other way set in a prominent position, apart from less exalted viewers. Furthermore, they occupied the only spot at which the perspective scenery created a perfect illusion of reality, and therefore one's appreciation of the performance depended on how closely he was seated to the royal dais.[169] The following illustrations show the seating for performance in two different royal theatres.

---

168 José Antonio Maravall, *La cultura del Barroco: Análisis de una estructura histórica*, (Barcelona: Editorial Ariel, 1980), pp. 487–498.

169 J. E. Varey, "L'Auditoire du *Salón Dorado* de l'*Alcázar* de Madrid au XVIIᵉ Siècle", in *Dramaturgie et Société: Rapports entre l'œuvre théâtrale, son interprétation et son public aux XVIᵉ et XVIIᵉ siècles*, ed. Jean Jacquot, (Paris: Editions du Centre National de la Recherche Scientifique, 1968), pp. 86, 91.

Figure 7-1: Audience Arrangement in the Salón Dorado of the
Alcázar[170]

The type of arrangement shown in the first illustration is described for a
performance in 1637 (apparently an ordinary private performance); for
that observer, the royal "box" is the primary spectacle, and is in fact
called a "teatro", while the play represented on stage is an "accessory".

> Tienen sus Magestades dos dias en la semana, como de tabla,
> comedia en el Salon, a cuyo festejo se combida a su Alteza [la
> Princesa de Carignano], y a mi la ocasion de noticiar a las
> naciones, la Magestad y grandeza de respetos con que venera
> España sus Reyes, aun en lo retirado, y mas domestica
> atencion de entretenimiento. Formase pues vn teatro, en cuyo
> frontispicio haziendole espaldas dos biombos, se pone el sitial
> a su[s] Magestades, silla al Rey, y cuatro almohadas, a la mano

170 From Varey, "L'Auditoire", p. 87. Sketch by Helen Reiss.

izquierda a la Reyna, pusieron a su Alteza dos, si bien dentro
dèl, con reconocimiento el asiēto, que pudiesse ver su Alteza
como en idea en los Reyes la representacion, y por acessorio lo
representado de la comedia. En los remates, que ya hazen
espaldas al Real assiento tienen su lugar sus mayordomos
mayores en pie, y por Grandes (que siempre lo son) cubiertos.
La Camarera mayor en almohada, sin ella la Guarda mayor, y
Dueñas de honor fuera del teatro, dentro dè diuididals [sic] a
dos coros en orden sucessiuo, adornan los dos lados: las
Damas y meninas galanteadas de Grandes, Titulos, Señores, y
Caualleros de entrada, q̃ por parte de afuera coronan el teatro
en pie, y cubiertos los Grandes. En la fachada los Mayordomos tocandole al de semana las ordenes, despejo y entrada
. . .[172]

The theatrical roles of the king and queen were further accentuated by
the solemn and elaborate ceremony accompanying entry to and exit
from the performances. Numerous spectators described the ceremony;
the following is a description by François Bertaut of the royal presence
at a performance in the Buen Retiro in 1659:

Le Roi, la Reine & l'Infante sont entrez après une de ces
Dames, qui portoit un Flambeau. En entrant il ôta son
Chapeau a toutes ces Dames, & puis il s'est assis contre un
paravant, la Reine à sa main gauche, & l'Infante aussi à la
gauche de la Reine. Pendant toute la Comédie, hormis une
parole qu'il a dite à la Reine, il n'a pas branlé ni des pies, ni des
mains, ni de la tête; tournant seulement les yeux quelques fois
d'un côté & d'autre, & n'aiant personne auprès de lui qu'un
Nain. Au sortir de la Comédie, toutes ces Dames se sont
levées, & puis aprés sont parties une à une de chaque côté, & se
joignant au milieu comme des Chanoines, que quittent leurs

---

171 From Shergold, *Stage*, p. 347, figures 7a and 7b. "Both drawings show the canopy
under which the King and Queen sat, and both indicate that spectators were
accommodated on seats facing the stage. Others stood at the sides, in front of
halberdiers of the King's guard. Halberds can also be seen, near the King, in the 'play'
drawing". The drawings were made by Harrewyn, a Flemish designer and engraver,
and are in the Bibliotèque Nationale, Paris, Series "Histoire de France", Qb4.

172 Andrés Sánchez de Espejo, "Relacion aiustada en lo possible, a la verdad, y repartida
en dos discursos. El primero, de la entrada en estos Reynos de Madama Maria de
Borbon, Princesa de Cariñan. El segundo, de las fiestas, que se celebraron en el Real
Palacio del Buen Retiro, a la eleccion del Rey de Romanos" (Madrid, 1637), fols. 9v.-
10r.; cited in Varey, "L'Auditoire", p. 80.

Figure 7-2: Two Scenes from Court Plays[171]

Chaises quand ils ont fait l'Office. Elles se sont prises par la main & ont fait leur Révérences, qui durent un demi quart d'heure & les unes après les autres, sont sorties, pendant que le Roi a été toujours decouvert.

A la fin il s'est levé, & a fait lui-même une Révérence raisonnable à la Reine en a fait une à l'Infante, & se prenant aussi, ce me semble, par la main, elles s'en sont allées.[173]

The potential political weight of the enactment of this myth of power was not lost on seventeenth-century aspirants to power. The outstanding example of the use of theatre as a means of legitimizing power was that of Richelieu, who made himself the chief patron of the Théâtre du Marais, formed his own theatre company, and constructed a special theatre in his Palais Cardinal for the performance of lavish spectacles, which he viewed on a dais in the middle of the hall, in the only position of perfect perspective in the theatre[174] – that is, in the royal position. He did so because, as Timothy Murray points out,

> Richelieu learned from the theater how a prince should show himself. Then he presented his portrait in a theatrical setting to profit from his viewers' . . . acknowledgment of legitimation. Richelieu seems particularly to have benefited from his deep sensitivity to the spectator's wish to be fooled by legitimation, to view ideal simulacra of authority instead of fallible people.[175]

No Spanish counterpart went as far as Richelieu in his use of the theatre to this end. Yet there were heated disputes, particularly in 1679, between the Alcaide of the Buen Retiro palace and the Condestable de Castilla over who controlled the distribution of boxes and their decoration for court *fiestas*.[176] Wealthy nobles would sometimes curry royal favor by sponsoring lavish performances, and Varey notes that the Principe de Astillano, wishing to become *valido*, "buscó el camino al poder a través de las lúcidas representaciones que costeó, tal como la del 19 de enero de 1672 . . ."[177] He did not succeed, but Fernando de Valenzuela did climb

---

173 Letter of Bertaut to his sister, Françoise Langlois de Mottesville, cited in her *Mémoires*, V, 58–59; cited in Varey, "L'Auditoire", p. 90.

174 Timothy Murray, "Theatrical Legitimation: Forms of French Patronage and Portraiture", *PMLA* 98 (1983), pp. 171–173.

175 Murray, "Legitimation", p. 177.

176 J. D. Varey, "La mayordomía mayor y los festejos palaciegos del siglo XVII", *Anales del Instituto de Estudios Madrileños*, 4 (1969), pp. 145–168.

177 Varey, "Mayordomía", p. 148.

to a brief tenure in that position in the mid-1670's, using as one means of currying favor with both nobles and the general populace of Madrid "an endless series of fabulous and spectacular entertainments."[178] The primary focus within the Spanish court theatre was, however, centered on the royal family itself, not on the aspiring *valido*.

The publication of the myth of royal power, inherent in the physical arrangement and ceremonial practices of court performances, was reinforced in the framework of the plays as such. The first visual plane presented would be a handsome stage curtain, decorated in some way with symbols of the royalty and/or pagan deities. In the case of *Las fortunas de Andrómeda y Perseo*, the names of Felipe, Mariana, and María Teresa appeared on the curtain.[179] The curtain for *Fieras afemina amor* displayed figures representing Mercury, Hercules and Cupid, as well as a lion and a tiger, signifying "el valor y la osadía."[180] The curtain would be raised in some dramatic way for the presentation of the *loa*, dedicated to the adulation of the royalty and usually specifying the occasion which the performance celebrated.[181] The *loa* for *Fieras*, for example, consists primarily of a musical competition between the twelve months of the year, with their associated zodiacal signs, for the title of the most important month. Since the occasion for the performance was the birthday of the queen mother, Mariana, on December 22, December wins the laurels because its generally sunless days saw the birth of the royal sun, Mariana, "a suplir del sol la ausencia".[182] The message proclaimed by this and other *loas* for court plays is that of an entire universe, and/or of all time, come to pay homage to the reigning Hapsburg kings.[183]

---

178 R. A. Stradling, *Europe and the Decline of Spain: A Study of the Spanish System, 1580–1720* (London: George Allen & Unwin, 1981), pp. 162–163; R. Trevor Davies, *La decadencia española, 1621–1700*, 2d. ed., (Barcelona: Editorial Labor, S.A., 1972), p. 138.

179 Pedro Calderón de la Barca, *Andrómeda y Perseo*, MS Typ 258H in Houghton Library, Harvard University.

180 Calderón, *Fieras afemina amor*, BAE IX, p. 530.

181 When the mythological plays were presented again, under different circumstances (as a number of earlier plays were staged again in 1679 for the marriage of Carlos II to María Luisa de Orleans), a new *loa* was generally written for the event. Calderón was paid 300 ducados for a new *loa* for *El hijo del sol, Faetón* that year. [Emilio Cotarelo y Mori], "Noticias inéditas de algunas representaciones palaciegas de las comedias de Calderón y otros", *Revista Española de Literatura, Historia y Arte*, 1 (1901), p. 182.

182 BAE, IX, 531c.

183 Unfortunately, most of the *loas*, including that for *La estatua de Prometeo*, have been lost, and it is therefore necessary to consider the technique on the basis of the few that remain.

The first stage setting in Calderón's last court play, *Hado y divisa de Leonido y Marfisa* (1680), places Carlos II and María Luisa literally at both poles of the spectacle:

> Subió la flor de lis, arrugando tras sí la cortina con tan hermoso desaliño, que quedaron sus extremos en forma de un pabellón, que asistía a un teatro que representaba un salón regio de arquitectura corintia, con la techumbre de artesones de florones de oro, que asistidos de todo el caudal de las luces, deslumbró la atención que aguardaba.
>
> Desde su primer término hasta el último había catorce reyes, siete á cada lado, los cuales eran figuras naturales adornadas con los aparatos regios de ricos mantos, cetros y coronas. Cargaban sobre unos orbes, teniendo cada uno por respaldo un pabellón en que se unía la púrpura y el oro.
>
> En la frente del salón, ocupando el medio de la perspectiva, se hizo un trono cubierto de un suntuoso dosel, debajo del cual había dos retratos de nuestros felicísimos monarcas, imitados tan al vivo, que como estaban frente de sus originales pareció ser un espejo en que trasladaban sus peregrinas perfecciones; y el ansia que desea verlos en todas partes, quisiera hallar mas repetidas sus copias.[184]

Neumeister reads this as a narcissistic self-indulgence of an increasingly isolated royalty:

> Die Selbstdarstellung des Herrscherpaares, in der sich ursprünglich das Gemeinwesen als Ganzes wiederkennen sollte, ist hier, am Ende des 17. Jahrhunderts, endgültig zu einer narzistischen Selbstbespiegelung fast ohne Außenbezug geworden.[185]

Undoubtedly, the setting is structurally narcissistic; nevertheless, its message was intended for the consumption not only of the royal couple themselves, but for the public as well, which was to see in them, in the sense that Richelieu understood, not the pathetic human figure of Carlos II and his attractive but ill-fated wife, but the rightful inheritors of a proud regal tradition.

Hado y divisa was not a mythological play, and it was therefore appropriate that the framework contain human kings. In the mythologi-

---

184 BAE, XIV, 358.
185 Neumeister, *Mythos,* p. 282.

cal plays, ennoblement by association links the kings not with earthly royalty but with the gods themselves. In the *loa* for *El golfo de las sirenas*, Felipe IV, regularly referred to as "el cuarto planeta", is called "Apolo destos valles" and Mariana is linked to Marte and Diana;[186] in that for *El laurel de Apolo*, the newborn prince Felipe Próspero is called a future Alcides;[187] and in the *loa* for *Las fortunas de Andrómeda y Perseo*, a gigantic figure of Atlante carrying the weight of the world is identified as Felipe IV, for whom all that weight was as nothing compared to the weight of concern during an illness of Mariana.[188]

The royal family is, in the framework provided by these *loas*, explicitly linked to the gods; implicity, they are honored by association with the deities who play out the central story itself. In this first system of meaning, the myth of royal power, the mythical figures equal the royal figures watching them.

Artistic propaganda linking the Spanish kings to the gods was of course not restricted to the theatrical sphere. The entire Hall of Realms of the Buen Retiro palace, so magnificently described by Brown and Elliott,[189] is constructed on the association of Felipe IV with the labors of Hercules. A more limited example is Rubens sketch of *Quos ego* – Neptune calming the stormy seas for the shipwrecked Aeneas – done for a ceremony celebrating the safe arrival of Prince Ferdinand in Antwerp in 1635. As Brower describes Rubens' sketch, "His *Quos ego* – bears a weight – perhaps too great a one – of historical and ideological reference: the heavens themselves, God and nature, further the purposes of the king of Spain and his emissary."[190] Brower, like most contemporary observer, is uncomfortable with the use of art for such self-serving political ends. Yet he continues in praise of Rubens' genius, saying that compared to lesser (and nonpolitical) translations of the myth, Rubens' sketch restores "the Homeric vision of human figures and gestures dramatically expressing events both natural and supernatural."[191] In the hands of a great artist, the political statement does not vitiate the work of art itself. Calderón was such an artist, and as we admire Rubens' work three and a half centuries later in a totally different political environment, so can we appreciate the enduring artistry of Calderón's mythological plays.

---

186 BAE IX, 618a.
187 BAE IX, 636c.
188 Harvard suelta.
189 Brown and Elliott, *Palace*, pp. 141–192.
190 Brower, "Translation", p. 178.
191 Brower, "Translation", pp. 178–179.

7.2 The Universal Myth

Present-day readers will almost certainly find this merit not in the first text of the performance, the myth of royal power, in which the mythological figures are equated with the royalty, but in the second text, the "universal myth," contained in the body of the play itself, in which the gods represent mankind in general. Perceiving that Calderón's mythological plays do indeed treat profound and permanent issues of human experience, critics tend to equate the mythic heroes of the works with Adam or Christ. This is, I believe, unnecessary, for to relate one symbol or myth to human experience by interposing another myth or symbol more often distorts than clarifies the issues. The Prometeo of *La estatua de Prometeo* is, of course, in a sense Adam, in that Adam represents to us all mankind; he and Epimeteo are also Abel and Cain, or every man struggling with a brotherly enemy, internal or external. If, however, we can fully comprehend the world view that Calderón presents through the Prometheus myth, we should not need to mediate it with another mythical tale.

Since no *loa* has survived for *La estatua de Prometeo*, we cannot glean from it any additional insight into the mythological play as a vehicle of the myth of power. What the play does offer is a complex and enduring story of conflictive human society. Its special genius resides not only in the value of that story as an explanation of the nature of man, but also in the subtlety with which Calderón has tied that universal myth to the political problems of late seventeenth-century Spain.

The central issue of *La estatua de Prometeo* is the duality of human existence: the inherent tension within man, and the ambiguity of his position in the traditionally-conceived hierarchy of the universe. Virtually all critics of the play have perceived the importance of dualism in the play, although their identifications of the axis of tension have differed. For example, Chapman, one of the first modern critics to recognize merit in the mythological plays, sees it as a conflict between reason and passions,[192] while Mujica reads it as reason against will or force;[193]

---

192 Chapman, "Las comedias mitológicas", p. 64.
193 Barbara Louise Mujica, *Calderón's Characters: An Existential Point of View* (Barcelona: Puvill, 1980), pp. 279, 286.

Pasero labels it an opposition between male and female principles;[194] and ter Horst considers the basic structural tension to be that between nature and culture.[195]

Calderón makes dualism central to his play through his major innovation in the interpretation of the Prometheus myth: that is, the linking of Prometheus and Epimetheus as twin brothers, and the doubling of the single goddess Minerva as twin goddesses, Minerba and Palas. Prometeo, whose Greek name means "forethought," is portrayed by Calderón as a man of reason, who seeks understanding and endeavors to bring the fruits of his learning to his uncivilized countrymen. Epimeteo, "afterthought" in Greek, is the man of passion and force, whose rivalry with Prometeo threatens all with destruction. By drawing the two together as twin brothers, the dramatist indicates to us that he considers them not separate and distinct types within the human race, but rather competing elements within one being: man[196] as a creature divided against himself. They are as inseparable as two sides of the same coin.[197] The counterpoised splitting of the goddess into Minerba as the goddess of wisdom and Palas as the deity of war suggests a parallel competition between countervailing forces at a determinative celestial level, in the nature of life as it is given to man. By his equally unique introduction of Discordia as a major character in the play, Calderón reinforces this image of a bipolar universe. As Apolo is the god of light and life, so Plutón reigns over darkness and death. Although Plutón does not appear himself to measure forces with Apolo, Calderón specifically links Discordia with him, calling her "bastarda Deydad . . . hija de Plutón" (III, 586–587). Up to the final scene, the play appears to present a virtually Manichean universe, in which every good impulse is counteracted by a corresponding evil, and ter Horst goes so far as to describe Calderón as a "Manichean fusionist."[198]

Calderón is of course not unique in his view of human dualism, nor in his externalization of the contrast in linked human figures. Its universality can be seen in tales as disparate as the Mesopotamian myth of

---

194 Anne M. Pasero, "Male vs. Female: Binary Opposition and Structural Synthesis in Calderón's *Estatua de Prometeo*", *Bulletin of the Comediantes*, 32 (1981), p. 111.

195 Robert ter Horst, *Calderón: The Secular Plays* (Lexington, Kentucky: The University Press of Kentucky, 1982), pp. 67–68.

196 Prometeo and Epimeteo are not titans but men – "dos nobles caudillos del pueblo" – in Calderón's presentation.

197 This central image was suggested to me by A. A. Parker in conversation in June, 1981. Pasero also views the brothers as one being in her interpretations.

198 ter Horst, *Calderón*, p. 68.

Gilgamesh and his ill-fated double Enkidu and Robert L. Stevenson's creatures, Dr. Jekyll and Mr. Hyde. The dualistic perception has yielded some of the greatest figures of Spanish literature: witness Critilo and Andrenio of Gracián's *El Criticón;* the beloved Don Quixote and Sancho Panza; or in a twentieth-century masterpiece, the two shoemakers of Pérez de Ayala's *Belarmino y Apolonio.* This idea of the internal warfare within man and his universe, a much-repeated topic in Golden Age Spain,[199] was one of Critilo's early lessons for Andrenio:

> Todo este universo se compone de contrarios y se concierta de desconciertos: . . . No hay cosa que no tenga su contrario con quien pelea, ya con vitoria, ya con rendimiento; todo es hazer y padecer: si hay acción, hay repasión. Los elementos, que llevan la vanguardia, comiençan a batallar entre sí; . . . los males assechan a los bienes, hasta la desdicha a la suerte. Unos tiempos son contrarios a otros, los mismos astros guerrean y se vencen, y aunque entre sí no se dañan a fuer de príncipes, viene a parar su contienda en daño de los sublunares vassallos . . . En la edad, se oponen los viejos a los moços; en la complexión, los flemáticos a los coléricos; en el estado, los ricos a los pobres; en la región, los españoles a los franceses; y assí, en todas las demás calidades, los unos son contra los otros. Pero qué mucho, si dentro del mismo hombre, de las puertas adentro de su terrena casa, está más encendida esta discordia.
> – ¡Que dizes?, ¡un hombre contra sí mismo?
> – Sí, que por lo que tiene de mundo, aunque pequeño, todo él se compone de contrarios. Los humores comiençan la pelea: según sus parciales elementos, resiste el húmedo radical al calor nativo, que a la sorda le va limando y a la larga consumiendo. La parte inferior está siempre de ceño con la superior y a la razón se le atreve el apetito, y tal vez la atropella. El mismo inmortal espíritu no está essento desta tan general discordia, pues combaten entre sí, y en él, muy vivas las passiones: el temor las ha contra el valor, la tristeza contra la alegría; ya apetece, ya aborrece; la irascible se baraxa con la concupiscible; ya vencen los vicios, ya triunfan las virtudes, todo es arma y todo guerra. De suerte, que la vida del hombre no es otro que una milicia sobre la haz de la tierra.[200]

---

199 See Otis Green, *Spain and the Western Tradition* (Madison: The University of Wisconsin Press, 1968), II, pp. 52–63.

200 Baltasar Gracián, *El Criticón*, Ed. Santos Alonso (Madrid: Ediciones Cátedra, S. A., 1980), pp. 90–91.

To present externally the internal conflict of "un hombre contra sí mismo" poses a problem for the dramatist. Calderón solves it by the device of twins, a refinement of a technique which he used in the *comedia El gran príncipe de Fez*, written shortly before the *Prometeo* in 1669, to solve the problem of presenting dramatically the internal conflict within a man's soul. In this story of the conversion of Baltasar de Loyola to Christianity, Calderón creates two characters, Buen Genio and Mal Genio, and has Buen Genio state explicitly the reason for their existence:

> representando los dos
> de su Buen Genio y Mal Genio
> exteriormente la lid
> que arde interior en su pecho . . .   (Aguilar I, 1412b)

The distribution of good and evil in *La estatua de Prometeo* is much more complex than in *El gran príncipe de Fez* – and more intriguing. Epimeteo and Prometeo are not simply black and white figures, but rather two forms of existence, two mutually dependent and inherently antagonic elements of man. They represent discordant dispositions which are congenital in man, with the effect, as Prometeo puts it, that the crib becomes "en vez de primer abrigo, campaña de primer lucha." (I, 63–4).

Calderón's Prometeo and Epimeteo are at once personifications of the war of man against himself, and of the suffering that afflicts "los sublunares vassallos" because the very stars which direct his existence "guerrean y se vencen". The conflictive stars in his play are the twin goddesses Minerba and Palas, who were born equal in power and beauty, but opposed in their inclinations, with Palas "auxiliando lides / dictando ella [Minerba] ciencias" (II, 660). Not only are they twins, but Calderón alters traditional mythical genealogy to make them sisters of Apolo. The sun god is the giver of life; as Minerba says, "el sol y el hombre / dan la vida" (III, 337–9), and his ray brings Pandora to life in the play. By making Minerba and Palas sisters of Apolo, Calderón indicates symbolically that reason and violence are genetically and inextricably linked to the gift of life itself; they are the positive and negative forces ever competing within man and without for control of his existence. The sister deities appropriate the twin brothers as their respective subjects in a competition to see which star pupil can achieve the greater stature, Prometeo with Minerba's gift of intelligence and learning, or Epimeteo with the force of arms.

Epimeteo has become the embodiment of man as the supreme hunter, the nemesis of every wild bird or beast in the forest. John Varey has observed that hunting is "an activity which normally signifies in the plays of don Pedro the discord which man introduces into the natural setting."[201] Epimeteo's accomplishments, as recounted by Prometeo, take on a negative coloration, as Calderón borrows Góngora's imagery to link him with the brute Polifemo. (See Note I, 69.) Epimeteo is the epitome of the man who controls his environment by the use of force. Prometeo disdains this "comerçio de la bruta" (I, 84) as demeaning to the noble nature of man; he has chosen to develop instead his specifically human capacity for reason because, as he says:

> Este anhelo de saber,
> ... es el que al hombre le ylustra
> más que otro alguno (supuesto
> que aquella distançia mucha
> que ay del hombre al bruto, ay
> del hombre al hombre, si junta
> la comferençia tal vez
> al que ygnora y al que estudia) (I, 97–103)

Not only does the use of reason distinguish man from animals but, says Prometeo, it also links him with the gods:

> Viendo, pues, en vna parte
> cuanto los hombres repudian
> la enseñanza, y viendo en otra
> cuanto los Dioses la ylustran,
> a su alto conoçimiento
> elebé la mente ... (I, 207–212)

Along with immortality, deities are characterized in Calderonian drama by their total understanding.[202] In *Apolo y Climene*, Apolo complains that his banishment from the heavens is not only a physical exile, but also an intellectual exile, for he finds himself "negado a todas las ciencias / que me acreditaron Dios." (Aguilar I, 1868a). The pursuit of knowledge, then, separates man from beasts and raises him toward the gods.

Scholarly figures, frequent protagonists in Calderón's dramas, generally fall into one of two categories: a) those who study in order to

---

201 J. E. Varey, "*Casa con dos puertas*: Towards a Definition of Calderón's View of Comedy", *Modern Language Review*, 67 (1972), p. 88.

202 Palas, the envious opponent of reason, is a partial exception to this rule. Epimeteo suggests that a goddess who is envious might be ignorant too (II, 133–135), and Palas does later display at least a partial ignorance of Epimeteo's true motives. (II, 539–542).

understand; and b) those who learn in order to control. Calderón always presents the first group in a positive light – as, for example, Cide Hamete (Baltasar de Loyola) of *El gran príncipe de Fez*, Licanoro of *Las cadenas del demonio*, or Carlos of *De una causa dos efectos*. He paints a dark picture of characters who employ knowledge for negative, controlling uses, as do many figures in the mythological plays – Medea in *Los tres mayores prodigios*, Circe in *El mayor encanto amor*, Liríope in *Eco y Narciso*, Fitón in *Apolo y Climene*, and the devil figure in various religious plays. A number of human figures are, however, borderline cases between the two groups, whose original motivations for study may have been laudable, but who, either from pride in their learning – e.g., Basilio of *La vida es sueño*, or diabolical influence – e.g., Cipriano in *El mágico prodigioso* – have attempted to play a God-like role which impinges unjustly on the liberty of other human beings. The question is, in which category does Prometeo belong. Do we place him with the first group and call the play "una exaltación del intelectualismo", as does Valbuena Briones,[203] or is he a more mixed figure representing, as Thomas O'Connor says, not only reason's power, but also its limitations?[204]

Prometeo's study begins with a laudatory quest for understanding. He leaves his homeland to study in Syria, "la más çelebrada curia de artes y çienzias" (I, 108–109), and devotes himself particularly to the study of astrology with the Chaldeans (see Note I, 129), for whom the heavenly bodies were gods who ruled the destinies of men and empires.[205] As he searches for an explanation of how brothers born under the same star could be so differently disposed, Prometeo questions how one cause could have diverse effects, a part of the inquiry into cause and effect which, as Calderón points out, was central to Scholastic philosophy (see Note I, 91–96).[206] Prometeo answers his question in astrological terms,

---

203 Aguilar, I, 2065b.
204 Thomas A. O'Connor, "Calderón and Reason's Impasse: The Case of *La estatua de Prometeo*", in *La Chispa '81: Selected Proceedings of The Second Louisiana Conference on Hispanic Languages and Literatures*, ed. Gilbert Paolini, (New Orleans: Tulane University, 1981), p. 229.
205 See Seznec, *Mythological Tradition*, p. 41.
206 Cipriano in *El mágico prodigioso* broaches a related problem as he reasons toward a concept of the existence of a single, supreme God:
       ¡no es cosa clara
   la consecuencia de que
   dos voluntades contrarias
   no pueden a un mismo fin
   ir? Luego yendo encontradas

attributing the differences between himself and Epimeteo to the rapid
revolutions of the heavens, which are such that although twins are born
under the same planet, their births may occur under different constellations (see Note I, 135). It should be pointed out that describing man's
fate in terms of astrological determinism – either in a symbolic or literal
sense – is not necessarily contradictory to Christian dogma. In the
Christian accommodation to the pagan astrological tradition, the stars
were often viewed as intermediaries through whom God's omnipotence
was made manifest.[207] As Calderón develops the tale, the differences
between Prometeo and Epimeteo result from their subjection to the
influences of Minerba and Palas, the contradictory goddesses who are
sisters of Apolo, the life-giver.

Viewed in the context of the play as a whole, this explanation is not an
answer to the cause of human difference and strife, but a begging of the
question. Palas will subsequently say that she and Minerba are:

> . . . vna cosa mesma.
> Pero aunque en deydad, en solio,
> en magestad y grandeza,
> naçimos las dos comformes,
> crezimos las dos opuestas
> en los diuididos genios
> de nuestras dos ymfluencias;   (I, 652–658)

Calderón leaves ambiguous whether these "dos ymfluencias" are the
effects the twin sisters exercise on their subjects, or two contrary powers
which shaped the divine beings. What, then, is the first cause of this
dualism? An old story tells of an Eastern prophet who preached that the
universe rests on the back of an elephant, which in turn rests on the back
of another elephant. When queried regarding the support of the second

---

> es fuerza, si la una es buena
> que la otra ha de ser mala.
> Mala voluntad en Dios implica el imaginarla:
> luego no hay suma bondad
> en ellos [opposing pagan gods], si unión les falta.
> (Aguilar I, 813b)

The ultimate question of cause and effect for Christian theology is that of the cause of evil:
if God is First Cause, and God is wholly good, then why and how does evil exist in
the world which He created? Prometeo does not pose this question, but it is implicit
in the search for the origin of dualism, considered a defect in comparison with the
philosophical perfection of unity, and is explicitly suggested in the refrain, "¡Ai de
quien el bien que hiço / en mal combertido vio!" (III, 1013–4, 1099–1104).

207 Seznec, *Mythological Tradition*, pp. 43–44.

elephant, he said, "There are elephants all the way down."[208] Does Prometeo's universe, then, consist of contrary pairs "all the way up?" In this work, Calderón provides no explanation of the first cause of dualism, beyond the symbolic sisterhood of Minerba and Palas with Apolo.

Prometeo, however, found the astrological explanation satisfactory, and feeling an obligation to make use of his newly-acquired knowledge, he then returned to the Cáucaso hoping to apply the fruits of his learning to civilize his barbarous homeland, through the application of "político gobierno". His efforts were a total failure. The populace rebelled, seeing him as an ambitious tyrant, and Prometeo retreated into solitude. Throughout the play, Calderón presents his man of reason as a solitary hero, divorced from the populace he aspires to lead. The play opens with Prometeo alone, on a hidden peak which the people find difficult to reach even when they attempt to answer his summons. Seeing his reforms rejected, the offended Prometeo had withdrawn into himself, symbolically retreating to a "melancólica espelunca", because "no ay / compañía más segura / que la soledad a quien/ no encuentra con lo que gusta". (I, 185–188). He later repeats the pattern of defeat and retreat, and when the populace divides into warring factions, his band is much smaller than that of his brother.

Epimeteo, in contrast, emerges as a natural leader. He first appears as the leader who instructs the populace to follow Prometeo's voice, and then organizes the "desmandadas cuadrillas" of the "tropel", uniting them "en seguimiento mío" (I, 38–406). When the people are astonished by the beauty of the statue of Minerba that Prometeo has created, Epimeteo says, "Yo responderé por todos" (I, 315), and it is he whom the mob follows in the scenes of trial and punishment. From the outset, then, Calderón suggests that Prometeo as a reasoning man is ineffective in communicating the fruits of his knowledge to the populace, which is more easily led by Epimeteo's passionate, forceful approach.

Calderón underlines the potentially isolating effect of reason by a fascinating symbolic device. He has Minerba appear disguised as a *fiera*. Such a wild figure frequently appears in the mythological dramas, as a sign of the threat to civilized society posed by the savagery and wildness that exists either just beyond the limits of civilized society, or more often, hidden within it in the anti-social passions of its individual members. Calderón, in this play, has the goddess of wisdom herself don

---

208 Cited by Wayne Booth, *A Rhetoric of Irony* (Chicago: University of Chicago Press, 1974), p. 242.

a beastly disguise to draw Prometeo apart from the populace where she can speak to him alone. The symbolic inference is that not only brutish passions, but reason itself can, at will, separate man from his society (see Notes I, 403 and 505).

It was precisely his withdrawal from a hostile society which led Prometeo to his worship of Minerba. Prometeo describes his relationship with the goddess as a somewhat distorted version of the mystical path of union with God, as related in Spanish mystical literature of the late sixteenth century. He has undertaken a variety of recollection (the removal of oneself from wordly distractions) by withdrawing physically from the world, and meditating first on the wonders of nature. This leads him to elevate his mind to speculating on the dominion of the gods. Finding himself particularly blessed with Minerba's gifts of wisdom, he dedicates to her an "ynterior culto" rather like the contemplative silent prayer described by Santa Teresa: "Tenía este modo de oración, que como no podía discurrir con el entendimiento procuraba representar a Cristo dentro de mí."[209] Prometeo describes a similar process:

> Y discurriendo en qué obsequio
> podría yo haçerla que supla
> a mi haçimiento de graçias,
> di en aprehender su hermosura
> tan viua en mi fantasía
> que no abía parte alguna
> en que no me pareçiese
> mirarla, con tan aguda
> vehemenzia que aun en las sombras
> de la noche siempre obscura
> (pues hasta aora no vio luz
> en ella humana criatura)
> jurara que vn vibo fuego
> para mirarla me alumbra.   (I, 237–250)

The result is an all-encompassing involuntary vision related to those some mystics describe as part of the *via illuminativa*. He sees it even in the darkness of the "noche siempre obscura" – which in this context must surely be considered a multiple reference, at once to the physical darkness of a world never illuminated by the light of fire, or of understanding, and to the dark night of the soul to which San Juan de la

---

209 Santa Teresa de Jesús, *Libro de su vida* (México: Editorial Porrúa, 1972), Cap. IX, p. 147.

Cruz refers in his poem "Noche oscura". His vision is illuminated by a "vibo fuego", which can similarly be associated with the light of understanding which mystics describe experiencing as they feel themselves close to God. He debates over whether it could be caused by madness, as Sta. Teresa and her confessors debated whether her visions were divinely or demoniacally inspired. Rather than following the Christian mystics in persevering to the final stage of the soul's true union with God, in which imaginary visions cease, however, Prometeo tries to dominate his vision by giving it corporeal existence, in the statue he shapes in its image. He has come to worship wisdom – yet at the same time, he tries to control it, as he had earlier tried to use his knowledge to direct the populace of the Cáucaso. In effect, Prometeo attempts to use reason to control the universe, as Epimeteo tries to dominate his environment by force.

Laudable as Prometeo's dedication to the goddess or reason might be, there is an ominously narcissistic element in his worship of Minerba, for he had been drawn to it by seeing "cuanto en mí las [the gifts of wisdom] distribuia". (I, 232). Furthermore, his exclusive attention to her is ill-advised. It is not only Minerba's jealous twin Palas who may be offended at his total devotion to her: Prometeo calls Minerba "de las çiençias/ la ynspirazión absoluta". (I, 229–230), and says that he dedicated his worship primarily to this deity, "oféndanse o no se ofendan/ las demás" (I, 235–236). According to Christian theology, it is God who is the ultimate source of true wisdom, which cannot be reached by purely human reasoning powers. Human reason is a good, but Prometeo's self-absorbed worship of it as an end in itself is a defect in the purity of that good, which makes it vulnerable to domination by self-centered passions. Prometeo's single-minded devotion to reason will trigger a countervailing effort by his "irrational" twin to redress the balance of power.

The immediate fruit of Prometeo's worship of reason is a positive one, however, as his intellectually inspired artistry yields a divinely beautiful creation. Ter Horst calls art "the resurrectionary principle" in Calderón, which triumphs over its hostile twin, nature, the "death-force".[210] The inspired artist is for Calderón endowed with semi-divine powers, capable of a creation like Prometeo's statue which is "algo menos que viba / con algo más que difunta" (I, 325-6). Of Pigmaleon's artistry he says, in *La fiera, el rayo y la piedra*, that he shares Jupiter's creative power, and in the *auto El pintor de su deshonra*, the artist who creates

---

210 ter Horst, *Calderón*, p. 24.

Naturaleza Humana is God himself. In Calderón's theocentric theory of art, God is the supreme artist, who shaped the beauty of the universe from chaos and portrayed man in his own image. The artist who creates lifelike forms from "nothing" – from the simple elements of nature – imitates the divine creativity. (See Note I, 264).

Seeing the beautiful product of Prometeo's reason, Epimeteo finds himself instinctively and passionately drawn to it. He appoints himself spokesman for the populace, and vows to build her a temple that will challenge the domain of the heavens, as a demonstration that "açepta lo sacro, quien lo político renunçia" (I, 338–340). The implication is that since the mass of men will not follow the dictates of reason, they are better governed by religion than law. The political utility of religion was generally recognized in the seventeenth century, as Maravall has pointed out. Religion, he says, was recognized as the first foundation of community.

> Una religión es necesaria como vínculo más eficaz que ningún otro para fundir en unidad las conciencias de los ciudadanos. Por otra parte, las relaciones de gobierno y obediencia que se han de dar en todo grupo social no pueden existir debidamente si no es sobre la base de una religión común. Saavedra Fajardo dedica la empresa XXIV a esta materia, y sostiene que hasta tal extremo es la religión lazo que une y fortifica el pueblo, "alma de las Repúblicas", que llegó a ser tenida por muchos impíos como mera invención política.[211]

Calderón was not such an "impío," but neither was he blind to the fact that the common man is more easily drawn to an emotionally-based religion than to a rationally-based code of law. As the embodiment of this passionate aspect of humanity, Epimeteo leads in the establishment of the rites and temples for the new "goddess".

As he does so, he exposes the fissures in his emotional soul. Epimeteo shows himself to be a proud, selfish and dissembling creature, in a series of impassioned asides that reveal the constant tug of war between his public and private faces. On seeing the marvelously lifelike statue, Epimeteo says with bravado, "Nothing scares me", only to whisper immediately, "Mal dije, que quizá a ellos / admira, y a mí me ofusca." (I, 317–8). Then he proclaims altruistically that the statue should be left in the grotto until the temple can be built, lest "familiarity breed contempt", but admits privately that his true motivation is a selfish

---

211 José Antonio Maravall, *La teoría española del estado en el siglo XVII* (Madrid: Instituto de Estudios Políticos, 1944), pp. 105–106.

desire to keep it safely in his own view (I, 349–50). Epimeteo's false
bravado does not cover physical cowardice, however, for when Timantes
announces the approach of a fearsome monster (Minerba in disguise), he
immediately sets out to conquer the "fiera" with the force of his arms, as
an offering to the new "goddess". Prometeo follows, vowing to prove
that it is not true "que se embotan los açeros / en el corte de las plumas"
(I, 427–8) – thus initiating as a contest between "armas y letras" the first
phase of the brotherly competition to honor the new creation. As the
competing twins exit, Timantes, whom Mujica rightly calls the voice of
knowledge acquired through experience,[212] suggests the use of harmony
to "sooth the savage beast", and leads the singing populace off stage.
The real "beast" remains on stage, however, in the person of the *gracioso*
Merlín. His name is an ironic commentary on the supremely ignorant
human being who has no desire to learn. If Prometeo embodies an
approach to life based on reason, and Epimeteo one of passionate (if ill-
directed) courage, Merlín is the negation of both in his ignorance and
cowardice. He displays blatantly all the duplicities that Epimeteo tried to
hide, along with a physical cowardice which sends him behind Libia's
skirts when he thinks the *fiera* is approaching. He is a willfully ignorant
and determinedly earthbound creature, with a finely-honed instinct for
self-preservation. Libia, in contrast, is a much more refined *villana*. She
shows her psychic linkage with Prometeo by composing the first hymn
of praise from Prometeo's own words (I, 380), and she displays a
curiosity about the workings of the universe, speculating on what the
sun says when it sets (see Note I, 802).
The contrasting attitudes of the twin brothers are demonstrated as each
has his first encounter with the goddess which has inspired his
development. Prometeo says factually that he will penetrate "al más
paboroso çentro" "desta bárbara montaña" (I, 469, 468), and quickly
encounters the goddess of reason, who removes her fierce disguise to
reveal her true "aspeto amable" (I, 485). Epimeteo, in contrast, struggles
fruitlessly to follow where Prometeo has led, and is overcome with
terror at the same surroundings, which he describes at length. He calls it
first a "coto, que de horrores lleno, / pisado no se vió, según espanta / de
bruta güella, ni de humana planta." (I, 587–9). He struggles on,
exclaiming as he tries to keep us his courage,

> qué estançia tan sin senda ni camino
> mi atrebimiento pisa,
> donde aun la luz del sol no se diuisa

---

212 Mujica, *Calderón's Characters*, p. 280.

cuanto y más Prometeo
ni fiera; pues tan solamente veo
a escaso viso la funesta voca
de vna entreabierta roca
por donde con pereza
melancólico del Cáucaso vosteza.
Sin duda éste es su albergue, y avn sin duda,
voraz, horrible, trájica, y sañuda
en él le oculta, ¡o pese a mi denuedo! (I, 601–12)

As Margaret Maurin has pointed out with regard to *La vida es sueño*,
Calderón often intertwines images of monsters or wild men, darkness
and tombs to suggest the death-in-life of a man whose passions dominate
his reason.[213] Epimeteo's search combines all these elements – the pursuit
of a monster through a dark, fearsome labyrinth to a cave which
Epimeteo describes as the "lóbrego panteón deste desierto" (I, 620).
In that cave, he encounters not a beautiful goddess disguised as a beast,
as had Prometeo, but another kind of monster, the goddess of force,
whose beautiful exterior conflicts with her monstrous, threatening
nature (I, 636–7, 643–4). While a grateful Minerba had descended to
earth to reward Prometeo with a heavenly gift for his adoration of her,
Palas comes inspired by jealousy, with threats of dire punishment for
Epimeteo's faithlessness. Appropriately, it is the envious goddess Palas
who tells the story of the competition initiated by the divine twins.
Calderón's poetry marvelously underlines the contrast between the two
goddesses, as he assignes a graceful, lyrical meter to Minerba, and a
heavy, pounding one to Palas (see Metrical Scheme). Taking full
advantage of the resources available to court spectaculars, Calderón uses
both the illusionistic scenery and the *tramoyas* to effect a symbolic and
superbly dramatic presentation of their divergent influences: while
Minerba takes Prometeo soaring upward on a heavenly shopping trip,
the result of the pursuit of knowledge, Palas draws Epimeteo into a black
cave of fear, the end of those who follow the road of passion and force.
The goddess of reason inspires creation, the goddess of force offers only
destruction. Divided against himself, man's pursuit of knowledge leads
him toward the heavens, while his selfish passions pull him down into a
hell on earth.
Prometeo reacts to Minerba's offer of any gift with pride, saying that he
already has the greatest gift the earth can offer, in the knowledge she has

213 Margaret Maurin, "The Monster, the Sepulchre and the Dark: Related Patterns of
    Imagery in *La vida es sueño*", *Hispanic Review*, 35 (1967) 161–178.

bestowed on him. Therefore, his ambition leads him to aspire to the sovereign domain of the heavens. He says self-confidently that he who travels with the goddess of reason will venture anything, and with her, he dares to "climb the wind". Despite this pride and ambition, Calderón's Prometeo is not the defiantly rebellious hero beloved of the Romantic period. He does not rail against the unjust division of goods and power between men and the gods. His animosity is directed downward, toward earth, rather than upward against the heavens, and his rebellion, if such it should be called, is against the brutish condition in which men live, and their resistance to improvement. He chooses to steal a ray of Apolo's life-giving light not in order to redress the balance of power, but because it will be useful to humanity, and will serve as a demonstration to men of the value of the gifts of reason, "pues moralmente se biera / que quien da luz a las gentes / es quien da a las gentes çiençia." (I, 852–4). He does not seek to challenge the power of the gods, but only to improve mankind.

Epimeteo is, on the other hand, left in torment by Palas' threat. He is torn between a positive passion, his attraction toward the beauty of the statue which he loves, and a negative passion, his fear of the vengeance of Palas (I, 724–739). The only solution which he can find is to "fingir", to attempt to kidnap the statue and keep it for himself, in the hopes that his imperfect patroness will possess an ungodly ignorance parallel to her jealousy (II, 133–4). He and Merlín are stumbling through the dark on their ignoble kidnapping mission when Prometeo approaches earth with the stolen light. Not seeing Prometeo, Epimeteo's reaction to the marvelous new light is egocentric; he says: "Sin duda Minerba trata / faboreçer mis deseos / agradeçida a mis ansias" (II, 168–9). When the stolen ray brings the statue to life, Epimeteo's interpretation of the miracle is similarly self-centered:

> . . . Que si sé
> que te di mi vida y alma
> en el punto que te vi,
> ¡qué mucho, si en dicha tanta,
> veo yo que viues con ellas . . . (II, 257–61)

She quickly disabuses him of that notion, offering him the animating flame so that he can reclaim his life and soul if they are contained therein. Epimeteo is terrified and blinded by the dazzling light, and flees to look for someone to explain the enigma to him (II, 269–80). Despite his bravado, it is not this supreme hunter who is truly brave; he possesses physical courage, but is frightened by what he does not understand, and blinded and put to flight by the concentrated flame of knowledge.

Prometeo, in contrast, possesses mental as well as physical courage, for his reasoning powers enable him to reach an understanding of what is an enigma to his twin. When he finds the "statue" (now called Pandora) animated, he first thinks it is Minerba herself who, offended for some reason, no longer speaks to him in the harmonies characteristic of deities, but in an ordinary mortal speaking voice. He is not frightened, however, and between the two they reason out that it is the torch which has brought her to life. Unlike Epimeteo, however, he does not take personal credit for the flame; he ignores Epimeteo's question as to where he has been (II, 422–4) and prefers to let the populace accept it as a gift of Minerba, his ideal goddess of reason.

The true source of the animating fire is, however, kept deliberately vague. When Epimeteo asks who gave life to the statue, offstage music like a divine chorus answers with the refrain:

> Quien triumpha para enseñanza
> de que quien da çiençias, da
> voz al barro y luz al alma. (II, 236–8)

The action in this first half of the drama thus establishes the basic human dichotomy between man as a reasoning being seeking knowledge and as a passionate beast acting on his instincts – between the philosopher and the superior hunter. The philosopher first tried to civilize mankind by the introduction of reason ruling directly through a rational code of law. When that failed, he created instead a beautiful image, which they accept, for the positive role played by the passions is their instinctive attraction toward the beautiful, the perceived good. Pandora represents, in Calderón's play, not the inevitable doom of mankind, but his potential salvation. Prometeo created her from all the beauty that Nature offers, shaped by all the creative artistry that reason inspires in man; the result is:

> la más perfecta hermosura
> que el arte y naturaleza
> en sus dos primores juntan. (I, 34–36)

Pandora is "la providencia del tiempo" – animated by the divine fire, "quien supla la falta / del sol para los comerçios de la noche" (II, 441–3); she is Civilization,[214] a product of reason refining itself away from the

---

214 This is one interpretation which Pérez de Moya gives to the Prometeo story, that Prometeo "boluiose a los Asirios, los quales aun no tenian orden de vida politica, mas medio saluage, a los quales trajo con leyes y costumbres a conuersacion ciuil. Por lo qual parece que de nueuo hizo a estos hombres, no siendo ellos antes hombres por su grosedad de entendimiento." *Philosophia*, p. 222.

bestial element of humanity and seeking to dwell with the gods, stealing from them the light of understanding that gives them control over their existence, over night and day, over life and death. Yet the animal nature of man persists, and its desire to possess the new life for its own selfish ends brings the threat of her destruction.

No sooner do the *villanos* begin to celebrate the miraculous life of Prometeo's creation, than they are interrupted by drums and trumpets and shouts of "¡Guerra, guerra, al arma, al arma!" (II, 447). This time, Epimeteo's egocentric reaction is right, as he interprets the shouts as that which "en baldón de Minerba, / es el enojo de Palas contra mí." (II, 450–2). The scene continues as a duel between the threatening war cries and the music celebrating "Que quien da las çienças, da / voz al barro y luz al alma." Minerba/Pandora concludes that:

> . . . el ver mezclados
> horrores y voçes blandas
> geroglífico es que diga
> que pacífica, esta llama
> será alhago, será alibio,
> será gozo, será graçia
> y colérica, será
> ynçendio, yra, estrago, y rabia;
> y así, temed y adorad
> al fuego cuando le exparza,
> o afable, o sañudo, a toda
> la naturaleza humana
> la estatua de Prometeo. (II, 460–72)

The flame of civilization is as ambivalent in its effects as the mankind that employs it – truth of which is only too evident in our nuclear age. While the concrete action of the play depicts Prometeo and Epimeteo as the human playthings of Minerba and Palas, its complex symbolism suggests that the goddesses may as well be read as creatures of human manufacture – as the embodiment of the disparate strivings of the contrary facets within mankind. When Minerba removed her fierce disguise, she appeared dressed exactly like the statue which Prometeo has created, a copy of his imagination. Similarly, the terror-stricken Epimeteo plunges through the underbrush and encounters exactly what he feared – a threatening, all-powerful monster.

Reading this way, we can then see in Discordia's arrival on the scene the embodiment of the conflict about to explode between man the philosopher and man the hunter. This infernal goddess is in Calderón's dramas the inherent and indispensable ally of war, for neither war nor discord can accomplish their ends without the assistance of the other. Palas says that she has summoned Discordia because:

> como la guerra no consta
> de solos los instrumentos
> mientras no ay en los vmanos
> desabenençias . . .
>
> . . .
>
> viendo cuanto neçesito
> de corazones opuestos,
> valerme de ti, Discordia,
> para mi venganza yntento. (II, 565–8, 571–4)

In the *auto El lirio y la azucena*, it is Discordia instead who summons her cohort Guerra:

> Tú, cuya furia al mundo introducida,
> en civil y campal vio dividida,
> no sólo entre el vasallo y enemigo
> cualquier mortal; pero entre sí y consigo,
> según de Job se indicia,
> pues el hombre doméstica milicia
> se llama, siendo en su confuso abismo
> (dentro de sí) batalla de sí mismo;
> oye mi voz.[215]

Discordia's powers have a diabolical origin: Minerba calls her "bastarda Deydad . . . hija de Plutón" (III, 586–7), and she describes herself as "aborted daughter of the first rebellion" in *El lirio y la azucena* (Aguilar III, 916b, 919b). As Mujica points out, she is capable both of divine song and human speech because she exists among men and among gods, at both an earthly and an eternal level.[216] Like her progenitor, she can assume a variety of deceiving and alluring disguises.[217]

She may have unearthly powers, but her personality traits are decidedly human. She has a nagging habit of interrupting while Palas is trying to

---

215 Pedro Calderón de la Barca, *Autos sacramentales*, ed. Angel Valbuena Prat, Vol. III of *Obras completas* (Madrid: Aguilar, 1952), p. 916a. Subsequent references to works in this volume will be cited as Aguilar III, with page and column citations.

216 Mujica, *Calderón's Characters*, p. 291.

217 In *Las cadenas del demonio* the devil appears in the first act disguised as a handsome *galán*, in the second as a beautiful woman, and only in the third is revealed in his true form, as a chained monster.

tell her story, and Palas finally explodes with a wonderful touch of
human irritation: "Gracias al çielo / que llegué a lo que no saues, / con
que me oirás con silençio." (III, 536–8). This same kind of verbal duel
occurs between the allies Culpa and Lucero in the *auto El pintor de su
deshonra*, linking Discordia both structurally and stylistically with the
figure Culpa; a subsequent song in *Prometeo*, "En la docta república
vuestra", couples her with the same figure in the *auto El pastor fido*.
Discordia explains her provenance in *El lirio y la azucena* in a speech
which, although long, merits quotation here, for its bearing on the
outcome of *La estatua de Prometeo*. She recounts her history to Guerra:

> Yo soy la Discordia (ya
> lo dijiste), del primero
> rebelión hija, abortada
> para escándalo del tiempo.
> Mi definición (según
> divinos y humanos textos)
> es íntimo odio del alma,
> que para mortal veneno
> de concordes voluntades,
> pasando a aborrecimiento
> el que primero era amor,
> en el corazón me engendro.
> Dígalo (¡ay de mí!) el que apenas
> me vi arrojada del Cielo,
> cuando en la Tierra avivé
> las cizañas de mi incendio,
> siendo la primera hoguera
> (en quien los duros alientos
> de la Discordia soplaron
> las ráfagas de sus cierzos)
> las entrañas de Caín,
> entre cuyos humos densos
> pavesa Abel introdujo
> mis sañas, pues por su pecho,
> para entrar al mundo, halló
> la muerte el camino abierto.
> Desde este, pues, primer triunfo
> de humanos ánimos dueño,
> perturbé la Natural
> Ley, en ella introduciendo
> no ser los bienes comunes;

con que así, como hubo ajeno
y propio, entró la Discordia
a partir el Universo,
hasta verse Babilonia
y Senaar, estableciendo
monarquías en Nembrot
e idolatrías en Belo;
entre cuyos aparatos
de rencores y de incendios,
de sediciones, de envidias,
tumultos y sacrilegios,
pasó la Ley Natural,
violados los dos preceptos
de amar a Dios (pues a mí
me dieron aras y templos,
por diosa de la Discordia)
y al Prójimo, pues me dieron
en ti el furor de las armas,
intentando y pretendiendo
ser de ti y de mí animados
todos más, ninguno menos. (Aguilar III, 919b–920a)

The two human weaknesses that give Discordia free rein in the world are pride and envy – the self-assertive pride of Lucifer's rebellion and the envy caused by inequality – which lead men to violate the two precepts of natural law: that of loving God and his fellow man. *La estatua de Prometeo* does not rely on theological explanations as the *auto,* but Calderón has built into Prometeo and Epimeteo the same psychological foundations for the operation of Discordia, giving her fertile ground for the implantation of jealousy, her "última sedición". Thus the second act ends dramatically with the joined threats of Discordia and Palas ringing over the background music of the peasants celebrating their new goddess.

The third act opens with a delightful comic speech by Merlín, welcoming Pandora, whom Timantes calls a "semi-diosa", as the rest of the populace takes up her praise in music and dance. The hostility between Epimeteo and Prometeo intrudes all too soon, however, as Epimeteo boasts of being Pandora's first worshipper and benefactor, and Prometeo, with a quieter pride in his modesty, refuses to claim credit and criticizes Epimeteo for doing so (see Note III, 147). While the brothers argue and threaten to proceed from words to swords, Discordia is present but silent. This is in keeping with the role played by the more familiar god Cupido and his brother Anteros in other Calderonian mythological plays; although the characters protest that they are helpless against such divine powers, the divine magic is generally only accentuating inclinations whose nascent presence the characters have already betrayed. The internal friction inherent in man's dual composition allows the demonic Discordia to take charge of humanity.

Hoping to cut off their dispute, the innocent Pandora prepares to open the golden urn which the disguised Discordia had given her, and to distribute the wealth of gifts it purportedly contains, in gratitude for the welcome she has been given. As she opens the urn, a cloud of smoke emerges, blocking out the sun, blinding everyone and setting Epimeteo, Pandora and Prometeo up in a classic love-hate triangle, while the populace divides into opposing factions, and nature repeats the human tumult with lightning, thunder, and an earthquake. Henceforth, the earthly characters live in the confusion of misunderstanding and strife so characteristic of the social world of the cape and sword dramas, with Epimeteo and Prometeo trying to discern which is the divine Minerba and which her human image, Pandora, and struggling to understand their own illogical emotions. Epimeteo questions the wrath that has taken possession of him, and the unreasonable, barbarous code of honor that requieres him to avenge his lady's disdain not on her but on his brother. When Pandora protests Prometeo's abhorrence of her, this previously rational being can give her no logical explanation, but can only say:

> ¡Cómo puedo, sin saberlo,
> deçirlo tampoco yo?
> pues si Deydad te contemplo,
> te adoro; si hermosa, te amo;
> si discreta, te venero;
> si prodijiosa, te admiro;
> y si todo, te aborrezco;
> que ay otro yo que sin mí
> manda en mí más que yo mesmo. (III, 848–56)

Dramatically speaking, the "otro yo" is Discordia, who could constitute the dramatization of Descartes' "demon theory" in his second meditation, in which he postulates the impossibility of relying on man's sense perception and rational faculties to reach a reliable standard of truth, because of the possibility that some demon might be working upon him, and twisting all he perceives and thinks to its own ends. The characters regain clear perception and harmony only in the final resolution when

Apolo, as the representative of Júpiter's supreme wisdom and justice, banishes Discordia.

Psychologically speaking, and focusing on Prometeo and Epimeteo as two aspects of a single being, the metaphor works equally well. Prometeo, as the reasoning capacity of man, disappointed in the human reality of the image he had created of his ideal, and horrified at the prospect of the destruction which his ambitious theft had brought about, has retreated into a death-like isolation:

> . . . me vi
> obligado a bolver
> la espalda para yr
> a nunca ver el sol
> (huiendo aora de ti
> si antes de ellos) a aquel
> del monte seno vil
> que fue mi albergue, donde
> su más hondo siuil
> sea mi tumba, siendo
> mi pira su cerbiz. (III, 554–64)

His retreat has left Epimeteo in virtual control of the "battlefield", which in this case is man himself – dramatically illustrating the cliché of the man whose reason is blinded by his passions.

The earthly civil war is paralleled by a celestial quarrel, as Palas condemns Prometeo's theft to Apolo, and Minerba comes to his defense. This debate is absolutely central to the telling of both the universal myth and its political counterpart, as Apolo's ray symbolizes at once the wisdom of God and the power of the king. For the second axis of tension in this play is that between man and the divine and temporal powers that rule over him. Man's dilemma is not only that he is divided against himself, but also that he exists in an ambiguous position, between heaven and earth, between animal and god. His reason rebels against the limitations imposed by his rude physical composition and leads him to aspire to divine understanding and power. The issue thus raised is whether the reasoning powers he possesses give him the right to control ever-increasing spheres of his own existence or whether such accretions to human power represent punishable treason toward God and king, the previous sole possessors of such powers.[218] Prometeo's theft of Apolo's

---

218 The persistence of this issue in the twentieth century is witnessed by the ongoing debate over questions such as abortion, euthanasia for the terminally ill, and genetic engineering.

ray raises precisely the same issue as the Adamic eating of the fruit of the
tree of knowledge; that is, whether man may rightly acquire "divine"
wisdom, or whether his attempts to do so represent a sinful attempt to be
"like God" and a challenge to the supreme authority.

Once advised of the theft by Palas, Apolo is angry not only with
Prometeo, but with the populace as a whole:

> . . . en mi yndignación
> todos son
> cómpliçes del robo el día
> que a nueba Deydad, con nueba alegría
> sabiendo que es hurto, le admiten por don. (III, 313–7)

By accepting his gift, they have incriminated themselves in his crime
against divine power. Calderón spelled out in his version of the
Prometeo myth exactly the ambiguity since pointed out by Donoghue,
who says:

> A gift of any kind starts a cycle of obligation . . . But a gift
> which has been stolen is a much more complex matter because
> it cannot release itself from its origin in violence, risk, and
> guilt; the receiver is incriminated in the donor's crime.

Donoghue considers the story essentially an account of the origin of
human consciousness and finds that "the interest of the myth consists in
the ambiguity with which it surrounds the lucidity of knowledge, the
moral darkness from which its brightness came."[219] As Calderón's gods
and goddesses debate the question, Palas emphasizes the moral darkness,
arguing that Prometeo's appropriation of the ray was robbery and that
robbery is always wrong. Minerba defends the ludicity, saying that
stealing to do good is not a crime, and that the loss of such a tiny ray did
not diminish Apolo's power, but rather perfected its goodness, by
extending it to a needy humanity, while preserving Apolo's dignity as
the essential source of its power. Palas counters with the charge of
treason, maintaining that it was solely Apolo's right to distribute his
powers, if and when he should choose to do so. Apolo finds both his
sisters' arguments convincing and finally chooses neutrality, leaving
reason and force to decide the issue between themselves on the human
battlefield. Apolo's neutrality is consistent with the doctrine of free will,
which reserves for man the obligation of electing the path to follow
between good and evil.

---

219 Denis Donoghue, *Thieves of Fire* (New York: Oxford University Press, 1974), pp.
   17–18.

The opposing forces are now aligned on earth. Prometeo has emerged from hiding, saying that he would hide to avoid a fight from starting, but will not flee as a coward from leading his followers once a fight is imminent. His band is smaller, but confident that with Minerba – reason – on their side, they are stronger, albeit fewer in number. Epimeteo criticizes Timantes for following Prometeo in opposing the goddess of war, and Timantes says that he prefers the risk of destruction in defense of Prometeo's honorable cause – the bringing of the ray which enlightens and warms man – to the dishonorable victory of Epimeteo's ingratitude. Epimeteo says that any possible good from Prometeo's accomplishment has been negated by the threat of Apolo's punishment. Timantes, the voice of wisdom acquired through experience, answers with a fascinating scientific metaphor:

> Los metheoros del ayre
> sin esa causa los vemos
> en condensados vapores
> conjelarse. (III, 909–912)

In other words, he says that it is not Apolo who keeps flaming meteors from reaching earth; we do not understand completely the ways of nature or the gods, and cannot be sure that Apolo will indeed punish Prometeo's theft. Fear of possible retribution by higher powers should not deter man from securing a certain good for humanity.

Epimeteo reacts impatiently to Timantes' reasoning, and urges his followers to battle. Discordia, unsure that even her larger force will enable her to prevail over Minerba's intelligence, intervenes again, disguising herself as an ambassadress of Júpiter, whom she claims requires either the sacrifice of the two principal offenders, Pandora by fire, and Prometeo by his traditional punishment, or the destruction of the whole Cáucaso. At this second, explicit threat, Timantes and the remaining members of Prometeo's band desert him; when he accuses them of treason, they reply that obedience to divine decrees is not treason (III, 1002–12), and aid Epimeteo in taking the two prisoner, covering their faces to deny all possibility of appeal or compassion. The man of reason has now been blindfolded literally as well as figuratively by his passionate brother, to prevent any possibility of his communicating with the rest of humanity or appealing for his right to exist. Prometeo has reached his nadir. Deserted by all his supporters, he and his creation seem totally at the mercy of the passions of his vengeful brother and a populace fearful of jealous deities. As O'Connor has said, the drama speaks as much of the limitation of unaided human reason as of its triumph.

As Epimeteo prepares the sacrifice of his brother and the woman he loves, he tries to distance himself from his cruel action, saying in an *aparte*, that it is the force of his passion and not he himself who accuses them:

> Si alguno culpa que soy
> quien de su castigo toma
> a cargo la ejecuzión
> ame aborreçido y tenga
> çelos, y verá que son
> çelos y aborreçimiento
> quien los acusa, y no yo. (III, 1010–16)

At the outset of the drama, Epimeteo's public face displayed courage and altruism, while his private face revealed fear and selfishness; now the situation appears reversed, as he calls determinedly for their sacrifice, while revealing inner pangs of guilt for his cruelty toward them.

Yet tragedy is averted.[220] As Epimeteo leads his brother and Pandora to prison, Minerba appears, to sing an appeal for justice to Júpiter that Prometeo's robbery, if such it is to be considered, was no crime compared to Discordia's treasonous theft of his voice and falsification of his decrees. When Palas descends to prevent Minerba from personally taking her appeal directly to Júpiter, the goddess of reason and the goddess of force themselves lock in battle and Minerba emerges triumphant[221] and leaves to take her claim to the highest court, proclaiming:

---

220 The dramatic transition which brings about the "happy ending" is as abrupt as the above sentence. Calderón did not allow any mythological court play to end in clear-cut tragedy, probably because the celebration of an occasion of state did not permit it. Yet the "felicity" of this ending seems an inorganic appendage to an essentially tragic tale. The drama contains all the philosophic elements to justify – intellectually – such an ending, but the emotional effect on either a reader or a spectator is, nevertheless, rather violently unsatisfying. It is tempting to speculate that this may result from a similar dichotomy within the playwright, between a fundamentally tragic sense of life and an intellectual – and inorganic – optimism.

221 If the goddess of reason herself resorts to violence, does this mean that reason itself is a disguised form of violence, as Cesáreo Bandera points out in the case of Basilio? Is Bandera right in saying that Calderón signals the omnipresence of violence as the central fact of human society? Bandera says: "La violencia, nos dice Calderón, no es nada externo, nada trascendente, nada sagrado. La violencia se origina siempre en el interior de la ciudad y en ella participan todos." [*Mímesis conflictiva* (Madrid: Editorial Gredos, 1975), p. 199.] This is surely an astute observation, yet the basic issue dramatized in *La estatua de Prometeo* is not the universality of violence, but the universal dualism which calls this violence into being.

> ... mortales,
> ved si entre yngenio y valor
> más que la fuerza del brazo
> vale la de la razón. (III, 1075–8)

Calderón described Discordia in *El lirio y la azucena* as the bastard offspring of Lucifer's rebellion against God, who flourishes in the world by reason of her introduction of inequalities and the resultant violation of the two precepts of Natural Law: that of loving God and one's fellow man. According to Thomistic philosophy, the principal roots of sin are pride, which causes man to turn away from God, and covetousness.[222] The obvious villains in *La estatua de Prometeo* are those who embody the second of these two sins, the jealous Palas and her protegé Epimeteo. Yet it is Prometeo, not Epimeteo, who must change in order to reassert his leadership and avert disaster. The defect in Calderón's philosopher Prometeo is a proud self-involvement which leads him to worship reason as an end in itself. As Minerba, in one sense a projection of Prometeo's aspiration, carries her appeal to Júpiter, she represents the recognition of final dependence on the supreme god as the ultimate source of wisdom and justice, a sign of man's return to obedience to the first precept of natural law as defined by Calderón. Prometeo manifests his beginning compliance with the second precept, that of loving his fellow man, when Epimeteo removes the blindfold and Prometeo, viewing Pandora, truly sees the suffering of another human being and learns compassion.

That Calderón has Epimeteo first place and then remove the blindfold is not a gratuitous detail, but a symbol vital to the structure of the play. Calderón has throughout depicted Prometeo as a solitary figure unable to relate to other human beings, while the passionate Epimeteo is eminently capable of such bonds. His blindfolding of Prometeo symbolizes the negative effect of passion when it dominates man's reason. That it is his removal of the blindfold which triggers Prometeo's love for Pandora and awakens the sympathies of all onlookers dramatizes the positive role that human emotions play in binding man to those with whom he shares the earth.

Apolo thereupon intervenes to convey Júpiter's inevitable pardon, to banish Discordia, and thereby to restore in all "razón y sentido / sentido y razón", (III, 1188–1189) and the twin brothers are restored to harmonious unity. Thus the final redemption of Prometeo is not a totally arbitrary intervention by a *deus ex machina*, but a response to modification occurring within Prometeo himself – or rather within the

---

222 *Summa Theologica*, Part I of Second Part, Articles 1 and 2.

complex protagonist, Prometeo/Epimeteo. That it is depicted as an unexpected and in large measure unearned event is in accord with the theological doctrine repeatedly dramatized by Calderón in the *autos*, that human salvation is a free gift from God which occurs only when man has come to recognize his dependence on the mercy of the supreme authority. Significantly, however, Calderón never depicts any active involvement by the supreme god, Júpiter, to avert the tragedy, but only a realignment of the lower deities (and their dependent human subjects) acting on their concept of Júpiter's code of justice. Taken in conjunction with Timantes' comment that man is not protected from meteors by Apolo's intervention, this suggests that it is not direct intervention of a supreme authority which governs human events, but rather the human conception of the possibility of such an intervention.

The "universal myth" Calderón tells in *La estatua de Prometeo* is, then, both a glorification of human reason *and* a recognition of reason's limitations. The progress of the individual and of human society depends on the creative and civilizing powers of man's reason, in ascendence over egocentric, destructive passions. Yet precisely because he is not an angel but a human being, living in society with other human beings, man cannot deny nor divorce himself from the emotional component of his dual nature, but must incorporate, under the guidance of reason, the positive bonding capacity which the passions contribute to human existence. If this delicate balance is maintained, man's attempts to perfect his condition are not punishable by death or expulsion from paradise like Adam, but rather merit the highest reward – marriage to the "semi-divine" beauty of his creation so that a new, civilized society may people the earth.

7.3 The Political Myth

The complexity of this universal myth of human dualism is yet enriched by a third system of meaning intermeshed with the universal system, a third text which we may call a political story. The myth of royal power is also, of course, a political myth, but it functions on a very different level and quite independently of this third text; the two are alike, however, in that both incorporate into their text the context of the courtly performance. The telling of the political myth works through the presence of the royal spectators, whose association with certain of the mythical figures links the problems depicted in the action on stage with tensions perceived in contemporary Spain.

We have seen earlier how the arrangement of the theatre made the royal audience and the stage the two poles of the spectacle, and how important the royal presence was in the mind's eyes, and often the physical eye, of the rest of the audience. Within this setting, the political myth was told by the process described by Stephen Orgel for the English court:

> Now there were, properly speaking, two audiences and two spectacles. The primary audience was the monarch, and the performance was often directed explicitly at him. Thus, early in Queen Elizabeth's reign the two political theorists gave the young queen counsel through the dramatic example of *Gorboduc;* and later, in *The Arraignment of Paris,* a poet created for her a crucial role in the mythology of the commonwealth. At these performances what the rest of the spectators watched was not a play but the queen at a play, and their response would have been not simply to the drama, but to the relationship between the drama and its primary audience, the royal spectator.[223]

Heroic or divine genealogies can be a two-edged weapon, as Judith Shklar has pointed out. Divine ancestors or associates are the ultimate source of honor; conversely, vulgar ones are a sense of disgrace, as the common language of insults reveals. Now the mythical figures in Calderón's plays are at once divine and imperfect, and thus furnish a perfect medium for simultaneously honoring the ruling powers and discretely discussing their imperfections. As Shklar says:

> It is because origins can glorify that they can also defame . . . Since Hesiod's day the myth of origins has been a typical form of questioning and condemning the established order, divine and human, ethical and political.[224]

Neumeister would surely reject the idea that such a political myth was intended by the playwright, as he rejects Charles Aubrun's suggestion of the political intentions of *La estatua de Prometeo.* For Neumeister, the absolutist theory of monarchy in Spain would admit of no such questioning of the limits or imperfections of kingly authority. Nevertheless, the use of art as a clearly political statement on the division of power within Spain is evident in Brown and Elliott's description of the Hall of

---

223 Stephen Orgel, *The Illusion of Power: Political Theater in the English Renaissance* (Berkeley: U. of California Press, 1975), p. 9.
224 Judith N. Shklar, "Subversive Genealogies", *Daedalus,* 101 (1972), pp. 129–130.

Realms. The arrangement of the entire hall is, as they point out, an argument for Olivares' pet project, the Union of Arms, by which kingdoms other than Castile would contribute to their mutual defense.[225] And while the conquering general is painted as the principal figure in most of the paintings in the hall depicting famous Spanish victories, in the Maino rendition of the *Recapture of Bahia*, the victorious general don Fadrique de Toledo, a determined foe of Olivares, is reduced to the second plane of the painting, and is shown presenting a tapestry in which it is precisely his arch-enemy Olivares who crowns the king with laurels.[226]

> If God was on Philip's side, so too was the count-duke. In a motif of considerable audacity, Olivares had himself depicted with Minerva as the joint author of Philip's victories. With one hand he lays the laurel wreath on the king's brow, and with the other he holds a sword and the olive branch, a symbol both of the olive groves of his title and of reconciliation. Olivares offered victory to his sovereign and clemency to his defeated enemies; a merciful king offers them peace and reconciliation. And behind it all, in this perfect representation of the concept of rule by favorite, or *valimiento*, is the figure of the minister.[227]

Orgel provides us with a clear example of the use of court theatre as an explicitly political statement directed toward the autocratic Charles I of England as he consolidated royal power in the 1630's:

> In 1634 the Inns of Court took the remarkable step of retaining Inigo Jones and James Shirley in an attempt to speak to the king in his own language. The lawyers presented a masque at Whitehall that was, for all its courtly splendor, diplomatically but unequivocally critical of the royal policies, and undertook, through the power of poetry and the marvels of spectacle, to persuade the royal spectator to return to the rule of law.[228]

Charles I, perhaps paying attention not to the criticism but the adulation, not only accepted the masque, but ordered it repeated. He then countered, two weeks later, with his own version of the proper

---

225 Brown and Elliott, *Palace*, pp. 168–170.
226 Brown and Elliott, *Palace*, pp. 172–174, 185.
227 Brown and Elliott, *Palace*, p. 190.
228 Orgel, *Illusion*, p. 79.

kingly role in a masque by Thomas Carew and Inigo Jones which Orgel calls "the greatest theatrical expression of the Caroline autocracy."[229] The courtly theatre evolved from early masques in which the royal family often participated directly to the sophisticated court plays of the later seventeenth century, in which they were involved by association. I believe that Calderón's deliberate integration of a political text within the mythological court plays was also a gradual evolution, as he became aware of the political implications inherently associated with such productions.

Although this is not the place for a detailed history of his development of the technique,[230] I will mention at least a few clues to the evolution. The idea for the first mythological court play composed solely by Calderón, *El mayor encanto amor,* did not originate with the dramatist, but with the scene designer Cosme Lotti, as a vehicle for displaying an enormous assortment of spectacular effects. Calderón reduced and reorganized the devices used, in order to make the production dramatically coherent.[231] Although the resulting play is logical and pleasing enough, it remains strangely flat and superficial, as Calderón presents the story of Ulysses' enchantment by Circe without exploring the moral implications of the story. One might speculate that Calderón hesitated to develop the issues inherent in the tale precisely because of his awareness of their pertinence to the contemporary criticism of Felipe IV for his multiple love affairs.[232] By 1661, Calderón had apparently become considerably less timid politically. Between the play *Apolo y Climene* and its sequel, *El hijo del sol, Faetón,* Calderón changed the identity of Climene's father. Only two explanations seem logical: 1) that Calderón was careless – which seems doubtful, since he planned the plays as a pair; or 2) that he altered the identity of the father figure to underline its relevance to the problems arising from Felipe's ambivalent treatment of his bastard son, don Juan José de Austria. And in 1669, Calderón wrote *Fieras afemina amor,* a strange, dark play which is esthetically satisfying only when read in light of the factional struggles rending the court under Mariana's regency.

---

229 Orgel, *Illusion,* p. 83.
230 I will treat this in detail in a forthcoming book on the Calderonian mythological court plays.
231 Shergold, *History,* p. 280.
232 For a superb evaluation of the play, and a comparison of it with the *auto Los encantos de la culpa,* see Richard LeVan, "From Tradition to Masterpiece: Circe and Calderón", Unpublished Ph. D. Dissertation, U. of Texas at Austin, 1981. LeVan points out the political relevance of the Circe story, as did Prof. William R. Blue, in a paper read at the Modern Language Association Convention in Los Angeles, December, 1982.

La estatua de Prometeo is a masterpiece, I believe, not only because of the themes developed in the telling of the universal myth, but because of the superb artistry with which Calderón has interwoven that system of meaning with another system of immediate political import. When the mythological plays are read with a full realization of the three texts involved, the myth of power, the universal myth, and the political myth, the total effect is, I submit – in an analogy that would horrify the ceremonious Hapsburg court – rather similar in its social function to the Balinese cockfight described by Clifford Geertz.[233] It is the acting out and pretended resolution of the conflicts of a society, within the protective and restrictive order of a rigid ceremonial frame.

The central villain of *La estatua de Prometeo*, Discordia, was a familiar figure in the Hapsburg court of the 1670's, both literally and figuratively speaking. In the frankly political *auto*[234] *El lirio y la azucena*, Calderón calls the court her natural habitat, as Discordia says to her partner Guerra:

> Aunque en el fin uno no más seamos,
> somos dos en las sendas que pisamos,
> pues cuando hacia las cortes van mis sañas,
> van tus furores hacia las campañas: (Aguilar III, 916b)

She had long since become a familiar figure in the iconography of court-commissioned art, and looms large in the 10-picture Hercules cycle painted by Zurbarán for the Hall of Realms of the Buen Retiro, as Brown and Elliott point out:

> Religious and political struggles of this period, and the divided loyalty of a sovereign's subjects, made the threat of discord loom large over the times. The extension of the Herculean metaphor to include the power to stifle rebellion was almost inevitable, and by the mid-sixteenth century the usual form for the symbol showed Hercules vanquishing a monster. By the time that Cesare Ripa published his influential encyclopedia of emblems *Iconologia* (1603), the identification between monster and Discordia was universally understood. Discordia, he writes, is a woman in the form of an infernal demon, *furia infernale,* dressed in multicolored clothes, with snakes in her hair.[235]

---

233 "Deep Play: Notes on the Balinese Cockfight", *Daedalus* 101 (1972), pp. 1–37.
234 Celebrating the peace concluded between France and Spain in 1659.
235 Brown and Elliott, *Palace*, p. 160.

Six of the 10 pictures of the cycle show Hercules defeating various monsters, "feats which were understood to symbolize the triumph of the just sovereign over his domestic and foreign enemies."[236] Furthermore, Discordia is one of the "unholy triumvirate" crushed by Felipe IV and Olivares in Maino's *Recapture of Bahía* in the same hall.

> At the king's feet lie in defeat the personifications of his enemies – Heresy, holding a broken cross in its hands and mouth; Discord, the *"furia infernale,"* with snakes in her hair; and Treachery, or Fraud, a two-faced creature, with left and right hands reversed, who offers peace and then stabs in the back.[237]

Interestingly, while Heresy lies under Felipe's feet, it is Olivares who is painted with his foot crushing Discordia's neck.

With no strong foot to crush her, Discordia – or factional struggle – grew to truly monstrous proportions in the Spanish court after Felipe IV died in 1665, leaving his widow Mariana and a junta of ministers to rule for his retarded 4-year-old son Carlos. In a decade, the Spanish governmental system, which was designed to function around the person of a mature monarch, degenerated from being one of the most stable and orderly in Europe to one of the most chaotic and vacillating, and pure politics filled the vacuum left by the absence of an effective sovereign in Madrid.[238] At the center of this struggle stood Felipe's illegitimate son, don Juan José de Austria, whom Kamen calls "la personalidad más poderosa del reino y una de las figuras más importantes de toda la historia de la España de los Austrias."[239] Stradling describes his role as follows:

> The single most significant political fact during the subsequent decade was the existence of the new king's adult halfbrother, Don Juan José. Even whilst his father had lived, this prince had made no secret of his claim to share power, and now publicly advanced a cause which amounted to a demand for the regency itself. The politics of this period were dominated by his campaign, and the faction fighting which it encouraged in Madrid. By the late 1660's, Don Juan provided an alternative centre of allegiance for many individuals and sectional

---

236 Brown and Elliott, *Palace*, p. 161.
237 Brown and Elliott, *Palace*, p. 188.
238 R. A. Stradling, *Europe and the Decline of Spain: A Study of the Spanish System, 1580–1720* (London: George Allen & Unwin, 1981), p. 147.
239 Henry Kamen, *La España de Carlos II* (Barcelona: Editorial Crítica, 1981), p. 522.

interests, like the "court" of the Prince of Wales in Hanoverian England.[240]

Don Juan José, born on April 7, 1629, was the son of Felipe IV by the actress María Calderón, called "la Calderona"; he was a handsome, energetic and intelligent individual who was the only one among Felipe's numerous bastard children to be publicly recognized by his father.[241] Felipe recognized him as his illegitimate son in May, 1642, and the following year he was accepted as a prince, with the title of "Serenidad". He was made a *caballero* of the ecclesiastical order of San Juan, with the title of Gran Prior of the order in Castilla and León, which had its seat in Consuegra, south of Toledo. In 1647, he was named "Príncipe de la Mar", and took command of the fleet headed for Naples to put down an uprising in Massaniello. Succeeding in this, he remained in Sicily as Viceroy from 1648 to 1651. In 1650, he was named to the Consejo de Estado. Returning from Sicily in 1651, he assumed command of the campaign to end the Catalán separatist movement, and brought it to a successful conclusion, both militarily and politically, as Kamen describes:

> El 10 de octubre de 1652 el *conseller en cap* de Barcelona fue a ofrecerle la sumisión de la ciudad, postrándose a los pies del general. Don Juan le impidió arrodillarse, haciéndole levantar. Era un símbolo de la generosidad que había de conquistarle el constante apoyo de los catalanes.[242]

He was named Viceroy of Cataluña, and subsequently served as Viceroy in the Low Countries from 1656 to 1659. From 1661 to 1664, he served as commander in chief of the forces combatting the secession of Portugal, with a lack of success, however, which disappointed his father.[243]

Don Juan José was not only a political and military leader, but also the principal patron of the introduction of new scientific information in Spain. José María López Piñero, in his study of scientific renovation in Spain, maintains that it did not begin with Feijóo, as is commonly thought, but had its roots in the late seventeenth century, despite the common image of the reign of Carlos II as Spain's period of greatest

---

240 Stradling, *Decline*, p. 147.
241 R. Trevor Davies, *La decadencia española, 1621–1700* (Barcelona: Editorial Labor, 1972), pp. 67–8, 126.
242 Kamen, *España*, pp. 522–523.
243 Kamen, *España*, p. 523.

cultural decadence. During the last 25 or 30 years of the seventeenth century, the first really modern Spanish scientists appeared and began the process of breaking with traditional principles, and introducing modern science, earning in the process the negative title of *novatores* from their traditional opponents.[244] Don Juan José was a vital patron of this group, as López Piñero points out:

> Al no tener prácticamente cabida en las instituciones existen-tes, los *novatores* tuvieron que depender de la protección de nobles y clérigos de mentalidad preilustrada, y agruparse en "tertulias" independientes o en torno a sus mecenas. Entre estos últimos destaca, por su importancia y sobre todo por su prioridad cronológica, el varias veces citado Juan José de Austria. Si se tiene en cuenta su papel dentro de la historia política española, resulta extraordinariamente ilustrativo cono-cer su interés por la ciencia moderna. Seguía con gran atención la producción astronómica y física de su tiempo, manejaba con gran destreza los instrumentos de observación astronómica, y era un gran aficionado a la mecánica, llegando a construir personalmente varios aparatos. Su postura acerca de la aplica-ción de los nuevos conocimientos y técnicas a la resolución de los problemas colectivos, se refleja en dos significativas dedicatorias a su persona: la del *Discurso físico y político* (1679) de Juan Bautista Juanini, primer texto español en el que se utilizan los saberes médicos y químicos "modernos" para enfrentarse con un problema de higiene pública, y la *Arquitec-tura civil, recta y oblicua* (1678) de Juan Caramuel, fundamen-tación matemática al día de las técnicas de construcción. Su apoyo es, sin duda, una de las claves explicativas de la pujanza del grupo de novatores y tradicionalistas moderados de Zaragoza.[245]

Six years after the death of don Juan in 1679, Juanini, who had been his personal physician for six years, wrote in glowing praise of his intellectual interests and talents:

> no he hallado otro Príncipe que como su Alteza tuviesse talentos tan universales y eminentes ... El tiempo que le

---

244 López Piñero, *La introducción de la ciencia en España* (Barcelona: Ediciones Ariel, 1969), pp. 8–9, 12, 34.
245 López Piñero, *Ciencia*, p. 42.

> sobrava de los manejos públicos, no lo entregava al descanso
> del cuerpo, lo aplicava al divertimiento honesto y erudito del
> espíritu . . . En todas la partes de Mathemática era versadíss-
> simo; conocía y manejava con gran destreza y acierto los
> Instrumentos . . . Distinguía las doctrinas de todos con incom-
> parable claridad, y lo bueno, dudoso y Religioso de ellas,
> dando a Aristóteles, Ptholomeo, Thico Brahe, Copérnico,
> Galileo y otros lo que les tocava. En la Geometría, Geogra-
> phía, Cosmografía, hablava y obrava con la misma excelencia.
> Y como el mando del Mar era el primer empleo a que le
> destinó la prudente atención del Señor Rey su Padre, tenía el
> Arte Náutica tan sabida que el Padre Lasalle de la Compañía
> de Jesus dixo al Rey: no sabía ya qué enseñarle . . .[246]

Don Juan José, benefitting from his experience in governing Cataluña in
particular, was also the proponent of substantial economic and political
reform; some of those which were actually initiated during his brief
tenure as prime minister between 1677 and 1679 include: monetary
reforms aimed at producing a stable Spanish currency; limiting the
growth of ecclesiastical orders; and the establishment of a Junta de
Comercio which worked toward the modernization of the industrial
system, by breaking down the ancient guild system, increasing trade, and
declaring nobility compatible with participation in industry.[247]
Despite his talents, preparation and widespread popular support,
nevertheless, don Juan José remained in an anomalous position when
Felipe IV died on 17 September 1665, refusing on his deathbed to grant
an audience to his illegitimate son.[248] As Kamen puts it:

> Al final del reinado de su padre, don Juan se encontraba en la
> curiosa posición de ser el general más distinguido de su patria,
> pero al que se le negaban todos los honores políticos corre-
> spondientes a su rango. La negativa de Felipe IV de legitimarlo
> efectivamente le cerraba el paso a toda dignidad superior.
> Siendo el candidato más evidente para actuar como jefe de
> Estado, quedaba excluido de la Junta de Gobierno.[249]

The center of opposition toward don Juan rested in Felipe IV's Austrian

---

246 J. B. Juanini, *Nueva Idea Physica* (Zaragoza, 1685), pp. 2–6; cited in Kamen, *España*,
p. 546.
247 Kamen, *España*, pp. 170, 202, 350, 442–3.
248 Kamen, *España*, p. 517.
249 Kamen, *España*, p. 523.

widow, Mariana, who saw in the illegitimate prince a threat to her own authority and to the future rule of her pathetic son Carlos, who at four years of age could not yet walk, had only recently been weaned, and who at nine years of age still seemed incapable of learning to read and write.[250]

Lacking the intellectual gifts or political acumen to rule herself, Mariana sought a strong man on whom to rely, but her two choices of *valido* were almost universally unpopular. Her first choice was her confessor, Juan Everardo Nithard, an Austrian Jesuit who had accompanied her to Madrid when she married Felipe IV in 1649. Mariana maneuvered to have him naturalized in 1666, because her husband's will had specified that no foreigner could hold office in the councils of state. Succeeding in that, she arranged for his appointment as Inquisitor General on 22 September 1666. Kamen describes the result:

> El nombramiento de un desconocido extranjero para los más altos cargos de estado fue la causa directa de las crisis constitucionales de los dos años siguientes. Pero la chispa que encendió la llama fue la acalorada impaciencia de don Juan, que aguardaba en Consuegra la llamada que no llegaba.[251]

Mariana and Nithard arranged to have don Juan appointed commander of the forces in Flanders, to remove him from the center of power. But alleging various difficulties, he refused the post. In August, 1668, he was exiled to Consuegra and forbidden to come within 20 leagues of Madrid. Alerted to an attempt by don Juan's secretary to kidknap Nithard, the Junta de Gobierno voted on 19 October 1668 to arrest him, but he escaped and eventually fled to Cataluña, a stronghold of support for him dating from the days of his viceregalty. From there, he began a war of pamphlets and letters, seeking to use public opinion as a means of achieving control of the country.[252] As the various councils of state turned toward support of don Juan, he began a triumphant march from Barcelona toward Madrid in early 1669, with a troop of 400 cavalryman which he claimed to need as a personal escort. He entered incognito and as a private person in Zaragoza, yet received a tumultuous welcome from the crowd, and excited students burned the effigy of a Jesuit in front of the Jesuit residence.[253] Don Juan's approach, even with this small force,

---

250 Kamen, *España*, pp. 41–42.
251 Kamen, *España*, p. 524.
252 Kamen, *España*, pp. 525–527.
253 Kamen, *España*, p. 531.

threatened civil war, and with it he achieved "lo que acaso se pueda llamar el primer pronunciamiento de la historia moderna de España: un golpe militar contra Madrid con la ayuda de las provincias."[254] The Junta de Gobierno at last met all his demands, Nithard left for Rome, a Junta de Alivios was created to carry out reforms, all recent legislation against don Juan was removed from the records, and don Juan, unable to achieve more, accepted the post of Vicario General of the crown in Aragón.[255] Mariana's subsequent choice for *valido* was Fernando Valenzuela, a member of the lesser nobility who rose to power through his charm and marriage to one of the queen's ladies-in-waiting. As the queen appointed him to ever more honored posts, the resentment of the old nobility increased. The tension reached a climax in November, 1675, when Carlos reached his majority at 14 years of age. According to his father's will, the Junta de Gobierno was to be suspended automatically on his birthday, but the young king was obviously incapable of ruling alone, and don Juan's cause was raised again. The secretary of the Junta presented Carlos with a decree continuing its powers another two years, but Carlos refused to sign, and informed his mother on November 5 that he had summoned don Juan.

> Aquella mañana el príncipe cabalgó por entre la multitud enfervorizada en dirección al alcázar; fue recibido como infante de España e introducido, a la hora convenida, a la presencia del rey. Los hermanos se abrazaron mutuamente y Carlos garantizó a don Juan su protección. Después de la misa y el *Te Deum* el príncipe se dirigió al Buen Retiro y el monarca fue a visitar a su madre.
>
> Carlos estuvo encerrado con Mariana durante dos horas, saliendo con lágrimas en los ojos . . . Costó varias horas ejercer con éxito la presión sobre el rey. Poco después de las seis el duque de Medinaceli se encaminó a ver a don Juan al Buen Retiro, con una orden escrita del rey para que inmediatamente se dirigiera a Italia . . .
>
> Don Juan salió de Madrid aquella misma mañana [7 November]. En una carta del 8 de noviembre a la Diputación y ciudad de Zaragoza, relatando el repentino cambio de los acontecimientos y que tuvo plena publicidad como todas las cartas del príncipe, don Juan explicaba que se había retirado con el fin de

---

254 Kamen, *España*, p. 532.
255 Kamen, *España*, pp. 532–3.

evitar un enfrentamiento. Para "sacar la persona de Su
Magestad del estado en que se halla" habría necesitado el
auxilio de la nobleza, pero una minoría de ella le había sido
hostil.[256]

Valenzuela was also ordered out of Madrid, being made Capitán General
of the kingdom of Granada, but he returned in April of 1676, with the
support of the Queen, who appointed him Caballerizo Mayor, a post
supposedly reserved for the highest nobility. The majority of the
nobility went on strike and circulated a public petition demanding the
permanent separation of the queen from her son, the imprisonment of
Valenzuela, and the designation of don Juan as "colaborador inmediato"
of the king. Valenzuela began gathering troops in the capital and armed
conflict threatened again. As don Juan marched from Zaragoza to
Madrid, volunteers from Valencia, Cataluña, and Aragón swelled his
forces, which came to number more than 15.000 men, including "ocho
grandes de Castilla, la flor y nata de la nobleza aragonesa y varios otros
nobles; es posible que fuera la fuerza mayor que nunca se hubiera
reunido en España en tiempo de paz."[257] The king sent troops to arrest
Valenzuela, who had fled to El Escorial, and at 6:00 AM January 23,
1677, don Juan entered the Buen Retiro palace, had the king awakened
and offered him his services.

The events of January, 1677, were, as Kamen says:

> más que un pronunciamiento: era un golpe de estado, el
> primero de la historia moderna española. Pero a diferencia de
> tantos otros posteriores, éste contó con el abrumador apoyo
> tanto de las clases dirigentes como del pueblo de España. En
> contraposición con Valenzuela, vulgar valido sin relieve histó-
> rico, don Juan poseía la importancia única de ser el primer
> líder real de la historia de España. En todas partes era
> considerado el salvador de la patria.[258]

The savior proved disappointing. Don Juan found the obstacles to
reform even more intractable than the obstacles he had overcome on his
way to power. His own authority was dependent on the continued favor
of the king, on whom Mariana continued to apply pressure against the
prince. In the end, his tenure proved too brief to effect any real change,
as he died in September of 1679, at the age of 50.

---

256 Kamen, *España*, pp. 535–6.
257 Kamen, *España*, p. 538.
258 Kamen, *España*, p. 539.

We cannot be sure of the exact year in which Calderón wrote *La estatua de Prometeo* – only that it was sometime between 1670 and 1674. As the above account demonstrates, in any one of those years, the principal issue in the court at Madrid was the power struggle between the factions supporting and opposing don Juan José de Austria. It is very probable, then, that Calderón, in writing a play about a contest between "los dos nobles caudillos del pueblo" and their heavenly patronesses, was addressing that issue.

It is equally likely that Prometeo, whom Calderón draws as the man of reason, the student of science, who had studied abroad and returned to institute a new rule of law in his own country, was in some way to be related to don Juan José. He creates Pandora, civilization – in political terms, a new Spain – a beautiful product of human reationality which he brings to life with power stolen from Apolo – ever the symbol of the king. When Prometeo, representative of "forethought" or progressive forces, has created the new Spain, his brother Epimeteo, representing "afterthought" or memory, the reactionary leader who had led the populace to reject rational new laws for the simple old ways, becomes enamored of the new creation and wishes to possess it. Pandora rejects his advances and follows Prometeo, whereupon the jealous conservative leader turns his vengeance on her "galán" – the progressive leader – and threatens to destroy both him and his new Spain.

Whether Calderón intended his audience to identify Epimeteo with any specific opponent of don Juan is questionable. While certain features of characterization might suggest certain figures,[259] the political myth which Calderón constructed was, I believe, both more subtle and more universal than such a simplistic, one-to-one allegorical message, limited by specific identification of Epimeteo with don Juan's current opponent. Rather, Calderón structured the drama to convey the idea that as each individual is divided by the discord between his reason and his passion,

---

259 It is possible to see Prometeo as don Juan José, and Epimeteo as the recently fallen Nithard or the rising Valenzuela, or a blend of both. His enthusiastic championship of new religious rites might link him with the Jesuit *valido*, while his espousal of building a magnificent temple could recall the image of Valenzuela as a builder. Epimeteo says:

> . . . yo
> voto haçer que se construia
> templo a Minerba que exçeda
> en riqueza y escultura
> al del gran Saturno nuestro,
> donde aquesa ymagen tuia
> se venere; . . .

every country is torn by the strife between progressives and conservatives, and every political movement by the contest between reason and force. This broader structuring makes the myth applicable to an almost infinite variety of conflictive political situations. Aubrun mentioned three: the 1669 peace between Spain and Portugal; the struggle between don Juan and Valenzuela; and that between Carlos II and Louis XIV of France.[260] The list could be expanded well beyond the seventeenth century, and beyond the borders of Spain. Certainly this story of the contest between progressives and conservatives, between reason and force, is equally applicable three centuries later to the problems of Spain since the death of Franco.

The superb subtlety of this myth is that the dominant political figure of the period, don Juan José *is*, on the one hand Prometeo, and his opposition Epimeteo; yet he also is both Prometeo and Epimeteo – he is every man divided internally between reason and passion, and his pursuit of power reflects both the positive use of human reason and the negative threat of force. Both were clearly applicable to don Juan, who was at once the patron of science and modernization, and the focus for the threat of civil war. Calderón assigns a similar double personality to the second crucial figure of the period, Mariana. As don Juan José is both Prometeo and Epimeteo, so Mariana can be related to the twin goddesses in her controlling influence over the fate of "earthly" *caudillos* and their followers; in Minerba and Palas Calderón created for her two role models, obviously suggesting Minerba as the preferable image of the two. Nor is Mariana the only one whom Calderón is tactfully lecturing with his play. Tragedy is averted at the end of the drama because Prometeo has learned humility and compassion for his fellow man. He

---

           ... aquí vendremos por ella
           luego que la arquitectura
           del templo a la región media
           sobre dóricas columnas
           de bronzeados capiteles
           en piramidal abuja
           crezca de suerte que el ayre
           dude, cuando la sacuda,
           si es vracán que se abate,
           o fábrica que se encumbre. (I, 341–347, 360–370)

Along with the provision of spectacular entertainment, Valenzuela used an ambitious program of building and public works to impress the public. (See Kamen, *España*, pp. 233, 534.) On the other hand, Epimeteo's passionate ignorance might be seen as linking him instead with the feeble-minded Carlos.

260 Aubrun, *Prometeo*, p. vii.

is then rewarded by marriage to Pandora so that in the product of their union the new civilization might continue. So too must the dominant political leader justify his ascendency by demonstrating not a proud or possessive self-assertion, but a genuine concern for the people he governs.

The peculiarly vacillating role of Apolo in the play also becomes understandable in the reading of the political myth. The sun god is the traditional symbol of kingship, both human and divine. Calderón underlines this symbolism emphatically in *La estatua de Prometeo*, calling Apolo:

> . . . *árbitro* del día y la noche,
> *monarca* de los planetas,
> *rey* de los signos, y *dueño*
> de luzeros y de estrellas,
> vida es de frutos y flores,
> y alma de montes y selbas. (I, 837–842; emphasis mine)

In the play, civil war threatens because the indecisive Apolo cannot choose to side with either one of his two sisters. As Stradling pointed out, the basic political problem of the time was the lack of a decisive, mature king in a system designed to function around such a figure. The validity of the Apolo scenario would therefore have been clear to a contemporary audience, even before they witnessed the dramatic spectacle in November, 1675, of Carlos II pulled back and forth between his half-brother and his mother.

Calderón's play addresses in two different symbolic actions the issue of the threat which don Juan's bid for power represented to the authority of Carlos and Mariana. The first is the end of the first act, in which the audience saw Apolo crossing the stage singing, while Prometeo stole a ray of his light:

> No temas, no, desçender,
> que si en todo es de sentir
> que naçe para morir,
> tú mueres para naçer. (I, 877–885)

Felipe IV, "el cuarto planeta," was the king most regularly identified with the sun god, but the image of the sun setting only to be reborn was a standard motif in the funerary art of other Hapsburg kings as well. The idea thus suggested is that the transference of power is not the "death" of the Hapsburg monarchy, but only its regeneration through the natural process of periodic renewal.

Calderón treats the more immediate and more eternal issue – that of whether Prometeo's theft of regal authority is a praiseworthy advance for mankind or a damnable act of treason – through Apolo's actions at the end of the drama. After Minerba appeals to Júpiter and Prometeo demonstrates compassion for Pandora, Apolo intervenes to pardon Prometeo, and thus banish the villanous Discordia. Apolo justifies his last-minute decision to intervene by saying that he wants to be the bringer of the pardon which he knows Júpiter will grant:

> . . . al ver que Minerba
> al solio subió
> de Júpiter, donde
> pide su perdón,
> y que el conçederle
> es preçisa acçion,
> porque nunca niega
> piedades vn dios,
> venir e querido
> a traerle yo;
> débanmele a mí,
> y a Júpiter no. (III, 1162–1173)

His action accords with the theory of the divine right of kings, by which kings are the representatives through whom God's wisdom and justice are dispensed on earth. As Calderón phrases this speech, the process works not because the supreme god actually orders earthly affairs through a regal intermediary, but because the king's conception of Júpiter's ultimate goodness makes him eventually act in accord with his understanding of that goodness.

Significantly, Júpiter never actively intervenes. The final verdict is not dictated by a *deus ex machina* in the classic sense of a supreme being who swings in on stage machinery to arrange human affairs, but by invocation of a supreme authority who remains totally outside the works. Apolo is, of course, a machine-born god, but as he had earlier abjured his regal authority to settle the dispute between Minerba/Prometeo and Palas/Epimeteo, so now he invokes not his own authority, but his conception of an invisible supreme being. This king-figure who had first refused to act, now acts only as an intermediary for an absent authority principle whose presumed judgment Apolo explains only in the flat, unrevealing and unsatisfying phrase, "nunca niega / piedades vn dios." (III, 1168–69).

In the end, Calderón's Prometeo is not condemned to either divine or regal punishment for his usurpation of power, nor expelled from paradise like Adam. Instead, he emerges a wiser, triumphant figure, rewarded with marriage to Pandora and once again in ascendance over his contrary brother, who is restored to allegiance to him. The accretion of regal or "divine" power to the human sphere of control is, then – if properly motivated and guided – not to be condemned, but generously applauded.

How does this accord with the theory of Maravall, that Golden Age theatre, while superficially modern, was in ultimate intent and effect an important force toward immobilization and the maintenance of an authoritarian *status quo*? Maravall states:

> Shakespeare o Ben Johnson no representan una cultura que hiciera imposible la revolución industrial. Racine o Molière tal vez contribuyeron a preparar los espíritus para la fase renovadora del colbertismo. Pero de las condiciones en que se produjo el teatro de Lope o el de Calderón y que en sus obras se reflejaron – con no dejar de ser ellos modernos –, no se podría salir, sin embargo, hacia un mundo definitivamente moderno, rompiendo el inmovilismo de la estructura social en que el teatro de uno y otro se apoyaban – a pesar de lo mucho que para la primera aparición de una modernidad contribuyeran. Tan sólo cuando, a pesar de todo, entran en la Península Descartes o Galileo, y con ellos la ciencia moderna, se puedan descubrir algunas novedades en el pensamiento que, no obstante la noble polémica que representa la Illustración dieciochesca, no lograrían tampoco triunfar.[261]

For Maravall, Golden Age theatre assists in undermining the forces of human liberty set in motion by the Renaissance. For ter Horst, on the other hand, the expression of that force provides the life of Calderonian drama:

> A departure from orthodoxy . . . is . . . of absolutely fundamental and crucial importance to the life and function of Calderonian drama. To rise up in rebellion against the mandates of governing powers, paternal and divine, is an essential role which man constantly creates for himself, in contradistinction to the part that God or one's father would have one passively play. In this sense, though an oversimplification, it might help

---

261 Maravall, *Barroco*, p. 77.

to say that the pressures towards paternalistic conformism are
the medieval dogmatic continuum in Calderón's theatre, while
the irrepressible urge of the gifted man to fashion his own fate
constitutes a Renaissance corollary. Both impulses are
required. They engage each other so as to give voice to the
contrapuntal melody of struggle that always informs Calderón's plays. Disobedience, there, can be original, creative, and
can ultimately be reconciled to the world harmonic.[262]

Both these statements are at least partially valid with regard to other
works of Calderón; neither, however, adequately describes the fundamental attitude toward authority which is embodied in the structure of
La estatua de Prometeo.

Ter Horst's interpretation is subconsciously influenced by the rebellious
Prometheus of Aeschylus and Romantic writers. As pointed out above,
Calderón's Prometeo is not driven by a rebellious attitude toward
superior authority. He complains of being limited not by the restrictive
pressure of divine beings, but by the ignorant and conservative barbarity
of those below him. He expresses boundless admiration for the gods (I,
207–230), and commits his theft under the tutelage of a goddess; when
he thinks that Apolo threatens retribution, he first withdraws from
conflict and then joins the fray only in self-defense, when the battle has
become inevitable.

On the other hand, and in contradiction of Maravall's view (in the case
of La estatua de Prometeo, based on a superficial reading of the play),
Calderón's hero in this work neither advocates nor yields to the status
quo. In this play it is the "villains" – Discordia, Epimeteo and Palas –
who advocate the maintenance of the status quo and constantly raise the
specter of divine retribution for human acquisition of knowledge and
power. Prometeo, in contrast, is an outspoken advocate for political
change and the introduction of new scientific knowledge. In a key
exchange, Timantes, the voice of experience, supports Prometeo precisely because he has brought the invaluable gift of fire to his people.
When Epimeteo objects that Apolo's punishment will negate that good,
Timantes replies with the enigmatic metaphor that it is not Apolo who
makes meteors dissolve before reaching earth. The implication is that
given his lack of understanding of the relationship between natural
phenomena and divine (or regal) will, man should not be deterred from a
proven good by a fear of possible punishment.

---

262 ter Horst, Calderón, p. 58.

In effect, the entire structure of the play demonstrates a fundamental uncertainty concerning the locus of power over human affairs. Calderón raised, then side-stepped the issue of the cause of dualism by naming Minerba and Palas as the efficient causes of the divergence between Prometeo and his alter ego, but specifying no first cause for the split between the heavenly pair. When various characters ask who brought the statue to life, a off-stage chorus answers enigmatically:

> Quien triumpha para enseñanza
> de que quien da çiençias, da
> voz al barro y luz al alma.

Minerba and Palas appeal their quarrel to Apolo, only to have him renounce his monarchical role, and tell them to fight it out on earth. Lastly, the supreme authority, Júpiter, is an absent power, who shapes the outcome only as he exists as a concept of final justice in the minds of his subjects.

In spite of the multiple deities involved in this drama, authority is notable in *La estatua de Prometeo* as much for its absence as for its presence. Certainly this reflects the vaccuum of royal authority which characterized Hapsburg Spain after the death of Felipe IV. In this situation, Calderón does not postulate as a model a return to immobility and absolutism, but rather political change and the introduction of precisely the "ciencia moderna" whose lack Maravall laments. The artificial and unsatisfying suddenness of the happy resolution which Calderón gives to the Prometheus story we may perhaps attribute to the fact that for him, as for the rest of the late Hapsburg court, the destructive conflict caused by the dualism of human nature was a lived experience; in the absence of a strong authority and depending on decidedly human resources, the channeling of that conflict toward the path of peace and progress could be at best a hypothetical scenario.

Prometeo's human counterpart, don Juan José de Austria, the would-be reforming savior of late-Hapsburg Spain, too soon succumbed to the illness of his own body and that of the complex Spanish state. Yet Calderón's play survives as a witness that even in those bitter years, the aging playwright could still construct a scenario in which the power of true human wisdom might change the established order and build a better future.

TEXTUAL INTRODUCTION

8 TEXTUAL TRANSMISSION

8.1 Printed Editions

During Calderón's lifetime, twelve collected volumes of his *comedias* were published, in five *Partes*, each of which appeared in two or more editions.[263] All these *Partes* were quite careless editions, with little or no editorial intervention by Calderón.[264] Although Calderón complained bitterly about the compounding of errors in his plays as they passed through the pens of scribes, careful or careless, and from the hands of *autores,* actors, or various kinds of artistic pirates to and through the hands of the printer, only the second edition of the *Quarta Parte* of 1674 shows any evidence of extensive editorial intervention on his part. Nevertheless, these often-corrupt *Parte* texts are the only source we have for a substantial number of Calderonian *comedias.* Furthermore, the process of corruption has continued with the onlay of "corrections" – some justified, many arbitrary or erroneous – by subsequent editors.

8.1.1 The "Barcelona" *Quinta Parte*

Of the five *Partes,* the *Quinta Parte,* which contains *La estatua de Prometeo,* possesses the distinction of being the most defective. In 1677, only months apart, two different editions of this *Parte* appeared, one purporting to have been printed in Barcelona by Antonio la Cavallería (hereinafter referred to as "B"), the second in Madrid by Antonio Francisco de Zafra. (Bibliographic descriptions of editions are included at the end of this section.) In the prologue to his *Primera parte de autos sacramentales,* also published in 1677, Calderón condemns the "Barcelona" edition as:

---

263 A number of plays were also published in volumes of the *Comedias escogidas* series begun in 1652, which regularly published collections of plays by various popular playwrights.

264 D. W. Cruickshank, "The Textual Criticism of Calderón's *Comedias*", in Edward M. Wilson and D. W. Cruickshank, *The Textual Criticism of Calderón's Comedias*, Vol. I of Pedro Calderón de la Barca, *Comedias: A Facsimile Edition*, ed. by D. W. Cruickshank and J. E. Varey (London: Gregg International Publishers Limited, 1973), pp. 1–12.

> vn libro intitulado: *Quinta parte de Comedias de Calderon*,
> con tantas falsedades, como auerse impresso en Madrid, y
> tener puesta su impression en Barcelona, no tener licencia, ni
> remission, ni del Vicario, ni del Consejo, ni aprobacion de
> persona conocida . . .[265]

Furthermore, he asserted that four of the ten plays of the collection were
not his (although in reality only two are by other playwrights), and went
on to disclaim the other six, because they were so inaccurate, adulterated
and defective. Calderón does not mention the Madrid edition, which
probably appeared after he had written his prologue.[266]

Cotarelo, who believed that the Madrid edition was the *princeps*, and the
Barcelona one a pirated copy of it, suggested that Calderón, at 77 years
of age, had confused the two editions.[267] S. E. Leavitt argues for the
priority of the Barcelona edition, which he assumes to be authentic.[268]
Subsequent investigations by Cruickshank and Jaime Moll, however,
have demonstrated that Calderón was right: The "Barcelona" edition is
a falsification, probably motivated by the desire to avoid the legal
requirements of the Consejo de Castilla. By studying the decorative
woodblocks and the type founts, Moll and Cruickshank have demonstrated that the volume was produced in Madrid by two printers, one of
whom almost certainly was Melchor Sánchez and the other possibly
Bernardo de Hervada.[269] A careful reading of *La estatua de Prometeo* in
this *Parte* reveals that Calderón was also justified in rejecting this volume
for its defective texts, as the play contains a number of very confused
passages.

8.1.2 The Madrid *Quinta Parte*

The Madrid edition of the *Quinta Parte* ("M") a page-for-page reprint
of B, was a duly authorized edition, apparently produced quickly to

---

265 Pedro Calderón de la Barca, *Autos* (Madrid: Imprenta Imperial, por Ioseph Fernández
de Buendía, 1677); cited in D. W. Cruickshank, "The Two Editions of Calderón's
Quinta Parte (1677)", in Wilson and Cruickshank, *Textual Criticism*, p. 201.

266 Cruickshank, "Two Editions", p. 204.

267 E. Cotarelo y Mori, *Ensayo sobre la vida y obras de Don Pedro Calderón de la Barca*
(Madrid: Tip. de la Revista de Archivos, Bibliotecas y Museos, 1924), p. 336, note.

268 S. E. Leavitt, "The *Quinta parte de Comedias* ascribed to Calderón de la Barca",
Hispanic Review, 40 (1972), 209–211.

269 Cruickshank, "Two editions", and Jaime Moll, "Sobre la edición atribuida a
Barcelona de la *Quinta parte de Comedias* de Calderón", *Boletín de la Real Academia
Española*, 53 (1973), 207–213.

capitalize on the success of the first edition. In seventeenth-century Spain, a *Privilegio de impresión* (approximately equivalent to a copyright), protected a book only in the kingdom for which it had been issued, not in other kingdoms, unless separate privileges had also been secured for those areas. It was easier to secure approval for a printed work than for an unedited one, and, as Moll says,

> Legalmente, una obra editada en un reino podía ser reeditada en otro. Y para el editor resultaba más barato pedir licencia para editar una obra de éxito y beneficio seguros, cuya primera edición había salido en un reino distinto del suyo... que comprar a un autor el privilegio de una obra de acogida dudosa. No se trata de ediciones piratas, sino de un escaso desarrollo de propiedad intelectual.[270]

The printer of M makes some attempt to improve on his copytext, correcting some 20 minor errors of B. He also modifies extensively the punctuation, orthography, accentuation and capitalization. At the same time, he commits a new series of errors which facilitate the identification of subsequent editions based exclusively on the Madrid *Parte*. The most notable of these errors is the omission of a line in B (corresponding to III, 385 of the text of my edition), "esse rayo sutil." Of the remaining errors, four can be found on folio 46, which reads "vagas" for "vayas" (II, 331), "me rindo" for "merezco" (II, 346), "leño" for "ceño" (II, 358), and "tu Estatua llama" for "tú esta llama" (II, 371).

8.1.3 The Vera Tassis *Sexta Parte*

After Calderón's death, Juan de Vera Tassis y Villarroel, who had been a friend of the playwright, undertook the publication of the majority of Calderón's *comedias* in nine *Partes,* beginning with the *Verdadera Quinta Parte* in 1682, working up through an eighth *Parte,* then re-editing the first four *Partes* published during Calderón's lifetime, and finally publishing a ninth *Parte* in 1691. A second edition of this nine-volume series was published between 1698 and 1730.

Vera Tassis includes *La estatua de Prometeo* not in the *Verdadera Quinta Parte,* but in his *Sexta Parte* published in 1683 ("V"). We can see that he based his text on B (perhaps with reference to M), rather than on M alone, because he restores the line "ese rayo sutil" missing in M. Furthermore, where B and M have different readings, his text follows B 40 times, and follows M only 24 times (see Table of Variants below); the

---

270 Moll, "Sobre la edición atribuida", p. 208.

variants in which he follows M are readings which Vera Tassis would quite likely have introduced without the authority of M. Although the Vera Tassis text differs in many readings from both *Parte* texts (a total of 276 variants, not including stage directions), there is no evidence that he possessed in this case another manuscript as the basis for his corrections, as he did for a number of other dramas. Although he correctly (by comparison with the Biblioteca Municipal manuscript) restores a line at the beginning of the play (I, 6) – "¡Ha del valle! ¿Quién nos busca?" – the rhyme scheme demands this line, which is virtually a formula in Calderón's works. Vera Tassis did not need any other source than his own familiarity with Calderón's style for such a reconstruction. With regard to the other 275 readings, and again using the manuscript as a base of reference, 130 or 47 % are accurate, and 53 % are either arbitrary or erroneous. This is a percentage of accuracy almost identical to that which E. W. Hesse found when he compared the Vera Tassis versions of the first four *Partes*, for which Hesse said that 52 % of the alterations were arbitrary.[271]

Vera Tassis has been much maligned as an editor precisely because of such arbitrary changes. The criticism of his editions may have been unduly harsh (particularly in regard to the lax standards of subsequent editors of Calderón), as Cruickshank points out:

> By the standards of the seventeenth century, Vera was a comparatively good and conscientious editor. He knew that he was working from very faulty texts, so it is not surprising that when he found a passage that seemed badly written, his great admiration for Calderón led him to assume that the text was corrupt rather than that the master had nodded, and he altered the passage accordingly. No doubt he also considered that his task of correction extended quite properly to words actually written by Calderón. This is extremely reprehensible by today's academic standards, but it is not unknown among friends turned editor. Hartzenbusch, with an advantage of 160 years and none of the handicaps of friendship, was no more sophisticated in his editorial technique.[272]

When an alternative line of textual authority is not available, Vera Tassis's reading must surely be considered seriously in correcting errors in the

---

271 E. W. Hesse, "The Publication of Calderón's Plays in the Seventeenth Century", *Philological Quarterly*, 27 (1948), 50.

272 Cruickshank, "Textual Criticism", p. 13.

earliest texts; he was right 40 to 50 % of the time. Nevertheless, the difficulty is that in attempting to clear up confused passages, Vera Tassis sometimes draws us away from the original text, furnishing a rational but erroneous version which impedes finding the correct reading, as for example in the *gracioso* Merlín's speech in Act III of the *La estatua de Prometeo*.

8.1.4 Other Editions

Along with the collected volumes, Calderón's plays were also published as *sueltas,* or "separate" editions, three or four gatherings in quarto, usually without date or imprint, at least in the seventeenth century.[273] A number of copies have survived of a *suelta* of *La estatua de Prometeo* bearing the number 194, which appeared in several editions, containing the same text and carrying the same number 194, but not typographically identical. Its text follows that of M. Like many other *sueltas,* it circulated not only separately, but also as part of collected volumes, in this case, the *Parte XVII* of the *Jardín ameno,* a collection of plays by various authors. Kurt and Roswitha Reichenberger have presented evidence that the number 194 derives from its inclusion in that numerical position in this series, begun in 1686.[274]

Suelta No. 194 is also included in the fake Vera Tassis *Sexta Parte.* In order to capitalize on the popularity of the genuine Vera Tassis editions of Calderón's plays, a large number of fake copies of all nine volumes were prepared, probably sometime early in the eighteenth century.[275] They were composed of *suelta* editions bound together with reprints of some of the preliminaries from the corresponding genuine Vera Tassis editions. They are easily identifiable, since the preliminaries are not complete and the pages or folios are numbered by individual plays, rather than consecutively through the volume as a whole.[276] Unfortunately, uninformed editors of Calderón on occasion continue to accept fakes as genuine editions.[277]

---

273 See E. M. Wilson and Don W. Cruickshank, *Samuel Pepy's Spanish Plays* (London: The Bibliographical Society, 1980), especially Chapter IV, "The *comedia suelta*: History of a Format".

274 The Reichenbergers kindly communicated this information to me by letters of November 4. 1983 and September 19. 1984.

275 Wilson and Cruickshank, *Samuel Pepy's Spanish Plays,* pp. 115–116.

276 For a fuller description of the differences, see Cruickshank, "Textual Criticism", pp. 16–17.

277 A recent example of this error is the edition of *Celos aun del aire matan* prepared by Matthew Stroud (San Antonio, Texas: Trinity University Press, 1981).

The Vera Tassis text, more polished and physically attractive than the original *Partes*, prevailed, and it is this basic version of the *La estatua de Prometeo* which was passed down to the present day, collecting additional layers of more or less arbitrary corrections by subsequent editors as it was handed down. Francisco Suriá and Carlos Sapera published it in Barcelona in 1765 as Number 65 in their series of numbered *suelta* editions of the 108 *comedias* from the nine *Partes*, and the same *suelta* was subsequently reedited, undated, by Francisco Suriá y Burgada.[278] It has also appeared in the collected editions published by Juan Fernández de Apontes (1762),[279] Juan Jorge Keil (1829),[280] Juan Eugenio Hartzenbusch (1856),[281] and in the most recent edition of Calderón's *comedias* by Angel Valbuena Briones (1959).[282] Although Valbuena Briones states in a footnote that his edition of the *La estatua de Prometeo* is based on B, he incorporates only stage directions from B, and follows the text inherited from Vera Tassis.

Charles Aubrun, who published *La estatua de Prometeo* with notes and an introduction in 1965,[283] also based his edition on the Vera Tassis text: "Notre édition est fondée sur B' commun a Vera Tassis, Apontes et Suriá y Burgada." He also stated that he was incorporating in his text variants taken from the version which carries "the mysterious number" 194 in a Vera Tassis *Sexta Parte* preserved in the Bibliotèque Nationale de Paris, without realizing that that *Parte* was a fake Vera Tassis. Aubrun asks whether this text might not be related to the *princeps* of 1677,[284] apparently unaware that there were two versions published in the same

---

278 Jaime Moll, "Las nueve partes de Calderón editadas en comedias sueltas (Barcelona 1763–1767)", *Boletín de la Real Academia Española*, 51 (1971), p. 287.

279 *Comedias del célebre poeta español don Pedro Calderón de la Barca*, 11 vols. (Madrid: Fernández, 1760–1763). *La estatua de Prometeo* is in Vol. VIII (1762), pp. 181–221. The volumes of the second Vera Tassis edition which, based on censorial signatures and other marks, Jaime Moll believes to have been used as copytexts for this edition, are in the Biblioteca de la Real Academia.

280 *Las comedias de D. Pedro Calderón de la Barca*, 4 vols. (Leipsique: Ernesto Fleischer, 1829). *Prometeo* is in Vol. III, pp. 321–342.

281 *Comedias de Don Pedro Calderón de la Barca*, 4 vols.: Vols. 7, 9, 12 and 14 of the *Biblioteca de Autores Españoles* (Madrid: M. Rivadeneyra). *Prometeo* is in Vol. 12 (1856), pp. 701–718.

282 *Obras completas*, 3 vols. (Madrid: Aguilar, 1952–1960). Vol. 3, containing the *autos sacramentales*, was edited by Angel Valbuena Prat. *La estatua de Prometeo* is in Vol. 1 (1959).

283 (Paris: Centre de Recherches de l'Institut d'Études Hispaniques, [1965]).

284 Aubrun Introduction to *La estatua de Prometeo*, by Pedro Calderón de la Barca, pp. x–xii.

year. Ironically, he would have been closer to the original of Calderón had he used the fake as his base, because, as we have seen, the *suelta* 194 contains the Madrid *Quinta Parte* text.

La estatua de Prometeo has also been published in translation: in French, by H. Fourtoul in 1838;[285] in German, by K. Pasch in 1887 and 1893, and in an apparently anonymous earlier translation in 1867; and in Czech, by J. Vrchlický in 1901.[286]

8.2 Manuscripts

According to the recent bibliography of Kurt and Roswitha Reichenberger, only two manuscripts of *La estatua de Prometeo* are known to exist. One is in the Biblioteca del Instituto del Teatro, in Barcelona.[287] Although the Reichenbergers follow the Simón Díaz bibliography[288] in saying that the manuscript is written in a seventeenth-century hand, on the first page of the manuscript it is stated that the play is the work of Calderón de la Barca, "arreglada nuevamente para representarse en el Teatro Cómico de Granada por D. Juan Marujan, año de 1768." The confusion may derive from the fact that the manuscript is bound with another manuscript of *La española de Florencia*, undated and in a hand that could be seventeenth century.

The other manuscript, on which my edition is based (hereinafter referred to as Ms) is Ms. 1–110–12 of the Biblioteca Municipal de Madrid. Although that library possesses numerous autograph manuscripts of Calderón's *autos sacramentales,* its collection of *comedias* contains primarily copies used by the actors in the public theatres from the eighteenth century on; some of these copies are manuscripts, but the majority are printed editions, or editions ripped out of *Partes,* with the first or last page hand-copied. It would seem most likely, then, that the manuscript of *La estatua de Prometeo* would be a late copy, taken from Vera Tassis or the *Quinta Parte.* However, even a quick examination of its text reveals that this is not the case; it is clearly closer to the *Quinta Parte* than to V, but it contains 30 lines which are not in the *Parte,* and the stage directions are much more detailed.

---

285 Aubrun Introd., *La estatua de Prometeo,* p. xi.
286 Kurt and Roswitha Reichenberger, *Bibliographisches Handbuch der Calderón-Forschung* (Kassel: Verlag Thiele & Schwarz, 1979), I. 257.
287 Pedro Calderón de la Barca, *La estatua de Prometeo,* Biblioteca del Instituto del Teatro Ms. No. CDXCVII.
288 José Simón Díaz, *Bibliografía de la Literatura Hispánica* Vol. VII (Madrid: Consejo Superior de Investigaciones Científicas, 1967).

Table 8–1: Table of Variants[289]

Number of Variants	B	M	V	Ms
290	X	X	X	Y
130	X	X	Y	Y
76[290]	X	X	Y	X
59	X	X	Y	Z
31	X	Y	X	X
19	Y	X	X	X
8	X	Y	X	Z
8	X	Y	Z	A
4	X	Y	Y	Z
3	X	Y	Z	Z
1	Z	X	Y	Z
1	Y	X	X	Y
1	X	Y	X	Y

Of these variants, 14 common to BMV were incorporated as corrections to the Ms; 5 occuring only in V were incorporated, as well as 2 from BM, 1 from BV end 1 from MV.

What, then, is the source of the manuscript? It is in rough *pasta* paper, in quarto, with 60 folios (20 in the first act, 14 in the second and 26 in the third), plus blank folios between acts, and a covering sheet. It is written in a clear hand, with minor additions by another hand or hands. The manuscript is undated, and cannot be dated by the paper, as the same watermarks appear from the second half of the seventeenth century through the mid-eighteenth century.

The only true clue which the manuscript offers us is the name "Mosquera" written on the cover sheet, below the title. The only Mosquera whose name appears in connection with the theatrical world of the epoch is Manuel de Mosquera.

---

289 Each letter indicates a reading of the text. Thus, in 59 instances, B and M have the same reading "X", V has a different reading "Y", and Ms a third reading, "Z". This tally includes only variants in the text itself, not differences in stage directions, speakers, line divisions or punctuation. Lines added or deleted are counted as one variant per line.

290 This figure does not include the division of 21 12-syllable lines into 42 6-syllable lines. See Metrical Scheme.

Partially
obscured
by binding

Figure 8-1: Manuscript Watermarks

Manuel de Mosquera was a well-known, but not first-rate, actor in the principal theatrical companies of Madrid from sometime in the 1660's at least to 1689; from 1684 to 1689, as director of his own troupe as well, he was one of the main theatre company owners to perform for the court in the Buen Retiro palace. Since he and his first actress-wife, Antonia del Pozo, were members of the principal theatrical troupes in the 1660's and 1670's, it is very possible that one or both of them might have acted in the original production of the *La estatua de Prometeo*.[291]

As *autor de comedias*, in conjunction with the company of Rosendo López, Mosquera presented *La estatua de Prometeo* in the Palace on December 22, 1685, in celebration of the birthday of the Queen Mother, Mariana.[292] There are some subsequent references to performances by Mosquera's troupe, either in public theatres or the Palace, until 1689, but after that date his name does not reappear in the theatrical records of the era. The most logical deduction would therefore seem to be that Mosquera secured the manuscript in connection with the performance of 1685, which allows us to assign it an approximate date – and in any case no later than 1689.

---

291 For a fuller account of Mosquera and his family, with citations of manuscript and
     secondary sources from which it is drawn, see my article, "Manuel de Mosquera y su
     manuscrito de *La estatua de Prometeo*", in *Actas del "Congreso Internacional sobre
     Calderón y el Teatro Español del Siglo de Oro"*, *Madrid, 1981* (Madrid: Consejo
     Superior de Investigaciones Científicas, 1983), pp. 265–276.
292 J. E. Varey and N. D. Shergold, *Teatros y comedias en Madrid. Estudios y documentos,
     1666–1687* (London: Tamesis Books Ltd., 1975), p. 188.

Figure 8-2: Ms Title Page

Since the manuscript obviously does not derive from Vera Tassis or the *Quinta Parte*, only two possibilities remain: either it is a copy, if not of the dramatist's original, at least closer to it than the *Parte* text; or it is an adaptation made for the 1685 presentation. The second possibility seems dubious. Adaptations were not careful, word-for-word revisions of the text; the process of adaptation consisted rather in cutting out whole passages of the text, adding lines or a new speech here and there to fill the resulting holes. Another Biblioteca Municipal "manuscript"[293] of *Las fortunas de Andromeda y Perseo,* which also belonged to Mosquera, follows this technique of adaptation. Some 50 passages are marked for deletion, thus cutting approximately 400 lines, and one speech and about 30 scattered lines are added to mend the gaps. Although the *La estatua de Prometeo* manuscript differs from the readings of BM in over 500 instances, the discrepancies are not of the sort characteristic of adaptations – with the one exeption of the altered division between the second and third acts, which will be discussed below.

I have not been able to identify positively the principal copyist of the manuscript, although there is some circumstancial evidence that the hand might be that of Mosquera himself. A manuscript copy of Calderón's play *Los tres mayores prodigios* in the Biblioteca Nacional[294] with approvals dated June and July, 1669, contains a number of interesting additions. The title page of the second act bears a number of notes and scribbles in various hands; one of these is the following: "Adios Senores oficios de [?]/Mosquera," written in a hand resembling that of the *La estatua de Prometeo* manuscript; another hand has written "Loescribio Anton de Utrera[?] en Madrid/Ano de mill y 69 años." Obviously, the manuscript was used for more than one performance, and Mosquera was somehow associated with one of them. On the *verso* of this same folio, a large, childish hand has written in spidery-thin letters, "yo mosquero," and another hand has written, between flourishes: "Señor Manuel de mosquera/Señor de Galicia." Furthermore, a page has been inserted in the manuscript, apparently by being glued to the previous page in the inside margin, containing a number of lines written in a hand very like that of the *La estatua de Prometeo* manuscript. It seems to be a song intended either as a replacement for a five-line one sung by Flora in the text, or as a two-stanza addition to that song. With its crossouts and

---

293 BM 83-8 – really a printed edition pulled out of the Vera Tassis *Sexta Parte*, wrapped in   a covering sheet containing a handwritten list of characters and the actors and   actresses who would portray them.
294 BN Ms. 16.641.

rewrites, the addition was obviously being composed on the spot. In the following transcription, words and lines within brackets were crossed out or otherwise marked for deletion:

[Si la pena del sentir]
      debo
[no la (puedo) Remediar]
[para q quiero – vibir]
[pues no la puedo alibiar]
[con mas cura q El morir]
La pena de mi Sentir
no la deuo Remediar
[Y asi]
[(pues) ni quiero El vibir]   q mas muerte es El vibir
[que si no la e de alibiar]   Sin q la pueda alibiar
[mas Remedio es El morir]   q no llegar a morir
no mi discurso se mida
      dolor
a Sentir [pena] tan fuerte
      [compuesta]
que cuando [El alibio] pide la vida
[sea El alibio la muerte]
me de El remedio La muerte
aun con mas Rigor q La herida

There are two other substantial sections of this manuscript in which a number of lines have been crossed out with black lines so heavy that the writing beneath is hard to read; a decision was apparently made to reinstate those lines, and they were copied in the hand like that of the *La estatua de Prometeo* manuscript.

I have also found the same hand in documents in the Archivo del Palacio in Madrid. One is a "Memoria de los particulares[295] que ha hecho La compañia de Manuel de Mosquera A su Mg^d que dios g^e desde el año de 1684."[296] The hand is a somewhat less careful version of that of the *La estatua de Prometeo* manuscript, and the name "Manuel de Mosquera" in the heading and summary of the document are very similar to the name on the coverpage of the *La estatua de Prometeo* manuscript. The handwriting in the name is also quite similar to Mosquera's signature (if

---

295 *Particulares* were private performances of a popular play staged at the Palace for members of the royal family and court.
296 Caja 11.744, Expediente 56; see Figure 8–3.

indeed he personally signed it) on a "Lista de la Compañia de Manuel de Mosquera para las Representaciones [del Auto de Corpus] del año de 1685" in the Archivo Municipal de Madrid,[297] and a similar list for 1684.[298] (The lists were written in a different hand.) On the other hand, there is also in the Archivo del Palacio a shorter list in the same hand of the *La estatua de Prometeo* manuscript of *particulares* performed by the company of Guillermo García in 1680.[299]

Based on this evidence, it would appear that if the principal hand in the *La estatua de Prometeo* manuscript is not that of Mosquera himself, then it is that of a copyist who worked closely with him on several occasions. That an *autor de comedias* would be copying plays personally might seem questionable, yet this is precisely what Lope has an *autor* do in his play *Lo fingido verdadero*. When the emperor Carino asks the *autor de comedias*, Ginés, what he has been doing, he replies, "Sacando estaba / de una comedia papeles."[300] It is also conceivable, however, that Mosquera had copied the play years previously, when he held a less exalted position in the Madrid theatrical community.

While we cannot be sure whether the copyist was Mosquera or an associate, we can tell that he was a careful copyist who reread and corrected his finished copy. We can deduce this from the variations in the color of ink used, for it is darker in the second act, while the corrections are in the lighter ink used at the beginning and at the end, which reveals that they were made in a re-reading. There is another indication that this scribe was trying to copy faithfully another manuscript which was not always easy to read. At the beginning of the third act (III, 72), when Discordia, disguised as a peasant girl, has mixed in with the populace honoring Minerba, the text in the *Parte* has her saying, "Yo también que de la *tierra* / con mi Don he descendido". [Emphasis mine.] The line is a problem, because she cannot have descended "from the earth"; it would have to be either "del cielo", which does not fit the rhyme scheme, or "a la tierra". The manuscript has instead of "tierra", "fieRa" – which makes even less sense – but the

---

297 Legajo 2-199-5. These were lists made annually of the members of the two companies officially named by the Villa de Madrid to perform the Corpus Christi *autos sacramentales*. The members of the companies were required to remain in Madrid, at a season when others went on tour, to ensure they would be available for the performances.

298 Legajo 2-199-6.

299 Caja 11.744, Expte. 63.

300 *Comedias de Vidas de Santos*, ed. Marcelino Menéndez Pelayo, Vol. IX of *Obras de Lope de Vega*, BAE, Vol. CLXXVII (Madrid: Ediciones Atlas, 1964), pp. 63b–64a.

Figure 8-3: "Memoria de los Particulares"

copyist has drawn a rectangle around the word "fieRa" and has written "sierra" beside it. His second reading is the correct one, because Discordia is disguised as a peasant girl, and therefore says that she is descending not from heaven but from the hills. A second case of "s-f" confusion occurs in Act II, 405, where the scribe has either changed the word "fiel" to "Si él" or vice-versa (the logical reading would be "si él"), and he has written an unusual "s" in line III, 1042, which may have

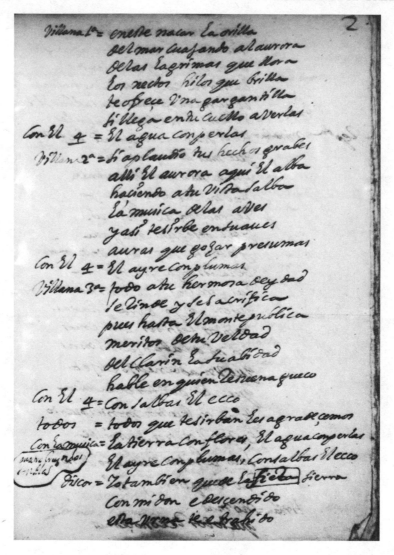

Figure 8-4: Ms Act II, Folio 2

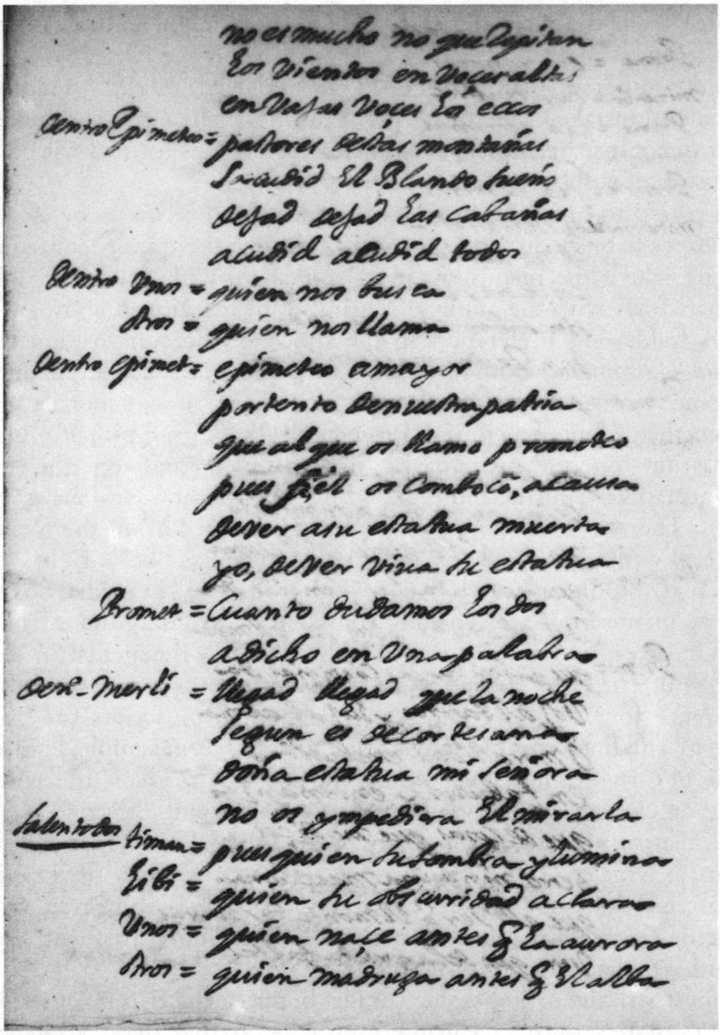
no es mucho no que dexen
los viendos en voces altas
en vestas voces los ecos
Dentro Epimeteo = pastores destas montañas
escuchad el blando sueño
dejad dejad las cabañas
acudid acudid todos
Dentro Unos = quien nos busca
Otros = quien nos llama
Dentro Epimet = epimeteo a mayor
portento de vuestra patria
que al que os llamo prometeo
pues si él os convocó, a la suya
de ver a su estatua muerta
yo, de ver viva su estatua
Promet = Cuando dudamos los dos
a dicho en una palabra
Dent. Merli = llegad llegad que la noche
segun es de cortesana
doña estatua mi señora
no os ympediera el mirarla
salen todos Timan = pues quien su sombra ylumina
Libi = quien su oscuridad aclara
Unos = quien nace antes q la aurora
Otros = quien madruga antes q el alba

Figure 8-5: Ms Act II, Folio 9v

resulted from the same difficulty. These cases might indicate that the manuscript is closer to Calderón's original than is the *Parte*, for judging from the autograph manuscript of *El gran príncipe de Fez*,[301] it would be difficult to mistake Calderón's "s" for his "t" as the *Parte* has done, but easier to confuse his initial "s", which is sometimes formed with a long downstroke, with his "f".

With regard to orthography, the manuscript also seems to be closer to Calderón's habits than are B, M and V, although there are peculiarities of spelling which the manuscript does not share with Calderón. I have compared Ms with the autograph manuscript mentioned above, which shows Calderón's preferences in the epoch of the composition of *La estatua de Prometeo*. Both manuscripts vaciliate in the use of "t" or "th" in some words. In *La estatua de Prometeo*, one generally reads "Prometheo", but sometimes "Prometeo". In *El gran príncipe*, Calderón writes on the first page "matematicos" and on the third, "mathematicos"; furthermore, he writes "Balthazar" as often as "Baltazar". The two manuscripts also omit the initial "h" in the forms of "haber," writing "e" and "as" where the *Parte* has "he" or "has".

With regard to the use of "b" or "v" rather than "u" in medial position, the two manuscripts are generally consistent in avoiding the use of "u" (with the exception of the forms of "saber"), while the medial "u" is the norm in B. The *La estatua de Prometeo* manuscript is more extreme in its preference for "b", nevertheless. While both manuscripts use "b" in "nuevo" and the forms of "mover" and "haber", for example, in Ms, the forms of "vivir" and other words appear with medial "b", whereas Calderón chooses "v" or vaciliates between "v" and "b".

A peculiarity of Calderón is the frequent use of "j" in such words as "jenio", "ymajen", or "yntelijencia". The *La estatua de Prometeo* manuscript does not follow this example. It does, however, follow Calderón in scarcity of punctuation, despite more frequent use of parentheses than the printed versions.

The most striking orthographic parallel between the two manuscripts is their absolute consistency in the use of "y" rather than "i" in initial position; the printed versions of *La estatua de Prometeo* always use "i". Since this preference for initial "y" is a generalized characteristic of manuscripts of the period, it cannot be considered significant, however. In fact, spelling evidence must be treated very carefully, in general, since printers customarily imposed their own accidentals on their copy;

---

301 BN Res. 100.

copyists also tended to impose at least some of their spelling habits as well. The manuscript of *Los tres mayores prodigios* gives us an interesting evidence of this in the case of the *La estatua de Prometeo* scribe. In the two passages that were lined out and then copied in by him, he has followed the spelling of the original lines for the most part, including maintaining the spelling with initial "v" of "vela" and "vista", despite the preference he exhibits elsewhere for "b". His own preferences have crept into a few words, however, as he changes "hoxas" to "hojas", "viendo" to "biendo", "açul" to "azul", and "se aoga" to "se ahoga". This example confirms for our scribe what Cruickshank has suggested for compositors: that the spelling of the source text will affect the habits of the compositor, and that spelling analysis can therefore be of some use in indicating the source from which the compositor was working.[302] While the orthographic similarities between the *La estatua de Prometeo* manuscript and *El gran príncipe* cannot prove that the scribe was copying from a Calderonian autograph, they do demonstrate that he was closer to it than were the printed texts.

Although the entire *La estatua de Prometeo* manuscript was copied by one scribe, other hands made scattered additions and alterations to it, mainly in connection with the stage directions. On folio 9v of the first act (line 386), a large, spidery hand has written "Builtas," and the same hand may have added the speaker "Min" in Act III, line 805. The samples are too small to allow any identification of this hand. The majority of the changes, however, were made in a hand that is almost certainly that of Juan Francisco Sáez de Tejera.[303]

Sáez de Tejera – or as he was more commonly listed, Juan Francisco Tejera – was a scribe/prompter associated with the theatrical world from at least 1672 to 1695. In 1672, in Murcia, he made a copy pf Calderón's play *Afectos de odio y amor*[304] which he signed and dated on the title pages of the second and third acts. The same year, in Valencia, he copied and signed Calderón's *Apolo y Climene*.[305] Thereafter, we find him working in Madrid. He was paid for copying out the "Fiesta de Siquis y Cupido," (Calderón's *Ni amor se libra de amor*) in 1679,[306] and in 1680 for *Hado y divisa de Leonido y Marfisa* and for *Entre bobos anda el*

302 D. W. Cruickshank, "Some uses of paleographic and orthographical evidence in *comedia* editing", *Bulletin of the Comediantes*, 24 (1972), pp. 40–45.
303 I owe this identification to an inspired intuition of Louise Stein.
304 BN Ms. 16.835.
305 BN Ms. 16.883.
306 Archivo de Palacio, Caja 11.744.

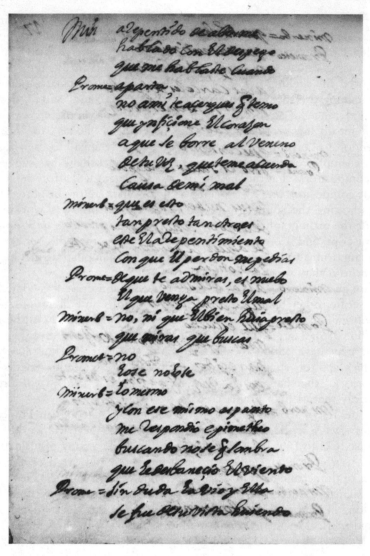

Figure 8-6: Ms Act III, Folio 17v

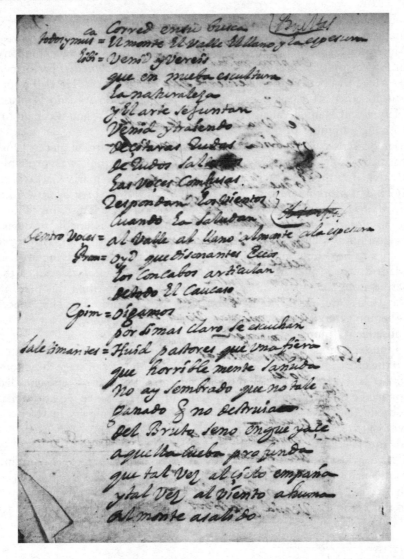

Figure 8-7: Ms Act I, Folio 9v

juego and *El celoso extremeño*, as well as six *entremeses*.[307] He was included in the Corpus list for 1684 as the *apuntador* in the company of Mosquera[308] and was apparently associated with the Mosquera company in 1685 as well, as there is a list in his hand of seven *comedias* performed by Mosquera between January and March of that year.[309] He also wrote out documents for other companies (including Simón Aguado, Agustín Manuel and Manuel Vallejo) in the 1680's and 1690's,[310] and was paid for copying a number of plays.

Sáez de Tejera also composed at least two minor theatrical pieces. One, entitled *Sarao de la minué franzés*, a two-folio *sarao*, was probably written after the arrival of María Luisa de Bourbon to marry Carlos II in 1679. The more interesting piece is a five-folio *Mojiganga de las Cassas de Madrid*.[311] In this piece, the first character on stage is a scribe, talking to an *alcalde* who is threatening suicide because he is unable to devise "algun donoso chiste" for the Corpus Christi festivities. An astrologer comes to help him, and with his magic takes the *alcalde* flying around Madrid. To be prepared for sudden inspiration, the *alcalde* takes the scribe along "en ancas". Sáez de Tejera must have written this piece in the 1670's, during Carlos II's youth, as it is dedicated to the "clabel soberano/pimpollo oloroso del arbol de Austria," and there were no subsequent "pimpollos" of that family tree.

In the *La estatua de Prometeo* manuscript, Sáez de Tejera wrote the title on the title pages of Acts I and II, and added a number of stage directions in Act III.[312] He also added in the left margin a number of verses needed to change the division between Act II and Act III. Since we know that Sáez de Tejera was associated with the Mosquera company in 1684–85, we can reasonably conclude that this manuscript was used for Mosquera's presentation of the play in 1685.

That conclusion, if valid, provides some insight into the proper handling of the major editorial problem in this play – the altered division between the second and third acts. As the play was first copied, and is presented in this edition, the second act ends two-thirds of the way through what

---

307 "Noticias inéditas de algunas representaciones palaciegas de las comedias de Calderón y otros", *Revista Española de Literatura, Historia y Arte*, 1 (1901), pp. 247, 374.
308 Archivo Municipal Leg. 2-199-6; he may have held the same position in 1685 and 1686, as the lists of Mosquera's company for those years do not name an *apuntador*.
309 Archivo de Palacio, Caja 11.744, Expte. 56.
310 See Archivo de Palacio Caja 11.744, Expedientes 32 and 63.
311 BN Ms. 16.700; see Figure 8–8.
312 See Manuscript Notes for Act III, lines 30, 69, 207, 306, 308, 471 and 886.

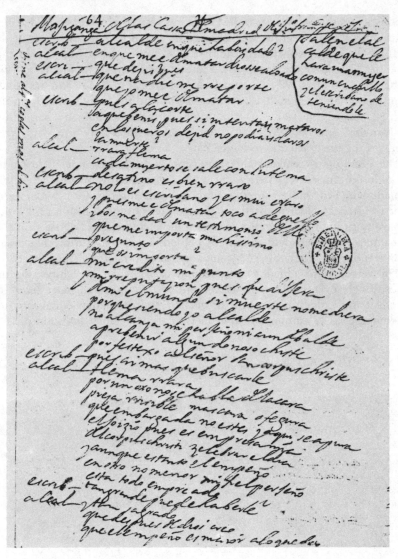

Figure 8-8: Sáez de Tejera *Mojiganga*, Folio 1

constitutes the second act in BMV. The manuscript then begins its third act with a new sheet, as was Calderón's practice. The last third of the BMV second act constitutes the first 298 lines of Act III in Ms. At that point, Sáez de Tejera has drawn a line in the left margin as if to box off for omission lines 299–305, which do not appear in BMV, and has added in the margin the nine lines which in BMV end the second and begin the third act. In the right margin, by lines 306 and 308, he has added "Jornada" and "3a Xda/zielos ette" to indicate where and with what verses the third act was to begin.[313]

The question is whether this alteration reflects a change of heart by Calderón himself, carried down to this scribal copy or whether it was made with – or more probably without – his authorization by an *autor de comedias*. Calderón often did change the endings of his plays,[314] but I have not found any instance in which he altered the act division in this manner. As the acts were originally copied in this manuscript, they are of uneven length, containing 916, 636, and 1238 verses, respectively. If the 298 verses were added to the second rather than the third act, the resultingly even count of 916, 934 and 940 would seem more likely to reflect the Calderonian norm of acts of approximately equal lengths. Nevertheless, a number of other factors argue against this solution.

---

313 See photocopy of Act III, folio 7, in Figure 8–9.
314 See my article "Calderón, Copyists and the Problem of Endings", *Bulletin of the Comediantes* 35 (1984), 71–81.

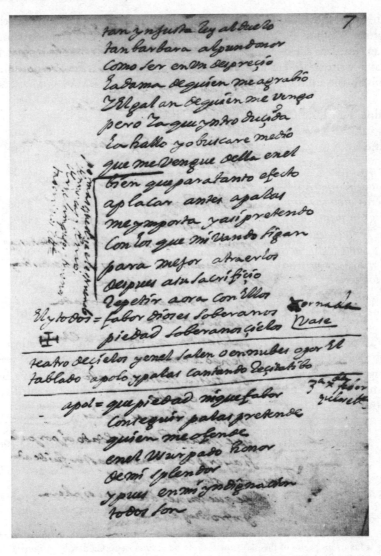

Figure 8-9: Ms Act III, Folio 7

However the acts are divided, the total line count of the manuscript (which contains 30 lines missing in BMV) is only 2790, much shorter than any late Calderonian play edited from an autograph manuscript. Plays written in 1650 or later for which we have such manuscripts contain the following numbers of lines:

Table 8–2: Late Calderonian Play Lengths

Title	Act I	Act II	Act III	Total
Basta callar[315]	1317	1336	1254	3907
Cada uno para sí[316]	1332	1264	1200	3796
Fieras afemina amor[317]	1022	1116	1226	3364
El gran príncipe de Fez	1253	1392	1400[318]	4045
En la vida todo es verdad y todo mentira[319]	1318	1315	1208	3841
El mayor monstruo los celos[320]	1208	1219	1205	3632
El postrer duelo de España[321]	1007	1286	1324	3617

In all probability, La estatua de Prometeo, in BMV and Ms, reflects an abbreviated version of an original that was closer to 3,400 to 3,800 verses long. As Ms was first copied, its first act would appear to have been somewhat shortened, and the second drastically cut, while the third act is about the normal length.

315 Figures based on adding to the Hartzenbusch edition the lines supplied by S. N. Treviño, ["Versos desconocidos de una comedia de Calderón, *PMLA* 52 (1937), 682–704] as belonging to the full early version of the play; not included are the 27 lines about the recapture of Barcelona by don Juan José de Austria, added in a later revision.

316 D. W. Cruickshank kindly supplied me with these figures from the just-published edition by J. M. Ruano de la Haza (Kassel: Edition Reichenberger, 1982), as well as the figures for *Fieras afemina amor*.

317 Although we do not have an autograph manuscript for this play, the edition, based on a luxurious *suelta* of the play, must surely be very close to Calderón's original. See E. M. Wilson, "The first edition of Calderón's *Fieras afemina amor*", in Wilson and Cruickshank, *Textual Criticism*, pp. 183–200.

318 A rough count taken from a microfilm copy of the manuscript in the Biblioteca Nacional. The third act count would vary, depending upon the inclusion of lines from two ending variants.

319 Ed. by D. W. Cruickshank (London: Tamesis Books Ltd., 1971).

320 Ed. by Everett W. Hesse (Madison: The University of Wisconsin Press, 1955).

321 Ed. by Guy Rossetti (London: Tamesis Books Ltd., 1977).

The list of "Personas" in the play provides further evidence that shortening has occurred. BMV include "Soldados" in their lists, although there is no part for soldiers in the play; Ms also has "Soldados" entered, but then crossed out of its list. Since these unnecessary soldiers persist in two separate lines of transmission, it seems probable that a part for them was deleted at some point, but the deletion not carried through to the list of characters.

It is possible that certain musical parts have also been deleted. In act I, 473, the scribe wrote an echo by "Música" of Minerba's line "No/las dispares" and then deleted the echo (see Manuscript Notes), probably as he copied, because the syllable count for the line would be wrong if they were included. Perhaps the passage was not clearly marked for deletion in his copytext, and he entered the half-line, and then realized it was to be omitted. There is no other mention of "Música" in that scene.

There are lingering clues of a possible deletion in Act II, line 499, where another line is needed to complete a section of *romance* in a-a or begin the following section in e-o. One could reasonably guess that a section in some other kind of verse was deleted here, along with, inadvertently, one line of *romance*; Calderón does sometimes link two sections of *romance* in different assonance, but he is more likely to have an alternate verse form between them.

Even disallowing all this evidence of shortening, it is difficult to imagine why an *autor de comedias*, (or Calderón), if he had a play with three even acts, would want to change to an uneven division. A much more plausible scenario would be that some *autor* cut the original by about one-fourth, deleting the greatest number of lines from the second act (perhaps nearly half the act, since most acts of late plays contain at least 1200 verses), and that he or a subsequent *autor* then realized how unbalanced the acts were, and altered the division between the second and third acts. Since the Mosquera manuscript reflects the two states, one could then surmise that the scribe was working from a manuscript on which the deletions were marked, before the act division was changed; if the BMV act division had been indicated on his copytext, he would almost surely have noted it in his own hand, but the alteration in Ms was not done by the original scribe, but by Sáez de Tejera.

If one grants that the first state of Ms reflects Calderón's original act division,[322] then the metrical scheme gives additional evidence that Act II

---

322 If one does *not* grant this, then the metrical argument becomes a case of circular reasoning, because Calderón did write a number of acts with 600 or more verses in undivided *romance*: e.g., *Darlo todo y no dar nada*, with over 800 verses in the third act, or *En la vida*, with 848 verses opening the first act.

has been shortened. With the exception of a three-line song and a two-line refrain, the entire act is in *romance*. No other three-act Calderonian play has any act entirely in *romance*. Probably one or more scenes, more reflective and decorative, in another verse form, have been cut, leaving only the *romance* sections necessary to the advancement of the action.

Given the above evidence, I believe the most plausible sequence of events is the following:

1) That for the 1685 performance Mosquera, aware of the deficiency of the *Parte* texts, either made (or had his associated scribe make) a copy either of Calderón's original marked for shortening or, more probably, of a manuscript copy of that original similarly marked. As noted above, it is also possible that the manuscript was made considerably earlier; and

2) That he had Sáez de Tejera copy from either B, M, or V the changes necessary to even out the acts. According to Cruickshank, there is evidence from other manuscripts that *autores* sometimes turned to printed texts to correct problems in a manuscript.[323]

---

323 I thank him for this suggestion, contained in a letter of 3 September 1982.

Assuming this to be the case, the stemma for the text would be as follows, with X being a manuscript or manuscripts between Calderón's original and the Mosquera manuscript, and Y being one, or probably several manuscript states between the original and B:

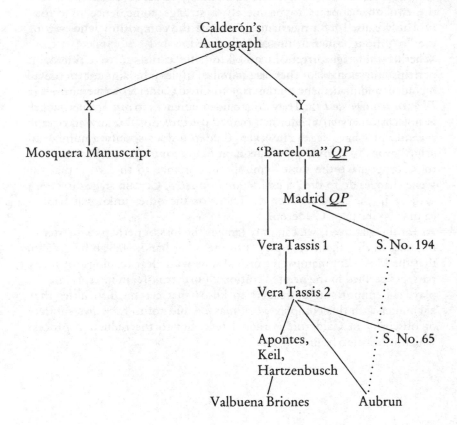

Figure 8-10: Transmission of the Text – Stemma

(Corrections incorporated from a source other than the basic copytext are indicated by a dotted line.)

One small and puzzling variant might possibly cloud this scheme. In Ms an ink blot in Act III folio 26 has seeped through the page and blotted out the "so" of "dichoso" in line 1217, so that on microfilm the word appears to have been corrected to "dicho", which makes no sense. A close examination of the manuscript itself reveals that the deletion was accidental. Strangely, B also reads "dicho". Since the great disparity in texts between B and Ms seems to rule out any direct connection between the two, this appears to be merely a strange coincidence of errors, probably caused by a mechanical error of the compositor who, setting the "o", thought he had finished the word.

Whether the stage directions of Ms can be attributed to Calderón is perhaps questionable. They are similar in length, amount of detail included, and placement on the page to those Calderón wrote himself in *El gran príncipe de Fez*. They do include references to *mutaciones*, which is not customary in Calderón's own stage directions in any autograph manuscript I have seen. However, Calderón does specify a number of stage "props" – books, a globe, etc., in *El gran príncipe*, perhaps because these props have the same symbolic importance to the work that the scene changes do to the *La estatua de Prometeo*. Certain stage directions – those in the hand of Sáez de Tejera or the other unknown hand – cannot be those of Calderón.

As for the text itself, we can only lament the loss of perhaps a quarter of the lines in this significant play. On the other hand, we can be grateful that the Mosquera manuscript provides us with clear readings for many passages garbled in the printed editions. Furthermore, in interpreting the play, it is important for readers to know that certain difficulties they encounter with this complex work may be due not to excessive subtlety or obscurity in Calderón's original text, but to the reduction process which it has clearly undergone.

8.3 Bibliographic Descriptions[324]

1. "Barcelona" *Quinta Parte*

I have examined two copies of this edition, the facsimile edition taken from the copy in the Library of Wadham College, Oxford, and the Biblioteca del Instituto del Teatro copy in Barcelona.

[Title Page]: [In black and red, within a triple frame of black and red type-ornaments: inner and outer frames of black conventional foliage; center frame of red fleur-de-lis.] QVINTA PARTE / DE / COMEDIAS / DE D. PEDRO CALDERON DE / la Barca, Cavallero de la Orden de Santiago. / [Woodcut ornament 87 × 69 mm; ornamented medallion of falcon on fist, and lion, with motto POST TENEBRAS SPERO LVCEM] / CON LICENCIA / [single rule in 10 divisions] / En Barcelona, Por Antonio la Cavalleria, / Año de 1677.

Title-page verso blank.

¶2r: *APROBACION DEL R^{MO}. P. M. Fr. IAYME* [Swash R's, second A swash] / *Castellar del Orden de N. Señora de la Merced, Redemp- / cion de Cautiuos, Calificador del Santo Oficio.* / POr comission del Ilustrissimo señor Don Luis de Iosa, [P three lines high] / . . . 10 de Iulio de 1676. / *Fr. Iayme Castellar.* / Die 15 Iulij 1676. / Imprimatur, / DeIosa, Vic. Gen & Offie. / [line of type-ornaments] / TASSA. / TAssaron los Señores del Consejo este libro, [T two lines high] / *Quinta parte de Calderon*, a seis marauedis ca-/ da pliego, como consta de su Original. Madrid, y / Março 18. de 1677.

Collation: 4°. ¶², A–D⁸, E⁴, F–Z⁸, Aa–Ff⁸ [¶2 signed; $1–4 signed (–E3, 4, T1, Bb1; Q1,2 missigned P,P2; R4 missigned Q4 in facsimile copy. In Instituto del Teatro copy, Bb1 is signed, and only Q2 and R4 are missigned; S3 is signed with an inverted 3.)]

Foliation: [i–ii], 1–14, 51, 16–49, 48, 51–76, 80, 78–116, [117], 118, [118 bis], 119–121, 123–143, [144], 145 [146], 147–149, 14[?], 14[?],

---

324 For an explanation of symbols used in description, see Philip Gaskell, *A New Introduction to Bibliography* (New York: Oxford University Press, 1972), pp. 321–335. This is a condensed presentation of the standards set in Fredson Bowers' *Principles of Bibliographic Description*. I have deviated from these conventions only in using the / to indicate line endings.

152–153, 145, 155, 143, 157–167, 169–171, 171[bis]–197, 189, 199–212, 21[3?7?], 220, 219, 220–232.

[Running Titles]:   [Title of individual play] / *De Don Pedro Calderon de la Barca*. No running titles on preliminaries. Numerous exceptions, as follows: LOA.: A1v, A2v, A3v, A4, A4v, A5; LOA: A2, A3; [Head titles of plays]: A1, F1, H5, L3, [Q1], Dd4; *DE IVAN RANA.*: B7–B8; *De D. Pedro Calderon de la Barca.*: A6–B6, C1–E4 [C3: "De" missing in Instituto de Teatro copy; below line of type in facsimile); *De Don Pedro Calderon*. I4, [Q2]–Q4, Q6, Q8, R2–[R4], R6–S8, T2; *De Don Pedro Calderon de la Barca.*: I5, K1, K4, L8, M3, N6; De *Don Pedro Calderon de la Barca.*: N7, O2, P5; *De Don Pedron Calderon.*: Q5, Q7, R1, R5; *De Don Pedro Calderon*: T1, V2, V6; *De Don Pedro Calderon,*: Y1]

[¶2v]: TITVLOS DE LAS COME-/dias que tiene este libro, quinta / parte de D. Pedro Calderon / de la Barca. / [*La estatua de Prometeo* is second].

2. Madrid *Quinta Parte*

I have examined two copies of this edition: the facsimile based on the copy in the Biblioteca Apostolica Vaticana, and the Instituto del Teatro copy.

[Title Page]: [In frame of conventional foliage type-ornaments]: QVINTA PARTE / DE / COMEDIAS / DE D. PEDRO CALDERON / DE LA BARCA, CAVALLERO DE / LA ORDEN DE SANTIAGO. / AL EXCELENTISSIMO / Señor D. Iñigo Melchor Fernandez de Valasco y / Tovar, Condestable de Castilla, y de Leon, Camarero Mayor del / Rey N. Señor, su Mayordomo Mayor, su Copero Mayor, su Ca- / çador Mayor, de sus Consejos de Estado, y Guerra, Duque de la / Ciudad de Frias, Marques de Verlanga, Conde de Haro, Conde / de Castilnovo, Señor de las Casas de Velasco, de la de Tovar, y / de la de los siete Infantes de Lara, de las Ciudades de Osma, y / Arnedo, Villas de Villalpando, Pedraça de la Sierra, Villalva del / Alcor, y San Vicente de la Sonsierra, Comendador de la / Encomienda de Vsagre, de la Orden, y Cavalleria / de Santiago, y Treze de ella, &c. / *FVE GOVERNADOR, Y CAPITAN GENERAL DEL / Estado de Milan, General de la Cavalleria de Cataluña, Go- / vernador, y Capitan General del Reyno de Galicia, Governador, / y Capitan General de los Paises Bajos de Flandes, / y Governador de los*

Reynos de Castilla. / CON LICENCIA. / [single rule] / EN MADRID: Por Antonio Francisco de Zafra, *Y à su costa.* / Vendese en su casa en la Calle de los Negros. Año 1677.

Collation: 4º. [¶²], ¶⁴, A–D⁸, E⁴, F–Z⁸, Aa–Ff⁸ [¶2 unsigned; ¶bis 1,2 signed; $1–4 signed (–E3,4; Aa2 missigned Aa in facsimile; Instituto del Teatro copy missing folios K3–K6.)]

Foliation: [i–vi], 1–17, 16, 19–34, 55, 36–44, 54, 46–86, [87], 88–133, 136, 135–145, 164, 147–215, 226, 217, [218], 219–228 [3 of 63 did not print, and 178 is illegible, in facsimile copy; 218 is not visible in that copy, but 2 and faint 8 did print in Instituto del Teatro copy; Instituto del Teatro missing folios 71–74.]

[Running Titles]: [Title of individual play] / *De D. Pedro Calderon de la Barca.* [No running titles on preliminaries; Variations as follows: *LOA.*: A1v–A5; *DE IVAN RANA.*: B7–B8; [Comedia Head Title]: A1, F1, H5, L3, Q1, Dd4; *De D. Pedro Calderon.*: S7, T8; *De Don Pedro Calderon de la Barca.*: R2, S1, S8, T2, T5, V1, V4, X2, Y1, Y6, Z5, Z7, Aa5, Aa7, Bb2, Bb4, Bb8, Cc2; *De Don Pedro Calderon de la Barca*: Dd3, Ff8; / *La Critica del Amor.*: M3P.]

Title-page verso blank.

[¶2]: *SVMA DE LA LICENCIA.* / TIene licencia de los Señores del Consejo Real de su Magestad [T two lines high] / . . . Madrid 10 de Abril de 1677. / à que me remito. / *Diego de Vrueña* / *Navamuel.* / [line of ornamental foliage type-ornaments] / *FEE DE ERRATAS.* / PAg. 19. b . . . [P two lines high] / Madrid, y Iulio 27. de 1677. / *Licenciado D. Francisco* / *Forero de Torres.* / [line of ornamental foliage type-ornaments] / *SVMA DE LA TASSA.* / TAssaron los Señores del Consejo de su Magestad este libro intitu- [T two lines high] / lado *Quinta parte de Comedias de D. Pedro Calderon,* à seis marave-/dis cada pliego, como consta de su Original. Madrid, y Iulio 30. / de 1677.

[¶2v]: TITVLOS DE LAS COME- / dias que tiene este libro, quinta parte / de Don Pedro Calderon de la / Barca. / [*La estatua de Prometeo* is second].

¶[bis]–[¶4r]: AL EXCELENTISSIMO / SEÑOR DON IÑIGO MELCHOR FER-/nandez de Velasco y Tovar, . . . / Criado de V. Exc. que S.M.B. /*Antonio Francisco de Zafra.*

[¶4v]: blank.

3. Vera Tassis *Sexta Parte* – First Edition

I have examined two copies of this edition: the facsimile prepared from a copy in the University Library, Cambridge (pressmark Hisp.5.68.6) with additions from another copy in the same library, and the copy in the Rare Books Collections of the University of California at Los Angeles.

[Title Page]: SEXTA PARTE / DE COMEDIAS / DEL CELEBRE POETA / ESPAÑOL [N in smaller cap] / DON PEDRO CALDERON / DE LA BARCA, / CAVALLERO DEL ORDEN DE SANTIAGO, / Capellan de Honor de su Magestad, y de los señores Reyes / Nueuos de la Santa Iglesia de Toledo, [. in facsimile] / SACADAS DE SVS ORIGINALES / QVE PVBLICA LA AMISTAD / DE / DON IVAN DE VERA TASSIS / Y VILLA-RROEL, / *DEBAXO DE LA PROTECCION* [swash A's] / *DEL EXCELENTISSIMO SEÑOR* [swash R] / *Don Francisco Antonio Casimiro Alfonso Pimentel de* / *Herrera Ponce de Leon Velasco Quiñones y Benauides,* / *Conde-Duque de Benauente, Conde de Luna,* / *Marquès de Xaualquinto,* / *y Villa-Real, &c.* / CON PRIVILEGIO, / [Line of type ornaments] / EN MADRID: Por *Francisco Sanz,* Impressor del Reyno, / y Portero de Camara de su Magestad. Año de 1683. [final, en facsimile]

Collation: ¶⁴, ¶ ¶ –¶ ¶ ¶ ¶⁸, ¶ ¶ ¶ ¶ ¶⁶, A–Z⁸, Aa–Nn⁸, Oo⁴; [Copper plate portrait of Calderón bound in UCLA copy facing title page, so that the order is: ¶1v, plate; ¶2r, title page; ¶2v blank; ¶3r– ¶4v – as described below for pages makes ¶2–(¶3); Facsimile copy has plate bound as (¶4v), with (¶3v– ¶4r) blank.] ¶2 signed, ¶ ¶ – ¶ ¶ ¶ ¶1–4 signed, ¶ ¶ ¶ ¶ ¶1,2,3, signed, $1–4 signed (¶ ¶ ¶ ¶ ¶3 signed like reversed D's; Gg3 missigned Gg2).

Pagination: (i–lxviii), 1–48, 46, 59–152, 154, 154bis–164, 195, 166–174, 145, 176–180, 161, 182–184, 189, 186–187, 192, 189–194, 203, 200, 197–236, 273, 238–311, 362, 313–320, 329, 322–387, 396, 389–390, 393, 384, 393–410, 399, 412, 414, 414bis–417, 408, 419–429, 422, 431–433, 438–439, 436–446, 443, 448–521, 520bis–521bis, 524–555, 524, 557–561, 592, 563–579, [580–584] (Facsimile copy: 105 marked 123, 330 marked 230, 496 marked 469; UCLA copy: only part of 5 printed.)

[Running Titles]:   [Title of individual play] / *De Don Pedro Calderon de la Barca.* [No running title on preliminaries or (580–584); exceptions as follows: [Comedia Head Title]: 1, 91, 137, 179, 269,

533; *De D. Pedro Calderon de la Barca.*: 67, 85, 93, 107, 111, 121, 125, 139, 143, 159, 163, 171, 183, 195 [marked 203], 203, 219, 223, 225, 233, 241, 257, 263, 275, 297, 307, 315, 323, 327, 341, 351, 353, 361, 385, 389, 397, 415, 425, 427, 431, 433, 457, 461, 475, 479, 487, 495, 503, 511, 515, 519, 537, 543, 555, 559, 569, 577; *De D. Pedro Calderon de la Barca,*: 105 [marked 123], 113, 123, 149, 161, 167, 187, 199, 205, 215, 227, 231, 245, 259, 287, 311, 319, 331, 335, 339, 345, 355, 373, 381, 397, 407, 419–423, 445, 449, 453, 467, 471, 483, 491, 499, 507, 521bis, 527, 535, 541, 557, 561, 579; *De Don Pedro Calderon de la Barca,*: 333]

[¶1v]:   blank.

¶2r–[¶3r]:   AL EX^{MO}. Señor / DON FRANCISCO / ANTONIO CASIMIRO ALFONSO / . . . / Su mas obligado seruidor. / *Don Iuan de Vera Tassis / y Villarroel.*

[¶3v– ¶4r]:   blank [in facsimile copy].

[¶4v]:   Copper plate, portrait of Calderon, framed by angel and cherubim, the latter holding a banner: D. PETRVS CALDERON / DE LABARCA. / AEtat suae 81. / [With motto below] Sapientia hominis lucet in Vultu eius, / et potentissimus faciem illius commutabit / *Ecclesi. Cap. 8. V. 1. / G.º Fosman f. Matriti. 1682.*

¶ ¶ –¶ ¶ ¶ ¶8]:   *APROBACION DEL R^{MO.} / Padre Maestro Fray Manuel de Guerra, / y Ribera,* . . . / Madrid, 14, de Abril de 1682. / *Fr. Manuel de Guerra / y Ribera.*

¶ ¶ ¶ ¶ ¶ :   LICENCIA DEL ORDINARIO. / NOS El Doctor Don Antonio Pasqual, [N two lines high] / Arcediano de las Seluas, . . . *Doct. D. Antonio Pasqual.* / Por su mandado, / *Iuan Aluarez de Llamas,* Notario.

¶ ¶ ¶ ¶ ¶v: *APROBACION DE DON IVAN / Baños de Velasco y Acebedo, Chronista General* / . . . Madrid, y Mayo 6. de 1682. / *Don Iuan Baños de Velasco / y Acebedo.*

¶ ¶ ¶ ¶ ¶2:   *SVMA DEL PRIVILEGIO.* / TIene Priuilegio Don Iuan de Vera [T two lines high] / Tassis y Villarroel, . . . en Madrid à veinte y cinco / de Mayo de mil seiscientos y ochenta y dos / años.

[¶ ¶ ¶ ¶ ¶2v]:   FEE DE ERRATAS. / . . . *Don Francisco Murcia / de la Llana,* / Corrector general por su Mag.

¶ ¶ ¶ ¶ ¶3r–[¶ ¶ ¶ ¶ ¶4v]:   *EN OCASION DE SACAR A LVZ / Don Iuan de Vera Tassis y Villarroel las Obras* / . . . oy Martes 16. de Febrero de 1683. / B.L.M. de Vmd. / Su mas seguro, y fino seruidor. / *Don Marcos de la Nuza* [swash Z] / *Mendoza y Arellano.* [swash Z]

[¶ ¶ ¶ ¶ ¶5]:   SVMA DE LA TASSA. / . . . En Madrid à / veinte y

siete de Febrero, de mil seis- / sientos y ochenta y tres años.
[¶ ¶ ¶ ¶ ¶5v– ¶ ¶ ¶ ¶ ¶6r]:   A LOS DISCRETOS. / . . . VALE.
[¶ ¶ ¶ ¶ ¶6v]:   TABLA DE LAS COMEDIAS / Que contiene esta
Sexta / Parte. / [*La estatua de Prometeo* is fifth.]
[580–4]:   COMEDIAS   *COMEDIAS*
                 Verdadera de D. Pedro   *Supuestas, que andan debaxo*
                        Calderon.   *de su nombre.*
[In two columns, with divided rule separating them]

9 Editorial Policy

We know that Calderón vigorously denounced many of the editions of
his work printed in his lifetime. Our goal in this edition is to produce a
text such as Calderón would have wished to see reach his reading public.
Substantives, therefore, should be as nearly as possible identical to his
hypothetical final draft or fair copy of the text as intended for its
performance.[325] Since the Biblioteca Municipal manuscript is clearly
closer to that stage of the text than any other edition, I have chosen it as
my copy text and have followed its readings in all cases except those
which are demonstrably due to scribal error. Emendations introduced to
correct such errors are enclosed in square brackets, and the original
manuscript version is included in Manuscript Notes.
I have also resolved a number of abbreviations, enclosing the added
letters in square brackets. No mention is made of such resolution of the
standard abbreviation "q" for "que", but the original manuscript
abbreviation of other words, both in the text and stage directions, is
given in Manuscript Notes. The scribe was inconsistent in his abbreviation of speakers' names, and these have been written out in full, without
brackets or other notations.
Variant readings from the first three printed editions are listed in
footnotes. Chronologically, these are the only editions that could
conceivably be linked to the transmission of the play from the time of its
composition in the early 1670's to its usage by Mosquera in the mid-

---

325 This ignores the complicating and very real possibility of revision during rehearsal or
for subsequent performances, with varying degrees of authorial involvement in the
revision. The aesthetic problems involved have been thoughtfully treated by James
Thorpe in "The Aesthetics of Textual Criticism", *PMLA* 80 (1965) 465–482, and are
pertinent to the question of the division between the second and third acts of this
play. See my article "Calderón, Copyists and the Problem of Endings", *Bulletin of
the Comediantes* 35 (1984) 71–81.

1680's. They are: the "Barcelona" *Quinta Parte* of 1677 (B), the Madrid *Quinta Parte* also of 1677 (M), and the first edition of the Vera Tassis *Sexta Parte* of 1683 (V). Any variation in a word which could cause a different pronunciation has been considered a variant, as for example "escuras" and "obscuras", and any difference in the number of words, even if it does not change the pronunciation, as in the case of "desso" and "de eso". Other spelling differences which would not affect pronunciation have not been listed as variants.

The proper procedure with regard to accidentals poses a number of problems for the editor, since it was the standard practice of seventeenth century printers to impose their own accidentals on manuscripts. Calderón's own punctuation was very scant, beyond his fairly heavy use of parentheses, and he would have expected printers to add punctuation needed by a reading public. The punctuation of the *Prometeo* manuscript is similarly scant, with a parallel reliance on parentheses, and what punctuation does exist is quite often misleading, by present-day standards. The punctuation of B, M and V would also confuse a modern reader in some cases, particularly in the use of semicolons. I have therefore added punctuation, following that of the manuscript whenever possible, and noting any changes to the manuscript punctuation in Manuscript Notes. Any significant divergences in the resulting text and that of the early printed versions are listed as variant footnotes.

Capitalization and accentuation have also been modernized, without notation, except when the manuscript has accents which have been deleted. These are listed in Manuscript Notes. (When the scribe did add accents, he wrote a tilde where modern practice calls for an accent, and vice-versa.)

The old spelling of the manuscript has, however, been maintained, with its considerable inconsistencies in spelling habits. Not only does this help to preserve the flavor of the original text, but it also makes possible the discovery of alternative readings which might not be visible in an modern spelling text. The only related alteration necessary has been that of word division, since the scribe writes a number of words without a pen lift. When a variant form is incorporated in the text or a stage direction, I have followed the spelling of the earliest edition in which it appears. Similarly, variants listed in footnotes are given in their earliest printed form, without notation of changes in spelling and punctuation in later editions. When I have added stage directions, or words to the text, as for example line repetitions omitted with an Ettc., I have followed the spelling practice of the scribe. In writing out the speakers' names, Minerva has been spelled with a "b", because the scribe is consistent throughout in that spelling, but Prometeo has been spelled without the "h", since the scribe vacillates in its use.

Lines have been numbered and lineated, with divergences of lineation noted as footnotes only where they might affect the line count.

The location of stage directions has been altered, since all but the longest stage directions are given in the right (and occasionally left) margins of the manuscript, often extending over a number of lines. When a change has been made, the original location is noted in Manuscript Notes, and variant locations in B, M and V are given in footnotes. In the case of suppression of redundant stage directions such as "sale" or "canta" by the speaker in the left margin, the original form is also given in Manuscript Notes.

Other silent editorial changes include rendering both the tall and short "s" as short "s", printing all accents as acute, rather than the accent grave preferred in B, M and V, and translating the occasional internal "R" of the manuscript as "rr".

10 METRICAL SCHEME

Act I

Lines 1–30	*Romance* u-a
31–32	*Estribillo*
33–36	*Romance* u-a
37	*Estribillo*
38–45	*Romance* u-a
46	*Estribillo*
47–380	*Romance* u-a
381–398	Song, hexasyllabic lines with intercalated *estribillo*, lines 387 and 398.
399–432	*Romance* u-a
433	*Estribillo*
434–467	*Romance* u-a
468–499	*Redondillas abrazadas*, abba.
500–529	*Estancias*. Heptasyllabic and hendecasyllabic lines, abbaA.
530–557	*Redondillas abrazadas*, abba.
558–577	*Estancias* with *quintilla*-type stanza, rhyming abbaA, last abbAA.

578–632	*Silvas pareadas* with varying arrangements of seven- and eleven-syllable verses.
617	Extra verse apparently added on, throwing off the rhyme scheme from aabb to ababb.
633–644	*Romance* e-a
645–709	Song; Six lines of *romance* e-a, followed by 2 lines of 12 syllables. See explanation below.
710–815	*Romance* e-a
816–820	Song; *Quintilla* rhyming aabba
821–828	Six lines of *romance* e-a, followed by 2 12-syllable lines, as 645–709.
829–854	*Romance* e-a
855–862	As 645–709
863–874	*Romance* e-a
875–876	Two 12-syllable lineas in 645–709.
877–886	Song; *quintilla* of lincs 815–819; each line repeated.
887–916	Gloss on preceding song: *décimas* with last two lines repeating those of *quintilla*.

Act II

1–280	*Romance* a-a
281–293	*Romance* a-a, with repeated verses.
294–499	*Romance* a-a
499–630	*Romance* e-o; Line 499 is needed both to properly complete the section of a-a *romance*, and to begin the e-o section. (See Notes and Manuscript Notes.) Sung by Palas and Discordia. Intercalated *estribillo*, 619–620.
633–636	Song

Act III

1–6	Song; 10- to 12-syllable lines rhyming in e-o.
7–13	*Romance* in e-o. Line 13 has 3 extra syllables. Vera Tassis has therefore shortened the following line and added the second "Pandorga" ("Pandorra" in his edition) to it.
31–36	Song (as lines 1–6), rhyming e-o.
37–40	*Romance* e-o
41–80	Song. Gloss on the last two lines of the act-opening song, "La tierra con flores, el agua con perlas/el ayre con plumas, con salbas el ecco."
81	Hendecasyllabic line. One line transition.

82–307	*Romance* e-o
308–367	Song. *Décimas* of 4, 8 and 12 syllable lines, rhyming abbaaccddc, with last 10 lines cddccccddc.
368–469	*Romance heptasílabo* í
470–471	*Estribillo*
472–564	*Romance heptasílabo* í
565–628	*Romance* í
629–658	*Espinelas*
659–943	*Romance* e-o
944–982	Song
983–1161	*Romance* ó
1162–1193	Song. *Romance hexasílabo* ó
1194–1199	*Estribillo* (with repetition)
1200–1235	*Romance* ó
1236–1238	*Estribillo*

The song sung by Palas, Act I, 645–709, has 7 stanzas, consisting of six lines of *romance* rhyming in e-a, followed by two lines of 12 syllables each, both ending with the e-a assonant rhyme. Vera Tassis has divided each of these long lines into two lines, making the stanzas consist of 10 lines rather than eight, 6 lines of normal *romance*, and 4 lines of *romance* hexasílabo. This is probably how Calderón's listeners would have heard the lines, accustomed as they were to both the normal and abbreviated *romance* line. Nevertheless, I believe it is proper to conserve the long lines. Since both the manuscript and the *Quinta Partes*, representing separate lines of textual transmission, have the long lines, this almost certainly is the way the lines appeared in Calderón's original. Furthermore, when printed this way, the lines offer an interesting contrast to Minerva's first song. While the goddess of wisdom sings in a graceful, lyrical meter combining 7- and 11-syllable lines in 5-line strophes, the martial goddess Palas sings in 8-line stanzas of 8 and 12 syllables, a heavier, pounding rhythm. This juxtaposition of the parallel meters heightens the contrasting caracterization of the rival goddesses in their first appearances in stage. Conserving the long lines should make it easier for the reader to perceive this skilled use of meter for dramatic characterization.

Calderón also employs a variety of traditional dramatic meters to shape the changing moods throughout the play. The work opens with the traditional dramatic *romance*, rhyming in u-a assonance, a resonant sound appropriate for the stately effect that should set the tone of this courtly mythological drama. As Prometeo first meets Minerva, the goddess he has worshipped, the meter changes to *redondillas,* which Lope recommended as appropriate for "las [cosas] de amor."[326] After Minerva sings, as described above, Prometeo answers in *redondillas.* The two then alternate in *estancias,* with Prometeo speaking and Minerva singing.

The 7–11 syllable combination continues as the frightened, and perhaps breathless, Epimeteo appears, but in an irregular combination of short and long lines, creating a rougher effect appropriate to his emotional state. Palas then appears, and as Epimeteo asks who she is, the meter changes back to *romance,* now in e-a assonance, a somewhat tighter sound suited to the "thickening plot." This assonance continues through the rest of the first act, with the mortals speaking in the normal *romance,* and the goddesses singing in the 8–12 combination.

Apolo, too, sings in his own meter, the *quintillas* of lines 816–820, and 877 886, which are then glossed in *décimas* as the act closes.

The entire second act is in *romance,* in an a-a assonance, which changes to e-o as Discordia makes her first appearance, and continues through the first third of the third act (in fact, part of the second act in all other editions).

As Apolo and Palas discuss Prometeo's offense, Calderón changes to a song composed of 4, 8 and 12 syllable lines in *décimas,* the verse form Lope deemed good for complaints.[327] When Minerva comes to Prometeo's defense, Calderón changes the meter to *endechas* rhyming in í, an even stronger tone of complaint for the impassioned debate between the three.

These sharp, short lines continue as the quarrel passes down to the earthbound mortals, then relaxes slightly to normal 8-syllable *romance* lines as Minerva descends to assure Prometeo that he need not fear Apolo's wrath.

Calderón employs the traditional complaint meter of 8-syllable *décimas* (or *espinelas*) for Epimeteo's fruitless courting of Pandora, then returns to the normal e-o *romance* until Discordia sings, purporting to report Jupiter's will. Her song is in long (9- to 12-syllable) unrhymed lines, appropriate for the pomposity of a feigned ambassador.

As she leaves, and the crowd seizes Prometeo and Pandora, the meter is *romance* in ó, subsequently shortened to hexasyllable *romance* in ó as Apolo comes to sing of his pardon, then lengthened again to normal *romance* for the close of the play.

---

326 Lope de Vega, "El arte nuevo de hacer comedias", in *Obras completas,* ed. Federico Carlos Sainz de Robles (Madrid: M. Aguilar, 1946) II, 1447.

327 Lope de Vega, "El arte nuevo", p. 1447.

BIBLIOGRAPHY OF WORKS CITED

Manuscripts and Archival Sources

Anonymous. *Baile de Júpiter y Calixto*. Biblioteca Nacional Ms. 15.788.

Anonymous. *Genealogia, Origen y Noticias de los Comediantes de España*. 2 vols., Biblioteca Nacional Ms. 12.917–12.918.

Pedro Calderón de la Barca. *Afectos de odio y amor*. 1672. Biblioteca Nacional Ms. 16.835.

Pedro Calderón de la Barca. *Apolo y Climene*. 1672. Biblioteca Nacional Ms. 16.883.

Pedro Calderón de la Barca. *Basta callar*. Biblioteca Nacional Res. 91.

Pedro Calderón de la Barca. *La desdicha de la voz*. Biblioteca Nacional Res. 108.

Pedro Calderón de la Barca. *La estatua de Prometeo*. 1768. Biblioteca del Instituto del Teatro Ms. CDXCVII.

Pedro Calderón de la Barca. *La fiera, el rayo y la piedra*. 1690. Biblioteca Nacional Ms. 14.614.

Pedro Calderón de la Barca. *Las fortunas de Andromeda y Perseo*. Biblioteca Municipal Ms. 83–8.

Pedro Calderón de la Barca. *El gran príncipe de Fez*. 1669. Biblioteca Nacional Res. 100.

Pedro Calderón de la Barca. *El mayor encanto amor*. Biblioteca Nacional Ms. 21.264.

Pedro Calderón de la Barca. *El mayor monstruo los celos*. Biblioteca Nacional Res. 79.

Pedro Calderón de la Barca. *El secreto a voces*. Biblioteca Nacional Res. 117.

Pedro Calderón de la Barca. *Los tres mayores prodigios*. 1669. Biblioteca Nacional Ms. 16.641.

Corpus Christi documents. Archivo de la Villa de Madrid Legajos 2–199–5, 2–199–6.

Diplomatic correspondence of Tuscan ambassador to the Secretary of State of the Grand Duke in Florence. 1670. Mediceo, *filza* 4980.

Antonio Draghi (?). *Il Prometeo*. (1669?). Ms. of two acts of music. Österreichische Nationalbibliothek, Vienna.

Mathias Godos? *Bailes*. Biblioteca Nacional Ms. 16.571.

Juan Francisco Saez de Tejera. *Mojiganga de las Cassas de Madrid*. Biblioteca Nacional Ms. 16.700.

Juan Francisco Saez de Tejera. *Sarao de la minue franzes*. Biblioteca Nacional Ms. 14.090.

Theatre documents. Archivo del Palacio Caja 11.744.

Theatre documents. Archivo Municipal Legajo 2–456–3.

Published Works and Dissertations

José Luis Abellán. *Historia crítica del pensamiento español*. Vol. II: *La edad de oro*. Madrid: Espasa-Calpe, S.A., 1979.

Aeschylus. *Prometheus Bound*, Trans. James Scully and C. J. Herington. London: Oxford University Press, 1975.

Aeschylus. *Prometheus Bound*, Ed. George Thompson. Cambridge: Cambridge University Press, 1932.

Alciato. *Emblemas*, Prologue by Manuel Montero Vallejo. Madrid: Editora Nacional, 1975.

José Luis Alonso Hernández. *Léxico del marginalismo del Siglo de Oro*. Salamanca: Universidad de Salamanca, 1977.

Othón Arróniz, *La influencia italiana en el nacimiento de la comedia española*. Madrid: Editorial Gredos, 1969.

Cesáreo Bandera. *Mímesis conflictiva*. Madrid: Editorial Gredos, 1975.

Janet E. Beat: "Monteverdi and the Opera Orchestra of His Time", in *The Monteverdi Companion*, Ed. Denis Arnold and Nigel Fortune. London: Faber and Faber, 1968, pp. 277–301.

Wayne Booth. *A Rhetoric of Irony*. Chicago: University of Chicago Press, 1974.

Reuben A. Brower. "Visual and Verbal Translation of Myth: Neptune in Virgil, Rubens, Dryden", *Daedalus*, 101 (1972), pp. 155–182.

Jonathan Brown and J. H. Elliott. *A Palace for a King: The Buen Retiro and the Court of Philip IV*. New Haven: Yale University Press, 1980.

Donald C. Buck. *Theatrical Production in Madrid's Cruz and Principe Theaters during the Reign of Felipe V*. Doctoral dissertation, University of Texas at Austin, 1980.

Pedro Calderón de la Barca. *Obras completas*, eds. Angel Valbuena Briones (Vol. I–II); Angel Valbuena Prat (Vol. III). Madrid: Aguilar, 1952–1960.

Pedro Calderón de la Barca. *Autos*. Madrid: Imprenta Imperial, por Ioseph Fernández de Buendía, 1677.

Pedro Calderón de la Barca. *Comedias del célebre poeta español don Pedro Calderón de la Barca*, Ed. Juan Fernández de Apontes. 11 vols., Madrid: Fernández, 1760–1763.

Pedro Calderón de la Barca. *Las comedias de D. Pedro Calderón de la Barca*, Ed. Juan Jorge Keil. 4 vols. Leipsique: Ernesto Fleischer, 1829.

Pedro Calderón de la Barca. *Biblioteca de Autores Españoles*. Vols. 7, 9, 12 and 14: *Comedias de Don Pedro Calderón de la Barca*, Ed. Juan Eugenio Hartzenbusch. Madrid: M. Rivadeneyra, 1850–1856. Vol. 14 is 1st ed. (1850); Vols. 7–12 are 2d ed. (1851–1856).

Pedro Calderón de la Barca. *Andromeda y Perseo*. n.p., n.d. (c.1653). *Suelta* numbered MS Typ 258H in Houghton Library, Harvard University.

Pedro Calderón de la Barca. *Celos aun del aire matan*, Ed. Matthew Stroud. San Antonio, Texas: Trinity University Press, 1981.

Pedro Calderón de la Barca. *En la vida todo es verdad y todo mentira*, Ed. D. W. Cruickshank. London: Tamesis Books Ltd., 1971.

Pedro Calderón de la Barca. *La estatua de Prometeo*, Ed. Charles V. Aubrun. Paris: Centre de Recherches de l'Institut d'Études Hispaniques, 1965.

Pedro Calderón de la Barca. *La hija del aire*, Ed. Gwynne Edwards. London: Tamesis Books Ltd., 1970.

Pedro Calderón de la Barca. *El mayor monstro los çelos*, Ed. Everett W. Hesse. Madison: The University of Wisconsin Press, 1955.

Pedro Calderón de la Barca. *El postrer duelo de España*, Ed. Guy Rossetti. London: Tamesis Books Ltd., 1977.

Pedro Calderón de la Barca. "La selva confusa", *Revue Hispanique*, 21 (1909), pp. 168–338. Ed. G. T. Northup.

Luis de Camoens. *Os Lusiadas*, Ed. Frank Pierce. Oxford: Clarendon Press. 1981.

W. G. Chapman. "Las comedias mitológicas de Calderón", *Revista de Literatura*, 5 (1954), pp. 35–67.

José María de Cossío. *Fábulas mitológicas en España*. Madrid: Espasa Calpe, S.A., 1952.

Emilio Cotarelo y Mori. "Actores famosos del Siglo XVII: Sebastián de Prado y su mujer Bernarda Ramírez", *Boletín de la Real Academia Española*, 3 (1916), pp. 1–38, 151–185.

Emilio Cotarelo y Mori. *Nueva Biblioteca de Autores Españoles.* Vol. 17: *Colección de Entremeses, Loas, Bailes, Jácaras y Mojigangas desde fines del siglo XVI a mediados del XVIII.* Madrid: Casa Editorial Bailly-Baillière, 1911.

Emilio Cotarelo y Mori. *Ensayo sobre la vida y obras de D. Pedro Calderón de la Barca.* Madrid: Tipografía de la Revista de Archivos, Bibliotecas y Museos, 1924.

(Emilio Cotarelo y Mori). "Noticias inéditas de algunas representaciones palaciegas de las comedias de Calderón y otros", *Revista Española de Literatura, Historia y Arte,* 1 (1901), pp. 141–6, 179–82, 212–14, 245–7, 263–4, 295–6, 327–8, 372–6.

Sebastián Covarrubias Orozco. *Tesoro de la Lengua Castellana o Española,* Facsimile of 1611 edition, Madrid: Ediciones Turner, S. A., n. d.

D. W. Cruickshank. "Calderón's Handwriting", *MLR,* 65 (1970), pp. 65–67.

D. W. Cruickshank. "Some Uses of Paleographic and Orthographical Evidence in *Comedia* Editing", *Bulletin of the Comediantes,* 24 (1972) pp. 40–45.

D. W. Cruickshank. "The Textual Criticism of Calderón's Comedias", in *The Textual Criticsm of Calderón's Comedias,* Ed. D. W. Cruickshank, *Pedro Calderón de la Barca, Comedias: A Facsimile Edition,* Vol. 1. London: Gregg International Publishers Ltd., 1973, pp. 1–35.

D. W. Cruickshank. "The Two Editions of Calderón's *Quinta Parte* (1677)", in *The Textual Criticism of Calderón's Comedias,* Ed. D. W. Cruickshank, *Pedro Calderón de la Barca, Comedias: A Facsimile Edition,* Vol. 1. London: Gregg International Publishers Ltd., 1973, pp. 201–210.

Ernst Robert Curtius. "Calderón und die Malerei", *Romanische Forschungen,* 50 (1936), pp. 90–97.

Ernst Robert Curtius. *European Literature and the Latin Middle Ages.* Princeton: Princeton University Press, 1973.

R. Trevor Davies. *La decadencia española, 1621–1700,* 2nd ed. Barcelona: Editorial Labor, 1972.

José Deleito y Piñuela. *La mujer, la casa y la moda (en la España del Rey Poeta),* 3rd ed. Madrid: Espasa-Calpe, S.A., 1966.

Denis Donoghue. *Thieves of Fire.* New York: Oxford University Press, 1974.

(Antonio Draghi?). *Benche vinto, vince amore. O Il Prometeo.* (Vienna): Mateo Cosmerovio, Stampatore di Corte, (1669?).

John Louis Emil Dreyer. *A History of Astronomy from Thales to Kepler,* 2nd ed. n.p.: Dover Publications, Inc., 1953.

Peter N. Dunn. "The Horoscope Motif in *La vida es sueño.*" *Atlante,* 1 (1953), pp. 187–201.

Manuel Durán and Roberto González Echevarría. "Calderón y la crítica", in *Calderón y la crítica: Historia y antología,* Ed. Manuel Durán and Roberto González Echevarría, Vol. I. Madrid: Editorial Gredos, 1976, pp. 13–123.

Hans Flasche, ed. *Konkordanz zu Calderón.* 5 vols. New York: George Olms Verlag, 1980.

Dr. Alfred Francis Pribram and Dr. Moritz Landwehr von Pragenau, eds. *Fontes Rerum austriacarum.* Vol. 56–57: *Privatbriefe Kaiser Leopold I an den Grafen F. E. Pötting: 1662–1673.* Wien: Aus der Kaiserlich-Königlichen Hof- und Staatsdruckerei, 1903–1904.

Luis de Góngora y Argote. *Sonetos completos,* Ed. Biruté Ciplijauskaité. Madrid: Clásicos Castalia, 1969.

Antonio Gallego Morrell. *El mito de Faetón en la literatura española.* Madrid: Consejo Superior de Investigaciones Científicas, 1961.

Carlos García Gual. *Prometeo: Mito y tragedia.* Pamplona: Ediciones Peralta, 1979.

Philip Gaskell. *A New Introduction to Bibliography*. New York: Oxford University Press, 1972.

Clifford Geertz. "Deep Play: Notes on the Balinese Cockfight", *Daedalus*, 101 (1972), pp. 1–37.

Luis de Góngora. *Obras poéticas*. 3 vols. New York: The Hispanic Society of America, 1921.

Luis de Góngora. *Polyphemus and Galatea: A Study in the Interpretation of a Baroque Poem*, Ed. by Alexander A. Parker. Austin: University of Texas Press, 1977.

Baltasar Gracián. *El Criticón*, Ed. Santos Alonso. Madrid: Ediciones Cátedra, 1980.

J. Gray. "Ophir", in *Dictionary of the Bible*, Ed. Frederick C. Grant and H. H. Rowley, Rev. ed., New York: Charles Scribner's Sons, 1963, pp. 713.

Otis Green. *Spain and the Western Tradition*. 4 vols. Madison: University of Wisconsin Press, 1968.

Margaret Rich Greer. "Calderón, Copyists and the Problem of Endings", *Bulletin of the Comediantes*, 35 (1984), pp. 71–81.

Margaret Rich Greer. "Manuel de Mosquera y su manuscrito de *La estatua de Prometeo*", *Anejos de la Revista "Segismundo"*, 6 (1983), pp. 265–276.

Erwin Haverbeck O. *Colección de Anejos de Estudios Filológicos. El tema mitológico en el teatro de Calderón*. Valdivia, Chile: Universidad Austral de Chile, 1975.

Fernando de Herrera. *Poesías*. Madrid: Ediciones de "La Lectura", 1914.

Hesiod. *Hesiod*, Trans. Hugh G. Evelyn-White. New York: The Macmillan Co., 1914.

E. W. Hesse. "The Publication of Calderón's Plays in the Seventeenth Century", *Philological Quarterly*, 27 (1948), pp. 37–51.

Harry Warren Hilborn. *A Chronology of the Plays of D. Pedro Calderón de la Barca*. Toronto: The University of Toronto Press, 1938.

Ana Ivanova. *The Dancing Spaniards*. London: John Baker, 1970.

Henry Kamen. *La España de Carlos II*. Barcelona: Editorial Crítica, 1981.

Hayward Keniston. *The Syntax of Castilian Prose: The Sixteenth Century*. Chicago: University of Chicago Press, 1937.

G. S. Kirk. *Myth. Its Meaning and Functions in Ancient and Other Cultures*. Berkeley: U. of California Press, 1970.

S. E. Leavitt. "The *Quinta parte de Comedias* ascribed to Calderón de la Barca", *Hispanic Review*, 40 (1972), pp. 209–211.

John Richard LeVan. *From Tradition to Masterpiece: Circe and Calderón*. Doctoral dissertation, The University of Texas at Austin, 1981.

Willy Ley. *Watchers of the Skies: An Informal History of Astronomy from Babylon to the Space Age*. New York: The Viking Press, 1966.

M. R. Lida de Malkiel. *La tradición clásica en España*. Barcelona: Editorial Ariel, 1975.

Ann Livermore. *A Short History of Spanish Music*. London: Duckworth, 1972.

José María López Piñero. *La introducción de la ciencia moderna en España*. Barcelona: Ediciones Ariel, 1969.

Erika Lorenz. "Calderón und die Astrologie", *Romanistisches Jahrbuch*, 12 (1961), pp. 265–277.

Lucian, *Lucian*, Trans. A. M. Harmon. Cambridge, Mass.: Harvard University Press, 1968.

David Norris Mackinnon. *The Mythological Dramas of Pedro Calderón de la Barca*. Doctoral dissertation, University of Kentucky, 1977.

James E. Maraniss. *On Calderón*. Columbia, Missouri: University of Missouri Press, 1978.

José Antonio Maravall. *La cultura del Barroco: Análisis de una estructura histórica*. Barcelona: Editorial Ariel, 1980.

José Antonio Maravall. *La teoría española del estado en el siglo XVII*. Madrid: Instituto de Estudios Políticos, 1944.

L. Martínez Kleiser. *Refranero general ideológico español*. Madrid: Real Academia Española, 1953.

Phyllis Dearborn Massar. "Scenes for a Court Play by Baccio del Bianco", *Master Drawings*, 15 (1977), pp. 365–375.

Margaret Maurin. "The Monster, the Sepulchre and the Dark: Related Patterns of Imagery in *La vida es sueño*", *Hispanic Review*, 35 (1967), pp. 161–178.

Marcelino Menéndez y Pelayo. *Calderón y su teatro*, 3rd ed. Madrid: Imprenta de A. Pérez Dubrull, 1884.

Manuel Milá y Fontanals. *Obras completas*. Barcelona: Librería de Álvaro Verdaguer, 1893.

Jaime Moll. "Las nueve partes de Calderón editadas en comedias sueltas (Barcelona 1763–1767)", *Boletín de la Real Academia Española*, 51 (1971), pp. 259–304.

Jaime Moll. "Sobre la edición atribuida a Barcelona de la *Quinta parte de Comedias* de Calderón." *Boletín de la Real Academia Española*, 53 (1973), pp. 207–213.

Paul Arthur Mooney. *A Reevaluation of Past and Current Critical Opinion on the comedias mitológicas of Pedro Calderón de la Barca*. Doctoral dissertation, Pennsylvania State University, 1973.

Barbara Mujica. *Calderón's Characters: An Existential Point of View*. Barcelona: Puvill, 1980.

Timothy Murray. "Theatrical Legitimation: Forms of French Patronage and Portraiture", *PMLA*, 98 (1983), pp. 170–182.

Sebastian Neumeister. *Mythos und Repraesentation*. Munich: Wilhelm Fink Verlag, 1978.

Thomas A. O'Connor. "Calderón and Reason's Impasse: The Case of *La estatua de Prometeo*", in *La Chispa '81: Selected Proceedings of The Second Louisiana Conference on Hispanic Languages and Literatures*, Ed. Gilbert Paolini. New Orleans: Tulane University, 1981, pp. 229–237.

Stephen Orgel. *The Illusion of Power: Political Theater in the English Renaissance*. Berkeley: U. of California Press, 1975.

Stephen Orgel. "The Royal Theatre and the Role of the King", in *Patronage in the Renaissance*, Ed. Guy Fitch Little and Stephen Orgel. Princeton: Princeton University Press, 1981, pp. 261–273.

Steven N. Orso. *In the Presence of the "Planet King": Studies in Art and Decoration at the Court of Philip IV of Spain*. Doctoral dissertation, Princeton University, 1978.

Ovid. *Metamorphoses*, Trans. Rolfe Humphries. Bloomington: Indiana University Press, 1972.

Dora and Erwin Panofsky. *La caja de Pandora: Aspectos cambiantes de un símbolo mítico*, Rev. ed. Barcelona: Barral Editores, 1975.

A. A. Parker. *The Allegorical Drama of Calderón*. London: The Dolphin Book Co. Ltd., 1943.

A. A. Parker. "*El monstruo de los jardines* y el concepto calderoniano del destino", in *Hacia Calderón*, Ed. Hans Flasche, Cuarto Coloquio Anglogermano, Wolfenbüttel, 1975. Berlin: Walter de Gruyter, 1979, pp. 92–101.

Anne M. Pasero. "Male vs. Female: Binary Opposition and Structural Synthesis in Calderón's *La estatua de Prometeo*." *Bulletin of the Comediantes*, 32 (1980), pp. 109–115.

Juan Pérez de Moya. *Philosofia secreta*. Madrid: Francisco Sanchez, 1585.

Plato. *Protagoras*, Trans W. R. M. Lamb. New York: G. P. Putnam's Sons, 1924.

Cynthia Munro Pyle. *Politian's Orfeo and the favole mitologiche in the Context of Late Quattrocento Northern Italy*. Doctoral dissertation, Columbia University, 1976.

Real Academia Española. *Diccionario histórico de la lengua española.* Madrid: Real Academia Española, 1972.

Real Academia Española. *Diccionario de Autoridades,* Edición Facsímil. 3 vols. Madrid: Editorial Gredos, 1979.

Kurt and Roswitha Reichenberger. *Bibliographisches Handbuch der Calderón-Forschung.* Kassel: Verlag Thiele & Schwarz, 1979.

Hugo Albert Rennert. *The Spanish Stage in the Time of Lope de Vega.* New York: Hispanic Society of America, 1909.

L. Rouanet. "Un Autographe inédit de Calderón", *Revue Hispanique,* 6 (1899), pp. 196–200.

Jack Sage. "The Function of Music in the Theatre of Calderón", in *Critical Studies of Calderón's Comedias,* Ed. J. E. Varey, *Pedro Calderón de la Barca, Comedias: A Facsimile Edition,* Vol. 19. London: Gregg International Publishers Ltd., 1973, pp. 209–230.

Jack Sage. "Nouvelles lumièrcs sur la genèse de l'opéra et la zarzuela en Espagne", *Baroque,* 5 (1972), pp. 107–114.

Jack Sage. "Texto y realización de *La estatua de Prometeo* y otros dramas musicales de Calderón", in *Hacia Calderón,* Ed. Hans Flasche, Coloquio Anglogermano, Exeter, 1969. Berlin: Walter de Gruytcr, 1970, pp. 37–52.

Agustín Salazar y Torres. *Cythara de Apolo. Segunda parte.* Madrid: Francisco Sanz, 1681.

Augustus William Schlegel. *A Course of Lectures on Dramatic Art and Literature,* Trans. John Black. London: Bell & Daldy, 1871.

Rudolf Schnitzler and Herbert Seifert. "Antonio Draghi", in *The New Grove Dictionary of Music and Musicians,* Ed. Stanley Sadie, Vol. 5. London: Macmillan Publishers Ltd., 1980, pp. 602–606.

Jean Seznec. *The Survival of the Pagan Gods: The Mythological Tradition and Its Place in Renaissance Humanism and Art,* Rev. ed. Trans. Barbara F. Sessions. New York: Pantheon Books, 1953.

N. D. Shergold. *A History of the Spanish Stage from Medieval Times until the End of the Seventeenth Century.* Oxford: Oxford University Press, 1967.

N. D. Shergold and J. E. Varey. *Representaciones palaciegas: 1603–1699. Estudios y documentos.* London: Tamesis Books Ltd., 1983.

N. D. Shergold. "Calderón and Vera Tassis", *Hispanic Review,* 23 (1955), pp. 212–218.

Judith N. Shklar. "Subversive Genealogies", *Daedalus,* 101 (1972), pp. 129–154.

José Simón Díaz. *Bibliografía de la Literatura Hispánica.* Vol. vii. Madrid: Consejo Superior de Investigaciones Científicas, 1967.

R. A. Stradling. *Europe and the Decline of Spain: A Study of the Spanish System, 1580–1720.* London: George Allan & Unwin, 1981.

Roy Strong. *Splendour at Court: Renaissance Spectacle and Illusion.* Boston: Houghton Mifflin Co., 1973.

Francisco Suárez. *Disputaciones metafísicas,* Ed. y trad. de Sergio Rábada Romeo, Salvador Caballero Sánchez y Antonio Puigcerver Zanón. 7 vols. Madrid: Editorial Gredos, 1960.

Rosita Subirats. "Contribution a l'Etablissement du Repertoire Théâtral à la cour de Philippe IV et de Charles II", *Bulletin Hispanique,* 79 (1977), pp. 401–479.

Robert ter Horst. *Calderón: The Secular Plays.* Lexington, Kentucky: The University Press of Kentucky, 1982.

Santa Teresa de Jesus. *Libro de su vida.* México: Editorial Porrúa, 1972.

Thomas Aquinas. Vol. 11, 15: *Summa Theologica.* New York: McGraw-Hill Company, 1970.

Lynn Thorndike. *History of Magic and Experimental Science.* 8 vols. New York: Columbia University Press, 1923–1958. First 2 vols. published by The Macmillan Co.

James Thorpe. "The Aesthetics of Textual Criticism", *PMLA*, 80 (1965), pp. 465–482.

S. N. Treviño. "Versos desconocidos de una comedia de Calderón." *PMLA*, 52 (1937), pp. 682–704.

S. N. Treviño. "Nuevos datos acerca de la fecha de *Basta callar.*" *Hispanic Review*, 4 (1936), pp. 333–341.

Raymond Trousson. *Le Thème de Prométhée dans la littérature européenne.* 2 vols. Geneva: Librairie Droz, 1964.

Richard W. Tyler and Sergio G. Elizondo. *The Characters, Plots and Settings of Calderón's Comedias.* (Lincoln, Nebraska): Society of Spanish and Spanish-American Studies, 1981.

Angel Valbuena Prat. *Calderón: Su personalidad, su arte dramático, su estilo y sus obras.* Madrid: Editorial Juventud, 1941.

J. E. Varey and N. D. Shergold. *Teatros y comedias en Madrid. Estudios y documentos, 1666–1687.* London: Tamesis Books Ltd., 1975.

J. E. Varey. "*Casa con dos puertas:* Towards a Definition of Calderón's View of Comedy", *Modern Language Review*, 67 (1972), pp. 83–94.

J. E. Varey. "L'Auditoire du *Salon Dorado* de l'*Alcázar* de Madrid au XVIIe Siècle", in *Dramaturgie et Société: Rapports entre l'œuvre théâtrale, son interprétation et son public aux XVIe et XVIIe siècles.* Ed. Jean Jacquot. Paris: Editions du Centre National de la Recherche Scientifique, 1968, pp. 77–91.

J. E. Varey. "La mayordomía mayor y los festejos palaciegos del siglo XVII". *Anales del Instituto de Estudios Madrileños*, 4 (1969), pp. 145–168.

Lope de Vega Carpio. *La Arcadia*, Ed. Edwin S. Morby. Madrid: Clásicos Castalia, 1975.

Lope de Vega Carpio. *Lírica*, Ed. José Manuel Blecua. Madrid: Clásicos Castalia, 1981.

Lope de Vega Carpio. *Obras escogidas.* Vol. 2: *Poesías líricas, Poemas, Prosa, Novelas*, Ed. Federico Carlos Sainz de Robles. Madrid: M. Aguilar, 1946.

Juan Vélez de Guevara. *Los celos hacen estrellas.* Ed. by J. E. Varey and N. D. Shergold. London: Tamesis Books Ltd., 1970.

Baltasar de Vitoria. *Primera parte del Teatro de los dioses de la gentilidad.* Madrid: Juan de Ariztia, 1738.

Robert Lamar Weaver. "Giulio Rospigliosi", in *The New Grove Dictionary of Music and Musicians*, Ed. Stanley Sadie, Vol. 16. London: Macmillan Publishers Ltd., 1980, pp. 210.

Hayden White. "The Forms of Wildness: Archaelogy of an Idea", in *The Wild Man Within*, Ed. E. Dudley and M. Novak. Pittsburgh: University of Pittsburgh Press, 1972, pp. 3–38.

E. M. Wilson and Don W. Cruickshank. *Samuel Pepy's Spanish Plays.* London: The Bibliographical Society, 1980.

Edward M. Wilson and Duncan Moir. *Golden Age Drama. 1462–1600.* New York: Barnes & Noble, Inc., 1971.

E. M. Wilson and Jack Sage. *Poesías líricas en las obras de Calderón.* London: Tamesis Books Ltd., 1964.

E. M. Wilson. "The first edition of Calderón's *Fieras afemina amor*", in *The Textual Criticism of Calderón's Comedias*, Ed. D. W. Cruickshank, *Pedro Calderón de la Barca, Comedias: A Facsimile Edition*, Vol. 1. London: Gregg International Publishers Ltd., 1973, pp. 183–200.

R. P. Winnington-Ingram. "Pythagoras", in *The New Grove Dictionary of Music and Musicians*, Vol. 15. London: Macmillan Publishers Ltd., 1980, pp. 485.

LA ESTATUA DE PROMETEO

La E[s]tatua de Prometheo Fiesta de Años
de D. Pedro Calderón
de la Barca

Personas

Prometheo, Galán	Palas
Epimeteo, Segundo	Discordia
Timantes, Barba	Libia
[Merlín]	Músicos
Apolo	Billanos
Minerba	Billanas

[XORNADA PRIMERA]

Mutaçión de bosque sobre peñascos, y el foro a de ser vna gruta de peñascos pelados y en ella vna puerta de la misma peña capaz de vna persona, hasta q[ue] a su tiempo se abre todo el foro, y sale della Prometheo, dando voçes.

PROMETEO   Moradores de las altas
cumbres del Cáucaso, en cuia
ynhiesta çeruiz descansa
todo el orbe de la luna.
¡A del monte!

Title: B COMEDIA/FAMOSA. / DE LA ESTATVA / DE PROMETEO. / REPRESENTOSE A LOS ANOS / de la Reyna nuestra Señora. / *De Don Pedro Calderón de la Barca.* M COMEDIA / FAMOSA. / DE LA ESTATVA / de Prometeo. / REPRESENTOSE A LOS ANOS /de la Reyna nuestra Señora. / *De Don Pedro Calderón de la Barca.* [Museo del Teatro copy: *AÑOS*] V COMEDIA FAMOSA, / LA ESTATVA / DE PROMETEO, / REPRESENTÓSE A LOS AÑOS DE LA REYNA / Madre nuestra señora. / *DE DON PEDRO CALDERON / de la Barca.*
List of Characters: BM Hablan en ella las personas siguientes. V PERSONAS QVE HABLAN EN ELLA. Merlín is missing in the manuscript list of characters, and Soldados are crossed out. "Soldados, y Musicos" appears in the lists of BMV, although there is no further reference to Soldados in the text. Billanos and Billanas are called "Zagales" y "Zagalas" in BM and "Coro de Zagales" and "Coro de Zagalas" in V. BMV list Epimeteo as "Galan", Timantes as "Viejo", Merlín as "Villano", and Libia as "Villana".
First st.d. BM *Abrese vn peñasco, y sale Prometeo.* V *Abrese vn peñasco, y por él sale Prometeo.*
  3 BM inculta cerviz V cerviz inculta

Dentro [Vnos]   ¿Quién nos llama?   5
Prometeo   ¡A del valle!
[Dentro] Otros   ¿Quién nos busca?

Prometeo   Prometheo soi; venid,
                  que ya es tiempo que os descubra   (folio 1v)
                  el alto empleo que en esta
                  triste paborosa gruta   10
                  tantos días de vosotros
                  [tuvo] mi persona oculta.
                  Venid, pues, venid trayendo
                  de buestras zampoñas rudas,
                  de buestros rudos albogues,   15
                  las armonías comfusas
                  que en culto de las Deydades
                  festibos aplausos vsan.

Dentro   ¿Prometheo dijo? Todos
Epimeteo   seguid su voz, que sin duda   20
                  a grande efecto oy se deja
                  ver.
Dentro Merlín   Y más cuando pronunçia
                  que alegremente festibos
                  vamos todos en su busca.

Dentro Liba   Pues perzeuir no podemos   25
                  adonde la voz se escucha,
                  por varias sendas, en varias
                  tropas, la maleza ynculta
                  penetremos.
[Dentro] Voz 1ª   Sea diziendo,
                  para bolberse a hallar juntas: 30

                       [*Cantado*]

---

   5 BMV *Vnos*. Quien nos llama?
   5 V adds st.d. *Dentro otros*. after line 5
   6 omitted in BM
  12 BMV tuvo
  15 BM alvergues
  20 BM omit "que" V writes "pues"
  25 BMV percibir

[*Dentro*] 1ª Vna   ¡Al monte!   (folio 2)
[*Dentro*] 2ª Otra   ¡Al balle!
[*Dentro*] 3ª Otra   ¡Al llano!
[*Dentro*] 4ª Otra   ¡A la espesura!

                              [*Todos, y música*]

[*Dentro*]   Al monte, al balle, al llano, a la espesura.
Todos y Ellas
Prometeo   Llegad, llegad, y veréis
                           la más perfecta hermosura
                           que el arte y naturaleza   35
                           en sus dos primores juntan.

[*Dentro*] Música   Al monte, al balle, al llano, a la espesura.

Den[*tro*]   No en desmandadas cuadrillas
Epimeteo   vago ya el tropel discurra,
                           sino en seguimiento mío,   40
                           a esta parte se reduzcan,
                           que en lo yntrincado de aquel
                           risco le e visto.

Den[*tr*]o Merlín   Pues vnan
                           sus lígneas a vn punto el fiero
                           afán dejando en su busca.   45

                              [*Todos, y Música*]

[*Dentro*]   El monte, el llano, el valle, la espesura.
El y Todos

                 Salen todos y todas con arcos y flechas

-----

31 speakers and st.d. BMV omit *1a Vna*; BM al monte. / 2 Al valle. *Cantan*. / 3. Al llano.
   / 4. A la espesura. *Todos, y Musica*. V al monte. *Cantando*. / *Voz 2*. Al valle. / *Voz 3*. Al
   llano. / *Voz 4*. A la espesura. *Todos, y Musica*.
32–36 omitted in BMV
41 BMV reduzgan
43 BMV Pues vna
44 B punto nuestro MV punto, nuestro
45 BMV add. st.d.: BM *Todos, y Musica*. V *Todos, y la musica*
46 BMV speakers *Music*.
46 BMV Al monte, al valle, al llano, á la espesura
46 st.d. BMV *Sale Epimeteo con arco y flechas*. After line 48, BMV add another st.d.: BM
   Salen dos tropas de Villanos, y Villa-/nas, con instrumentos. V *Salen dos tropas de
   Zagales, y Zagalas, / con instrumentos*.

Epimeteo	Ya, Prometheo, a tu voz	
	apenas ay quien no acuda.	
Vnos	Dinos, pues, a qué nos llamas.	
Otros	Sepamos a qué nos juntas.	50
Todos	Corriendo a la voz tuia	
	el monte, el valle, el llano, y la espesura.	
Prometeo	Ya sabéis que de Japeto	
	y Assia, en cuio lustre y cuia	(folio 2v)
	velleza se compitieron	55
	naturaleza y fortuna,	
	de vn parto naçimos yo	
	y Epimetheo, sin duda	
	para ejemplar de que puede	
	aber estrella que ymfluia	60
	en vn punto tan distantes	
	afectos, que sea vna cuna,	
	en vez de primer abrigo,	
	campaña de primer lucha.	
	Opuestos crezimos, no	65
	en la volumptad que anuda	
	nuestros corazones, pero	
	en la ynclinazión, que muda	
	los genios; de suerte que	
	dada a los montes la suia,	70
	no ay fiera que por la saña,	
	no ay bruto que por la fuga,	
	la piel redima, o la testa,	
	de las açeradas puntas	
	de su benablo o su aljaba;	75
	pues testa y piel le tributan	
	lo feroz a sus cuchillas,	
	o lo veloz a sus plumas.	(folio) 3
	Yo, dada mi ynclinazión	
	a la paz de la lectura,	80

49–52 omitted in BMV
54 BMV de Asia,
63 BMV primero
76 BMV testa, o V tributa

culpando cuanto a la noble
naturaleza la ynjuria
quien la razional aplica
al comerçio de la bruta,
mobido quizá de aquella   85
razón de dudar que vna
estrella en vn mismo ynstante
vn mismo oróscopo ymfunda
dos afectos tan contrarios,
con ansia de ver si apura   90
el yngenio que vna causa
varios efectos produzca,
me di a la especulazión
de causas y efectos, suma
dificultad en que toda   95
la filosophía se funda.
Este anhelo de saber,
que es el que al hombre le ylustra
más que otro alguno (supuesto
que aquella distançia mucha   100
que ay del hombre al bruto, ay   (folio 3v)
del hombre al hombre, si junta
la comferençia tal vez
al que ygnora y al que estudia)
me mobió en jouen hedad   105
a dejar la patria en busca
de maestros, y como es
la más çelebrada curia
de artes y çienzias la Siria,
donde de toda Assia cursan   110
los más floridos yngenios,
con ellos me mezclé, en fuçia
de que ya a lo menos saue
algo el que al sauer se ajusta.
La lógica natural,   115

---

91 BM al ingenio
92 BMV produzga
109 M Ciencia
114 BMV á saber
114–115 punctuation BM se ajusta, / la Lógica V se ajusta; / la Logica. See Manuscript
    Notes.

que estaba en el alma ymfusa
sin saber della, ylustrada
de la clara lumbre pura
de la enseñanza, me abrió
sendas que hasta allí comfusas   120
pisaba, bien como çiego
que anda tropezando a escuras,
y como puerta de çienzias
se difine o se yntitula   (folio) 4
vna vez abierta, pude   125
trascender de sus clausuras,
por los prinçipios de todas,
a la profesión de algunas.
La escuela de los Caldeos,
en que es prinçipal lectura   130
la astrología, con más
afecto que otra ninguna
seguí, porque como en ella
abía empezado mi duda,
no descansé hasta saber   135
cuánto en vn ynstante mudan
al rapto curso del sol,
veloz siempre y tardo nunca,
los astros semblante, pues
entre primera y segunda   140
ymfluençia se diuiden,
no sólo, aunque nazcan juntas,
las ynclinaçiones, pero
la desdicha y la bentura.
Rico, pues, de artes y çienzias,   145
biendo cuanto el cuerdo acusa
al que adquiere en patria agena   (folio 4v)
y no lo logra en la suia,
a ella bolbí, con deseo
(la sabia judicatura   150
de otras gentes obserbada)
de ver si hiçiese mi astuçia
que buestra rustiçidad

---

122 V á obscuras,
126 BMV transcender

a preçeptos se reduzca
de político gobierno, 155
lastimado de la ruda
barbaridad que os mantiene
sin leyes que os constituian
raçionales, mayormente
cuando en los polos se fundan 160
de paz y justiçia, siendo
pocas, guardadas, y justas.
Apenas proposiçión
tan digna os hiço mi yndustria
cuando temiéndoos de que era 165
alhagüeñamente astuta,
sólo a fin de abasallaros,
con çiega popular furia,
notándome de ambiçioso,
de la no ympuesta coyunda 170
sacudisteis la ceruiz, (folio) 5
con tan ymfame calumnia,
como torçer el sentido
de vn benefiçio en ynjuria.
Hasta aquí e dicho, porque 175
la admiraçión os comfunda
de ver cuánto en mi fabor
buestro despreçio resulta;
pues ofendido de ver
lo que vn tumulto repugna 180
la obediençia, ynterpretando
el buen çelo como culpa,
a viuir conmigo en esta
melancólica espelunca
me reduje; que no ay 185
compañía más segura
que la soledad a quien
no encuentra con lo q[ue] gusta.

---

154 BMV reduzga
162 punctuation BM pocas guardadas, y justas.
165 BMV omit "de"
170 BMV la aun no impuesta
174 BMV omit "vn"
180–181 punctuation BM vn tumulto repugna, / la obediencia interpretando,

Aquí no sólo del sol,
no sólo aquí de la luna,   190
las liçiones repasaba
que en esa plana cerúlea
me dieron el día y la noche,
leyendo a hedades futuras,
líneas de dorados rayos,   (folio 5v) 195
en pautas de estrellas rubias,
pero de plantas y flores
en la silbestre cultura
naturales cualidades,
y aun de las aves q[ue] surcan   200
el ayre, cantos y buelos,
pues las q[ue] a la luz saludan,
y las q[ue] a la sombra aplauden,
a mi ymbocazión anunzian
vatiçinios como faustas,   205
y agüeros como nocturnas.
Viendo, pues, en vna parte
cuanto los hombres repudian
la enseñanza, y viendo en otra
cuanto los Dioses la ylustran,   210
a su alto conoçimiento
elebé la mente, en cuia
especulazión hallé
las monarchías difusas
del çielo y la tierra, dando   215
de Júpiter a la augusta
magestad el çielo, el mar
a Neptuno, sus espumas
a Venus, luego la tierra   (folio) 6
a Saturno, sus fecundas   220
miesses a Çeres, sus flores
a Aura, a Pomona sus frutas,
los abismos a Plutón,
a Eolo, vientos y llubias.

---

191 BMV lecciones
194 BMV omit "a"
196 V de luzes rubias
200 BMV sulcan
222 BM frutos

a Mercurio los comerçios, 225
a Apolo, nimphas y musas,
a Marte y Palas las lides;
y para deçirlo en suma,
a Minerba, de las çiençias
la ynspirazión absoluta. 230
Con que obligado de ver
cuanto en mí las distribuia,
liberal, ynterior culto
más que a otra Deydad ninguna,
(oféndanse o no se ofendan 235
las demás) rendí a la suia.
Y discurriendo en que obsequio
podría yo haçerla que supla
a mi haçimiento de graçias,
di en aprehender su hermosura 240
tan viua en mi fantasía
que no abía parte alguna (folio 6v)
en que no me pareçiese
mirarla, con tan aguda
vehemenzia que aun en las sombras 245
de la noche siempre obscura
(pues hasta aora no vio luz
en ella humana criatura)
jurara que vn vibo fuego
para mirarla me alumbra. 250
Bien ser locura pensé;
pero como a la locura
es tal vez el complazerla
çierto género de cura,
complaçer quise la mía, 255
siguiendo su tema en vna
estatua que me dictaba
el arte de la escultura,
creyendo que con tenerla
siempre a la vista segura, 260

233 punctuation BM liberal interior culto,
238 BMV podia
245 V la sombra
248–251 punctuation BM criatura. /Iurara, que vn viuo fuego / para mirarla me alumbra, V
criatura; /jurara, que vn viuo fuego / para mirarla me alumbra;

çesaría el verla en sombras
de fantásticas figuras.
Ya conzebida esta ydea,
para que mejor la esculpa,
me dio su dóçil materia   265
la tierra, al agua conjunta,
con que siguiendo el dictamen   (folio) 7
del ayre que la dibuja,
de su vago original
fui copiando vna estatura   270
al natural, aplicando
en simétricas mensuras
partes al todo, de suerte
que avn ymformemente bruta
la semejaba, y más cuando,   275
para que la labre y pula,
me franqueó la primauera
de su varia agricultura,
liquidados los matizes;
díganlo dos tezzes juntas,   280
pues para que de su rostro
sonrrosease la blancura,
la cándida dio el jazmín,
y la rosa la purpúrea.
Laurel y oliba, bien como   285
premio en literales justas,
aquél sus rizos corona,
ésta su siniestra ocupa.
Lo demás de sus adornos,
ropajes, y vestiduras,   290
se bordan de varias flores,   (folio 7v)
tanto que le disimulan
la tosca materia al barro,
según cuajado le ocultan.
Pero ¿para qué la voz   295
se detiene en su pintura

---

261 M al verla
282 BMV sonrosasse
283 BM candidal
294 BMV le ocupan

oçiosa, cuando la vista
mejor que ella lo dibulga?
Llegad, pues, llegad, veréis
su efigie, y pues mi cordura   300
ya no os da leyes, sino
simulacros, sobstituian
a políticos consejos
sagrados ritos; construia,
pues, buestro çelo ara y templo   305
a la sabia Deydad pura
de Minerba en su primera
estatua del mundo, y suban
açeptados buestros ruegos
a mejorar de fortuna   310
al sagrado solio, donde
viue, reyna, venze, y triumfa.

*Descubre[se] la estatua, abriendo la gruta, q[ue] estará como la pintan los
versos y pareçida a la q[ue] hiçiere el papel de Minerba.*

Vnos	¡Qué prodigio!	(folio) 8
Otros	¡Qué portento!	

Prometeo Pues ¿qué os asombra? ¿Q[ué] os turba?

Epimeteo Yo responderé por todos,   315
pues a mí nada me asusta.
(Mal dije, que quizá a ellos   *Ap[ar]te*
admira, y a mí me ofusca.)
Prometheo, que tu yngenio
es grande, nadie lo duda;   320
y cuando alguien lo dudara,
retóricamente muda
le desmintiera esa estatua,

---

302 BMV sostituyan
308 BMV omit "y"
312 st.d. [in BMV, following line 304] BM *Descubrese vna estatua en la gruta, / como la
han pintado los versos, pareci- / da á la que ha de hazer á Minerua.* V *Descubrese en la
gruta vna estatua, / como la hán pintado los versos, parecida / á la que haze á Minerua.*
314 BM assombra? ó q̃
317–318 BMV omit parentheses and place st.d. *Ap.* on line 318
321 V lo negára
323 for "le", BM have "les", V has "lo"

puesto q[ue] a todos perturba
verla, algo menos q[ue] viba   325
con algo más que difunta.
Pero vna cosa es, (¡Qué mal
el corazón disimula!)
pero vna cosa es, que no
admitamos leyes tuias,   330
contentos con nuestras leyes,
que son las dos q[ue] ejecuta
el pueblo, cuando castiga
al que mata y al que hurta;
y otra es, que no admitamos   335
sagrados ritos que yncluian
adorazión a los Dioses;   (folio 8v)
y porque mejor se arguia
que açepta lo sacro, quien
lo político renunçia,   340
de parte de todos, yo
voto haçer q[ue] se construia
templo a Minerba q[ue] exçeda
en riqueza y escultura
al del gran Saturno nuestro,   345
donde aquesa ymagen tuia
se venere; pero en tanto
que mi ofreçimiento cumpla,
(Esto es para no perderla   Ap[ar]te
de vista, mi nueba angustia.)   350
hasta su colocazión
no la saques desta gruta,
porque el trato, que es quien más
las estimaziones frustra,
no como al sol la desdeñe,   355
pues por ver cuanto madruga
regular a vna hora siempre,
ya no nos admira nunca.
Y así, otra vez lo repita
aquí, hasta entonçes la oculta,   360

---

346 BMV Imagen suya
349–350 BMV omit parentheses and place st.d. *"Ap."* on line 350
352 BM dessa V de essa
354 V has "sus" for "las"

	que aquí vendremos por ella,	
	luego q[ue] la arquitectura	
	del templo a la región media,	
	sobre dóricas columnas	(folio) 9
	de bronzeados capiteles	365
	en piramidal abuja	
	crezca de suerte que el ayre	
	dude, cuando la sacuda,	
	si es vracán que se abate,	
	o fábrica que se encumbra.	370

MERLÍN   Y para que veas q[ue] todos
         lo que él a votado juran,
         ya que voçes y ynstrumentos
         a su llamado se avnan,
         empieze su aclamazión   375
         desde luego.

LIBIA   Acción es justa,
         y yo me obligo a que el himno
         de las mismas voçes tuias
         se componga.

PROMETEO   ¿De mis mismas
         voçes?

LIBIA   Sí.

PROMETEO   Di cómo.

LIBIA   Escucha.   380

                 Cantan y baylan

Canta   Venid, moradores
          del Cáucaso, en cuias
          zerbiçes descansa
          sus orbes la luna.
          Venid, y festibos   385
          corred en su busca.   *Builtas* (folio 9v)

---

364 BM colunas
366 V "abuja" changed to "aguja"
366–367 punctuation B abuja. / Crezca M abuja, / crezca V aguja; / crezca
374 BM tu llamado V tu llamada
377 BM igno
380 st.d. BM add *Canta.* following "Escucha."; BMV st.d. following line 380: *Cantando, y baylando.; Canta* omitted on line 381
381 speaker V *Music. y Libia.*

[Todos y Música]

TODOS Y MÚSICA	El monte, el valle, el llano, y la espesura.

[Canta]

LIBIA	Venid y veréis	
	que en nueba escultura	
	la naturaleza	390
	y el arte se juntan.	
	Venid, y traiendo,	
	de çítaras rudas,	
	de rudos salterios,	
	las voçes comfusas,	395
	respondan los vientos	
	cuando la saludan.	

Dentro VOÇES	Al valle, al llano, al monte, a la espesura.	

PROMETEO	Oýd, ¿qué disonantes eccos	
	los cóncabos articulan	400
	de todo el Cáucaso?	
EPIMETEO	Oigamos,	
	por si más claro se escuchan.	

[Sale Timantes viejo]

TIMANTES	Huid, pastores, que vna fiera	
	que horriblemente sañuda,	
	no ay sembrado que no tale,	405
	ganado q[ue] no destruia,	
	del bruto seno en que yaçe	
	aquella cueba profunda	
	que tal vez al çielo empaña,	
	y tal vez al viento ahuma,	410
	al monte a salido.	

---

386 BMV omit "Builtas", and add following st.d. *Todos y Musica*.
387 speakers BMV *Music*.
387 BM omit "y" V El monte, el llano, el valle, y la espesura.
387 st.d. BM *Canta Libia*.
388 speaker V *Canta Libia*.
398 BMV Al monte, al valle, al llano, á la espesura.
402 BMV se escucha.
402 st.d. BMV *Sale Timantes viejo*.
408 V de aquella

TODOS	Todos	(folio) 10
	discurren, puestos en fuga.	

Dentro [VOÇES]	Al monte, al valle.
TODOS	¡Qué asombro!
Dentro [VOÇES]	Al llano, al bosque.
TODOS	¡Qué angustia!

EPIMETEO   Salirla al paso me toca,   415
que es bien mi valor presuma,
por más veneno que exsale,
por más ponzoña que escupa,
que en loor de Minerba tubo
sacrificada su furia,   420
la primer víctima mía,
la primer estatua suia.   *Vase*

PROMETEO   Primero, tomando yo
mi arco y çerrando la gruta,
sabré por donde atajarla,   425
desmintiendo a quien murmura
que se embotan los açeros
en el corte de las plumas.   *Vase*

TIMANTES   Por si es verdad que a las sierpes
las músicas las conjuran,   430
venid, repitiendo todos,
cláusulas y voçes juntas.

TODOS	Al monte, al valle, al llano, a la espesura.	
Y MÚSICA	[*Vanse*]	(folio 10v)
LIBIA	¿No vas tú, Merlín?	
MERLÍN	No, Libia.	
LIBIA	¿Por qué?	
MERLÍN	Porque no me gusta,	435
	por yr a ver su fiereza,	
	dejar de ver tu hermosura.	

---

412 BMV discurran
417 BMV exale
426 BM mormura
433 speakers BM *Music.*
433 st. d. BV add *Vase.*

Libia	Si eso es ser gallina, no
	fundes en mí tu disculpa.
Merlín	¿Cómo gallina? si es sólo 440
	porque tú huias segura
	el quedarme yo, pues cuando
	esa horrible fiera adusta
	viniese haçia donde estás,
	vieras en defensa tuia 445
	lo que haçía.
Dentro Voçes	Al monte, al llano.
Libia	Pues tiempo es de que lo cumplas,
	que haçia aquí viene.
Merlín	¿Qué diçes?
Libia	Que veamos qué procuras
	en mi defensa haçer.
Merlín	Ponte 450
	delante tú; verás vna
	herioca gloriosa acçión.
Libia	¿Delante? (folio) 11
Merlín	Sí.
Libia	¿A qué?
Merlín	¿Eso dudas?
	A que dando antes contigo
	çebe en ti presas y vñas, 455
	y pueda afufallas yo,
	mientras ella a ti te engulla. *Vase*
Libia	¡Aprobechada fineza!
	Pero aténgome a la suia,
	pues por otra parte buelbe 460
	acosada de l[a] bulla,
	siendo Prometheo el que más
	en su alcanze se apresura,
	pues él sólo diçe, cuando
	todos los demás dibuglan . . . 465

439 V fundes en esso disculpa.
441 BMV tu viuas segura
443 V fiera ruda
446 speaker V *Vnos.*
461 BMV de la
465 BMV add. st.d. *Ella, y todos.*

VOÇES [*Dentro*], Al monte, al llano.   [*Vase*]
Y ELLA

Dentro   Por más,
PROMETEO   [o] fiero bestiglo, que huias
               desta bárbara montaña
               al mas paboroso çentro,
               sabrán alcanzarte dentro   470
               de su yntrincada maraña
               mis ardientes flechas.

     Sale Minerba de fiera y canta, [y tras ella Prometeo].

MINERBA   No
               las dispares.
PROMETEO   Blando açento.   (folio 11v)
               que a mí me paras, y al viento,
               ¿quién te a pronunçiado?
Canta MINERBA   Yo.   475

     Quítase las pieles y queda como la estatua de la gruta

PROMETEO   ¿Quién heres, o tú, veldad
               de tan no esperado asumpto,
               que lo que a vn monstruo pregunto,
               me responde vna Deydad?
               Pues para que tú lo seas   480
               sobre ser la q[ue] admiré
               en sombras, la que copié
               en fantásticas ydeas,
               y la q[ue] trueca el feroz
               aspecto en aspecto amable,   485
               nada lo haçe más probable
               que lo dulçe de tu voz;

---

466 speakers BMV *Todos.*
466 BMV add. st.d. *Vase* after "llano", and on following line: *Sale Minerva vestida de fiera, y tras ella Prometeo.*
466 BM *Por mas, ó*
467 BM *vestigo* V *ó fiero vestiglo*
472 st.d. omitted in BMV [Minerva had appeared before Prometeo's speech.]
473 M *la*
475 st.d. BMV *Desnudase las pieles, y queda con el / mismo vestido y demás señas que se / vió la estatua.*
477 V *assunto*

        pues los horrores que das
        quitas con las suabidades;
        siendo así que las Deydades   490
        no hablan como los demás,
        sonando siempre a armonía
        cuanto pronunçia su açento.
        Y en fin, Deydad, sombra, viento,
        ylusión o fantasía,   495
        que aparentemente vi,   (folio) 12
        que realmente retraté,
        si tu culto procuré,
        ¿qué es lo que quieres de mí?

        [Canta] rezitatibo [Minerba]

MINERBA   Yo soi, o Prometheo,   500
        Minerba, que a tu vida,
        no sólo agradeçida
        por su estudioso empleo,
        mas por la ara en que ya arde tu deseo,
        en aquel propio trage   505
        que tu ydea me copia,
        porque de ser yo propia
        cualquier duda se ataje,
        quiso mi amor q[ue] en busca tuia vaje.
        Y por no dilatarte   510
        las graçias que te debo,
        a rebestir me atrebo
        tal dizfraz, q[ue] te aparte
        de todos donde a solas pueda hablarte,
        trayéndote a esta esphera   515
        que la luz no la dora,
        que el pájaro la ygnora,

---

491 BM have "las" for "los"
492 BMV omit "a"
493 V has "cuando" for "cuanto" and "tu" for "su"
494 BMV sombra, ó viẽto
499 st.d. BMV *Canta recitatiuo Minerua.*
503 BMV por tu
504 BMV omit "ya"
513 B aparté [in Museo del Teatro copy; no accent is visible in the facsimile edition of the
      Wadham College copy] M aparta

el bruto la venera,
negada al sol, al ave, y a la fiera.
Mira, pues, qué don quieres   520
que mi agradeçimiento   (folio 12v)
rinda a tu pensamiento,
persuadido a que heres
dueño de cuanto ymaginar pudieres
no en el abaro anhelo   525
del çentro de la tierra,
pero en cuanto en sí ençierra
debajo de su velo
toda esa azul república del çielo.

PROMETEO   Al verte y oírte lucho   530
con segundo debaneo;
si dudo cuando te veo,
¿qué creeré cuando te escucho?
Pero ya que tu fabor
el sobresalto destierra,   535
y no puedes en la tierra
darme tesoro mayor,
que el que ya me diste, pues
me diste sabiduría,
aspire la ambiçión mía   540
al soberano ynterés
del çielo.

Cantado MINERBA   ¿Qué quieres dél?

PROMETEO   Si yo, Minerba, supiera
lo que contiene la esphera,
de su estrellado dosel   (folio) 13   545
vn don te pidiera ygual
al poder que en ti se mide,
que el que acobardado pide
haçe abaro al liberal.
Mas si bien no sé (aunque sé   550

---

525 BMV omit "en"
529 BV Republica de el M replica de el
530 BM y al oirte
540 M aspiré
542 MBV add st.d. *Canta Minerua* after "çielo", and omit *Cantado* from following line.

                    bien sus ymágenes vellas)
                    lo que puedes darme dellas,
                    ¿cómo pedirte podré
                    lo que ygnoro? llegue a oír
                    qué ay allá particular,   555
                    y enseñaréte yo a dar,
                    pues me enseñas tú a pedir.

                    [Recitatiuo Minerua.]

Canta MINERBA   Son tan raras, tan vellas,
                    sus altas marabillas,
                    que no es bastante oíllas,   560
                    Prometheo, sin vellas,
                    para saber lo q[ue] se yncluie en ellas.
                    Mas si tú te atrebieras
                    a penetrar osado
                    conmigo su dorado   565
                    alcázar, en él vieras
                    lo que quieras traer de sus espheras.

PROMETEO   ¿Si me atrebiera diçes?
                    ¿Qué abrá a que no se atreba
                    quien consigo te lleba?   570

Cantado   Pues no te atemoriçes   (folio 13v)
MINERBA   si arrancando [d]este tronco sus raíçes
                    deja la tierra dura
                    por escalar el viento.

                    Suben asidos a vn árbol

PROMETEO   En tan glorioso yntento   575
                    tu deydad los temores asegura.

TODOS CON EL   Al monte, al llano, al valle, a la espesura.

---

554 BMV lo que yo no llegué a oír?
557 BM me enseñaste á V me enseñas a
557 st.d. BM *Recitatiuo Minerua.* V *Canta Minerua recitatiuo*
567 V que intentas traer
572 BM de este tronco V á este tronco
574 st.d. [after line 576 in BMV] BM *Desaparecen los dos, él, y todos.* V *Buelan sobre vn
      tronco los dos, y dizen todos.*
577 speaker BM *Todos.* V *Dentr.*
577 BMV Al monte, al valle, al llano, á la espesura.

Dentro   No fatiguéis en vano
EPIMETEO   el monte, la espesura, el valle, el llano,

          Sale despaborido

que el valle, el llano, la espesura, el monte,   580
en todo su orizonte,
talado tronco a tronco y peña a peña
no os pueden dar ni huella, rastro, o seña,
ni de la fiera, ni de Prometheo,
que ambiçioso de haçer suio el tropheo,   585
a lo lejos le vi romper el seno
tras ella al coto, que de horrores lleno,
pisado no se vio, según espanta,
de bruta güella, ni de humana planta.
Y pues no es bien se diga   590
que él siguió el riesgo sin q[ue] yo le siga,
arrójese a su çentro mi destino,
que morir en su amparo determino,
no tanto ya (¡ay de mí!) por ser mi hermano
cuanto por ser autor del soberano   595
simulacro de aquella
veldad tan ymposible como vella   (folio) 14
a quien dejé su víctima ofreçida;
y así en su nombre, ¿q[ué] a de auer q[ue] ympida
mi altibez? mas, o Júpiter diuino,   600

      Entra y sale p[or] otra parte,
y ábrese otra gruta en el foro, más horrorosa q[ue] la otra.

qué estançia tan sin senda ni camino
mi atrebimiento pisa,
donde aun la luz del sol no se diuisa
cuanto y más Prometeo
ni fiera; pues tan solamente veo   605

---

579 st.d. BM *Sale como despauorido*. V *Sale como assombrado*.
583 BM nos pueden dar allá rastro, ni seña V no pueden dar allá rastro, ni seña
591 BMV yo á él le
594 BMV omit "ya"
595 BM omit "ser"
600 st.d. omitted in BMV
604 BMV omit "y"
605 B solamen [sic]

a escaso viso la funesta voca
de vna entreabierta roca
por donde con pereza
melancólico del Cáucaso vosteza.
Sin duda éste es su albergue, y avn sin duda,   610
voraz, horrible, trájica, y sañuda
en él le oculta, ¡o pese a mi denuedo!
Acuérdate, valor, de que no ay miedo
que te estorbe a que entres
hasta donde le encuentres   615
con espíritu altibo,
bien q[ue] al asombro yerto,
para librarle si le hallares vibo,
para vengarle si le hallares muerto.
Lóbrego panteón deste desierto,   620
a pesar del terror q[ue] en ti se ençierra,
e de ver . . .

     Dentro de la cueba con cajas y trompetas   (folio 14v)

MÚSICA   ¡Arma, arma, guerra, guerra!

EPIMETEO   ¿Qué desusado estruendo
de mal ruidoso ydioma q[ue] no entiendo
mezcla a vn tiempo en su cóncabo veloçes   625
roncos açentos y sonoras voçes?
Si lo horrible, bramido es de la fiera,
¿cúia será la dulçe lisongera
cláusula q[ue] diçiendo al ayre yerra . . .

                 Cajas

---

607 BM entre otra roca
609 BMV add. st.d. *Entra por vna puerta, y sale por otra.*
612 BMV se oculta
618 BMV hallare
619 BMV hallare
622 st.d. BMV *Oyese dentro de la cueva musica, caxas y clarines.*
627 BMV la tierra
628 V dulce sonorosa
629 BM clausula que diziendo al ayre, guerra. V clausula, que repite belicosa / en lisonja
    del ayre.
629 st.d. BMV omit

MÚSICA	¡Arma, arma, guerra, guerra!	630

Sale cantando Palas, armada

PALAS ¿Cúia a de ser sino de q[uien] ynspira
al valor, puesta en música la yra?

EPIMETEO ¿Quién eres, vello prodijio,
de tan encontradas señas
que tu voz diçe Deydad, 635
y no Deydad la aspereza
de tu semblante? ¿Quién heres,
otra vez a dudar buelba,
y otras mil, o tú q[ue] a un tiempo
çeñuda y afable muestras 640
rayo de azerada nube,
parto de ynfausta quiebra?
que no deja de ser monstruo
quien es monstruo de velleza.

Cantado PALAS De Júpiter y Latona 645
hermanas del sol, Minerba
y yo naçimos, gozando (folio) 15
tan vna la ynfançia nuestra
que el número no podía
distinguirnos, de manera 650
que ya vbo quien dijo, q[ue] equíbocas eran
o Minerba o Palas, vna cosa mesma.
Pero aunque en deydad, en solio,
en magestad y grandeza,
naçimos las dos comformes, 655
crezimos las dos opuestas

---

630 V Arma, arma, guerra?
630 BM *Canta Palas, y sale con vengala, y plumas.* V *Sale Palas, con vengala, y plumas, y canta.*
636–637 punctuation BM aspereza? / De tu semblante quien eres, V aspereza / de tu semblante? Quien eres,
644 BM add. st.d. *Canta recitatiuo Palas a tonada corriente, punto por letra.*
645 BM la Tona
651–652 V divides each of these lines, and lines 659, 660, 667, 668, 675, 676, 683, 684, 690, 691, 699, 700, 707, 708, 709, 827, 828, 861, 862, 875 and 876 into two hexasyllabic lines. See introductory section on metrical scheme.
653 omitted in BM V En valor, y en hermosura,

en los diuididos genios
de nuestras dos ymfluençias;
blanda ella lo diga, dígalo seuera
yo, auxiliando lides, dictando ella zienzias.   660
Y siendo así que de vn parto
visteis las luçes primeras
Prometeo y tú, ymitando
nuestra fortuna en la buestra,
partimos los dos asumptos,   665
trabada la competençia,
de cual mayor lustre, mayor exçelençia
da al vno en las armas, q[ue] al otro en las letras.
A este efecto, en tanto que
te asista en altas empresas,   670
te yncliné a la caza, bien
como ymagen de la guerra;
pero biendo cuan yngrato   (folio 15v)
al ymflujo que te alienta,
a vna ynnanimada, fingida velleza   675
víctimas dediques, y altares ofrezcas,
mayormente, abiendo dicho
la sacrílega soberbia
de aquese ygnorante sabio
que en obsequio de Minerba,   680
todas las demás Deydades
se ofendan, o no se ofendan,
al son de mis voçes, cajas, y trompetas,
que tu ánimo ynspiren, tu espíritu enzienda[n],
quise abatirte a este abismo,   685
en tanto q[ue] al çielo eleba
ella a su alumno, oponiendo
a su lisonja mi ofensa;
no tanto ayrada por q[ue] él
culto a su Deydad prebenga,   690
cuanto porque tú, tan villano seas
q[ue] la propia olbides, y aplaudas la ajena.

---

659 BMV digalo soberuia
668 BMV have "ciencias" for "letras"
676–677 punctuation BMV ofrezcas. / Mayormente
679 BM aqueste

¡Minerba, primera estatua,
primero templo, primera
víctima, primera pira,   695
siendo quien más la engrandezca
el héroe q[ue] elijió Palas,   (folio) 16
y que Palas lo consienta?
¡No sólo es desaire, no sólo es vajeza,
pero es furia, es rabia, es yra, es biolençia!   700
Y así dispónte a que tú
as de ser quien desbanezca
toda su pompa, exparziendo
al ayre en polbos deshecha
la estatua, o prebente a que   705
por enemiga me tengas,
bolbiendo a mezclar, de Deydad y fiera,
extremos que digan en voçes diuersas
contra Prometheo,

[TODOS, Y MÚSICA]   ¡Arma, arma, guerra!

Desapareçe [Palas]

EPIMETEO   ¡Oye, espera! No es posible   710
seguirla, porque me çierran
el paso troncos y ramas.
¿Quién se abrá visto en tan çiega
comfusión como buscar
a vn hermano y a vna fiera,   715
y en vez de fiera y hermano,
hallar Deydad tan violenta
que se explique faborable,
para declararse adbersa?
Que rompa la estatua dijo,   720
esparçida en tan pequeñas
partes que la llebe el viento
en sus ráfagas embuelta.   (folio 16v)

697 punctuation BM Palas; V Palas?
707 BMV omit "de"
708 BM add. st.d. *Todos, y Musica.*
709 speaker BM *Music.* V *Tod. y Mus.* Contra Prometeo
709 st.d. BMV *Vase*
713 BMV Quien avrá visto tan ciega
722 BMV el ayre

¿Cómo, çielos, (si al mirar
tan hermosa, tan perfecta   725
estampa, con el dolor
de que alma y vida no tenga,
la ofreçí mi vida y alma
por si vibiese con ellas)
podré obedeçer a Palas?   730
Pues en ygual conferençia,
si la obedezco, peligran
vna y otra en la obedienzia,
y en la amenaza, si no
la obedezco; de manera   735
que expuesto a vn sagrado çeño
o a vna dominante estrella,
obedeçerla es el mismo
riesgo que no obedezerla.
¿O no vbiera vn medio en que,   740
partida la diferençia,
complazer supiera a Palas,
sin ofender a Minerba?
Mas ¿qué dudo? q[ue] sí abrá,
si no me miente la ydea   745
de vna ymaginada yndustria:
Yo e de fingir . . .

Dentro   Haçia aquella   (folio) 17
TIMANTES   parte está.
[*Dentro*] TODOS   Lleguemos todos.

EPIMETEO   Quede la yndustria suspensa
                hasta otra ocasión.

Salen [Timantes, Libia y Merlín, y] todos los villanos

TODOS   Los brazos   750
                nos da.

---

726 V efigie, con
728 BMV la ofreci mi alma, y mi vida,
729 BMV con ella
724–731 punctuation BMV omit parentheses; BM have "ellas?" and begin a new sentence
    with "Podré", line 730, not "pues", line 731.
731 V igual competencia
740 BMV omit "en"
750 st.d. BMV *Salen Timantes, Liuia, y Merlin.*

LIBIA   Montañas y selbas
                    hasta hallarte emos corrido.

TIMANTES   Dónde as estado nos cuenta,
                    y si al monstruo o Prometheo
                    as visto.

EPIMETEO   Mi duda es ésa,   755
                    que ni a Prometheo ni al monstruo,
                    con llegar hasta su cueba
                    y exsaminarla, no vi
                    ni sé daros más respuesta
                    de que salgáis deste sitio,   760
                    ¡huid, huid de su maleza,
                    que ay más prodijios en él
                    que pensáis!   *Vase*

MERLÍN   Bien aconseja
                    quien aconseja q[ue] huiamos.

LIBIA   Aunque él no te lo dijera,   765
                    supieras haçerlo tú.

MERLÍN   Aý verás, o Libia vella,
                    lo que me debes, pues siendo   (folio 17v)
                    tú mi vida, fue fineza
                    guardar la tuia en la mía.   770

TIMANTES   Pues ya ynnútil dilijençia
                    es buscar a Prometheo,
                    puesto que la noche çierra,
                    vamos de aquí.

MERLÍN   También es
                    buen consejo, si te acuerdas   775
                    de que mi amo dijo q[ue] ay
                    prolijos por aquí çerca.

LIBIA   Harto desconsuelo es
                    el yrnos sin que parezca
                    Prometheo.

---

754 BM have "ó" rather than "y", and V omits it
758 BMV examinarla
761 BMV omit "de"
770 BMV guardar tu vida en la mia.

TODOS   ¿Qué abrá sido   780
          dél?
MERLÍN   Bien presto, si dijera
          yo lo que pienso, sería
          saberlo.
TODOS   Pues, di, ¿qué piensas?

MERLÍN   Que sin duda combidados
          en otra parte la fiera   785
          tenía, y para su banquete
          voló con él.
LIBIA   ¿De qué, bestia,
          lo ymfieres?   (folio) 18
MERLÍN   De que sin duda
          sería gran plato en su mesa,
          porque el que crudo sabía   790
          tanto, forçoso es que sepa
          más, o cozido o asado.

TIMANTES   Luego vi que sería neçia
          frialdad tuia; de aquí vamos,
          que ya el sol en la eminençia   795
          de aquella elebada cumbre,
          en que el rumbo de sus ruedas
          suele rozarse, según
          sobre las nubes descuella,
          sus altas çimas transmonta   800
          su carroza.   *Vase*
LIBIA   ¡O quien supiera
          lo que al verse desçender
          del çénit de su grandeza
          dirá al despeñarse al mar!

MERLÍN   ¿Qué dificultad es ésa?   805
          pues con saber q[ue] es cochero,
          sabrás q[ue] vota y reniega,
          y que da al diablo a su amo,
          porque nunca el coche presta.

LIBIA   ¡Que en tu vida digas cosa   (folio 18v)   810
          que vna neçedad no sea!

—————————————
800 BMV trasmonta

MERLÍN   ¿Mayor neçedad no es

                Aquí puede aber mutazión de çielo

                querer tú desde la tierra
                oír si dirá o no dirá
                Apolo cuando se acuesta?   *Vanse*   815

A su tiempo apareçe el sol, q[ue] va pasando de vna a otra parte, y estarán
Minerba y Prometeo sobre vna nube, y al pasar, le quita vn rayo.

Dentro,   No temas, no, descender
Canta APOLO   vellísimo rosicler,
                que si en todo es de sentir
                que naçe para morir,
                tú mueres para naçer.   820

Canta MINERBA Ya que sobre el pedestal
                de tupida nube densa,
                del transparente çafir
                las diáfanas vidrieras
                as penetrado, obserbando   825
                cuanto se contiene en ellas,
                mira qué don quieres que yo te conçeda,
                ya que mi palabra cumplírtela es fuerza.

PROMETEO   De cuanto e visto y de cuanto
                e notado en sus espheras,   830
                nada me suspende, nada
                me admira, pasma y eleba
                tanto como el explendor,
                mirado desde tan cerca,
                deste corazón del çielo,   835
                de ese aliento de la tierra,   (folio) 19
                que árbitro del día y la noche,

---

812 st.d. BMV omit
815 st.d. BM omit *Vanse* and write *En tonada canta Apolo, a quien se ve / en lo alto y á otra*
     parte Minerua, / y Prometeo. V *Apolo en lo alto canta, y al otro lado está / Minerua, y*
     Prometeo.
818 BMV omit "en"
819 V nazca
820 st.d. BM add *Recitatiuo Minerva.*, omitting *Canta*
821 V pedrestal [sic]
824 V la [sic] diafanas
835 BMV de esse

              monarca de los planetas,
              rey de los signos, y dueño
              de luzeros y de estrellas,   840
              vida es de frutos y flores,
              y alma de montes y selbas.
              Si yo pudiera llebar
              vn rayo suio, que fuera
              su actibidad aplicada   845
              a combustible materia,
              ençendida lumbre, que
              desmintiendo las tinieblas
              de la noche, en breue llama
              supliese del sol la ausençia,   850
              fuera don bien como tuio,
              pues moralmente se biera
              que quien da luz a las gentes
              es quien da a las gentes çiençia.

Canta Minerba Mucho pides, mas por mucho   855
              que pidas, a más me empeña
              la palabra q[ue] te·di;
              y pues que ya el sol se azerca,
              embozado en pardas nubes,
              que se te transponga deja   (folio 19v) 860
              para que al pasar, sin ser visto puedas,
              hurtándole vn rayo, llebarle a la tierra.

                    Ynstrumentos

Prometeo   La armonía de los orbes,
              a cuio compás su tierna,
              dulçe voz va dibirtiendo   865
              la continuada tarea
              que de la eclíptica pasa

              Va pasando el sol, poco a poco

---

839 BM omit "y dueño;" V Astros y Signos,
841 BMV omit "es"
843 V pudiesse
856 BM pidas, en mas V pides, en mas
860 BV que se trasponga le dexa M que se transponga le dexa
862 st.d. BMV omit
867 BM eclipta
867 st.d. BMV omit. See note, line 876

atrabesando la senda
al Zodíaco, a quien siguen
de sus ymágenes vellas   870
las cláusulas arrebata
mis sentidos de manera
que no sé si e de tener
acçión q[ue] no se suspenda.

MINERBA   Pues yo te apadrino en tan alta empresa,   875
              atiende a su luz, no a su voz atiendas.

APOLO   No temas, no, desçender . . .

MÚSICA   No temas, no, desçender . . .

APOLO   . . . vellísimo rosicler . . .

MÚSICA   . . . vellísimo rosicler . . .   880

APOLO   . . . que si en todo es de sentir . . .

MÚSICA   . . . que si en todo es de sentir . . .

APOLO   . . . que naçe para morir,
              tú mueres para naçer.

MÚSICA   . . . que naçe para morir,   885
              [tú mueres para naçer.]

APOLO   No temas ver que la aurora   (folio) 20
              delante de ti falleçe,
              pues en los rumbos que dora,
              si a cualquier ora anocheçe,   890
              amaneçe a cualquier ora.
              Y pues nunca anocheçer
              puede, sin amaneçer,
              ¿quién podrá contradeçir . . .

870–871 punctuation BMV bellas. / Las
871 speaker V *Prom.* [superfluous, since Prometeo was already speaking]
871 V arrebatan
874 BM add st.d. *Descubrese Apolo, y canta.*
875 speaker BM omit *Minerva* [lines assigned to Prometeo]
876 BMV atiende a su voz, no á su luz atiendas.
876 V adds. st.d. *Va atrauessando Apolo el teatro en su carro, y canta.*
882 B tdoo [sic]
883–886 BMV *Apol.* Que nazca para morir. / *Music.* Que nazca para morir. / *Apol.* Tu
     mueres para nacer. / *Music.* Tu mueres para nacer.
887 BM el Aurora
890 M anoche
892 M anocher
893 M pueden

A 4   . . . que naçe para morir,   895
                       y muere para naçer?

APOLO   No temas, no, pues adquiere
                       nueba luz la luz q[ue] yaçe,
                       y tanto a todas prefiere,
                       que muere de la que naçe,   900
                       y naçe de la que muere.
                       Y así no temas caer
                       desde el cenit al nadir,
                       pues es tan otro tu ser . . .

A 4   . . . que naçe para morir,   905
                       y muere para naçer.

                       Al enparejar el carro, le quita vna luz.

PROMETEO   Perdone, Apolo, esta ofensa,
                       y tú, gran Minerba, piensa
                       que a consagrarte voi fiel
                       este rayo; huio con él   910
                       pues quedas en mi defensa,
                       y te sabré agradeçer,
                       si llega en tu culto a arder,   (folio 20v)
                       que por él puedan deçir . . .

CON EL 4   . . . que naçe para morir,   915
                       y muere para naçer.

                    Repite toda la copla la música, y pasa el carro,
                    y Prometeo vaja, Minerba sube, y acaba la jornada.

---

895 speaker omitted in BMV [Apolo speaking]
897 speaker omitted in BMV [lines previously assigned to Apolo]
905 speaker BMV *Musica, y él* [Apolo]
906 st.d. BMV *Al emparejar con los dos, quita / Prometeo vna hacha del Carro.*
910 BMV huya
911 BMV pues quedas tu en mi defensa
912 BMV y podrás agradecer,
913 B omits "a"
915 speaker BMV *El, y Music.*
916 BMV add a repetition of the *estribillo*, as follows: *Repiten todos.* [V*Repiten todos, y
     musica.*] / *Todos. No temás no descender, / que si en todo es de sentir, / que nazca para
     morir, / tu mueres para nacer.*
916 st.d. BMV *Con esta repeticion buela Prometeo / con la luz, y desaparece el carro con /
     Apolo, y se dá fin á la primera / Iornada.* [B has written á Tolo for Apolo]

SEGUNDA JORNADA DE LA ESTATUA DE PROMETHEO

Empieza con la mutación de bosque y peñascos de la Primera Jornada con la misma gruta, y a vn lado, a su tiempo se verá Prometeo sobre vn peñasco, y la q[ue] haçe a Minerba estará en lugar de la estatua dentro de la gruta.

Salen como a escuras Epimetheo y Merlín.

EPIMETEO	Haçia esta parte a de ser,	
	si la noche no me engaña,	
	la [estancia] de Promethco.	
MERLÍN	Si as dicho que en su comarca	
	ay prolijos, ¿cómo a ella	5
	bienes? y más cuando baja	
	la noche, sus verdes riscos	
	vistiendo de sombras pardas.	
EPIMETEO	Calla, y sígueme, Merlín,	
	ya que hiçe comfianza	
	de ti, más que de otro alguno.	10
MERLÍN	El fabor te perdonara,	
	porque seguirte y callar	
	son dos cosas mui contrarias;	
	y ya, señor, que el seguirte	15
	en mis pies esté, repara	
	que el callar no está en mi voca.	
	y así la duda se parta,	(folio 1v)

Act title B IEGVNDA IORNADA. MV SEGVNDA IORNADA
First st.d. omitted in BMV
Second st.d. BM *Salen Epimeteo, y Merlin como á escuras.* V *Salen Epimeteo, y Merlin, como á obscuras.*
2 BMV si el deseo
3 BMV estancia
7 V verdes troncos
13 BM porque guiarte
18 M se aparta

que pues te sigo y no enojo,
no es justo quitarme el habla;   20
sepa a qué efecto buscando
vas de Prometheo la estançia.

EPIMETEO   Que sea fuerza q[ue] el más cuerdo   [*Aparte*]
de algún criado se valga,
el día que por sí solo   25
a sus motibos no vasta;
mayormente el día que es
fuerza también q[ue] a dar vayan
a su casa sus motibos,
donde del ladrón de casa   30
el thesoro de vn secreto
o nunca, o tarde se guarda.
Y pues por ambas razones
déste e de valerme, haga
comfianza desde luego.   35
Quizá podrá ser q[ue] aya
tal vez villano en q[uie]n tenga
mérito la comfianza.
Yo, Merlín, biendo q[ue] eres
hombre honrrado . . .

MERLÍN   Sí, a Dios graçias.   40

EPIMETEO   . . . y que a tanto que me sirbes . . .   (folio) 2

MERLÍN   Cuanto a que tú no me pagas.

EPIMETEO   . . . pretendo, atento a tu buena
ley . . .

MERLÍN   Lo primero es el alma.

EPIMETEO   . . . fiar de ti vn noble secreto.   45

MERLÍN   Mejor fuera que fiaras
de mí vn villano vestido.

EPIMETEO   Oye, y sabrás con qué causa.
Entre los raros acasos
que en este monte me pasan,   50
en busca oy de Prometheo,
el mayor fue que llegara

---

42 BMV Como ha que

	a la voca de vna cueba	
	en cuias duras entrañas,	
	con dulçes y horribles voçes,	55
	superior Deydad me manda	
	que la estatua de Minerba,	
	en vez del templo y el ara	
	y víctima que ofreçí,	
	la rompa, quiebre, y deshaga.	60
MERLÍN	¿Mandóte más?	
EPIMETEO	¿Esto es poco?	
MERLÍN	Y [tan] poco q[ue] no es nada;	
	que puesto que Prometeo	
	de todo el contorno falta,	(folio 2v)
	y la estatua se está allí,	65
	qué enfecultad abrá en darla –	
	pues el mandato no es barro,	
	y es varro la tal estauta –	
	con vn canto en el cogote,	
	con otro canto en la cara,	70
	con otro canto en los pechos,	
	y con otro en las espaldas,	
	y cátala aquí deshecha.	
EPIMETEO	¡No lo digas, calla, calla!	
	que vltrages de ygual prodijio	75
	aun sólo dichos agrabian.	
MERLÍN	Pues ¿no vas a deshaçerla?	
EPIMETEO	No, Merlín, sino a robarla;	
	que esto es lo más que de ti	
	fío, pues para llebarla	80
	a esconder entre los dos	
	te traigo.	
MERLÍN	¿Cómo, si manda	
	superior Deydad que la rompas?	

---

56 BMV Deydad superior
58 BMV Templo, Altar, y Ara,
62 BM tampoco V tan poco
68 BM y es barro lo de la estatua V y es barro lo desta Estatua
69 BMV el copete
75 BMV de tal prodigio
83 V omits "que"

EPIMETEO   Como no es posible que aya
              obediencia a vn cruel preçepto   85
              en que me van vida y alma;
              pues desde el ynstante que
              vi marabilla tan rara,   (folio) 3
              ydolatré su hermosura.

MERLÍN   Eso, señor, no me espanta,   90
              como esas estautas ay
              por aý q[ue] se ydolatran.

EPIMETEO   ¿Cómo, si ésta es la primera
              que a visto el mundo?
MERLÍN   Te engañas,
              que yo e visto muchas.
EPIMETEO   ¿Dónde?   95
MERLÍN   En bobas de buena cara;
              y esto aparte, por que creo
              que ya está dicho, ¿qué trazas?

EPIMETEO   Llebarla donde escondida,
              no sabiendo della, no aya   100
              quien templo la dé, ni culto,
              con que satisfago a Palas,
              que fue la Deydad que dije,
              y sin llegar a vltrajarla,
              la reserbo para mí,   105
              contento con adorarla,
              teniéndola en mi poder.

MERLÍN   Con que tendraś vna dama
              para la comodidad,
              de notables zircunstançias,   110
              pues no te pedirá el coche,   (folio 3v)
              ni la joya, ni la gala,
              ni el cayrel, ni el perendengue,
              el relámpago, la enagua,
              la vngarina, y cuanto al plato,   115

_____
  91 BMV estatuas
  95 BM En donde?
 105 BMV rescato
 113 BM pelendengele
 115 BMV omit "la;" BM anguarina

no hará costa en las viandas,
pues dellas te pagará
el escote en la garganta;
y en fin, no te dará celos,
pues siempre metida en casa,   120
no dirá esta calle es mía.
mas sobre esto, ¿no reparas
que Palas se ofenda, y biendo
el que para ti la guardas,
ayrada se buelba en   125
Dios Palos la Diosa Palas?

EPIMETEO   No lo sabrá, que la noche
siempre en sus sombras ampara
hurtos de amor.

MERLÍN   Eso es dar
ygnorancia en soberanas   130
Deydades.

EPIMETEO   Esa objeçión
pondrá alguno, pero es vana;
que Deydad que tiene embidia
¿por qué no tendrá ygnorancia?   (folio) 4
Y pues por aquí es la gruta   135
de Prometheo, a la escasa,
trémula luz de la luna
la busquemos; que el hallarla,
ya ves cuanto ymportaría,
antes que amanezca el alba.   140

MERLÍN   Que a escuras encuentre vn hombre
alguna sima en que caiga,
vaya, mas que encuentre sima
en que galantear, no vaya.

EPIMETEO   No me repliques.
MERLÍN   ¿Qué hiciera   145
Minerba, pese a su alma,
en alumbrarnos?, supuesto
que el yr a buscar su estauta

---

119 BMV no tendrás
141 V obscuras
146 BM pesie
148 BMV estatua

es hacerla el agasajo
de no deshaçerla.

EPIMETEO   Aguarda,   150
que apenas lo as dicho cuando
vn nuebo splendor jurara
que me abía dado luz.

En lo alto, Prometeo con la luz.

MERLÍN   Yo también.
EPIMETEO   Ves en la alta
cumbre del Cáucaso vn vello   155
nuebo explendor, cuia llama   (folio 4v)
ni es relámpago que brilla,
ni es exsalaçión que pasa,
sino desasida estrella
del firmamento q[ue] vaga   160
a elección del viento que
de su epiciclo la arranca.

MERLÍN   Y como que lo veo, y veo . . .

EPIMETEO   ¿Qué?
MERLÍN   Que de la altura baja.

EPIMETEO   Diçes bien, pues de la cumbre   165
cay, alumbrando la falda.

MERLÍN   Haçia nosotros se azerca.

EPIMETEO   Sin duda Minerba trata
faboreçer mis deseos,
agradeçida a mis ansias,   170
porque tan no vista luz
de estos montes, en la opaca

---

152 BM explendor V esplendor
153 st.d. omitted in BMV
158 BMV exalacion
160 BMV baxa
161 BM "a" omitted; releccion
162 BM Epicielo
163 V la veo
164 BMV la almena
172 BMV destos

obscuridad de la noche,
¿quién duda que sea embiada
(pues perziuimos que viene,   175
sin perzibir quien la traiga)
de alta Deydad?

MERLÍN   Clara cosa
es, puesto q[ue] es cosa clara.   (folio) 5

EPIMETEO   Hasta aberiguar qué sea,
retírate entre estas ramas.   180

Ocúltanse y sale Prometeo

PROMETEO   Hurtado rayo del sol,
ven donde otro sol te aguarda,
que para ser sol Minerba,
ser su retrato la vasta.

[Prometeo] atrabiesa el tablado

EPIMETEO   Pues sin distinguir q[ue] bulto   185
es el que la muebe, pasa
por delante de nosotros.
Sigámosla, Merlín, hasta
que apuremos de vna vez
en qué ygual portento para.   190

MERLÍN   Sea, señor, a lo lejos,
por que me çiega el mirarla.

Abrese la gruta

PROMETEO   Vella ymagen de Minerba . . .

EPIMETEO   ¿Ves que la gruta se abra,
y a la estatua en ella?

MERLÍN   ¡Y cómo   195
que lo veo!

EPIMETEO   Atiende y calla,
hasta apurarlo más.

---

180 st.d. BMV *Sale Prometeo con la hacheta.*
184 BMV le basta
184 st.d. BMV *Vá passando.*
192 st.d. BMV *Abre la gruta donde se vió la estatua, que ha de ser la misma Minerva.*
194 BM abre

Pónele la luz en la mano derecha

PROMETEO   . . . Este
rayo del sol te consagra
quien como el rayo en tu mano,
pusiera el sol a tus plantas.   200
Agora, porque las gentes
de todas estas campañas   (folio 5v)
crezcan la adoraçión tuia,
creyendo que de ti nazca
al mundo este benefiçio,   205
de que familiar se haga
al hombre la actiuidad
del fuego, y con más ynstancia
te labren el templo q[ue] oy
te an ofreçido, que vaya   210
será bien, a combocar
a todos, para q[ue] añadan,
con segunda admirazión,
sacrifiçios a tus aras.   *Vase*

MERLÍN   La luz dejando en su mano,   215
el bulto della se aparta.

EPIMETEO   Pues para que yo la vea
y llebe donde ocultarla
de Palas pueda, la luz
paró en su mano, ¿q[ué] tardas?   220
Llega conmigo, que ella,
dando el reflejo en su cara,
se deja ver, como quien
dice, pues me ves, ¿q[ué] aguardas,
para que en salbo me pongas?   225
Y así, entre los dos, a casa
la llebemos.   (folio) 6
MERLÍN   De esa parte
tú, señor, con ella carga,
y yo de estotra.

---

197 st.d. BMV *Ponele el hacha en la mano derecha.*
214 st.d. omitted in BM
215 BM tu mano
217 BMV lo vea

Al llegar, los asusta hablando Minerba

MINERBA   ¡Teneos!
No sacrílegos, con vana   230
presumción tocarme oséis.

MERLÍN   ¡Ay, q[ue] se enoja la estauta!

EPIMETEO   ¿Qué es lo que miro?   ¿Quién, Dioses,
nuebo spíritu la ymflama,
nuebo aliento y nueba vida?   235

Dentro MÚSICA   Quien triumpha para enseñanza
de que quien da ciencias, da
voz al barro y luz al alma.

Sale la estatua de la gruta

EPIMETEO   ¿Qué es esto, Merlín?
MERLÍN   Esto es,
que al compás q[ue] encanta, canta   240
Doña Estatua mi señora;
como vna persona, anda,
habla, ve, alienta, y respira.

EPIMETEO   ¡El gran Júpiter me balga!

MERLÍN   A mí, el gran Baco, Deydad   245
más devota, pues es llana
cosa que él solo entre todas
Deydad de vota es.

MINERBA   ¡Qué estancia
tan paborosa, tan triste,
tan trémula, obscura, y vaga!   250
Si no fuera por el astro   (folio 6v)
que me ymfluye . . . Mas, ¿quién anda
allí? ¿quién va? ¿quién es?

---

229 st.d. omitted in BMV
230 BM sacrilegios
232 BMV Estatua.
234 BMV espiritu
237 BMV ciencia
238 st.d. omitted in BMV
240 M qual compás que canta, canta
248 BM deuota V de-bota

MERLÍN   ¡No
              se llegue acá!
MINERBA   ¿Qué os espanta?
              ¿qué os retira?   ¿q[ué] os suspende?   255
              ¿qué os estremece?
EPIMETEO   A mí nada.
MERLÍN   A mí todo.
EPIMETEO   Que si sé
              que te di mi vida y alma
              en el punto que te vi,
              ¿qué mucho, si en dicha tanta,   260
              veo yo que viues con ellas,
              que veas tú que a mí me faltan?

MINERBA   ¿Yo, tu alma? ¿Yo, tu vida?
              ¿dónde, cómo, o cuándo hallarlas
              pude? si ya no es q[ue] estén   265
              dentro desta viua llama
              que me anima; y si son tuias,
              llega tú, llega a cobrarlas.

EPIMETEO   ¡No la azerques, no la azerques!
              ¡Aparta su ardor, aparta!   270
              que más que alumbra, deslumbra,
              y tanto pabor me causa,
              que arrojándome de sí,
              me fuerza a que a buscar vaya
              quien me desçifre el enigma   (folio) 7   275
              de vna escultura animada,
              vn ynnanimado fuego,
              que con calidad contraria,
              abrasa como que yela
              y yela como que abrasa.   280

---

255 V qué os turba? qué os retira
256 BM omit "que os estremeçe" V qué os suspende?
261 BMV ella
262 V falta
264 BMV hallarla
265 BMV sino es yá que estén
274 BMV add. st.d. *Sale de la gruta como admirado.*
275 M has "que" for "quien"; BM egnima
277 BM vn ignanimado

MERLÍN	Bien dices, llamemos jente.		
EPIMETEO	¡Pastores destas montañas . . .		
Dentro	¡Pastores destas montañas . . .		
PROMETEO			
MERLÍN	El ecco te faboreçe,		
	pues repite tus palabras.	[*Vase*]	285

Azercańdose vno, se aleja el otro, y queda Prometeo,
y se va Epimeteo, con estas voçes.

EPIMETEO	. . . venid, q[ue] ay nuebo prodijio . . .		
PROMETEO	. . . venid q[ue] ay [nuebo prodijio] . . .		
EPIMETEO	. . . que admirar en nuestra patria!		
PROMETEO	. . . que admirar en [nuestra patria!]		
EPIMETEO	Sacudid el blando sueño.		290
PROMETEO	Sacudid el [blando sueño.]		
EPIMETEO	Dejad, dejad, las cauañas.	[*Vase*]	
PROMETEO	Dejad, dejad [las cauañas.]		
Dentro TODOS	¿Quién a esta hora nos despierta?		
MÚSICA	Quien triumfa para enseñanza		295
	de que quien da çiençias, da		
	voz al barro y luz al alma.		
MINERBA	Músicas el ayre, espantos		
	la tierra, y el fuego ansias;		
	¿quién soi yo, Dioses, q[ue] e puesto		300
	el orbe en comfusión tanta?	(folio 7v)	
PROMETEO	Ya q[ue] a mi voz y a la voz		
	del ecco q[ue] la acompaña		
	despierta la gente queda,		

281 BM gentes
285 BM omit st.d.; V has only *Vase*.
287 BMV que ay nueuo prodigio.
289 BM omit V *Prom*. Que admirar en nuestra patria.
290 speaker omitted in BM [Epimeteo speaking because of omission of previous line
    assigned to Prometeo.]
290 M blanco
291 BV el blando sueño. M el blanco sueño.
293 BMV Dexad, dexad las cabañas.
298 speaker V adds st.d. *Sale* to speaker, *Minerba*
298 B espanta, M espantas, V inquietan,
299 BM omit "ansias" V la tierra, el fuego, y el agua;

	y es fuerza que aquí la traiga	305
	el nuebo ymán del reflejo,	
	adelántome a esperarla	
	para que me halle con ella	
	cuando llegue; mas ¿q[ué] rara	
	marabilla es ésta, cielos?	310
	¿Fuera de la gruta no anda	
	en agena mano? Vea	
	quien se a atrebido a quitarla.	
	¡Qué miro! ¡Sacra Minerba!	

MINERBA   ¿Qué oigo? ¿Yo, Minerba sacra?   315

PROMETEO   ¿En qué de mi amor te ofendes?
              ¿En qué de mi fee te agrabias?
              ¿Por qué el rayo que me diste
              para tu ymagen le traiga . . .

MINERBA   ¿Qué rayo, qué ymagen? Dioses,   320
              ¿qué es esto que por mí pasa?

PROMETEO   . . . si en honor tuio, en su mano
              le puse, ¿a qué efecto bajas
              a quitársele tú della?
              ¿Por qué te enoja el q[ue] arda   325
              en culto tuio?   (folio) 8

MINERBA   Dos cosas
              bien nuebas y bien estrañas,
              (o tú, quien quiera que seas,
              hombre, ylusión, o fantasma)
              admiro al oírte, y verte: 330
              vna, que huiendo no [vayas],
              deslumbrado deste ardor;
              y otra, mirar que me tratas
              como si me vbieras visto
              antes de aora.

---

305 M y el furor
307 BV adelanteme a esperarla M adelanteme auperarla
308 BMV en ella
312–313 punctuation BM mano vea: / quien se ha atrevido á quitarla?
318 BM distes
324 BM de ella
331 BV vayas M vagas
332 MB deslumbrando

PROMETEO   Otras dos, y ambas   335
bien estrañas y bien nuebas
tú, al verte y al oírte, causas:
vna, que siendo tu más
faboreçido, reparas
en que te conozca; y otra,   340
que vengas tan enojada
que te desmientas divina
para castigarme humana.
¿Qué se hiço la armonía?
¿Qué se hiço la consonançia   345
de tu voz? ¿Aun no merezco
aquella dulzura blanda
con que me hablabas?

MINERBA   ¿Qué dices?
¿Cuándo yo (dime) te hablaba?   (folio 8v)
si son éstas las primeras   350
razones q[ue] articuladas
fueron de mí, trasçendiendo
las rudezas de la ymfançia
a los discursos de joben.

PROMETEO   No el enojo, o soberana   355
Minerba, [desluzga] el don
más luzido, que es tirana
pena q[ue] a tu çeño muera,
sin saber yo de que nazca.
Dime en qué te deshobliga   360
el que en honor de la estatua
que te labró, aquese hurtado
rayo del sol te consagra?
Y ya que para su robo

---

335 M O traidor! y ambas,
342 BM desmienta
346 B aun merezco M aun me rindo
352 BMV transcendiendo
353 M las infancia
356 BMV desluzga
358 M tu leño
362 B labro
364 BM tu

me guardaste las espaldas,   365
¿en quién le pude emplear
mejor que en ti misma?

Minerba   Aguarda,
que no sé quien la razón
de dudar en mí adelanta:
¿mi estatua labraste tú?   370

Prometeo   ¿Eso dudas?
Minerba   ¿Tú, esta llama
al sol hurtaste?   (folio) 9

Prometeo   ¿Eso ygnoras?
Minerba   ¿Tú la trujiste?
Prometeo   ¿Eso estrañas?

Minerba   ¿Y es don de Minerba?
Prometeo   ¡Eso
admiras?

Minerba   ¿De qué te espanta   375
el que admire, estrañe, dude,
y ygnore, la q[ue] se halla,
sin saber cómo, con vida
tan recién naçida, sabia?

Prometeo   Pues ¿quién heres?
Minerba   No lo sé;   380
que sólo sé que ylustrada
desta antorcha, por mí dijo,
no sé si el Euro o el Aura...

Ella   Que quien da las çiençias, da
y Música   voz al barro y luz al alma.   385

_____

365 BM guardastes
366 V la
368 BM que no sé que en la razon V que no sé qué la razon
371 M Tu Estatua llama
373 V traxiste
374–375 BM Y es don de Minerva / *Prom.* Eso admiras. *Min.* De que te espantas V Y es
    don de Minerua. *Pro.* Esso / admiras? *Min.* De qué te espantas.
375 BMV espantas
377 BM omit "y"
378 B como combida M á quien combida
383 M Auna [sic]

PROMETEO   Que quien da las çiençias, da
              voz al barro y luz al alma.
              O moralidad embuelta
              en fabulosa enseñanza,
              qué de cosas que me diçes;   390
              pero ninguna más clara
              que al ver q[ue] el monte discurras,
              ver que de la gruta faltas.
              No es mucho, no, que repitan   (folio 9v)
              los vientos en voçes altas,   395
              en vajas voçes los eccos . . .

Dentro   ¡Pastores destas montañas,
EPIMETEO   sacudid el blando sueño!
              ¡Dejad, dejad las cabañas!
              ¡Acudid, acudid todos!   400

Dentro VNOS ¿Quién nos busca?
[Dentro] OTROS   ¿Quién nos llama?

Dentro   Epimeteo, a mayor
EPIMETEO   portento de nuestra patria
              que al que os llamó Prometeo;
              pues si él os combocó a causa   405
              de ver a su estatua muerta,
              yo, de ver viua su estatua.

PROMETEO   Cuanto dudamos los dos
              a dicho en vna palabra.

Dentro MERLÍN Llegad, llegad, que la noche,   410

---

388 BMV á moralidad
392 BM que al ver el monte discurrir, V que al ver discurrir el monte,
393 BMV falta
394 BMV y assi, que mucho que digan
398 B sueños
401 st.d. BMV omit "Dentro"
401 V adds st.d. *Sale Epimeteo, y pastores.*
402 BM Epimoteo, [sic] amador
405 BM fiel os convoco, á causas
407 BM viua á su
409 BMV de vna
409 V adds st. d. *Sale Merlin.*
410 st.d. BM *Sale Merl.*
410 BM omit second "llegad" V Llegad todos, que la noche,

según es de cortesana
Doña Estatua mi señora,
no os ympedirá el mirarla.

Salen todos

Timantes	Pues ¿quién su sombra ylumina?	
Libia	¿Quién su obscuridad aclara?	415
Vnos	¿Quién naçe antes q[ue] la áurora?	
Otros	¿Quién madruga antes q[ue] el alba?	
Todos con Música	Quien dando las ciencias, da voz al barro y luz al alma.	(folio) 10
Epimeteo	¡Prometeo!	
Prometeo	Epimeteo.	420
Epimeteo	¿A dónde hasta aora estabas?	
Prometeo	Para tanta comfusión ésa es noticia mui larga; después lo sabrás.	
Todos	Bien dice, que aora no ay para nada atençión que no sea asombro.	425
Minerba	Pues ¿qué os suspende? ¿q[ué] os pasma, que el rayo del sol me anime afuer de flores y plantas? mayormente cuando oýs que a merçed de soberana Deydad, Minerba le ymbíe y que Prometeo le traiga? Y pues ya en este vsurpado rasgo del luçiente alcázar,	430 435

413 BM impidirá
413 st.d. BMV omit
416 BMV el Avrora
418 speaker BM omit [lines 418–419 assigned to "Otros"] V *Mus*.
421 speaker BMV omit [line assigned to Prometeo]
422 speaker BMV *Epim*.
432 BMV embia
434 speaker BMV *Prom*.
434 BMV omit "y" V Pues yá que en
435 BMV de

en tres hedades del fuego,
pasando de luz a brasa,
y desde brasa a çeniza,
su actiuidad aplicada
a la dispuesta materia,   440
tenéis quien supla la falta   (folio 10v)
del sol para los comerçios
de la noche, en dignas graçias
de su doméstica lumbre,
repetid en voces barias . . .   445

Todos,   Que quien da las çiençias, da . . .
Ella y Música

Caja y clarín

Dentro Otros   ¡Guerra, guerra, al arma, al arma!

Todos   ¿Qué nuebo escándalo, cielos,
                        es el que los bientos rasga?

Epimeteo   Este, en baldón de Minerba,   450
                        es el enojo de Palas
                        contra mí.

Todos   Y avn contra todos.

Minerba   No temáis sus amenazas,
                        pues cuando diga el terror
                        de sus trompas y sus cajas . . .   455

Vozes   ¡Arma, arma, guerra, guerra!

Minerba   . . . dirán otras consonançias . . .

Música   Que quien da las çiençias, da
                        voz al barro y luz al alma.

---

445 BMV add st.d. *Todos, y musica.*
446 speaker BMV *Mus.*
446 BM omit "las"
446 st.d. BMV omit
447 speaker BMV *Dent.*
456 speaker BMV *Dētr.*
456 V Arma, arma, guerra *Mi.* Minerua
457 speaker V omits [line previously assigned to Minerva]
457 B Minerva dirá en otras cōsonācia M Minerva dirá en otras cōsonācias V dirá en otras
    consonancias.

Minerba	Si ya no es q[ue] el ver mezclados	460
	horrores y voçes blandas	
	geroglífico es que diga	
	que paçífica, esta llama	
	será alhago, será alibio,	
	será gozo, será graçia,	465
	y colérica, será	(folio) 11
	ynçendio, yra, estrago, y rabia;	
	y así, temed y adorad	
	al fuego cuando le exparza,	
	o afable, o sañudo, a toda	470
	la naturaleza humana	
	la estatua de Prometeo.	*Vase*

Vno	¡Oye!	
Otro	¡Espera!	
Otro	¡Escucha!	
Otro	¡Aguarda!	

Epimeteo	Por veloz q[ue] corra, yo,	
	fuerza es yr tras mi esperanza.	*Vase* 475

Prometeo	Yo tras mi admirazión.	*[Vase]*
Merlín	Yo	
	tras saber si algo me manda	
	Doña Estatua mi señora.	*[Vase]*

Timantes	Hasta ver adónde para,	
	seguidla todos.	
Libia	Y sea	480
	en haçimiento de graçias,	

---

460 BM mezcladas V mezclar
469 BM la esparça
470 BMV sañuda
473 speakers BM *Vnos. Oye. / Otros. Espera. / Otra. Escucha. / Otro. Aguarda.* V 1. Oye.
    2. Espera. / 3. Escucha. 4. Aguarda.
475 speaker BMV *Pro.*
475 st.d. BMV omit
476 speaker BMV *Tim.*
476 V Y yo
477 BMV saber que me manda
479 speaker BMV *Liu.*
480 speaker BMV omit [Libia already speaking]

	dando a su nueba Deydad,	
	con dones, bayles, y danzas,	
	la bienvenida.	
Timantes	Bien diçes,	485
	aunque en parte me acobarda	
	el oýr a vn tiempo a vna	
	de dos Deydades contrarias . . .	(folio 11v)
El y Música	Que quien da las çiençias, da	
	voz al barro y luz al alma.	
[Timantes]	. . . y a otra . . .	
Cajas y Otros	¡Arma, arma, guerra, guerra!	490
Timantes	. . . con que reçelo que nazca	
	la estatua de Prometeo	
	para escándalo del Assia.	
Libia	En tanto que el no suçeda,	
	mejor es deçir con ambas . . .	495
Con Todos	Que quien da las çiençias, da	
y Música	voz al barro y luz al alma.	
	¡Arma, arma, guerra, guerra!	

Vanse y salen Palas, p[o]r vna parte, y por otra la Discordia,
cantando rezitatibo, o en tramoyas como mejor parezca.

Discordia	Entre dulçes voçes blandas,	
	¿qué militares estruendos,	500
	conzeuidos de los montes,	
	y abatidos de los eccos,	

---

487 BMV add. st.d. *El, y Musica.*
488 speaker BMV *Mus.*
488 BM dá sus ciencias
490 speaker BMV *Tim.*
490 st.d. BMV *Caxa, y todos.*
491 speakers BMV *Tod.*
494 B el nos rueda M él nos ruede, V que dura el ruido
496 speakers BMV omit [Libia speaking]
496 BMV add st.d. BM *Caxa, todos, y Musica.* V *Caxa, clarin, y musica.*
497 speaker BMV *Mus.*
498 speaker BMV *Disc.*
498 st.d. BMV *Vanse, y sale Discorida cantando recitatiuo.* [following line 497]
499 speaker BMV omit [Discordia speaking]
502 BMV "abortados" for "abatidos"

| | tocan al arma sin mí?
¿De cuándo acá pudo, çielos,
aber guerra sin Discordia? | 505 |

PALAS Nunca, y así prebiniendo
que abías de ser primera
çentella de mis ynçendios,   (folio) 12
dejé mi sagrado solio
para salirte al encuentro.   510

DISCORDIA Pues ¿q[ué] te obliga oy a tanto
bélico marcial apresto?

PALAS Minerba y yo . . .
DISCORDIA   Ya lo sé-
partisteis valor y yngenio.

PALAS Ella en Prometeo . . .
DISCORDIA   Ynspiró   515
çiençias.
PALAS   Yo en Epimetheo
alto espíritu . . .
DISCORDIA   De ambos
sé el estudio y sé el esfuerzo.

PALAS Prometeo a su Deydad . . .

DISCORDIA Labró vna estatua, a q[uie]n luego,   520
dando el vno el simulacro,
el otro la ofreçió templo.

PALAS Agradeçida Minerba . . .

DISCORDIA Elebó su alumno al çielo.

PALAS Y embozado en pardas nubes . . .   525

DISCORDIA Le ocultó, para q[ue] vn vello
rayo al sol le hurtase.

---

505 BMV add st.d. *Sale Palas cantando recitatiuo.*
509 BMV dexo
517 speaker BM *Dis.* Alto espiritu / de ambos
521 BM dando vno
522 BM ofreció el Templo.
527 BMV omit "le"

PALAS	Este, al calor del sacro fuego ...
DISCORDIA	Ymfluió en la bruta forma alma, ser, vida, y aliento. (folio 12v) 530
PALAS	Abía a Epimetheo mandado ...
DISCORDIA	Romperla, y Epimetheo, al verla vibir, no pudo ejecutar el preçepto. Hasta aquí sé de esos raros 535 prodijios.
PALAS	Graçias al çielo que llegué a lo q[ue] no saues, con que me oirás con silençio. Epimeteo, no sé si la buscó con yntento de cumplir con mi obedienzia, v de cumplir con su afecto; dejemos aquí esta duda, y vamos a que los pueblos de esos rústicos villages, 545 de esos bárbaros desiertos, admirados de los dos tan nunca vistos suçesos, como que entre leño y barro, viba el barro y arda el leño, 550 en loor de Minerba no ay quien con dones y festejos no la çelebre, ymbentando bayles, músicas, y juegos, aclamándola con nombre (folio) 13 555 de Pandora, que en el griego bulgar frase significa

---

531 BM omit "a"
535 BMV destos; M qui [sic]
542 BMV con mi afecto
545 BM dessos rusticos villanajes V dessos rudos villanages
546 BMV dessos
549 BM que en tu leño, V en vn leño
553 BM y inuentando
557 BMV Idioma, aqui significa

la probidençia del tiempo;
con que desairada yo
de que aya Prometeo   560
conseguido a su auxsiliar
Deydad tan común obsequio,
por derramar sus solazes,
al arma les toqué, pero
como la guerra no consta   565
de solos los ynstrumentos,
mientras no ay en los vmanos
desabenençias, supuesto
que el ruido en trompas y cajas
no es más q[ue] alhaja del viento,   570
viendo cuanto neçesito
de corazones opuestos,
valerme de ti, Discordia,
para mi venganza yntento.
Y así, pues tú [sediçiosa]   575
deydad [eres], [siembra] en ellos
ojerizas, disensiones,
hodios y aborrecimientos.
Débate yo lo que tú
me deberás a mí, viendo   (folio 13v)   580
que de tus zizañas naçen
mis victorias, pues poniendo
el fuego Minerba, y yo
la sangre, verás cuán presto
no sólo el Cáucaso, el orbe,   585
agoniza a sangre y fuego.
Esto por mí . . .

DISCORDIA   No prosigas,
que se desdeña el respeto

---

559 BM desayradas
561 BM conseguido amansiliar V auxiliar
564 BMV solo
566 BMV solo
568 B desta Venencia, M dessa Venencia, V desavenencia,
575 BMV sediciosa
576 BMV eres, siembra
580 BMV deuieras
581 BMV destas ciçañas

de que se balga el mandato
de la sumisión del ruego. 590
Yntroduzida en su tosco
trage, mezclada con esos
villanos, y desmentido
mi açento entre sus açentos,
mi don la ofreçeré en vna 595
vrna q[ue] contenga dentro
los hados de la discordia;
con que en abriéndola, es çierto
que rota la cárçel, salgan
ymfestando el ayre, embueltos 600
en venenosos vapores;
mayormente contra esos
dos ribales como más (folio) 14
nobles caudillos del pueblo,
que le alteren, pues su nueba 605
Deydad, a vno aborreçiendo,
y faboreçiendo a otro,
es fuerza que entren los çelos,
vltima sediçión mía,
tocando al arma, si llego 610
por ti a turbar los mortales.

[PALAS]   Yo haré que en ese yntermedio
cuente sus rayos Apolo,
y echando el hurtado menos,
su luz les niegue eclipsado, 615
porque asaltados a vn tiempo,
digan al son de mis trompas
sus relámpagos y truenos . . .

---

590 BM de la cumsion [sic] del ruego V de circunstancias de ruego.
591 BMV en vn
595 BMV le
600 BMV embuelto
603 BM "Piuales" for "ribales"
609 BM ú estima, sedicion
611 speaker BM *Pal.*
612 speaker V *Pal.*
612 BMV "este" for "ese" BM omit "yo"
615 BMV le

Dentro música y gritos

MÚSICA   Al festejo, al festejo, zagales,
                zagalas, venid, venid al festejo.   620

DISCORDIA   ¿Es éste su aplauso?
PALAS   Sí.
                Pero ya dél no me ofendo,
                si atiendo a cuán poco dura
                la brebedad del contento;
                y más cuando vas, Discordia,   625
                tú a turbarle.

DISCORDIA   Así lo ofrezco.   (folio 14v)
PALAS   ¡Pues al arma!
DISCORDIA   ¡Pues al arma!

PALAS   . . . que yo aguardo . . .
DISCORDIA   . . . que yo espero . . .

LAS DOS   . . . giman mañana llorando,
                por más que oi canten riendo,   630

                [Dentro música]

CON   Al festejo, al festejo, çagales,
LA MÚSICA   çagalas, venid, venid al festejo
                que a la nueba Deydad destos montes
                la ofreçen en fee de ser hija del fuego
                la tierra con flores, el agua con perlas,   635
                el ayre con plumas, con salbas el ecco.

                Fin de [Segunda] X[orna]da

_____

618 st.d. BMV *Dentro Musica.*
620 BMV Zagales
621 speaker BMV *Pal.* Es este su aplauso? *Disc.* Si.
622 speaker BMV *Pal.*
622 V Pues yá de él
629 speaker M *Los dos*
629 BMV Verlos mañana
630 V canten, diziendo
630 st.d. BMV *Dentro Musica.*
631 speaker BMV *Mu.*
632 BMV Zagales
633 BMV de estos
634 BMV omit "la" BMV de el BM fé

TERÇERA JORNADA DE LA ESTATUA DE PROMETHEO

Mutaçión de selba, y saldrá de debajo vn peñasco como pira para poner los sacrifiçios, de forma que vn hombre pueda dar fuego a lo q[ue] se pusiere en él, y salen cantando y bailando, lo mismo con q[ue] se acabó la segunda jornada, todos los pastores y zagalas, y en medio, Minerba y Timantes biejo, Prometeo, y Epimeteo con todos.

MÚSICA	Al festejo, al festjo, çagales,	
	çagalas, venid, venid al festejo,	
	que a la nueba Deydad destos montes	
	la ofreçen en fee de ser hija del fuego,	
	la tierra con flores, el agua con perlas,	5
	el ayre con plumas, con salbas el ecco.	
LIBIA	Pues te tocó a ti la suerte	
	de aber de hablar el primero,	
	llega.	
MERLÍN	Debina Pandorga . . .	
LIBIA	Pandora as de deçir, neçio.	10
MERLÍN	¿Cómo?	
LIBIA	Pandora.	
MERLÍN	Está bien –	
	aparta, y como lo enmiendo	
	verás: Deuina . . .	
LIBIA	Pandora.	
MERLÍN	Pandorga.	

Third Act begins at this point in the text only in Ms. In BMV, the division occurs at Ms. III, 307. See Manuscript Notes

First st.d. BMV *Dentro la musica, vozes, y instru- / mentos, y salen en tropa Zagales, / y Zagalas, cantando, y baylando / con los demás que dieren despues / los versos, y detras Prometeo, / Epimeteo, y Minerua.* V *darán*

1–6 BMV omit
7 BM á ti, Lauerto
9 M Pundorga
10 BM Pandorga
11 M bjen [sic]
12 BMV le
13 M *Liu.* Pandorga. BM *Merl.* Pandora.

LIBIA   Gentil enmienda por çierto.

MERLÍN   Si otros an de e[n]quibocarse,   (folio 1v)   15
                       tan estraño nombre oyendo,
                       quizá es artimaña que
                       me enquiboque yo primero,
                       para que del sonsonete
                       no tengan q[ue] trobar ellos.   20
                       Y así, deuina Pandora –
                       si de tres la vna lo açierto –
                       sepa su merçed que todo
                       el Cacaoso mui contento
                       de estar tan faboreçido   25
                       y tan sobido de preçio
                       con su hermosura y su luz,
                       viene el q[ue] a sus patas puesto
                       le vendiga en su olor, vna
                       y mil veçes repitiendo . . .   30

                              Quatro Cornet[as]

CON   Al festejo, al festejo, [çagales,
LA MÚSICA   çagalas, venid, venid al festejo,
                       que a la nueba Deydad destos montes
                       la ofreçen en fee de ser hija del fuego
                       la tierra con flores, el agua con perlas,   35
                       el ayre con plumas, con salbas el ecco].

---

14 V *Merlin*. Pandorra. / *Lib*. Bien lo hazes cierto.
15 BM enquiuocarse
18 V equiuoque
19 BM solsonete
22 BMV la acierto
24 BM El cacao, me vi contento V el Caucaso muy contento
26 BMV subido
26–27 punctuation BM precio. / Con
28 BM vine, que aupatas puesto, V viue, y que á sus patas puesto
29 BM le bendiga en oloor vna, V la bendize en loor, vna
30 st.d. BMV omit. See Manuscript Notes.
31 speakers BMV *Musi*.
33 speaker BMV *Dis*.
34 BM de el
36 BM con su voz el eco
36 st.d. BMV *Con esta repeticion sale la Discordia / vestida de Villana, mezclada con las demás*. V *los demás*

Con esta repetizión, sale de villana la Discordia,
y se mezcla con ellos.

TIMANTES	Ya que aquí no ay otra pira	
	en que te sacrifiquemos	
	nuestros dones, sea este risco	
	trono tuio, y altar nuestro.	40
Canta LIBIA	En esta guirnalda vella,	
	para que en tu frente hermosa	
	la menos fragrante rossa	
	sea más brillante estrella,	
	te sirbe, çifrando en ella	45
	sus matizados primores . . .	
EL 4	La tierra con flores.	
VILLANA 1ª	En este nácar, la orilla	(folio) 2
	del mar, cuajando al aurora,	
	de las lágrimas que llora,	50
	los nectos hilos que brilla,	
	te ofreçe vna gargantilla,	
	si llega en tu cuello a verlas . . .	
CON EL 4	El agua con perlas.	
VILLANA 2ª	Si aplaudió tus hechos grabes	55
	allí el aurora, aquí el alba,	

---

41 speaker BM omit [Timantes speaking]
41 BM en nuestra guirnalda bella. *canta* V Con esta
42 speaker BM *Liu.*
43 V brillante rosa
44 V fragrante estrella
46 BM add. st.d. *canta*
47 speakers BM omit [Libia speaking] V *Tod. y mus.*
47 BMV La tierra con flores, la tierra con flores,
48 speaker BM omit [Libia speaking] V *Zagala 2.*
49 BM quaxado á la V cuaxando á la
50 BMV omit. V adds a compensating line, "que sea nueua marauilla", after line 52.
51 BM los Netos, y los que brilla V Netos
54 speakers BM omit [Libia speaking] V *Tod. y mus.*
54 BMV el agua con perlas, el agua con perlas.
54 BM add. st.d. *canta*
55 speaker V *Zagal. 3*
55 BM sus ojos graves V tus ojos graues

	haçiendo a tu vista salba		
	la música de las aves,		
	y así te sirbe en suaues		
	auras que gozar presumas.		60
Con El 4	El ayre con plumas.		
Villana 3ª	Todo a tu hermosa Deydad		
	se rinde y se sacrifica,		
	pues hasta el monte publica		
	méritos de tu veldad;		65
	del clarín la suabidad		
	hable, en quien resuena gúeco . . .		
Con El 4	Con salbas el ecco.		
Todos	Todos que te sirban les agradeçemos . . .		

Quatro cruzados en alas

Con	La tierra con flores, el agua con perlas,		70
La Música	el ayre con plumas, con salbas el ecco.		
Discordia	Yo también, que de la sierra		
	con mi don e desçendido,		
	esta vrna te e trahido,		
	en que verás q[ue] se ençierra	(folio 2v)	75
	más que en ecco, ayre, agua, y tierra		
	dan en sus ofrecimientos		
	la tierra con flores, el agua con perla[s],		
	el ayre con plumas, con salbas el ecco.		

---

59 BM te sirven suaves V te seruirá en mas suaues
61 speakers BM *Musi.* V *Tod. y mus.*
61 BMV El ayre con plumas, el ayre con plumas.
62 speaker BM *3* V *Zagala 4.*
68 speakers BM *Music.* V *Tod. y mus.*
68 BMV Con salvas el eco, con saluas el eco.
68 V adds st.d. *Cantando, y baylando.*
69 speakers V *Mus.*
69 st.d. BMV omit. See Manuscript Notes
70 speakers BM *Todos, y mus.* V omits
71 BM add st.d. *cantando.*
72 BMV la tierra
77 speaker B *Lodos y Dis.* M *Los dos, y Dis.* V *Todos y Disc.*
77 BMV Dã essos ofrecimiẽtos,

| Todos | Al festejo, al festejo, çagales, . . . | 80 |

Rep[resen]ta
Minerba

Tened, suspended, parad el festejo,
que más dilaçiones no
sufre mi agradeçimiento.
Dadme lugar en que yo,
reconoçida al obsequio,   85
y del obsequio quejosa,
yntente mezclar a vn tiempo
de la lisonja y la ofensa,
las graçias y el sentimiento.
¿Quién soi yo, para q[ue] hagáis   90
tantos festibos extremos
en mi alabanza? ¿Soi más
que vn adbenedizo objeto
que a los golfos de la vida
tomó en buestros montes puerto?   95
Entre vosotros, humilde,
sólo a haçer número vengo,
no excepsión y assí . . .

Timantes

                              No más,
que todos reconoçemos
la feliçidad que en ti   (folio) 3
nos partiçipan los çielos,
pues de Minerba y Apolo,
dando ella el retrato al cuerpo,
y él la luz al alma, eres
tan elebado conçepto   105
que ya que no Diosa, te haçe
semidiosa por lo menos.

Epimeteo

Dígalo yo, pues aun antes
de cobrar vida y aliento,
ynnanimada hermosura,   110
te adoré y ofreçí templo;
y después quizá a pesar

---

80 speakers BMV omit
81 speaker BMV *Miner.*
84 BMV "á" for "en"
93 V aduenecido
98 B exencion M exempcion V essempcion
103 BMV al retrato el

de algún soberano çeño,
librarte yntenté de otro
no menos costoso riesgo   115
que el de no llegar a ser
viuo animado portento.
Esto e dicho porque sepas
lo que me debes, a efecto,
si lo que me deues saues,   120
de saber lo q[ue] te deuo.

Minerba   ¿Cómo tú, tan retirado
               no me alegas, Prometheo,
               lo que a ti te deuo?

Prometeo   Como
               quien da en rostro lo q[ue] a hecho   (folio 3v) 125
               en seruiçio de vna dama
               desluçe el merecimiento.

Epimeteo   No es dar en rostro acordar.

Prometeo   No, mas es haçer acuerdo.

Epimeteo   El silençio en las finezas,   130
               fineza es a parte, pero
               serlo para no sabidas,
               ¿de qué les serbirá el serlo?

Prometeo   De complaçerse en sí mismo
               quien las hiçiere, supuesto   135
               que aunque a la dama las calle,
               a él se las dirá el silençio.

Epimeteo   Esa es modestia que oi es,
               en las maliçias del tiempo,
               virtud desaprobechada.   140

Prometeo   Esotra japtançia, al mesmo

---

129 V recuerdo
130 BMV la fineza
132 V sabida
133 for "les" BM have "te", V has "le"
136 BMV omit "a"
138 B Esta; BM oyes
140 BM virtudes aprouechadas
141 BM Es otra jactancia V Estotra jactancia

                          paso, viçio ynteresado,
                          supuesto que aspira al premio.

EPIMETEO   Sin esperanza, ninguno
                          sirbiera.
PROMETEO   Serbir es neçio,   145
                          porque, ¿qué más esperanza
                          el día que serbir merezco?

EPIMETEO   Eso es bueno para dicho.

PROMETEO   Eso es malo para hecho.   (folio) 4

EPIMETEO   Quien piense . . .
PROMETEO   Quien ymagine . . .   150

MINERBA   No más, que no es bien q[ue] a duelo
                          pase de la bolumptad
                          la lid del entendimiento.

EPIMETEO   Como yo no sé argüir,
                          sino lidiar.
MINERBA   ¡Qué soberbio!   155

PROMETEO   Yo, ni argüir ni lidiar
                          sé, mas sé sentir.
MINERBA   ¡Qué cuerdo!
                          Pues yo, porque mude asumpto,
                          pasando de vno a otro extremo
                          la cuestión, dejo la queja,   160
                          y a lo que es lisonja buelbo.
                          Tan agradeçida estoi
                          al no mereçido obsequio,
                          como antes dije, q[ue] en fee
                          de mostrar que le agradezco,   165

───────────────

143 speaker BMV *Epi.*
143 BM aspirara el premio V aspira al
144 speaker BMV omit [Epimeteo speaking]
144 BMV ninguna
145 BMV sirviera neçio;
149 BM omit "es"
153 BMV la luz
155 BM altivo
158 B porque mudé assunto MV porque mude assunto
165 BMV lo

e de repartir con todos
los dones que yncluye dentro
de sí esta dorada vrna,
que serán preçiosos, puesto
que ençierra cuanto obstentaron   170
ayre, agua, tierra, y ecco;   (folio 4v)
y así, en el nombre de todos,
para yrlos repartiendo,
la abro, mas ¡ay, ymfeliz!

Abre la caja y sale humo, y todos se barajan como ciegos

TODOS   ¿Qué es esto, Dioses?   ¿Qué es esto?   175

DISCORDIA   Si tenéis el fuego hurtado,
                 ¿qué admiráis el humo, siendo
                 tan natural consecuenzia
                 que aya humo donde ay fuego?

EPIMETEO   ¡En tí, mágica villana,   180
                 vengaré el pabor!

PROMETEO   ¡Primero
                 le castigaré yo!

VNOS   ¡Muera
                 a tus manos, Prometheo!

OTROS   ¡Muera, Epimeteo, a tus manos!

DISCORDIA   En vano procuráis, çiegos,   185
                 que ellos os venguen de mí,
                 cuando e de vengar yo en ellos
                 de Apolo . . .

PROMETEO   ¿Qué es lo q[ue] escucho?

DISCORDIA   . . .Y Palas . . .

EPIMETEO   ¿ Qué es lo q[ue] veo?

---

169 BM "pues" for "puesto"
170 BM omit "que" BMV encierran V ostentaron
174 BM omit "ay"
174 st.d. BMV *Abre la vrna, y sale humo.*
180 BMV "mi ira" for "magica"
181 V vengará
182 BMV la
186 B vengen

Discordia	. . . el sacrilegio del hurto,	190
	y del culto el sacrilejio,	
	con tan discordantes hados	
	como que tú, Epimetheo,	(folio) 5
	amarás aborreçido;	
	tú, al contrario, Prometheo,	195
	aborreçerás amado,	
	y todos en bandos puestos	
	arderéis en duras lides.	

Canta

Y pues ya en discordia dejo
puesto el monte, mientras yo   200
con segundo dizfrás buelbo
a turbarlo, acude Palas
a los enojos de Fçuo;
que a mí no me toca más
que aber sido humo y ser viento.   205

Desapareze

Vnos	¡Qué asombro!	
Otros	¡Qué comfusión!	
Los Dos	Aora nos diçe tu açento	
	ser Deydad de la discordia.	

Truenos

Minerba	Y aun no para aquí, q[ue] embuelto	
	el sol entre pardas nubes	210

196 BMV amando
198 st.d. BMV omit
199 BMV omit "y" B en cordiscordia M en cordiscordias V en Discordia os dexo
202 BM á turbarle aun de Palas, V á turbarle, y mueue Palas
206 BMV Vnos. Que confusion!
206 BM add st.d. Epimeteo, y Prometeo.
206 speaker for "otros" BM has Prom., V has Prom y Epi. BMV Qué assombro!
207 speaker BMV Min.
208 BMV ser Diosa
208 st.d. BMV omit and add st.d. Terremoto, on line 211. See Manuscript Notes.
209 speaker BMV omit [Minerva speaking]
210 BM muchas nubes V densas nubes

de negros obscuros belos,
deja al día sin el día.

PROMETEO   Que mucho, si son efectos
de Apolo, ayrado en mi robo,
que ellas, rasgando sus senos,   215
se quejen en culebrinas
de relámpagos, siguiendo

Terremoto

el aborto de los rayos,   (folio 5v)
el gemido de los truenos.

Obscurécese

TIMANTES   Antiçipada la noche,   220
tocando arma al vniberso,
desarrugad[a]s desdobla
tupidas sombras sin tiempo.

EPIMETEO   Qué mucho, si es la ojeriça
de Palas, a quien yo temo.   225

TODOS   El humo de la discordia
a todos çiega.

MERLÍN   No es bueno.

LIBIA   ¿Qué?

MERLÍN   Que con ser griegos todos,
pareçe que somos griegos.

LIBIA   ¿A quién del rigor con que   230

---

212 BM dexa el
215 BMV ellos
217 st.d. BMV omit
218 BMV al aborto
219 st.d. BMV omit
220 speaker BMV omit [Prometeo speaking]
221 BM have "el" for "al"
222 BMV desarrugadas
223 BM tapidas
225 BMV yo tiemblo.
226 speaker BM *Merl.*
227 speakers BM *Liu.* A todos ciega. V *Libia.* No es bueno
228 speakers BM omit "*Libia*" [Merlín speaking], V has *Me.* Qué / BMV *Liu.* Que con ser
       Griegos todos,
229 BM que los mas Griegos
230 speaker BMV omit [Libia speaking]

	amenazados nos vemos	
	acudiremos?	
TIMANTES	A sólo	
	el llanto, el gemido, el ruego;	
	y assí, con himnos y voçes,	
	clamad conmigo, diçiendo,	235
	¡Fabor, Dioses soberanos!	

TODOS   ¡Fabor, Dioses soberanos!
Y MÚSICA
TIMANTES   ¡Piedad, soberanos çielos!

TODOS   ¡Piedad, soberanos çielos!
Y MÚSICA

Con el terremoto, música, y voçes, se van p[o]r distintas partes, y quedan
Prometeo, Epimeteo, y Minerba.

EPIMETEO	A sacrificar a Palas	(folio) 6	240
	tras éstos, por si es que puedo		
	desenojarla, yré.		
PROMETEO	Yo,		
	siguiendo a estotros, yntento		
	sacrificar a Minerba,		
	pues a ella el rigor q[ue] temo		245
	de Apolo toca.		
EPIMETEO	Conmigo		
	ven, para q[ue] vean sus çeños		
	que si en ti tube la culpa,		
	en ti la disculpa tengo.		
MINERBA	¿Yo contigo? Antes, desde ese		250
	elebado risco exçelso		
	me preçipitara al mar,		
	y más cuando en seguimiento		

---

233 BM el llanto es temido el ruego,
234 BMV con gritos
236 BMV omit
237 speakers BM *Todos.*
238 BMV omit
239 speakers BMV *Music.*
239 st.d. BMV omit
243 V essotros
250 BM dudé esse V antes aquesse

	a los cultos de Minerba	
	puedo yr tras Prometheo.	255

PROMETEO   Eso sí, mas no, no vengas
tras mí, ymfausto asombro bello,
que al mirarte como causa
de las ansias q[ue] padezco,
te e cobrado tal horror,   260
tal sobresalto, tal miedo,
tal susto, tal pabor, tal,
no sé si aborreçimiento,
que sin atreberme a verte,
me atrebo a dejarte; çielos,   (folio 6v) 265
¿cómo, cuando me acobardo,
oso a dezir que me atrebo?   *Vase*

EPIMETEO   Ve tras él, aborreçida,
no tras mí, amada.

MINERBA   Eso yntento,
porque tengo por menor   270
dolor, menor sentimiento,
aborreçida, y amada
seguir entre ambos extremos
al que amo aborreçida,
que no al q[ue] amada aborrezco.   *Vase* 275

EPIMETEO   Al que amo aborreçida,
que no al q[ue] amada aborrezco.

        A lo lejos, todos y mús[i]ca

TODOS   ¡Fabor, Dioses soberanos!
Y MÚSICA   ¡Piedad, soberanos çielos!

EPIMETEO   Por mí pudieran deçirlo   280
aun mejor que por sí mesmos,

---

256 V mas nunca vengas
257 V infausto monstruo
267 V omits "a"
275 st.d. BMV omit
276–277 BMV omit
277 st.d. BM *Terremoto á lo lexos, y musica.* V *Terremoto, y musica á lo lexos.*
278 speaker BM *Ter.* V *Tod.*
279 BMV *Music.*
281 B mismos

        pues no sé qué espeçie de yra,
        qué género de veneno,
        qué linage de rencor,
        a yntroduçido en mi pecho,   285
        no tanto el q[ue] a mí me deje,
        cuanto el que vaya siguiendo
        a otro, que de su desaire
        me vengaré en él primero
        que en ella; ¿quién yntrodujo   290
        tan ynjusta ley al duelo,   (folio) 7
        tan bárbara al pundonor,
        como ser en vn despreçio
        la dama de quien me agrabio,
        y el galán de quien me vengo?   295
        pero ya que yntroduçida
        la hallo, yo buscaré medio
        que me vengue della en él;
        bien que para tanto efecto,
        aplacar antes a Palas   300
        me ymporta, y así pretendo,
        con los que mi vando sigan,
        para mejor atraerlos
        después a su sacrifiçio,
        repetir aora con ellos . . .   305

EL Y TODOS   ¡Fabor, Dioses soberanos!
               ¡Piedad, soberanos çielos!   *Vase*

---

282 BM especies
286 BM dexa
287 BM aya seguido
289 BMV vengara
291 BMV tan ilustre ley
294 BM agrauia
299–305 BMV omit, replacing them with the following lines ending the second and
     opening the third act: por mas que diga el estruendo / de musicas, y de rayos, / de
     relampagos, y truenos. / *Todos, él y Musica.* / *Todos.* Fauor, Dioses Soberanos. /
     Music. Piedad, Soberanos Cielos. / IORNADA TERCERA. [V TERCERA IOR-
     NADA.] / *Dentro Timantes* / *Tim.* Pues de Palas, y de Apolo, / aun dura el sagrado
     ceño, / duren tambien en nosotros / repetidos los lamentos. / *El, y todos.*
306 speaker BMV *Todos.*
307 st.d. BMV omit *Vase* at end of their second act
307 st.d. BMV *Sale Apolo, y Palas cantando recitatiuo.* [after repetition of "Fabor . . .
     çielos," lines 6–7 of their third act]

Teatro de çielos, y en él salen, o en nubes, o por el tablado, Apolo y Palas,
cantando reçitatibo.

APOLO   ¿Qué piedad ni qué fabor
                 conseguir, Palas, pretende
                 quien me ofende   310
                 en el vsurpado honor
                 de mi splendor?
                 Y pues en mi yndignación
                 todos son
                 compliçes del robo el día   (folio 7v)   315
                 que a nueba Deydad, con nueba alegría,
                 sabiendo q[ue] es hurto, le admiten por don,
                 perezcan todos, y vea
                 Minerba que te e deuido
                 aber sabido   320
                 que ella en mi agrabio se emplea,
                 por que crea
                 que hajadas en ti mis pompas
                 es bien rompas
                 altas espheras y bajas,   325
                 jimiendo mis nubes al son de tus caja[s],
                 bramando mis truenos al son de tus trompa[s].
                 A este fin, a su orizonte
                 di la primera alborada,
                 cuando fiada   330
                 la rienda a Flegón y a Etonte,
                 vengo al monte
                 en busca tuia secreto,
                 a cuio efecto
                 visto militares galas.   335
                 ¿Qué mucho q[ue] sea soldado oi por Palas,

_____

312 BMV esplendor
317 BMV have "perdon" for "por don"
318 BM Parezcan
320 BMV aborrecido
326 BM have "sus" for "tus"
328 B aun Orizonte MV á vn Orizonte
329 BMV de la primer alboreada
331 BMV y Etonte ["a" omitted] V has "Pyrois" in place of "Flegon"
334 M cuya V efeto
336 V sea oy Soldado por

si ayer por Climene pastor fui de Admeto?

PALAS   Tan ofendida me vi
               de que Minerba en tu esphera
               yntrodujera   340
               tal traiçión, q[ue] antes q[ue] a ti,   (folio) 8
               cuenta di
               a la Discordia, por quien
               todos se ven
               ya en sus ritos encontrados;   345
               mas, ¿cuándo, sañudos y adbersos sus hados,
               corriendo haçia el mal, pararon al bien?

APOLO   Pues si ecco y aire, agua y tierra
               la tributaron sus dones,
               y dispones   350
               tú en su discordia la guerra,
               valle y sierra
               verán arder su comfín,
               siendo, a fin
               de la lid q[ue] tu horror fragua,   355
               la caja la tierra, el pífano el agua,
               el ayre la trompa, y el ecco el clarín.

PALAS   Pues sea a fin
               de la lid que tu horror fragua . . .

A DUO   La caja la tierra, el pífano el agua,   360
               el ayre la trompa, y el ecco el clarín.

               Sale canta[n]do Minerba.

MINERBA   No sea a fin.

EL DUO   Sí sea a fin.

---

337 M Clemene
344 BMV omit "se"
345 B y a mis ritos MV ya mis ritos
352 BMV y Tierra
356 V pifaro
360 speaker BMV *Los dos.*
360 V pifaro
361 st.d. BM omit, but add *Canta* to speaker *Min.* in next line.
362 B omits "a"
363 speaker BMV *Los dos.*

MINERBA	No sea a fin		
	de la lid que su horror fragua,		365
	ni caja la tierra, ni pífano el agua,		
	ni el ayre la trompa, ni el ecco el clarín.		
	Que no es justiçia, Apolo,		
	que ençiendas tú la lid,		
	cuando q[ue] agradeçer	(folio 8v)	370
	tienes, más q[ue] sentir.		

APOLO   ¿Qué agradeçer, tirana,
          biendo robar por ti,
          para tu estatua, vn rayo
          de mi luçiente ofir?   375

MINERBA   Si en solo vn rayo tuio –
          y aun ése tan sutil
          que no le hechaste menos
          hasta ýrtelo a deçir
          esa traidora hermana –   380
          a los mortales di,
          en común benefiçio,
          la dicha más feliz,
          no haçiendo falta allá
          y aprobechando aquí,   385
          ¿qué te enoja? pues queda
          siempre tuio el luçir.

APOLO   Diçes bien, que la lumbre
          material desmentir
          la elemental no puede,   390
          que proçedió de mí.

PALAS   No diçe bien, que tú
          supieras exparçir,
          cuando tu probidençia
          quisiera repartir   395

---

366 V pifaro
376 BM Siendo solo V Si es solo
377 BM este
379 BMV sin irtelo
385 M omits; BV esse rayo sutil
389 punctuation BMV material desmentir,
392 BV No dizes tu que tu M No dize que tu

	su luz con los mortales,	
	no vn rayo, sino mil;	
	con que ellos te debieran	(folio) 9
	el benefiçio a ti.	
	Pero a despecho tuio,	400
	¿no es traiçión conseguir,	
	a costa de tu luz,	
	las graçias para sí?	
APOLO	Tú diçes bien también,	
	y pues llegó a ympedir	405
	mi liberalidad	
	su cauteloso ardid,	
	no dejando q[ue] haçer	
	a mi Deydad, sentir	
	deuo, que el luçir mío	410
	yntente desluçir.	
MINERBA	No deues, que el bien no	
	comunicado oý	
	que no es perfecto bien;	
	y siendo, Apolo, assí,	415
	que aquella perfección	
	que le faltó, añadí,	
	a mí me deue el ser	
	perfecto bien por mí.	
APOLO	Tienes razón.	
PALAS	No tiene,	420
	que cuando fuese assí,	
	hurtar para haçer bien	
	no es virtud, viçio sí.	

---

397 punctuation BMV mil?
401 BMV omit "no"
402 BMV have "su" for "tu"
410 BM dudo que
412 V debes tal, que
413 BM oir
417 BMV añadir
418 BM omit "me"
419 BMV por ti

Apolo	Así es.	(folio 9v)
Minerba	No es assí cuando	
	resulta en tan gentil,	425
	noble, glorioso empleo;	
	que si suelen deçir	
	que el sol y el hombre dan	
	la vida, y oi por mí	
	claro lo ven, ¿q[ué] sientes?	430

Apolo	También esso es assí,
	que yo a esa noble acción
	quien la dio el alma fui.

Palas	No des nombre de noble	
	acción [a] la más ruin,	435
	que lo vil del hurtar	
	siempre se queda vil.	

Minerba	Y yntroduçir discordias	
	traidoramente, di,	
	¿es por ventura, Palas,	440
	acción menos çiuil?	

Palas	Yo su honor . . .
Minerba	Yo su aplauso . . .

Apolo	¡Tened, parad, oíd!	
	que ambas sois mis hermanas,	
	y aunque pude venir	445
	ofendido del robo,	
	no sé, llegad[o] a oír,	
	a cual debo dejar,	

---

425 BM resuelta
427 BM Si se suele
431 V es esso assi
432 BM omit "a"
433 BM have "le" for "la" B dió el al alma
435 BMV á la accion mas ruin
438 speaker V *Merl.*
438 BMV Discordia
443 BM parad, y oid,
444 BM hermanos
445 BM pudo
447 BMV no os he llegado

	ni a cual deuo asistir;	(folio) 10
	y así a buestro albedrío	450
	obrad, que desde aquí,	
	neutral soi de las dos.	

PALAS   Eso me vasta a mí,
que si en otro disfraz
consigue diuidir   455
en vandos la Discordia
ese pueblo ymfeliz,
mejor partido tengo
en lidiar q[ue] argüir.

MINERBA   Yo también, que las letras   460
con las armas medir
sauen su ymperio.

PALAS   ¿Pues
a la lid!

MINERBA   ¡A la lid!

APOLO   Ya que ympedir no puedo
el duelo, proseguid;   465
que yo siendo, y no siendo,
ni auxsiliar, ni adalid,
sólo diré que sean
y no sean a vn fin . . .

LOS TRES   La tierra la caja, el pífano el agua,   470
el ayre la trompa, el ecco el clarín.

Súbese Apolo y las dos se entran, mudando el teatro de selba florida,
y a las voçes de Epimeteo, buelben a salir.

Dentro   Venid, todos, venid   (folio 10v)
EPIMETEO   conmigo al sacrifiçio
de Palas.

---

452 BM los dos
455 BMV consiguió el diuidir
457 BMV a esse
459 BM que en argüir
467 BM auxiliar
470 V pifaro
470 st.d. BM omit; V has only *Vase apolo.*
473 BM add. st.d. *Vase Apo.*

                              [Sale Palas]

Rep[resen]ta   Pues aquí
PALAS   Epimetheo me aclama,   475
                   ¿qué espero para yr
                   a asistirle? no ya
                   de él dudosa.   *Vase*
Dentro   Acudid
PROMETEO   de Minerba al obsequio
                   todos conmigo.

                            [Sale Minerba]

Rep[resen]ta   Allí   480
MINERBA   me aclama Prometheo;
                   pues para yrle a asistir,
                   ¿qué aguardo?

                         Dentro caja y vnos

Dentro VNOS   ¡Viua Palas!
[Dentro] OTROS   ¡Minerba viba!
Repres[entan]do   En fin,
MINERBA   con otro yncauto trage,   485
                   y otro traidor ardid,
                   consigue la Discordia
                   alentar su motín,
                   a cuia voz suspensa
                   quedo, al oírla deçir . . .   490

                   Representa la Discordia dentro

---

474 speaker "Pues aquí": BM omit [Epimeteo speaking]
475 speaker BM *Pal.*
476 BM add st.d. *Representando.*
477 BMV have "huyas" for "ya"
478 BMV dél
480 st.d. BMV omit *Representa*
482 BM omit "a"
483 st.d. BM omit; V *Dent.*
484 BM *Otros. Minerva viua.* / *Min.* En fin V *Dent. otros.* Viua Minerua. / *Mineru.* Enfin,
488 punctuation V motin?
489 BM cuya luz
490 BM quedó
490 st.d. BMV omit

Dentro	Si el enojo de Apolo		
DISCORDIA	es por ver aplaudir		
	el robo de su fuego,		
	¿cómo el bando seguís		
	de Minerba? que fue	(folio) 11	495
	quien dio el traidor ardid		
	al ladrón Prometheo,		
	y ya que os diuidís		
	en vandos, ¡Viua Palas,		
	que es Diosa de la lid!		500

Dentro TODOS   Diçes bien, ¡Palas viua!   *Vanse*

Sale Prometheo

PROMETEO   ¿Adónde, ¡ay ymfeliz!
               hallar podré consuelo? . . .

Encuentra con Minerba

mas si estabas tú aquí,	
prodijio ymfausto y vello,	505
diga vna vez y mil,	
¿qué mucho que los montes	
se caigan sobre mí?	
O nunca aquella sombra	
que fantástica vi	510
despertara la ydea	
para copiar en ti	
de Minerba el retrato.	
Nunca para pulir	

491–498 BMV omit
499 speaker BMV *Disc.*
499 BMV Viua Palas, que es [omitting "en vandos"]
500 speaker BM *Tod.* V *Ella, y todos.*
500 BV La Diosa de la lid M La Diosa; y la luz
501 speaker BM *Prom.* V *Palas.*
501 B Dizen
501 st.d. BMV omit *Dentro* and *Vanse* and place *Sale Prometeo* after line 500.
502 speaker BMV omit [Prometeo speaking in BM, Palas in V]
503 st.d. BMV omit
504 V omits "tú"
505 BMV bello infausto prodigio
506 BMV digo otra vez

tu rostro liquidara 515
su candor al jazmín,
su púrpura a la rossa,
y vno y otro matiz,
para vestirte vbiera
desnudado al abril. 520
Nunca, ¡ay de mí! Minerba,
obligada de mí, (folio 11v)
mi persona elebara
al orbe de çafir,
adonde transparente 525
su diáfano viril
me franqueó los ynmensos
tesoros de su ofir.
Nunca en nubes de gualda,
listadas de carmín, 530
liberal ella en dar,
abaro yo en pedir,
me alentara a que hurtase,
cuando ya del çéni[t]
traspuesto yba su carro, 535
en busca del nadir,
aquel luçiente, vello,
ençendido rubí
que ofreçido en tu mano
te animó; nunca en fin, 540
feliz me vbiera visto,
para verme ymfeliz.
Pues Apolo, enojado
del robo, contra ti
y contra mí amenaza, 545
no sólo a este comfín
mas del Cáucaso a todo

---

519 BMV vestirle
521 B Nunca ya de mi Minerva M Nunca ya, y mi Minerva V O nunca ya Minerua
526 BMV viuir
529 BMV nube
530 BMV listada
534 BMV Zenit
538 BM y encendido
546 BMV omit "a"
547 BMV omit "a"

el bárbaro país.
Dígalo el que queriendo   (folio) 12
a Minerba rendir   550
sacrifiçios, no vbo
quien quisiese seguir
en çeño tuio el vando
mío, con que me vi
obligado a bolber   555
la espalda para yr
a nunca ver el sol,
(huiendo aora de ti
si antes de ellos) a aquel
del monte seno vil   560
que fue mi albergue, donde
su mas hondo siuil
sea mi tumba, siendo
mi pira su çerbiz.

Vase a yr y canta ella, y se detiene

Cantando MINERBA	¡Oye, aguarda, escucha, espera! sabrás que no ai q[ue] sentir ya los enojos de Apolo.	565
PROMETEO	¿Qué voz es ésta que oí?	
Canta MINERBA	La voz de quien te escuchó hablar conmigo sin mí.	570
PROMETEO	Sin ti y contigo, otra vez hablando a tu estatua di adorazión, y pues oy al contrario repetir	(folio 12v)

---

551 BMV sacrificio
558 BMV y huyendo aora
559 BMV omit "a"; V dellos
560 BMV seno del monte vil,
564 st.d. BMV *Canta Minerva*.; BMV omit st.d. *Cantado* and *Canta* from subsequent
    speeches by Minerba in this scene.
565 B espear [sic]
570 speaker BMV *Prom.*
570 BMV contigo
571 speaker BMV omit [Prometeo speaking]
574 BMV have "a" for "al"; M repeti

	el trançe se ve, a tus pies	575
	humilde llego a pedir	
	perdón del despecho que	
	descomfiado de ti	
	y de Apolo amenazado . . .	
	mas no puedo proseguir,	580
	que a esta parte Epimeteo	
	viene.	

Canta MINERBA   Pues no me halle aquí,
y me conozca en la voz,
que no la podré fingir
como la Discordia, a quien,   585
bastarda Deydad, en fin,
hija de Plutón, le es dado
el cautelar y el mentir.

PROMETEO   Pues escóndete detrás
de esse enrredado jazmín,   590
para que sin que te vea
él, te puedas encubrir,
haciéndote espaldas yo,
que biéndome solo yr
por otra parte, ¿quien duda   595
que ponga el reparo en mí,
y a ti no te vea, teniendo
objeto en que dibertir   (folio) 13
la vista?

Canta MINERBA   Diçes bien.
PROMETEO   Pues,
retírate, y no de aquí   600
faltes, para que en pasando,
bolber pueda a proseguir
disculpas de aquel despecho,
y también, Minerba, a oír
porque el enojo de Apolo   605
no tengo ya que sentir.

Canta MINERBA Buelbe, pues, q[ue] aquí te aguardo.

---

580 B pudo
582 M hable
587 BM les ha dado
607 BM omit "que"

Escóndese y salen Epimeteo y Merlín

PROMETEO   Por delante dél e de yr,
           ocasionándole a verme.   *[Vase]*

EPIMETEO   ¿Tú la viste?
MERLÍN   Yo la vi,   610
           hablando con él.
EPIMETEO   Pues ¿cómo
           él solo se va, y aquí
           ella no está?
MERLÍN   ¿Qué sé yo?

EPIMETEO   ¡Calla, que mientes, Merlín!   615
           que ni él hablara con ella,
           pues aborreçerla oý,
           ni ella desapareçiera
           tan presto.
MERLÍN   Digo que sí,
           y que resí çien mil vezes,
           por señas de que haçia allí   (folio) 13v   620
           echó, y si quieres más señas,
           mejor las podrán deçir
           las rehendijas de aquel
           verde cançel.
EPIMETEO   Es assí.

Rep[resen]ta   Forçoso, si él me descubre   625
MINERBA   será, sin hablar, oýr,
           y a más no poder, forçoso
           desapareçer de aquí.

*Estos versos los dirá detrás de la estatua, q[ue] estará puesta en su lugar,
y en diciéndolos, se pasará a la otra parte del teatro.*

---

607   st.d. BMV [after line 606] BM *Retirase Minerva en vn bastidor de yer / ua, y sale*
      Epimeteo, y Merlin. / Canta Minerva. V *Retirase Minerua á vn bastidor, y sale /*
      Epimeteo, y Merlin. / Canta Minerua.
609   BMV add st.d. *vase.*
613   BMV se vé,
623   BMV redendijas
624   BM add. st.d. *Representa Minerva.*
628   st.d. BMV *Estos versos ha de dezir detras de la / Estatua, puesta ya en su lugar, y en /*
      auiendolos dicho, passe a la otra parte / del vestuario, y Epimeteo llega abrien- / do el
      bastidor, / y habla con la Estatua. ["E"s not italicized in B; V *llega á abrir el*]

EPIMETEO   ¿Por qué tú, diuina aurora,
                  tanto su luz desbaneçe,   630
                  que alumbra al q[ue] la aborreçe,
                  y se esconde al que la adora?
                  Y si en las flores que dora
                  la rosa en cualquier jardín
                  es la reyna, ¿por qué a fin   635
                  de tenerla sospechosa,
                  quieres que [en éste] la rosa
                  esté [a sombra] del jazmín?
                  Si de aborreçido a sido
                  darme la Discordia el hado,   640
                  mira como amara amado
                  quien adora aborreçido.
                  Y pues que ya no te pido,
                  que hagas de mi amor apreçio,   645
                  haz despreçio de mi amor,   (folio) 14
                  que no quiero más fabor
                  que el mérito del despreçio.
                  Mira cúal deue de estar
                  quien desea mereçer   650
                  el día que es su plazer
                  soliçitar su pesar;
                  mas, ¿qué tendrá que mirar
                  quien ve en sí mi ansia cruel,
                  aborreçida de ymfiel   655
                  amante? mas fía de mí,
                  pues él me venga de ti,
                  que yo e de vengarte dél.
                  ¿Qué es ésto? ¿aun para deçirme
                  que te canso, no merezco   660
                  oír tu voz? ¿de cuándo acá

---

631 BM a quien le V á quien la
632 BM a quien le V á quien la
637 BMV que en este
638 B este assombra del MV esté á sombra
640 BM deme la V en mi de Discordia el hado
641 BMV amaria
643 V que yo no
649 BM de ser

[añade daño] el silençio?
Habla, dime q[ue] te canso,
que te aflijo, que te ofendo,
que yo me yré consolado   665
con saber que te obedezco.
¿Qué es esto, Merlín? ¿as visto
tan callado, tan seuero
semblante jamás?

MERLÍN   No saues
lo que al verla muda pienso: 670
que deuemos de tener   (folio 14v)
algún natural secreto –
como los saludadores
que hasta vn caso, ygnoran serlo –
de haçer hablar y callar   675
estatuas; y si no es esto,
es que a vna dama vn galán
robó, púsola vn pañuelo
en la voca; ella mui alto
preguntó, ¿para qué efecto?   680
De que no des voçes, dijo,
y ella prosiguió mui quedo:
¿qué voçes tengo de dar,
si estoi ronca? aplica el cuento.
a robarla ybas, habló,   685
con que el dejarla sintiendo
del desdén de no robada,
quiere aora enmendar el yerro
callando, como quien diçe:
si el dejarme, majadero,   690
entonçes, fue por que hablé,
róbame aora q[ue] enmudezco.

EPIMETEO   Aunque es desatino tuio,
yo estoi tal q[ue] ha açer me atrebo

662 BM añade daño al V añade daño el
680 BM pregunta:
685 BMV ibas, te habló
686 BMV con que dexada sintiendo
687 BMV el desden de no robarla:
694 BM omit "ha"

	caso dél; llega conmigo,	695
	llega, q[ue] atreberme tengo	(folio) 15
	a lograr oy lo q[ue] entonçes.	

Sale p[o]r la otra p[ar]te Minerba, representado,
que aora haçe la estatua.

MINERBA   En tu busca, Epimetheo, . . .

EPIMETEO   Çielos, ¿qué miro y q[ue] admiro?
            ¡Aquí vna, allí otra!

MINERBA   . . . vengo   700
            a desaogar ofendida
            el bolcán q[ue] arde en mi pecho.

EPIMETEO   ¿Qué es esto?
MERLÍN   Despacho de Yndias,
            que [trae] duplicado el pliego.

MINERBA   ¿Cómo es posible, tirano,   705
            alebe, falso, soberbio,
            cruel, sediçioso, ynjusto,
            y en fin, dado a fieras, fiero,
            ¿cómo es posible . . .

EPIMETEO   Suspende
            la voz, q[ue] absorto y suspenso   710
            lo que oigo y no oigo me agrabia,
            pues cuando estaba pidiendo
            a otra tus despreçios y yras,
            bienes tú a doblarlos, puesto
            que siento los q[ue] ella calla,   715
            y los q[ue] tú diçes siento.

MINERBA   ¿Otra yo?
EPIMETEO   Otra tú.
MINERBA   Pues ¿cómo   (folio 15v)
                Desapareçe la estatua
            es posible?

---

697 B lograr lo oy que
697 st.d. BMV *Sale Minerva por otra parte / representando.*
700 BM aqui vna, y aqui otra. V y allí otra?
704 BMV trae
714 BMV doblarlas
717 st.d. BMV place it after line 720

EPIMETEO   Llega a verlo,
y verás como es posible.

MINERBA   ¿Dónde está?
EPIMETEO   Díselo al viento.   720

MERLÍN   O para representanta,
que buena hera, pues es çierto
no herrara el papel, y fuera
en las tramoyas sin miedo.

MINERBA   ¿Qué es della?
EPIMETEO   No sé, no sé.   725

MINERBA   ¿Qué ylusión, qué deuaneo
te turba?
EPIMETEO   No sé.
MINERBA   Pues yo
que sé mi pena, a ella buelbo.
¿Cómo es posible (otra vez
lo diga) que ynjusto, fiero,   730
tirano, y alebe, des
calor a que en vandos puesto
el pueblo, por superior
el tuio aya a Prometheo
de sí ausentado? Y . . .
EPIMETEO   Detén   735
segunda vez el aliento,
que si pedí a la otra tú,
ya fuese verdad, ya sueño,   (folio) 16
me diese despreçios, no
la pedí me diese çelos;   740
y pues sin çelos [serían]
gala de amor los despreçios,

---

724 BMV la tramoya
730 BM que la Diosa, injusto fiero V sedicioso, injusto, fiero
731 V tyrano, aleue, que dés
732 BMV color
734 BM omit "a"
735 BM dél ausentadose, y V del ausentado, y
737 BM pedia á
738 BMV ó sueño
741 BMV serian

y con ellos son agrabios,
ya q[ue] a tu amante echas menos,
ençendiendo nuebas sañas,   745
as de ver como me vengo
en él de ti, y en ti dél.
Y que a nunca ver, . . . mas esto,
mejor que yo te lo diga,
será, te lo diga el tiempo.   *Vase*   750

MERLÍN   Tiene razón q[ue] le sobra
de huir de ti, que es mal echo,
ya q[ue] otras son de dos caras,
ser tú muger de dos cuerpos.

MINERBA   ¿Qué culpa tengo q[ue] haga   755
amor en su pensamiento
caso la ymaginazión?

MERLÍN   Y yo q[ue] su amor no tengo,
pues sólo soi de su amor
curador alitem, puesto   760
que siempre me toca andar
a la vista de sus pleytos,
¿cómo la vi a ella por ella?

MINERBA   Mientes, villano.   (folio 16v)
MERLÍN   No miento,
el día que estoi viendo cosas,   765
que son cosas que estoi biendo.   *Vase*

MINERBA   ¿Qué es esto, Dioses? ¿quién vio
dos tan contrarios extremos
como dejarme el que amo,
y seguirme el que aborrezco?   770

---

745 V nueua saña
748 BMV anuncia ver
749 BM have "la" for "lo"
750 M has "la" for "lo"; V será que lo
750 st.d. BM omit
752 BMV dezir de ti
756 BM amor, amor en
760 BM ad liten V ad litem
766 st.d. BM omit
770 M aborezco [sic]

> ¿Dónde Prometheo se abrá
> retirado? ¿quién saberlo
> pudiera para yr?

Sale Prometeo

PROMETEO   Apenas
vi bolber a Epimetheo
haçia el monte, cuando en busca   775
tuia, no en las alas vengo
del deseo, que oi en mí
son alas de dos deseos.

MINERBA   ¡Albriçias, alma, que no   *[Aparte]*
se a ydo y afable le veo!   780

PROMETEO   Vno es pedirte perdón
de aquel pasado despecho
con que te hablé.

MINERBA   ¡Qué ventura!   *[Aparte]*

PROMETEO   Comfieso q[ue] estube çiego,
mas por disculpa me valga . . .   785

MINERBA   ¡Qué dicha!   *[Aparte]*   (folio) 17
PROMETEO   . . . que vn sentimiento
no es fáçil de reduçir
a las cárçeles del pecho
sin q[ue] se asome tal vez
a los labios.

MINERBA   ¡Qué contento!   *[Aparte]* 790

PROMETEO   Otro es sauer cómo Apolo
a serenado los çeños
de sus nubes. Logre, pues,
de ambos a tus plantas puesto,
de aquél el perdón y de éste   795

---

773 st.d. BM omit
780 BMV y que afable
785 BM valgo
789 M has "le" for "se" [B has an imperfect "s" which looks much like an "l" in the
    facsimile edition]
790 M sabios
795 BMV deste

                    la notiçia.

MINERBA   Alza del suelo,
llega a mis brazos.

PROMETEO   ¿Qué escucho?
Mal aya quien puso a objetos
pareçidos la distançia
en la voz, q[ue] al fin es viento.   800

MINERBA   Llega, pues, llega a mis brazos,
que es bien que te pague en ellos
las albriçias . . .

PROMETEO   ¡Qué pesar!

MINERBA   . . . de mirarte . . .
PROMETEO   ¡Qué tormento!

[MINERBA]   . . . arrepentido de aberme   (folio 17v) 805
hablado con el despego
que me hablaste cuando . . .

PROMETEO   Aparta,
no a mí te açerques, q[ue] temo
que ynfiçione el corazón
a que se borre al veneno   810
de tu voz, que [se] me acuerda
causa de mi mal.

MINERBA   ¿Qué es esto?
¿tan presto tan otro? ¿es
éste el arrepentimiento
con que el perdón me pedías?   815

PROMETEO   ¿De qué te admiras? ¿es nuebo
el que venga presto el mal?

MINERBA   No, ni que el bien huia presto.
¿Qué miras? ¿qué buscas?
PROMETEO   No
lo sé, no lo sé.
MINERBA   Lo mesmo,   820

---

798 BMV puso objeto
799–800 V parecido la distancia / de la voz
805 speaker BM omit [Prometeo speaking] V *Miner.*
810 BM y que se borre el veneno V y que le ocupe el veneno
811 V se me [Broken "s" in facsimile edition]
820 BM mismo

y con ese mismo espanto,
me respondió Epimetheo,
buscando no sé q[ué] sombra
que le desbaneçió el viento.

PROMETEO   Sin duda la vio, y ella   [*Aparte*]   825
             se fue, de su vista huiendo.

MINERBA   ¿A dónde vas?   (folio) 18
PROMETEO   A no verte.

MINERBA   ¿No dijiste, no a vn momento,
             que a verme venías?
PROMETEO   Sí dije,
             mas también dije q[ue] a efecto   830
             de pedir vn perdón que
             no pido, y añadí luego
             que a sauer el desenojo
             de Apolo; y pues dos deseos
             me trujeron, y ya al vno   835
             yo respondida te tengo,
             respóndeme al otro tú:
             ¿qué desenojo es?
MINERBA   Mal puedo
             deçir yo lo q[ue] no sé.

PROMETEO   Aý verás si te combenzo   840
             en si te busco o no, pues
             buelto en azar el encuentro,
             te hallo como daño cuando
             te busco como remedio.

MINERBA   ¡Oye, espera!
PROMETEO   ¡Aparta!
MINERBA   No   845
             as de yrte sin que primero
             me digas en qué te agrabio.

PROMETEO   ¿Cómo puedo, sin saberlo
             deçirlo tampoco yo?   (folio 18v)

---

830 BM efeto
835 MV traxeron; BM have "el" for "al"
836 BMV respondido

	pues si Deydad te contemplo,	850
	te adoro; si hermosa, te amo;	
	si discreta, te venero;	
	si prodijiosa, te admiro;	
	y si todo, te aborrezco;	
	que ay otro yo q[ue] sin mí	855
	manda en mí más q[ue] yo mesmo.	

MINERBA   Apuremos ese enigma:
               ¿no hiçiste mi estatua?
PROMETEO   Es çierto.

MINERBA   ¿No vibió al calor del rayo
               que robaste?
PROMETEO   No lo niego.   860

MINERBA   Pues ¿quién, dime, aborreçió
               obra que empezó su yngenio,
               que prosiguió su valor,
               y perfiçionó su çelo
               en fee de auxsiliar Deydad?   865

PROMETEO   Quien vio . . .

                    Caja y clarín

Dentro VOCES   ¡Viua Epimetheo!

[*Dentro*] OTRAS   ¡Viua Prometheo!
[*Dentro*] VNOS   ¡Arma!
[*Dentro*] OTROS   ¡Guerra!

PROMETEO   Por mí responda ese estruendo:
               quien vio naçer vn milagro,
               que ve en escándalo buelto.   870
               Los vandos que entre Minerba
               y Palas se dibidieron   (folio) 19
               en sus sacrifiçios ya

857 V este
859 BMV viuo
863 BMV su calor
865 BMV auxiliar
866 speakers and st.d. BM *Pro* Quien vio. *Caxas / Dentro vnos.* Viua Epimeteo. V *Pro*
     Quien vio. *Dentro caxas. / Dentro vnos.* Viua Epimeteo.
867 speakers BMV *Otros.* Viua Prometeo. / *Todos.* Arma, Guerra.
869 BM quien viene hazer vn V quien viene á hazer vn
873 BM y en sus sacrificios, y V en sus sacrificios, oy

                    a las manos del encuentro
                    an venido, y si notaren   875
                    que antes de ser lid, me ausento
                    de corrido, ya que es lid,
                    no an de notar que me buelbo –
                    los pocos que me apellidan –
                    de cobarde el rostro al riesgo;   880
                    con ellos moriré.   *Caja*

MINERBA   Y yo
                    contigo, porque aunq[ue] siento
                    tus despreçios, no ay valor
                    en vn generoso pecho
                    como del despreçio mismo   885
                    haçer yo misma despreçio.

                                                    Bosque

Vanse los dos, tocan cajas y clarines, y salen por vna parte Epimeteo
con algunos, y por otra Timantes con otros, todos de guerra.

VNOS   ¡Epimetheo viua!
OTROS   No
Y TIMANTES   viua, sino Prometheo.

EPIMETEO   ¡Cómo es posible, Timantes,
                    que sigas el desaçierto   890
                    de los q[ue] – abiendo pasado
                    los discordes bandos nuestros
                    de sacrifiçios a ruinas –   (folio 19v)
                    a Minerba aclaman, siendo
                    Palas Deydad de la guerra?   895

TIMANTES   Como más (con Prometheo

---

878 BMV notarme, que buelvo
881 st.d. BMV omit *Caja*, add *Vase*.
883 BMV tus despechos
885 BMV have "mio" for "mismo"
886 BMV aun yo mesma el desprecio. [V misma]
886 st.d. BMV omit *Bosque*
886 st.d. BMV *Sale por vna parte Epimeteo con vnos, / y por otra Timantes con otros, y /
    tocan caxas.* [after line 888.]
887 B Epimoteo [sic]
887 speaker BMV *Timantes y todos.*
890 for "sigas", BM have "rigas", V has "rijas"
893 BMV a lides

siguiendo su razón, que
tu desagradeçimiento)
quiero el honor de la ruina
que el triumpho del vençimiento.   900

EPIMETEO   ¿Qué razón?
TIMANTES   La de aber sido
por quien doméstico el fuego,
su abrigo le deue el día,
la noche su luçimiento.

LOS SEGUNDOS   Y el Cáucaso vn bien tan sumo.   905

EPIMETEO   ¿Qué ymporta, si todo eso
para en q[ue] Apolo castigue
en todos su atrebimiento?

TIMANTES   Los metheores del ayre
sin esa causa los vemos   910
en condensado vapores
conjelarse.

EPIMETEO   Ya no es tiempo,
si an de razonar las armas,
que lidien los argumentos.
¡A ellos, amigos, y no   915
temáis, que en auxsilio buestro
Palas, Deydad de las lides,   (folio) 20
milita!

                    Salen Prometeo y Minerba
                    y se mezclan con ellos.

PROMETEO Y   ¡Amigos, a ellos!
MINERBA, LOS DOS

SOLO TIMANTES   Que Minerba por nosotros
bolberá.

_____

902   BM domesticó
905   speaker BMV *Vnos.*
910   BM omit "esa" V sin causa alguna los vemos
916   BMV auxilio
918   st.d. BMV *Salen Prometeo, y Minerva.*
918   speaker BMV *Los dos.*
919   speaker BMV omit ["Los dos" speaking – Prometeo and Minerva]
920   speaker BMV *Tim.*

SEGUNDOS	Con tal esfuerzo	920
	más que ellos somos, aunque	
	seamos en número menos.	

[EPIMETEO   ¡Pues al arma!
Y] VNOS

LOS DOS   ¡Pues al arma!
Y OTROS

Van a embestirse y baja la Discordia
rápid[o] y canta lo sig[uien]te.

Cant[and]o   Tened, parad los açeros.
DISCORDIA

MÚSICA   Tened, parad los açeros.   925

DISCORDIA   Que el vencimiento sin sangre
                   es el mejor vençimiento.

Repite MÚSICA   Que el vencimiento [sin sangre
                   es el mejor vençimiento.]

EPIMETEO   ¿Quién eres, o tú, que paras   930
                   a tu voz furor y aliento?

PROMETEO   ¿Quien eres, o tú, q[ue] a todos
                   dejas a tu voz suspensos?

Rep[resen]ta   Esto es no auenturar   [*Aparte*]
DISCORDIA   a los trançes de vn encuentro,   935
                   dictando Minerba ardides

---

923 speakers BMV *Epim. y vnos. Pues al arma.* / *Prom. y otros.*
923 st.d. BMV *Tocan caxas, y en oyendolas se suspen / den, baxa cantando de rapido la /*
    Discordia. [after line 922]
924 st.d. BMV *Dent. Dis.*
925 BMV omit
926 speaker BM *Mus.* V omits [Discordia speaking.]
927 speaker BM *Dis.*
928 st.d. BMV omit *Repite*
928–929 BM que El vencimiento ettª. V Que el vencimiento sin sangre, / es el mejor
    vencimiento.
930 BM omit "o" V Quien eres tu, di, que páras
931 BM have "su" for "tu"
932 BM omit "o" V Quien eres tu, di, que á todos
934 BM Esto no es
936 MV add. st.d. *Ap.* [M *Ap* appears in the Museo del Teatro copy, but not in the facsimile
    edition made from the Vatican copy]

contra el valor al yngenio,
la victoria a Palas – Soi
quien del alto coro exçelso,
embajatriz de los Dioses   940
os habla, y en fee de serlo,
sea carta de crehençia   (folio 20v)
la suabidad de mi açento.

Canta En la ruda política buestra,
dos leyes tenéis, y tan justas las dos   945
como que muera el q[ue] fuere homiçida,
como que pene el que fuere ladrón.
Pues ¿qué más sacrílego hurto,
que más alebe, ynicuo y traidor,
que el que escalando del sol el alcázar   950
se atreue a robarle sus rayos al sol?
Y así, Júpiter, viendo que Apolo
entre Minerba y Palas, q[ue] son
sus hermanas, no quiere neutral
tomar la venganza ni dar el perdón.   955
Y porque el delito de vno no pase
a ruina de muchos, pronunçia en mi voz
que el agresor no más lo padezca,
encarzelado en obscura prisión,
donde funesto pájaro sea   960
alado berdugo, q[ue] hambriento y feroz,
su corazón despedaze de día,
criando la noche otro ygual corazón.
Y porque a Minerba no puede llegar
el cargo de ser quien las alas le dio,   965
sacrificada su estatua resuelbe   (folio) 21

---

942 BM have "canto" for "carta"
946 M como el que [See Manuscript Notes]
948 V Pues que mas injusto sacrilego hurto
949 BM que mas aleue injusto traidor V que mas aleue iniquo traidor [BMV all omit "y"]
951 BM omit "le"
955 B perdor [sic]
956 BMV omit "Y"
957 BMV omit "en"
961 M al hado
963 BMV criando de noche
964 BM pueda V y porque Minerua no puede negar

que ella dé a Apolo la satisfaçión.
Y pues que vibió de su fuego, en su fuego
que muera es justiçia, en cuia oblazión
la otra ley se ejecuta, pues es   970
también omiçida quien mata de amor.
Y así, temed que de no ejecutarse
entrambos decretos, los cómpliçes sois
de entrambos delitos, con que delinquentes
el Cáucaso todo, de Jobe al ardor,   975
Etna, Volcán, Monjiuelo, Vesubio,
de más viuo ynçendio, de más viuo ardor,
oguera será que llebe en pauesas
de leues çenizas el ayre veloz.
¡Temed su rigor!

MÚSICA   ¡Temed su rigor!   980

ELLA Y MÚSICA   Oguera será que lleue en pabesas
de leues cenizas el ayre veloz.   *Buela*

MINERBA   ¡Oye, aguarda!
Y PROMETEO

EPIMETEO   En vano es
querer alcanzarla, no
tanto porque ya del ayre   985
pasa la media región,
cuanto porque ya es forçoso
daros ambos a prisión.

PROMETEO   Primero daré la vida,   (folio 21v)
no en mi defensa, sino   990
desta ymfeliçe hermosura,

---

967 BM omit "a"
968 BMV que pues viuio
969 BM obligacion
972 BM omit "asi"
973 BM entre ambos
975 V al rigor
976 BM en bolcan mongibelo nube subio
980 speakers BM *Music*. Temed su rigor, / [speaker omitted – *Musica* doing repetition also] Temed su rigor.
981 speaker BMV *Disc.*
982 BMV add another line: *Music*. Hogera será, &c.
982 st.d. BM omit V *Vase.*

que aunque no me muebe amor,
de ser muger y yo noble,
me muebe la obligazión.

MINERBA   Y a mí, la de que a su lado   995
haga apaçible el dolor,
ya que e de morir por fuerza,
el morir por elección.

PROMETEO   Ea, Timantes, muramos
a las manos del valor,   1000
no de la ymfamia.

TIMANTES   Ya viste,
Prometheo, que tu acción
tomé ausente; pero vna
cosa es oponerme yo
a los empeños de vn vando,   1005
o a los decretos de vn Dios.

TODOS   Todos deçimos lo mismo,
y siendo fuerza el temor
de Júpiter, fuerza es
                Préndenlos
que vengáis presos los dos.   1010

PROMETEO   ¿Cómo, traidores?
TODOS   Donde ay
obediençia, no ay traición.

PROMETEO   ¡Ai de quien el bien que hiço   (folio) 22
en mal combertido vio!

MINERBA   ¡Ai de quien naçió milagro,   1015
para falleçer horror!

EPIMETEO   Con vnas bandas los rostros
les cubrid, para que no
al mirarlos, se conmueba
el pueblo, ni oiga su voz;   1020

1002 BMV si tu
1006 BM omit "a"
1007 BM mesmo
1009 st.d. V places it after line 1010
1011 B taidores [sic]

demás de que también es
vsada demostraçión
entre nosotros que diçe
que ya no ay apelaçión
el día q[ue] se les niega   1025
mirar las luçes del sol.
Guiad, pues, al templo con ellos
de Saturno, donde oy
la prisión y el sacrifiçio

Entranse con ellos, y al bolber a la llamada, sacan otra mug[e]r
vestida como la estatua, y cubierto el rostro, y atrabiesan
el tablado con ella.

se disponga; pero no,   1030
no vais al templo, volbed,
volbed; no la dilaçión
enoje a Júpiter, dando
a algún tumulto ocasión;
Y así, desde luego yr   1035
al monte será mejor,
puesto q[ue] su paborosa
cueba a de ser la prissión
dél, y della el sacrifiçio   (folio 22v)
en la desierta mansión   1040
del mismo monte, porque
donde si al fuego vibió,
muera al fuego, dando en propios
términos satisfaçión;   1045
– al mío diré mejor –   [*Aparte*]
Al monte, pues, guidad con ellos.

1022 BV demonstracion
1026 BM mirad
1029 st.d. BMV *Entranse los soldados con los dos, y al / llamarlos, buelven á salir como*
     entra- / ron, con vna muger, vestida con ves- / tido de la Estatua, cubierto el rostro, y
     / al entrarse con ella, atrauesando el ta- / blado, sale Minerva cantando. [V *bueluan;*
     con el vesti- / do; BMV place st.d. after line 1026]
1031 BM á el
1033 BM enojo sea á Iupiter,
1042 BMV á donde el fuego viuió
1043 BMV have "el" for "al"
1046 BMV have "el" for "al"
1046 BMV add st.d. *Aparte.*

TODOS   ¡Al monte!

                 Al entrarse, sale Minerba y canta

MINERBA   Tonante Dios,
                 ¿cómo permites q[ue] enmiende
                 a vna culpa otra mayor?   1050
                 ¿Es menos delito que
                 la Discordia hurte tu voz,
                 que el que hurte Prometheo
                 vn pequeño rayo al sol?
                 ¿Qué traición como falsear   1055
                 tus decretos, ni qué horror
                 como que tenga más pena
                 vn robo que vna traiçión?
                 A tu soberano solio
                 llegue este justo clamor;   1060
                 mas ¿para qué, si primero
                 llegar yo puedo?

                 Baja Palas rápid[o]

Canta PALAS   Eso no,
                 porque hasta q[ue] ejecutado   (folio) 23
                 esté en ambos mi rencor
                 y veas quien a su alumno   1065
                 puso en más estimazión,
                 para que tú no lo ympidas,
                 sabré detenerte yo.

                 Cantado todo este paso, y luchan

MINERBA   También yo sabré romper
                 tus lazos.

PALAS   ¡Qué pretensión   1070
                 tan vana! ¿con Palas, tú,
                 a fuerzas?

1048 speaker BMV omit *"Todos"* [Epimeteo speaking]
1048 st.d. BM ¡Al monte! *Vase. / Canta Minerva en voz de lamento.* V ¡Al monte! *Vase. /
      Sale Minerua cantando como lamento.*
1048 BM Tonantes
1062 st.d. BMV *Sale Palas cantando todo este passo.*
1067 B tu no impidas M tu no lo impidas V tu no le impidas
1068 st.d. BMV omit

MINERBA	Pues, por qué no?
PALAS	Porque a par del mismo Marte,
	Diosa de las armas soi.
MINERBA	Yo de las letras; mortales, 1075
	ved si entre yngenio y valor,
	más que la fuerza del brazo
	vale la de la razón:
	¡Suelta, tirana!

Vase, y sale la Discordia.

PALAS	No pude,
	¡ay de mí! ympedirla.
Canta	No 1080
DISCORDIA	aqueso te descomfíe,
	por más que buele veloz,
	que antes que a Júpiter llegue
	su llanto y mi acusazión,
	abrás conseguido tú (folio 23v) 1085
	de entrambos la destruizión,
	v díganlo en paborosos
	eccos de fúnebre son,
	ronca la trompa vastarda,
	destemplado el atambor, 1090
	a cuio compás que sirbe
	al suplizio de pregón,
	ella viene acompañada
	del jubenil escuadrón
	de las çagalas del valle 1095
	y [del] popular rumor,

1072 BMV add st.d. *Luchando.* after "á fuerças"
1075 punctuation B letras mortales, M letras, mortales V letras: mortales,
1079 st.d. BMV place it after line 1080, "impedirla"
1080 st.d. BMV omit *Canta*
1087 BMV have "O" for "v"
1088 BM omit "eccos"
1088 BMV add st.d. *Sordinas y caxas destempladas.*
1092 BMV add. st.d. *Salen cubiertas las caras ella con las / mugeres a vna parte, y el a otra con los /hombres, y detras Epimeteo, Merlin / y Timantes.*
1094 BMV de
1096 BM y del V y él del

del demás pueblo diçiendo

Bosque y Risco

de vnos y otros el clamor . . .

Sordinas y cajas destempladas y, las caras cubiertas, sacan a los dos, a vna
p[ar]te mugeres y a otra hombres, y salen todos los demás.

LOS DOS	¡Ai de quien vio . . .
MÚSICA	¡Ay de quien vio . . . 1100
LOS DOS	. . . el bien combertido en mal . . .
MÚSICA	. . . el bien combertido en mal . . .
LOS DOS	. . . y el mal en peor!
MÚSICA	. . . y el mal en peor!

Mésclase con ellos la Discordia, y sale Palas

EPIMETEO   Haçed aquí alto, a la vista   1105
                de la gruta que prisión
                a de ser de Prometheo,
                y del risco en que oblazión
                su viua estatua a de ser.
                Si alguno culpa que soy   [*Aparte*]   11̣10
                quien de su castigo toma
                a cargo la ejecuzión,   (folio) 24
                ame aborreçido y tenga
                çelos, y verá qué son
                çelos y aborrecimiento   1115
                quien los acusa, y no yo.
                Y aora, para que sea
                el mereçido dolor
                de ambos, sobre padeçer,
                el ver padeçer mayor,   1120
                los rostros les descubrid;

1097 st.d. BMV omit
1098 st.d. BMV place corresponding st.ds. after lines 1088 and 1092
1104 st.d. BMV omit
1110 BMV add st.d. *Ap.*
1116 BM auisa
1130 BMV convertido

logren, pues, su hodio y su amor,
ella viendo lo que quiso,
biendo él lo que aborreçió.

PALAS   No creerás, Discordia, cuanto   1125
gozosa al verlos estoi.

DISCORDIA   Y yo más, cuando repiten
lamento a vn tiempo y cançión . . .

LOS DOS   ¡Ay de quien vio
Y MÚSICA   el bien combertirse en mal   1130
y el mal en peor!

PROMETEO   ¡O nunca bolbiera a ver
los claros rayos del sol,
si era para ver tu pena!

MINERBA   ¡O nunca yo el resplandor   1135
a ver bolbiera del día
para mirar tu aflicçión!

PROMETEO   No sé, ay, ymfausta hermosura,   (folio 24v)
cómo ya en mi corazón
se a de çcuar boreal fiera,   1140
si al verte sin él estoi.

MINERBA   Más siento (pues en mi muerte
fin a mis desdichas doi)
lo que tú as de padeçer,
que lo que padezco yo.   1145

TIMANTES   ¡Qué lastima!
VILLANA [S]   ¡Qué desdicha!
LIBIA   ¡Qué pena!
TODOS   ¡Qué compasión!

MERLÍN   Si a de morir como vna,
¿para cuándo era ser dos?

EPIMETEO   Volbed, volbed a cubrirles,   1150
y vayan al ronco son,

1143 BMV mi desdicha
1149 BMV era el ser
1150 BMV cubrirlos

	él a la gruta, y ella	
	a la hoguera.	
TODOS Y	¡Ai de quien bio . . .	
MÚSICA	*Apolo baja, en sol, cant[and]o.*	

APOLO	Tened, parad, suspended el rigor;	
	veréis a mi vos	1155
	el mal combertido en bien	
	y el bien en mejor.	

EPIMETEO	¿Qué nueba voz será ésta?	

TIMANTES	Y di, ¿qué nuebo arrebol	
	es el que ylumina el día?	1160

TODOS	¿Quién causa este efecto?	
APOLO	Yo,	(folio) 25
	que al ver que Minerba	
	al solio subió	
	de Júpiter, donde	
	pide su perdón,	1165
	y que el conçederle	
	es preçisa acçión,	
	porque nunca niega	
	piedades vn Dios,	
	venir e querido	1170
	a traerle yo;	
	débanmele a mí,	
	y a Júpiter no.	
	Y pues ya sin parte	
	están, no ay razón	1175
	para que en supliçio	
	padezcan los dos.	
	Y para que sea	
	mi triumpho mayor,	

1152 BMV á la gruta él, y ella
1153 V adds two lines: el bien conuertido en mal, / y el mal en peor!
1153 st.d. BM *Apolo en vn Sol cantando*: V *Aparece Apolo en vn Sol cantando.*
1158 BMV have "luz" for "voz"
1159 BMV Dioses, que
1169 punctuation BMV Dios. / Venir
1172 BMV debamele
1175 BMV esta no es razon

	echizos que en humo		1180
	la Discordia dio,		
	en rayos de luçes		
	hará mi splendor		
	que desbaneçidos		
	huian su arrebol,		1185
	cobrándose en cuantos		
	ella perturbó,		
	razón y sentido,		
	sentido y razón.		
	Y así, mude buestra	(folio 25v)	1190
	fúnebre cançión,		
	el himno diçiendo		
	todos con mi voz:		
	Feliçe quien vio . . .		
MÚSICA	Felice quien vio . . .		1195
APOLO	El mal combertido en bien,		
	y el bien en mejor.		
MÚSICA	El mal [combertido en bien,		
	y el bien en mejor.]		
PALAS	Huiamos de aquí, Discordia.	*Vase*	1200
DISCORDIA	¡Ai de quien por ti fingió		
	leyes para q[ue] aora tema		
	de Júpiter el rigor!	*Vase*	
EPIMETEO	¿Qué es lo q[ue] pasa por mí?		
	¿quién mi juiçio enagenó		1205
	para aborreçerte, hermano?		
PROMETEO	¿Quién el mío perturbó		
	para que yo aborreçiese		
	a quien adorando estoi?		
MINERBA	Bálgame a mí por disculpa		1210
	el ejemplar de los dos.		

1182 BMV rayo
1183 BMV esplendor
1191–1192 punctuation V canción / el himno,
1194 BM add st.d. *Todos, y musica.*
1195 speaker V *Tod. y mus.*
1198–1199 BM El mal Ettª V El mal conuertido en bien, / y el bien en mejor.

| TIMANTES | Y a todos de aber tenido |
| | tan violenta oposiçión. |

| MERLÍN | Libia, en tu aborreçimiento |
| | solo me e quedado yo. | 1215 |

LIBIA	Y yo en el tuio.
MERLÍN	Buen medio.
LIBIA	Di, ¿qué es?
MERLÍN	Casarnos los dos,
	pues ya está la costa hecha,	(folio) 26
	de no tenernos amor.

EPIMETEO	Ya, pues, que a Apolo deuemos	1220
	la paz, en su adoraçión
	dediquemos este día.

TIMANTES	Y para que desta vnión
	en el Cáucaso no falte
	memoria ni sucesión,	1225
	de Prometeo y Pandora
	an de celebrarse oy
	también las bodas.
MINERBA	¡Qué dicha!

PROMETEO	Yo solo el dichoso soi
	de entrambas feliçidades.	1230
	Pues es día de perdón,
	pidamos el nuestro.
MERLÍN	Sea
	todos diçiendo a vna voz . . .

| TODOS | Si es que lo mal que serbimos |
| | mereçe algún galardón . . . | 1235 |

CON LA	Feliçe quien vio
MÚSICA	el mal combertido en bien,
	y el bien en mejor.

1212 speaker M *Pom.* [sic]
1212 V omits "de"
1220 B omits "a"
1223 speaker BMV omit [Epimeteo speaking]
1229 B dicho – See Manuscript Notes
1234 speaker BMV omit [Merlín speaking]
1236 speakers BMV *Music. y todos.*

TEXTUAL NOTES

I, 2:   "Cáucaso" – The location of the play is of course determined by the traditional placement of the myth. Hesiod does not give a geographical location, but Aeschylus mentions Scythia in the *Prometheus Bound,* and a fragment of the *Prometheus Unbound* identifies the mountain to which he is tied as the Caucasus. See commentary of George Thompson to *The Prometheus Bound,* by Aeschylus (Cambridge: University Press, 1932), pp. 132–133. The Caucasus is also named as the site of Prometheus' suffering by a number of later Greek and Roman authors, including Apollodorus, Cicero, Virgil, Hyginus, Strabo and Lucian. (See Trousson, *Prométhée,* I, p. 43.) Calderón does not set any other plays here. His most immediate probable sources, the Vienna opera *Il Prometeo,* and Pérez de Moya and Vitoria's mythological dictionaries, all speak of "el Monte Cáucaso" as if referring to one peak, while Calderón refers to the Caucasus as a region.

I, 3:   "ynhiesta" – The *Diccionario de Autoridades* definition of "enhiesto" is: "levantado en alto, erguido y derecho." All examples given refer to military uses; e.g., 1) "una ciudad derribada, sin dejar cosa enhiesta" or 2) "no hay lanza enhiesta". The dictionary cites an example from Fray Luis de Granada, "Hasta tener muerta y sepultada su propia voluntad, para que no haya lanza enhiesta, ni cosa que resista à la voluntad de Dios."

"Ynhiesta" is much more resonant of meaning than the "inculto" of BMV, signifying pride, military resistance, and – if one supposes Calderón to have been at least subconsciously influenced by Fray Luis de Granada's usage – the resistant human will.

Calderón uses the same phrase, "la enhiesta cerviz," in the closely related *auto El pastor fido.* (Aguilar III, 1591b)

I, 12 :   "tuvo" – The sentence structure requires "tuvo" as in
             BMV; "alto empleo" is the subject, and "mi persona" the
             direct object. The manuscript form "tuve" is probably an
             error caused by the proximity of "mi".

I, 14, 15 : "zampoñas" and "albogues" – two different types of
             pastoral flutes.

I, 16 :   The musical offerings with which the populace celebrates
             the deities are called "confused harmonies" because they
             are mortal, and of plebeian, rustic voices and instruments,
             and are thus far removed from the divine harmony. See
             note on Calderón's philosophy of music, Act I, lines
             487–493.

I, 27–45 :   This scene, of "search parties" arriving at or departing to
             the four points of the scenic compass, frequently occurs
             near the beginning of Calderón's mythological plays.
             Here the object of search is Prometeo's voice; in *Eco y
             Narciso* (at the beginning of the second act), it is for the
             mysterious Narciso; often it is hunters in search of a
             presumed "fiera," as in *El hijo del sol, Faetón, Celos aun
             del aire matan, La fiera, el rayo y la piedra* and others.
             For the drama as spectacle, such a scene sets up a perfect
             opportunity for a kind of dramatic ballet, with or
             without music, utilizing the perspective scenery to the
             full. Calderón uses it, however, as more than a delight to
             the eyes. In these highly symbolic plays, which explore
             the more remote, and often uncivilized recesses of human
             nature and society, these scenes present the dramatis
             personae departing on (or arriving from) a search of the
             outer limits of civilization as they know it, in pursuit of
             some mysterious being that either threatens or attracts
             them.
             The device is not limited to the mythological plays, and it
             may well serve a related use when it occurs in other plays.
             I have not found it in the urban settings of the cape and
             sword plays, but Calderón does employ it in *En la vida
             todo es verdad y todo mentira*, in which hunters cut in
             just as Astolfo is about to reveal to Eraclio and Leonido
             the story of their origins.

I, 29–32 :   [dentro] – No edition specifies that the four female voices and music are within, but all other characters are so listed, except Prometeo, who has come out summoning the others. According to the manuscript stage direction, they all emerge together at line 46.

I, 38–43 :   In this opening scene, we see Epimeteo emerge as the leader of the populace, while Prometeo appears as a solitary figure, isolated from others by his intellectual and artistic pursuits. Prometeo is, significantly, glimpsed on a "risco", while Epimeteo is hunting in the "maleza", or underbrush.

I, 43–46 :   The variants in lines 43 and 44 change the structure of the sentence. In BMV, "nuestro afán" is the subject, the verb ("vna") is singular, and Merlín's words must be linked with the musical refrain in line 46. In the manuscript version, the subject is an understood "Ustedes", the verb therefore plural, "El fiero afán" is the direct object, and the sentence ends with "busca". Either reading is possible. There has been no previous reference to the hunting of a wild beast in the manuscript as we have it, but according to the manuscript stage directions, at this point everyone comes on stage with bows and arrows (not just Epimeteo, as in the *Parte* text), which suggests that they were all hunting when Prometeo called them.

I, 53 ff :   In this monologue by Prometeo, Calderón sets forth the main issues of the drama, as he does in similar opening monologues by the protagonist in so many of his plays.

I, 53–54 :   Asia and Iapetus – Asia was the daughter of Oceanus and Tethys, and was named by some authors as the mother, by Iapetus, of Atlas, Prometheus, Epimetheus, and Menoetius. While all accounts name Iapetus as Prometeo's father, various mothers are named. The mother in Hesiod is Clymene; in Aeschylus, she is Themis. Herodotus also says Asia, which some have interpreted as meaning that Asia was the site of the origins of humanity. (See Trousson, *Prométhée*, I, p. 41, n. 140.) Iapetus was a Titan, son of Ge and Uranus. When Zeus overthrew Cronus and the other Titans, he was confined with them in Tartarus.

I, 59–64 :   Calderón's presentation of the influence of the stars in
              this and other mythological plays is consistent with his
              treatment of it in other dramas. Calderón insists that man
              possesses free will, and various characters in his plays
              repeat the orthodox view that "las estrellas inclinan, mas
              no fuerzan el albedrío." However, in the working out of
              the action in the plays, celestial determination is never
              contradicted; horoscopes are always fulfilled, although
              not in the way man's imperfect understanding has
              interpreted them. For conflicting views on the role of the
              stars in Calderón's work, see A. A. Parker, *"El monstruo
              de los jardines* y el concepto calderoniano del destino," in
              Hacia Calderón, Cuarto Coloquio Anglogermano, Wol-
              fenbüttel, 1975 (Berlin: Walter de Gruyter, 1979), pp.
              92–101, who maintains that horoscopes are always fulfil-
              led; and for interpretations of Calderón's plays as
              following the orthodox view: Peter N. Dunn, "The
              Horoscope Motif in *La vida es sueño," Atlante* (London)
              I (1953), 187–201; Erika Lorenz, "Calderón und die
              Astrologie," *Romanistisches Jahrbuch,* 12 (1961),
              265–277; and Otis Green, *Spain and the Western Tradi-
              tion* (Madison, Wisconsin: University of Wisconsin
              Press, 1968), II, 212–248, passim.
              Despite papal bulls condemning its practice, the science
              of astrology retained considerable support in Spain in the
              17th century, and continued to be taught at the Univer-
              sity of Salamanca into the 18th century. See Lynn
              Thorndike, *History of Magic and Experimental Science*
              (New York: The Macmillan Co.), Vol. VI, (1941), pp.
              165–166, and Vol. VII, (1958), p. 131.
              Within the context of this play, if stars do indeed have a
              determinative effect, then the problem is that of explain-
              ing how twins born under the same sign could be so
              different – or how the warning halves within man can
              derive from the same cause. See note I, 153 ff.

I, 62, 89 :   "afecto" – the Diccionario de Autoridades (hereinafter
              indicated as (A), defines "afecto" as "una passión del
              alma, en fuerza de la qual se excita un interior
              movimiento, conque nos inclinamos á amar, ó aborrecer,
              . . . á la ira, á la venganza, . . . y otras afecciones y efectos
              proprios del hombre."

I, 63–64: For other examples of the full form of "primero" before masculine nouns (as in BMV) and the apocopated form before a feminine noun, see Hayward Keniston, *The Syntax of Castilian Prose: The Sixteenth Century* (Chicago: University of Chicago Press, 1937), pp. 301–303.

I, 66: "Voluntad" here has the meaning of love or affection, not will.

I, 69–78: i. e., given Epimeteo's inclination to the wilds (huntings), there is no wild beast that by its ferocity or by flight can save its hide or head from the steel points of his arrows and javelins (darts), since they offer up to him their head and hide – their ferocity yielding to his knives, their velocity to his feathers, i. e., his arrows.

The passage is an echo of Góngora's *Polifemo*, lines 65–72, describing Polifemo's hunting skill:

> No la Trinacria en sus montañas, fiera
> armó de crueldad, calzó de viento,
> que redima feroz, salve ligera,
> su piel manchada de colores ciento:
> pellico es ya la que en los bosques era
> mortal horror al que con paso lento
> los bueyes a su albergue reducía,
> pisando la dudosa luz del día.

With this imitation, Calderón subtly links Epimeteo's prowess with that of the brute Polifemo, then specifically reinforces this idea by calling it a business unworthy of rational man in lines 81–84.

I, 69: "genio": (A) "La natural inclinación, gusto, disposición y proporción interior para alguna cosa: como de ciencia, arte o manifactura."
Covarrubias offers a long, and most relevant, definition: "Cerca de los gentiles sinificava el demonio, espíritu que residía con qualquiera hombre, y que cada uno tenía dos; uno que le animava para el bien y otro que le incitava para el mal; y ambos creyan nacer juntamente con el hombre. Díxose genio, según éstos, *a gignendo, vel quia nobiscum gignatur, vel quia illi procreandorum sacra divinitas*

commissa putatur. Cuentan Plutarco y otros autores, que una noche se apareció a Bruto una visión de una persona horrenda y fiera, y preguntándole quién era, y qué le quería, le respondió: *Tuus sum, o Brute, malus genius, me videbis postea in Philippis;* y con esto se desapareció. Llamando luego Bruto a sus criados que estavan en su antecámara, les preguntó si avían visto entrar o salir a persona alguna de su aposento, o si avían oydo algunas vozes; respondieron que no avían visto ni oydo nada. Otros dixeron que genio no era otra cosa que la symetría y conmensuración de los elementos, la qual conserva los cuerpos humanos y los de toda cosa viviente. Otros una virtud e influencia de los planetas que nos inclinan a hazer esto o aquello; y no sólo constituyan genios a los hombres pero también a las plantas y a los edificios, y como dixo Marcial, a los libros: *Victurus genium debet habere liber.* Según verdad, todo hombre en naciendo tiene un ángel bueno en su guarda, y según opinión de algunos, para exercicio, un malo que nos pretenda divertir; uno ni otro no pueden forçarnos, y en nuestra mano está el asentir o no asentir a lo que nos representaren en la fantasía. Y esto baste para quien no ha de seguir de propósito esta materia." [Sebastián de Covarruvias Orozco, *Tesoro de la Lengua Castellana o Española* (Madrid, 1611; Facsimile edition published by Ediciones Turner, S. A., Madrid, n. d.), p. 636.]

I, 70:   "monte" has two meanings: (A) 1) "una parte de tierra notablemente encumbrada sobre las demás," and 2) "la tierra cubierta de árboles que llaman monte alto, ú de malezas, que llaman monte bajo."

I, 81–84: i. e., . . . criticizing how much rational man denigrates his noble nature when he dedicates himself to the business of beasts . . .

I, 91–96: The problems of cause and effect are indeed of major importance in Scholastic philosophy. For example, in the principle textbook read in Catholic (and some Protestant) universities through the seventeenth century, the *Disputaciones metafísicas* of the Jesuit Francisco Suárez, 16 of 54 *disputaciones* are devoted to the issue, and the entire concept of God as First Cause is central to the whole structure. See Francisco Suárez, *Disputaciones metafísicas* (Madrid: Editorial Gredos, 1960), I, 9–16, II–IV; and José Luis Abellán, *Historia crítica del pensamiento español* (Madrid: Espasa-Calpe, 1979), pp. 628–629.

With this statement, Calderón points us to the primary issue of the play, the exploration of the causes and effects of dualism in man, the microcosm, and the universe – the macrocosm whose tensions he reflects.

Calderón had treated the issue lightheartedly years earlier, in the *comedia De una causa, dos efectos*, in which twin brothers as different as Prometeo and Epimeteo (one a scholar, the other an indolent rake) react in opposite ways to the influence of love.

I, 105 ff.: Calderón drew the idea of Prometeo's voyage in search of knowledge from Pérez de Moya. That author, after relating the basic Prometeo-Pandora story, adds:

"El sentido Historico, y Alegorico desta fabula. Es que Iapeto tenia a Prometeo y a otros dos hijos, y aunque Prometeo era el mayor, y abia de succeder en el mayorazgo de su padre, creciole desseo de saber, y para esto mejor alcançar fuesse a la provincia de Asiria, y despues de auer oydo la doctrina de los sabios Caldeos, fuesse al mõte Caucaso, en donde entendio el moui-miento de las estrellas, y sus naturalezas, y otras cosas de Philosofia natural, y despues de mucho tiempo boluiose a los Asirios, los quales aun no tenian orden de vida politica, mas medio saluage, a los quales trajo con leyes y costumbres a conuersacion ciuil. Por lo qual parece que de nueuo hizo a estos hombres, no siendo ellos antes hombres por su grosedad de entendimiento."

Pérez de Moya cites Pliny, book 37 preface, as his source for this addition. It is obviously related to Plato's retelling of the Prometheus myth in *Protagoras* as the origin of civilization based on Prometheus's provision of technical skill and fire, and Zeus's gift of conscience and justice.

For the possible parallel with Don Juan José of Austria, see Introduction, The Political Myth.

I, 112: "en fuçia" – (A) "en confianza". (A) terms it a "voz anticuada".

I, 113–114:   Expresses the same idea as several proverbial expressions.
              See L. Martínez Kleiser, *Refranero general ideológico
              español* (Madrid: Real Academia Española, 1953), 56.749,
              "La primera jornada del saber es querer aprender," and
              4.858, "El que desea aprender, muy cerca está de saber."

I, 115–128:   "Puerta de çienzias" (line 123) refers back to "la lógica
              natural" (115). The meaning is: Having opened the "door
              of the sciences" (knowledge), the natural reason which
              was inherent in his soul without his being aware of it,
              when once illuminated by the clear, pure light of
              teaching, opened to him paths which hitherto he had trod
              as a blind man, tripping, and he was able to proceed
              through their inner recesses ("clausuras") from the
              beginnings of all (sciences) to the mastery of some.
              Calderón extends the architectural imagery suggested by
              "puertas" through his references to the sciences as
              "clausuras".

I, 115 ff: Calderón follows the Thomistic doctrine that the intellect
              is inherent in man as a passive power (one of the three
              powers of the soul), by which he can acquire knowledge
              "internally" through speculation, or "externally",
              through instruction. States Aquinas: "The human under-
              standing, lowest among intellects and remotest from the
              perfection of God's mind, is in a state of potentiality in
              relation to what it can understand, and is initially *like a
              blank page on which nothing is written*, as Aristotle
              writes. Which is obvious from the fact that initially we
              are solely *able* to understand and afterwards we come
              actually to understand." Thomas Aquinas, *Summa Theo-
              logica*, Part Ia, Question 79, 2, XI, *Man*, trans. and ed.
              Timothy Suttor, (New York: McGraw-Hill Book Com-
              pany, 1970), p. 151. "Knowledge, however, is acquired in
              a man both from an internal cause (as is clear in the case of
              one who acquires knowledge through his own research)
              and from an external cause (as is evident in the case of one
              who is instructed). For there is in everyone a kind of
              cause of knowledge, namely the illumination of the active
              intellect, through which certain universal principles
              of all the branches of knowledge are known naturally
              and immediately. When, however, anyone applies these

universal principles to the particular cases, the memory
and experience of which he gets through the senses, then
he acquires knowledge by his own research of things of
which he was ignorant, thus proceeding from the known
to the unknown . . . The teacher directly causes neither
the illumination which makes things intelligible in the
learner, nor the intelligible impressions. But he moves the
learner by his teaching so that the latter forms intelligible
concepts by the power of his own mind, when the signs
of these concepts are put before him from outside."
Aquinas, Part Ia, Ques. 117, 2, XV, *The World Order*,
trans. and ed. M. J. Charlesworth (New York: Mc-
Graw-Hill Book Company, 1970), pp. 132, 134.

I, 129 :   The Chaldeans were the first "modern" astronomers in
the sense of being the first who observed the heavens for
the purpose of learning, rather than as astrologers, to
make predictions. They were a Mesopotamian tribe,
originally separate from, later fused with the Babylo-
nians. When the fusion took place, the term "Chaldean"
shifted from meaning the tribe to designating a member
of the priest-astronomer profession in the Babylonian
empire. See Willy Ley, *Watchers of the Skies: An
Informal History of Astronomy from Babylon to the
Space Age* (New York: The Viking Press, 1966), pp. 8–9.

I, 135 ff: The sense of the passage is: I didn't rest until I
understood how, following the ever rapid movement of
the sun, the stars change their aspect in an instant, and
therefore, despite being born together, not only inclinations, but also good fortune and misfortune are diffe-
rentiated between first and second influences.
In disputing astrologers' claims of the determining effect
of the stars on men's lives, St. Augustine and other
opponents of astrology posed the problem of twins, who
can differ in temperament and even in sex. The answer
given was that due to the lapse of time between their
births, twins were born under the same planet but under
different constellations, because of the rapid revolutions
of the heavens. See Thorndike, *History of Magic and
Experimental Science*, I, pp. 514–516.

I, 137:   "rapto": (A) defines "movimiento rapto" as "aquel con que el Sol, la Luna, y los demás Astros se mueven de Levante á Poniente, con el qual dan todos ellos cada dia una vuelta al Cielo. Llamase tambien Movimiento diurno."

I, 141:   "influencia" – (A) "Significa . . . la virtud y calidad de los Astros y cuerpos celestes, con que ocasionan varios efectos en los cuerpos sublunares, por medio de su luz y su calór."

I, 179–181:   i. e., offended by seeing how the crowd refuses obedience.

I, 183–185:   Prometeo's self-imposed exile after rejection of his political leadership has no basis in mythological tradition; it is Calderón's addition to the story.
Don Juan José was several times exiled from Madrid either by decree or by assignment to posts which removed him from the center of power. In August of 1668, he was exiled to Consuegra and forbidden to come within 20 leagues of Madrid, from whence he fled to Aragón and then to Cataluña, where he enjoyed great respect and support dating from his governorship of the region in the 1650's. After a fleeting reconciliation with Carlos II in November of 1675, don Juan was ordered to leave for Italy, and did leave the city, saying he wished to avoid a confrontation. See Henry Kamen, *La España de Carlos II* (Barcelona: Editorial Crítica, 1981), pp. 526–7, 535–6.

I, 189–196:   Calderón's conceit is based on an schoolboy's lesson book. A "pauta" is:
(A) "1. Tablilla lisa, en que se fixan en líneas rectas y paralelas, varias cuerdas de vihuela, que sirve para reglar el papel en que escriben los muchachos. 2. Cualquier instrumento, que sirve para governarse en la execución de alguna cosa. 3. En el sentido moral vale cualquier cosa que sirve de régimen, o exemplar, para la rectitud de las acciones."
A "plana" is "la cara o haz de una hoja de papel impresso u escrito"; and "en la Escuela se llama lo que escriben los niños en una cara del pliego, para aprender: y suele ser la

tarea del tiempo que dura la escuela, por mañana, ó
tarde."
The sense of the conceit therefore is, on this tablet of
golden stars, with lines of golden rays, I studied not only
the lessons of the sun and the moon given to me by the
day and the night on that cerulean page, but also (the
lessons) of . . . plants, birds, etc. Calderón employs
similar conceits in other plays, including *La vida es sueño*
(Aguilar edition, Vol. I, p. 372a), *Apolo y Climene*
(Aguilar I, 1876b), and *Eco y Narciso* (Aguilar I, 1965).

I, 200–206: Birds were traditionally viewed as material for divining
future events. Francisco Torreblanca, writing on divining
magic in the early seventeenth century, held that since
birds inhabit the air, they are more open to celestial
influence, and more apt to sense weather changes and
other future happenings than are men. See Thorndike,
History of Magic and Experimental Science, VIII, pp.
482-3.

I, 207 ff: There are related speeches by magicians and learned men
or women in a number of Calderón's plays, particularly
the mythological ones; e.g., *La vida es sueño* (Aguilar I,
372), *El mágico prodigioso* (Aguilar I, 833), *Apolo y
Climene* (Aguilar I, 1878-9), *El mayor encanto amor*
(Aguilar I, 1604-5), *Los tres mayores prodigios* (Aguilar I,
1646), *Eco y Narciso* (Aguilar I, 1965).
In this speech, however, Prometeo shows himself princi-
pally motivated by the laudable quest for understanding,
not by the *soberbia* and desire to control the universe in
inappropriate ways that characterizes most of the other
learned figures.

I, 208–210: In Calderón's mythological plays, deities are distinct
from mortals by virtue of their understanding (as are
angels from men in St. Thomas Aquinas and St. Augustine). When Apolo is expelled from heaven in *Apolo y
Climene*, he says he is: "En trage y persona humano, /
negado a todas las ciencias / que me acreditaron Dios."
(Aguilar I, 1878b).

I, 215 ff: Calderón's assignation of authority to the divinities listed
is largely traditional, except for the separation of Palas

and Minerba, discussed in the Introduction, and the attribution of flowers to Aura, the gentlest breeze, rather than to Flora. (This could be due to the same association of flowers and gentle winds that made Zéfiro the husband of Flora.) Venus is described by her origin, in the sea foam from which she emerged.

I, 230–262: Prometeo describes his relationship with Minerba as a somewhat distorted version of the mystical path of union with God, as described in Spanish mystical literature of the late sixteenth century. He has undertaken a variety of recollection (the removal of oneself from worldly distractions) by withdrawing physically from the world, and meditating first on the wonders of Nature. This leads him to elevate his mind to speculating on the dominion of the gods. Finding himself particularly blessed with Minerba's gifts of wisdom, he dedicates to her an "ynterior culto" rather like the contemplative silent prayer described by Santa Teresa: "Tenía este modo de oración, que como no podía discurrir con el entendimiento procuraba representar a Cristo dentro de mí." (Santa Teresa de Jesús, *Libro de su vida*, Mexico: Editorial Porrúa, 1972, Cap. IX, p. 147). The result is an all-encompassing involuntary vision related to those some mystics describe as part of the *via illuminativa*. He sees it even in the darkness of the "noche siempre obscura" (line 246) – which in this context must surely be considered a multiple reference, at once to the physical darkness of a world never illuminated by the light of fire, or of understanding, and to the dark night of the soul to which San Juan de la Cruz refers in his poem "Noche oscura". His vision is illuminated by a "vibo fuego", which can similarly be associated with the light of understanding which mystics describe experiencing as they feel themselves close to God. He debates over whether it could be caused by madness, as Sta. Teresa and her confessors debated whether her visions were divinely or demoniacally inspired. Rather than following the Christian mystics in persevering to the final stage of the soul's true union with God, in which imaginary visions cease, however, Prometeo tries to dominate his vision by giving it a corporeal existence.

For the significance of this similarity, and these distor-
tions, see Introduction, Myths and Texts.

I, 231–235: i.e., Feeling obligated in seeing how generously Minerba
had bestowed "las ciencias" on him, Prometeo dedicated
his private worship to her, heedless of whether other
deities might be offended.

I, 239: "hacimiento de graçias" – (A) "Es el acto devoto,
rendido, y humilde, con que se reconoce y da gracias a la
Magestad Divina por los beneficios recibidos."

I, 264 ff: i.e., "so that I could better sculpt her, the earth, together
with the water, lent me its docile material, with which,
following the dictates of the air that drew her, from her
vague original [i.e., his vision of her], I copied a
statue . . ."

In some versions of the myth, Prometeo was held to be
the creator of the human race, which he formed out of
clay. He retains this semidivine artistic capacity in
Calderón's telling of the tale.

In the *auto sacramental El pintor de su deshonra*,
Calderón portrays God the creator in a parallel role, as
the "Pintor" who shapes "la Naturaleza Humana":

Pintor: porque hoy en el soberano
             retrato que hacer desea
             mi Amor, quiero que se vea
             de mis Obras el Poder;
             y así, tú, Ciencia, has de ser
             la que me dicte la Idea;
             tú, Inocencia, la Pureza
             a sus costumbres darás;
             y tú, Gracia, añadirás
             perfiles a la Belleza,
             con que a la Naturaleza
             saldrán las colores fieles
             de rosas y de claveles,
             pues me da el tiento la Ciencia,
             los matices la Inocencia
             y la Gracia los pinceles. (Aguilar III, 833a)

In *La fiera, el rayo y la piedra*, Céfiro asks Pigmaleón:

> Sois vos aquel a quien dieron
> la pintura y la escultura
> tanto opinión, que es proverbio
> decir de vos que partís
> con Júpiter el imperio
> así al metal como al lienzo?
> (Aguilar I, 1747a)

In Calderón's theocentric theory of art, God is the supreme Artist, who shaped the beauty of the universe from chaos and portrayed man in his own image. The artist who creates lifelike forms from "nothing" – from the simple elements of Nature – imitates the divine creativity. See Pedro Calderón de la Barca, "Tratado defendiendo la nobleza de la pintura", in Ernst Robert Curtius, "Calderón und die Malerei", *Romanische Forschungen*, 50 (1936), 90–97, and Curtius, "Calderón's Theory of Art and the *Artes Liberales*", in *European Literature and the Latin Middle Ages* (Princeton: Princeton University Press, 1973), pp. 559–572.

I, 280:   "dos tezzes juntas" – here, the union of the white ("la cándida", 283) of the jasmine and the red of the rose.

I, 286:   "literales justas" – literary competitions.

I, 293-4:   "cuajado" – condensed, united, covering. The abundant flowers unite to hide the rough clay.

I, 322:   "retóricamente muda" – In defending painting as a noble profession, Calderón characterized it as the "Art of Arts" which dominates and makes use of the seven traditional Liberal Arts, Grammar, Dialectics, Rhetoric, etc. Of the latter, he says: "La Rethórica, . . . cuyo principal asunto es la persuasión, también la asiste con la energía de las locuciones; pues Retórica muda, no persuaden menos que pintadas sus voces, articulados sus matices, ¿qué mayor eloquencia que la que representa? Pues sabiendo que es un manchado lino de minerales, y licores, hace creer (ó quando no lo crean que lo duden) que se vé presente lo historiado, y real lo fabuloso." In Calderón, *Tratado*, p. 92.

I, 345: "Saturno" – The description of the dominions of the eleven spheres of the universe in the *auto El gran duque de Gandía* says of Saturn:

> A Saturno se encomienda
> de la tierra la labranza,
> que es el séptimo lugar,
> cuyas sienes coronadas
> de espigas le apellidaron
> el gran padre de la humana
> Naturaleza. (Aguilar III, 100a)

The ascription of the *auto* to Calderón is questionable, however. See Valbuena Prat's introduction to the *auto*, Aguilar III, 95.

I, 349: Epimeteo shows a duplicity here, voicing altruistic motives which hide his egocentric desires. Calderón also paints as duplicitous creatures Palas and Discordia, but not Prometeo, although in the earliest versions of the mythical tale, Prometeo does appear as an accomplished trickster, dividing the sacrificial animal into two halves, one for men and the other for the gods, and then tricking Zeus into taking the attractive but useless package of fat and bones.

I, 353–4: Proverbial idea expressed in the *refrán*, "El mucho trato es causa de menosprecio", (Martínez Kleiser 61.406).

I, 363: "a la región media" – translates roughly as the middle atmosphere. In the geocentric conception of the universe, the center was the earth, composed of the two heaviest elements, earth and water. Above it was the region of air, and above that the region of the fourth element, fire. See Otis Greene, *Spain and the Western Tradition* (Madison, Wisconsin: The University of Wisconsin Press, 1968), II, 31-35. The region of air was sometimes conceived of as subdivided into three regions, labeled by the *Diccionario de Autoridades* as "infima, media, y suma".
Calderón has the goddess Ifis descend to the *media región* in *El hijo del sol Faetón* (Aguilar I, 1940a), and speaks of a falcon that soars to the upper edge of the "región suprema", burning its wings on the sphere of fire

in *La selva confusa,* ed. G. T. Northup, *Revue Hispanique*, XXI (1909), 186.
Epimeteo vows to build a temple whose structure, on Doric columns with gilded capitals, will mount so high in the air with its pyramidal spire that the heavens will doubt, when shaken by it, whether it is a hurricane which descends or an edifice that mounts skyward.

I, 366:   "abuja" – or "aguja". The form "abuja" is a widespread vulgarism, which also occurs in literature. See Real Academia Española, *Diccionario histórico de la lengua española* (Madrid: Real Academia Española, 1972). Since "abuja" also appears in BM, I have maintained it, although Calderón did write "aguja" in a number of other works. See Hans Flasche, *Konkordanz zu Calderón* (New York: George Olms Verlag, 1980), I, p. 266. Vera Tassis corrected it to "aguja" in his edition.

I, 374:   "su llamado" – The choice of "tu" or "su" here depends on whom Merlín is addressing. If he is speaking to Prometeo, as were Epimeteo before and Libia after him, it should be "tu", because it was Prometeo's summons which brought them all together. If Merlín is visualized as addressing Epimeteo, then "su" is correct. The expression "lo que él ha votado" in line 372 does not clarify the situation, since both Epimeteo and Prometeo have made a vow to which Merlín could refer.
The Vera Tassis correction from "llamado" to "llamada" is undesirable; "llamado" is listed in *Autoridades* as an antiquated form of "llamamiento"; the first definition of the latter word is, "la convocacion que hacen los Reyes y Principes, de sus vasallos, y los Superiores de sus subditos, mandandolos venir á su presencia, o á otro lugar que los señalan: como sucede quando llaman á Cortes, ó se convocan las Milicias". Changing the word to "llamada" removes the suggestion of a regal summons.

I, 403 ff: Such threatening beasts or monsters in some guise emerge from the wilds in many of Calderón's mythological plays (e.g., *Eco y Narciso, Las fortunas de Andrómeda y Perseo, Los tres mayores prodigios, Celos aun del aire matan,* and others). They are signs of the threat to civilized society perceived by the poet and his audience as posed by the savagery and wildness that exists either just beyond the limits of their society, or more often, hidden within it in the anti-social passions of its individual members. (See Hayden White, "The Forms of Wildness: Archaeology of an Idea", in E. Dudley and M. Novak, *The Wild Man Within* (Pittsburgh: University of Pittsburgh Press, 1972), pp. 3–38, esp. pp. 6–7.

I, 409–410: These lines refer not to the cave but to the monster, painted thus as a fire-breathing beast who "fogs up the sky" and "smokes the wind".

I, 412: "discurren" – The imperative form "discurran" of BMV is perhaps the more logical reading, but it is also possible that Calderón meant this as a descriptive sentence, with the function of a stage direction; I have therefore preserved the manuscript reading.

I, 427–8: The traditional debate between literature and arms is expressed in a number of proverbs. See Martínez Kleiser 36.395–36.398, "Las letras no embotan la lanza", "Las letras del caballero no embotan la lanza, al contrario, la realzan", "Las letras no embotan la lanza; antes la acicalan". Calderón cites it in other plays as well; e.g., *El gran príncipe de Fez* (Aguilar I, 1410b).

I, 456: "afufallas" = "huirlas" (presas y vñas). "Afufar" is a vulgar, comic expression for "huir".

I, 459: "aténgome a la suia" – i.e., to the courtesy of the beast.

I, 464–5: "pues él sólo dice, cuando todos los demás dibulgan . . ." – The sense is: When all the others repeat everywhere, "al monte, . . ." only Prometeo says . . .

I, 487–493: Throughout Calderón's mythological plays, deities sing (with the exception of Discordia – see note below, III, 585, and the exiled Apolo in *Apolo y Climene*), while mortals speak. Since they participate in the celestial harmony of Pythagorean-Platonic theory, they reveal themselves to men in music. Calderón mocks his own practice in a dialogue between two *graciosos* in *El laurel de Apolo:*

> Bata: Los dioses, aun disfrazados
>   dan de quién son señas craras,
>   que no habran como mosotros.
> Rústico: Pues, ¿de qué manera habran?
> Bata: Con tan dulce melodía,
>   tan suave consonancia,
>   que siempre suena su voz
>   como música en el alma:
>   y así, en oyéndole que hace
>   gorgoritas de garganta,
>   cátale dios.
> Rústico: El sabello
>   es bien, porque todos hagan
>   esta distinción: Mas dime
>   ¿todo lo que dicen cantan?
> Bata: Cuando habran entre sí,
>   ¿que sé yo lo que les pasa?
>   (Aguilar I, 2179a)

See Jack Sage, "The Function of Music in the Theatre of Calderón", in Pedro Calderón de la Barca, *Comedias. A Facsimile Edition*, eds. D. W. Cruickshank and J. E. Varey (London: Gregg International Publishers Ltd., 1973), Vol. 19, *Critical Studies of Calderón's Comedias*, ed. J. E. Varey, pp. 209–230.

I, 493:   The Vera Tassis corrections are misleading in this line, transforming it from the meaning of BM and the manuscript that "whatever their [i.e., las Deydades] accent pronounces is harmonious" to "when your [i.e., Minerba's] accent pronounces . . ."

I, 503:   Either the "tu" (BMV) reading or the "su" of the manuscript is possible here. "Su" refers back to "tu vida" – i.e., she is grateful for the studious dedication of his life.

I, 501–509:   i.e., grateful for the studious dedication of his life and for the altar on which his desire burns (the statue he shaped in her honor), she came in search of him, attired in the same dress in which he had imagined her in order to avoid any doubts about her identity.

I, 505–515 :   The symbolic possibilities of Minerba's costume changing are fascinating. That she is attired as Prometeo has
imagined her might suggest that she is in some way a
projection of his image of her. Much more important
however, is her *fiera* disguise. As Margaret Maurin has
pointed out with regard to *La vida es sueño* [in "The
Monster, the Sepulchre and the Dark: Related Patterns of
Imagery in *La vida es sueño*," *Hispanic Review*, XXXV
(1967), 161–178], Calderón often intertwines images of
monsters or wildmen, darkness and tombs to suggest the
death-in-life of a man whose passions dominate his
reason. In this play, however, Calderón has the goddess
of wisdom herself don a beastly disguise to draw
Prometeo into a sunless solitude. (The third element – of
death/tomb references – is not associated with Prometeo,
but rather with Epimeteo, in lines 602–620). The symbolic inference is that not only brutish passions, but also
reason itself can, at will, separate man from his society.

I, 554 :   Although the BMV form of the line, "lo que yo no llegué
a oír" might seem a smoother reading for this one line, it
does not connect logically to the next two lines. The
version of the manuscript is clearly preferable.

I, 573–4 :   Leaving the solid ground to "climb the wind" might
suggest the idea of arrogance or ambition; one of the
metaphorical meanings of "viento" given in *Autoridades*
is "vanidad, y jactancia." See Gwynne Edwards' note in
his edition of *La hija del aire* (London: Tamesis Books,
Ltd., 1970), p. 273.

I, 574 st.d. :   A similar stage effect is employed at the ending of the
second act of *Fortunas de Andrómeda y Perseo*, in which
Perseo ascends on a cloud to receive the gifts with which
Palas provided him to fight Medusa. Whether it was
devised in that case by Calderón himself is somewhat
questionable, since the effect appears only in the sim-
plified version of the standard texts, not the original
reflected in the Harvard *suelta* edition.

I, 606-609 :   Calderón often uses this metaphor of a cave as a
melancholy yawning of the earth. As D. Cruickshank

notes in his edition of Calderón's *En la vida*, pp. 212–213, he probably drew it from Góngora: "De este, pues, formidable de la tierra / bostezo, el melancólico vacío/a Polifemo, horror de aquella sierra,/bárbara choza es, . . ." (Stanza 6, lines 41–44). As Cruickshank states, Calderón also uses it in many other plays: *El purgatorio de San Patricio, La virgen del sagrario, Las cadenas del demonio, Darlo todo y no dar nada, Los dos amantes del cielo. Los hijos de la fortuna, La fiera, el rayo y la piedra, Apolo y Climene, El hijo del sol, La puente de Mantible, El castillo de Lindabridis, Hado y divisa de Leonido y Marfisa, El pastor Fido, La selva confusa, El galán fantasma,* and *El monstruo de los jardines.*

I, 620: Epimeteo's speech contains the full range of imagery discussed by Maurin: monster, dark, and tomb. See Note I, 505–515.

I, 622: Calderón frequently leaves one character with a suspended sentence, cut off and completed by the words of another speaker, or by offstage voices or music, as in this case, rather like a Greek chorus, producing moments of striking dramatic irony. See examples in Cruickshank's note to *En la vida,* p. 210, and in this play, I, 629.

I, 627: The manuscript reading "fiera," clearly preferable to the "tierra" of BMV, is another indication of the "f-s-t" confusion in the transmission of this text. See Manuscript Notes.

I, 630 st.d.: The added description of Palas given by BMV is similar to that given in the deluxe *suelta* edition of *Fortunas de Andrómeda y Perseo,* which has Palas appear in Act I "en trage militar, con espada, plumas, y vengala". The edition of that play in the Vera Tassis *Sexta Parte* describes her differently: "Palas armada con vna asta en la mano, y embrazado vn escudo, en que ha de estar vn espejo . . ." (p. 8).

I, 631–2: According to the humanistic ideas of music which became widespread in the sixteenth century, different modes of music could produce a variety of effects on listeners – joy or sadness, attraction toward love or

toward war. (See Sage, "Function of music," p. 210)
Calderón repeatedly puts this theory to dramatic use,
often having a hero pulled in opposite directions by the
music of love and war. He qualifies the power of music,
however, by stating that it can only be effective if the
listener's spirit is somewhat inclined in the appropriate
direction. See II, 565–574.

I, 641–642 :   The point of reference for these two lines is obscure; one
can easily explain Palas as "born of an unfortunate
ravine," since she appears in this fearful grotto, but the
reference to her as a "lightning bolt from a steely cloud"
is difficult. Aubrun explains it by saying, "La mise en
scène avec son nuage qui porte Minerve et avec son antre
rend compte de cette double image." [Charles Aubrun,
ed., *La estatua de Prometeo* (Paris : Centre de Recherches
de l'Institut d'Etudes Hispaniques, [1965]), p. 16, n. 1.]
However, neither in the manuscript stage directions nor
in BMV has there been any reference to a cloud. Minerva
appeared dressed as a *fiera*, and in that costume would
not have been lowered on a cloud *tramoya*; her heaven-
bound departure with Prometeo is described as follows :
Manuscript – "Suben asidos a vn arbol"; BM – "Desaparecen los dos"; V – "Buelan sobre vn tronco los dos".
Nevertheless, Aubrun might possibly be right, if a scene
has been cut which included cloud *tramoyas*.

I, 644 :   A number of characters are called "monstruo de velleza"
in Calderón's plays : e.g., Semíramis in *La hija del aire*,
Part I, lines 778–784, 2384–2385 [Ed. Gwynne Edwards,
(London : Tamesis Books, 1970)], and Cupido in *Ni amor
se libra de amor* (Aguilar I, 2031a).

I, 645 ff :   Latona was indeed in classical myths named as the
mother of twins by Jupiter – not of Prometheus and
Epimetheus, but of Apolo and Diana. Calderón's version
of the divine genealogy therefore makes Palas and
Minerba full sisters of Apolo.
This division of Palas and Minerba into two separate
personalities is Calderón's addition to the myth. It may
have been suggested by the Vienna opera, *Il Prometeo*.
See Introduction, Sources for *La estatua de Prometeo*.
Although Minerba had already appeared to Prometeo,

Calderón does not have her recount the rivalry of the two goddesses, but leaves the telling to the jealous Palas.

I, 649:   "número" – (A) "muchedumbre indeterminada."

I, 657–658:   The direction in which the "ymfluencias" are acting is not clearly stated. It could be read as meaning that the diverse development of the two goddesses was subject to some higher power(s), as was that of Prometeo and Epimeteo; or as indicating the influence that she and Minerba have on mortals.

I, 669–692:   The general sense of this long sentence is: In order to assist you in great deeds, I guided you towards hunting, the image of war, but seeing you so ungrateful towards the influence that inspires you that you promise altars and dedicate sacrificial victims to a false, lifeless beauty – especially after the sacrilegious pride of that ignorant "wise man" [Prometeo] has said that in honor of Minerba, let all the other deities be offended – at the sound of my voice, drums and trumpets that inspire your courage and ignite your spirit, I wanted to bring you down to this abyss, while she raises her pupil to the heavens, thus opposing my offense to her adulation; [I am] not angry so much because he worships his goddess, as because you are so base as to forget your own deity and celebrate another.

I, 683–4:   See note I, 631–2.

I, 685:   "abatirte" – "abatir" means (A) "derribar, derrocar, echar por tierra algun edificio, arbol ú otra cosa" and, in the reflexive form, "humillarse, envilecerse".
              Calderón's choice of words in lines 685–6 makes dramatically clear the negative force of Palas. While the parallel words of Minerba to Prometeo are the relatively neutral "apartar – solas – esfera" (I, 513–519), for Palas he uses "abatir", which has connotations of humiliation and debasement as well as a physical pulling down, and "abismo", abyss. While Minerba draws Prometeo apart, and then upward, Palas draws Epimeteo apart and down.

I, 694:   "primero templo" – See Note I, 63–64.

I, 709:   For the assignment of this line, see Manuscript Notes.

I, 724–729: Calderón earlier used the same idea of giving one's soul to a statue in *La fiera, el rayo, y la piedra,* in which Pigmaleón says to the statue:

> que al ver cuán perfecta estás,
> que alma te falta, no más,
> te has valido de la mía.
> La elección estimo: no
> duren tus ansias esquivas;
> que a precio de que tú vivas,
> ¿qué importa que muera yo?
> Y pues mi afecto te dio
> el alma, ¡oh estatua bella!,
> que ella no te sirva a ti,
> y a mí me dejes sin ella.
> O para verme y hablarme
> el alma que te di emplea,
> o para que te hable y vea
> vuelve, volviendo a animarme
> el alma que te di a darme;
> mira que es desdén indino,
> si a ti fue y a mí no vino,
> creer que algún tirano dios,
> poniéndose entre los dos,
> nos la ha hurtado en el camino.
> (Aguilar I, 1754a)

I, 731: "conferençia" – A subordinate meaning, listed by (A) as out of use, is "cotejo de una cosa con otra", a more interesting reading than that which results from the arbitrary Vera Tassis "correction". Calderón uses the same phrase, "en igual conferencia", in a similar situation in the *auto ¿Quién hallará mujer fuerte?* (Aguilar III, 662a).

I, 733: "vna y otra" refers to "mi vida y alma", as Aubrun suggests (p. 17, n. 2); i.e., if Epimeteo obeys her, he puts his soul in jeopardy by destroying the statue he loves, and if he disobeys her, he puts his life in danger before the wrath of Palas.

I, 736–7: "vn sagrado çeno" – the wrath of Palas; "vna dominante estrella" – that which determines his love for the statue.

I, 767–770:   Merlín's speech makes a nice parody of Epimeteo's offer
of his life and soul to the statue.

I, 777:   "prolijos" – Standard comic devices in Golden Age
theatre are the mispronunciations and malapropisms of
the *gracioso*, and despite his learned name, Merlín is no
exception. Here Merlín twists the "prodigio" into a
tiresome creature – with some reason, as the cowardly
gracioso certainly found burdensome the menace of a
monster's presence.

I, 788–791:   These lines constitute a possible link between this play
and the Vienna opera *Il Prometeo*. See Introduction,
Sources for *La estatua de Prometeo*.
Ter Horst points out a fascinating relationship between
Merlín's joke and the Lévi-Strauss analysis of myth as
built around the opposition between nature and culture,
the "raw and the cooked". See ter Horst, *Calderón*, pp.
67–68.

I, 794:   "frialdad" – (A) "necedad, dicho, ú despropósito, sin
gracia ni viveza, que deja frio al que lo oye."

I, 795–801:   The image is, of course, that of Apolo driving the chariot
of the sun; i.e., the sun's chariot is already passing behind
the high peaks of that towering summit which its wheels
brush as it surpasses the clouds.

I, 800:   "transmotar" or "trasmontar" – (A) "Passar del otro
lado de los montes ... Dicese particularmente del Sol,
quando en su ocaso se oculta de nuestro Horizonte detras
de los montes."

I, 802–804:   The speculative interest which Libia expresses in the
preceding exchange with Merlín is unusual for a female
counterpart of the *gracioso*. The exchange can be
explained in two ways: (1) that it is essentially a "filler",
allowing time for the chariot-*tramoya* to transport Apolo
through the air to the proper point above the stage; and/
or (2) that it expresses an interest in the role of the sun in
the structure of the universe – an interest immediately
condemned by the supremely anti-intellectual Merlín as
inappropriate stupidity for earthly mortals. Calderón
would of course not espouse, or openly support, the

heliocentric view of the universe condemned as heretical in 1616 and 1630. Yet there was contemporary interest in the new astronomical theories. As Cotarelo points out, Calderón may have studied the Copernican theory at Salamanca [Emilio Cotarelo y Mori, *Ensayo sobre la vida y obras de D. Pedro Calderón de la Barca, Parte Primera,* (Madrid: Tipografía de la Revista de Archivos, Bibliotecas y Museos, 1924), pp. 83] and it was supported as an ingenious and useful, although condemned, doctrine in the three-part astronomical treatise *Esphera en común, celeste y terráquea* published in 1675 by José de Zaragoza, who was awarded the chair of mathematics, at the Jesuit Colegio Imperial de San Isidro in Madrid in 1670. See José María López Piñero, *La introducción de la ciencia moderna en España* (Barcelona: Ediciones Ariel, 1969), pp. 137–144, and Abellán, *La edad de oro,* pp. 390–392.

I, 819–820: Calderón used the same refrain as early as 1622, in *décimas* written for a *certamen poético* that was part of the festivities sponsored by the Villa de Madrid to celebrate the canonization of San Isidro, Santa Teresa, San Ignacio de Loyola and San Francisco Javier:

> Ya el trono de luz regía
> el luminoso farol,
> el fénix del cielo, el Sol,
> ya desde la tumba fría
> en su fuego, buelve a ser
> hoy, lo mismo que era ayer,
> que si en todo es de sentir
> que nace para morir,
> él muere para nacer.

He creates variants of the refrain in *La sibila de Oriente* (Aguilar I, 713a), *Las manos blancas no ofenden* (Aguilar II, 1093b – referring to the phoenix, rather than the sun), and in the *autos A tu prójimo como a ti* (Aguilar III, 1422a – second version) and *El gran duque de Gandía* (Aguilar III, 102a). All cited in E. M. Wilson and Jack Sage, *Poesías líricas en las obras de Calderón* (London: Tamesis Books, Ltd., 1964) pp. 88–89. See also Cotarelo y Mori,

Ensayo sobre la vida y obras de D. Pedro Calderón de la Barca, pp. 103–104.

I, 837: Aubrun notes the variant "arbitrio" in the peseudo-Vera Tassis *Sexta Parte.* It does not occur in M, the source for this *suelta* No. 194 text. See Introduction, Textual Transmission.

I, 860: "transponer" or "trasponer" – One meaning is (A) "ocultar, ó esconder alguna cosa con maña, y presteza." The reading of the manuscript is that Prometeo is to let the sun pass in front, while he, hidden by enveloping clouds, steals a ray. The BMV readings might be read as meaning "let the sun go down", as in another meaning of "transponerse", (A) "Se dice tambien del Sol, ú otros Astros, quando se ocultan á nuestro horizonte."

I, 863: A reference to the doctrine associated with the Pythagorean school, that each planet revolving in its sphere produces a certain note determined by its velocity, and that the combination of the notes of all the planets creates a celestial harmony. See R. P. Winnington-Ingram, "Pythagoras", *The New Grove Dictionary of Music and Musicians,* 1980 edition.

I, 863–874: This complex sentence has troubled many editors (see following note and I, 870–1). The basic structure is: "La armonía de los orbes . . . arrebata mis sentidos . . ." The image is of harmony produced as the sun, with its sweet voice, travels continually along its orbit ("eclíptica"), crossing the path of the Zodiac, whose beautiful planets follow him, emitting their own musical notes. Prometeo says this celestial harmony so enthralls his senses that he is paralyzed by it.

I, 866: "tarea" – (A) "Figuradamente se toma por el afán, cuidado, ó penalidad, que causa un trabajo continuo."

I, 867: "la eclíptica" – (A) "Círculo máximo, que se considera en la esphera celeste, el qual corta obliquamente á el equatór, haciendo con él un angulo de veinte y tres grados y medio, y el Sol anda siempre por ella."

I, 869: "Zodíaco" – (A) "Uno de los Circulos máximos, que consideran los Astrónomos en la Esphéra en forma de

banda, ancha de doce grados, segun los Antiguos, y de
diez y seis, segun los Modernos, y es el camino, y espacio,
en que andan los Planetas con su curso natural, y proprio
de Poniente á Oriente, yá retirandose, y ya acercandose á
la Equinoccial, ó Equadór, que corta obliquamente,
haciendo un angulo de veinte y tres grados y medio, que
es lo que distan los circulos Solsticiales de dicho Equadór.
Se divide en doce partes iguales, que llaman casas,
contando cada una de treinta grados, colocando en ellos
los Signos, cuya Eclíptica le divide á lo largo por la mitad,
quedando los seis, u ocho grados hacia un Polo, y los
otros seis, ú ocho hacia el otro. Tambien le dividen en
quatro partes iguales, dando tres Signos a cada una por la
diferencia de las estaciones del año."

I, 870–1 :   Aubrun notes, "Tous les textes donnent: 'Las claúsulas
             arrebatan'." This is surprising, because the plural form of
             the verb was introduced by Vera Tassis and would not be
             expected in the pseudo-Vera Tassis (*suelta* No. 194) *Sexta
             Parte* which Aubrun says he collated with the Vera Tassis
             text. Both the copy of the *suelta* in the University of
             Texas collection and D. W. Cruickshank's personal copy
             read "arrebata". Aubrun notes and discards Hartzen-
             busch's proposed substitution of "con sus claúsulas
             arroba," and makes the verb singular (as it should be),
             saying, "Notre solution respecte la grammaire et le style
             de l'auteur." (p. 20, n. 8) Yet he adopts without comment
             another change made by Hartzenbusch in the previous
             line, that of substituting "doce" for "de sus." (In so
             doing, he is following only part of the Hartzenbusch
             emendation, for the latter writes the line, "Doce imáge-
             nes de estrellas".) The substitution of "doce" does not
             respect either the author's style or grammar – or his
             meaning: the "imágenes vellas" are not the twelve
             constellations but the seven planets, which follow the
             sun, contributing their own characteristic notes
             ("claúsulas") to the celestial harmony.

I, 910 :   Aubrun deduces correctly that the subject of the verb
             huir was "yo", meaning that Prometeo will flee with the
             ray, rather than an imperative form used by Prometeo
             directing Minerba to take it. What he could not know

was that the puzzling form "huya" of BMV and subsequent editions apparently derived from an error in the
transmission of the text, and that the original reading was
"huyo", as the manuscript reflects.

II, 18: "se parta" – i. e., "let the doubt be resolved", using one
meaning of "partir" given in (A): "resolverse ú deter-
minarse el que estaba suspenso ú dudoso."

II, 30–32: Many proverbs name the servant as "el ladrón de casa."
See Martínez Kleiser 14.220–14.225, 14.227, 14.229–
14230; e. g., 14.230, "Para el ladrón de casa, no hay
puerta cerrada."

II, 44: Epimeteo means "ley" in the sense of "lealtad,
fidelidad".

II, 68: Merlín mispronounces "estatua" several times, all of
which were lost in B and derived editions.

II, 105: The change from "reserbo" to the form "rescato" of
BMV involves a significant change of meaning; "reserbo"
expresses more clearly Epimeteo's egotistical possessive-
ness.

II, 113: "cayrel" – (A) "cerca de cabellera postiza, que imita el
pelo natural para que le supla."

II, 113: "perendengue" – "pendientes".

II, 114: "relámpago" – (A) "la parte del brial que se veía,
trahiendo la basquiña enteramente abierta por delante."

II, 115 "vngarina" – (A) "especie de casaca hueca, llamada assi
per ser á la moda de los Ungaros."

II, 118: "escote" - Play on words between the two meanings of
"escote" - "decolleté" and "one's share of the bill", as
defined by Covarrubias: "Es la cantidad que por rata
cabe a cada uno de los que han comido de compañía,
repartiendo entre todos, por partes iguales, lo que se ha
gastado".

II, 127–129: Related to the proverb, "La noche es amiga de los
ladrones". (Martínez Kleiser, 45.693).
Referring to "hurtos de amor" is not a purely rhetorical
device, however, as Epimeteo does intend a sort of
kidnapping.

II, 130:   See note I, 208–210.

II, 158:   "Exhalaçión que pasa" - i.e., a comet. The explanation
given for comets, handed down from Aristotle, was that
they were fires in the air, produced when, under certain
climatic conditions (particularly dry and windy weather),
vapors rise from the earth to the uppermost, fiery part of
atmosphere, where they catch fire from the sun's influence, and following the daily east-west rotation of the
heavens, appear as comets, lasting until the combustible
material is consumed. See Ley, *Watchers of the Sky*, pp.
136–137, and John Louis Emil Dreyer, *A History of
Astronomy from Thales to Kepler*, 2nd ed. (n.p.: Dover
Publications, Inc., 1953), p. 121.

II, 159:   Technically speaking, stars were considered to have a
fixed position; only planets would have an orbit, from
which they could be detached. See note II, 162.

II, 162:   i.e., in modern terms, its orbit. In the geocentric view of
the universe, the theory of epicycles helped to reconcile
the apparently irregular motion of the planets around the
earth with the idea that celestial bodies could only travel
in perfect circles and in perfectly uniform motion.
According to this theory, planets travelled in a sort of
double orbit, moving along a small orbit, which in turn
revolved around the earth on a large orbit, the deferent,
as is depicted in the following diagram from Ley,
Watchers of the Sky, p. 76.

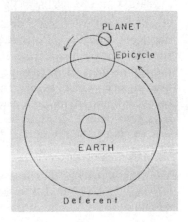

That this was a sophisticated term not in the normal vocabulary is evident from the modification to "epicielo" in BM.

II, 177–178:   Play on words based on two meanings of "claro" – "understandable" and "light".

II, 194:   "abra" – The normal form here would be the indicative "abre" of BM; however, the a-a assonance requires "abra", which can perhaps be justified as expressing uncertainty. See Keniston, *Syntax of Castilian Prose*, (29.532), p. 390. See Note II, 462.

II, 246–247:   Following the traditional *gracioso* fondness of wine, Merlín considers Bacchus the most devout ("devota") deity, since he is the "deidad de vota", the "god of the wineskin".

II, 257–262:   See note I, 724–729.

II, 285–292:   The stage directions present a problem. BM have no indication of when Merlín and Epimeteo leave. The manuscript indicates that Epimeteo exits, presumably after line 292, but not when Merlín leaves. Since the manuscript stage direction after line 285 speaks only of one person exiting after the "duet" between Epimeteo and Prometeo, the Vera Tassis solution, of having Merlín exit at line 285, seems reasonable.

II, 290:   Although it is doubtful that Calderón drew directly from the Aeschylean tragedy (see Introduction, The Prometheus Story), this scene presents an interesting coincidence of imagery. Prometeo and Epimeteo literally summon the populace from sleep to see the new marvel; the Prometheus of Aeschylus says that he awakened the human race, which before receiving his civilizing gifts, had been "like shapes in a dream dragging out their long lives bewildered", (Aeschylus, *Prometheus Bound*, trans. and ed. James Scully and C.J. Herington, (New York: Oxford University Press, 1975), p. 50.)

II, 298–299:   Vera Tassis patches up these lines to compensate for the missing "ansias" and the garbling of "espantos" by adding in the only one of the four elements that is absent from the lines – "el agua". It is an ingenious solution, in accord with a standard technique in Calderón of indicating chaos by the disturbance of the four elements, but it is inaccurate in this context, as there is no sea change presented or even mentioned in the play.

II, 306: "ymán del reflejo" – i.e., they will be attracted to the "magnet" of light, a terrestrial reflection of the sun's light.

II, 307: "la" refers to "la gente" (line 304); Aubrun, in his edition of the play, (p. 29, n. 1) surmised correctly that the meaning requires "adelántome" despite the BMV form "adelanteme".

II, 318–319, 322–324: Although they do not so appear in any other edition, these lines should be read as one sentence, interrupted by Minerba's question:
"The ray which you gave me so that I might bring it to your image (the statue) . . ." and ". . . if in your honor I put it in her hand, to what end do you descend to take it away from her?"
An accomplished actor could play up the lovely dramatic irony of this scene, gesturing back to the grotto where he supposed his statue to be, while the audience knows that he is addressing her "in person".

II, 338–339: "siendo tu más faborecido" – i.e. Prometeo being her favorite. Ter Horst has misread and misquoted this phrase as "tú más favorecida", and has consequently given an incorrect translation of it: "since our worship of you has increased". See ter Horst, *Calderón*, p. 35.

II, 342 ff: See I, 487–493.

II, 353–354: i.e. transcending the ignorance of infancy, to the reasoning of youth.

II, 357–359: i.e., it is cruelty that the most brilliant gift should perish, without my knowing what gave rise to it [i.e., "tu çeño"].

II, 378–379: i.e., not knowing how, so newly born to life [yet] wise.

II, 383: "el Euro, o el Aura" – The east wind or the gentle breeze.

II, 388–389: These two lines encapsulate the traditional justification for the retelling of "fabulous" (i.e., fictitious in the sense of untrue) myths.

II, 392 :   "discurrir" = "andar".

II, 405 :   "si él" – See Manuscript Notes, II, 405, and Introduction, Textual Transmission.

II, 421–422 :   The line assignment in BMV confuses the scene, as it makes Prometeo ask Epimeteo where he has been, and Epimeteo answer that he will tell him later.

II, 434–445 :   The BMV assignation of these lines to Prometeo is plausible; however, the manuscript quite specifically says that the next line is spoken by "Todos, ella y música", the "ella" indicating continuation of the preceding speaker.

II, 436 :   "tres hedades del fuego" – As there are three ages, or stages of man – youth, maturity and old age, so there are of fire – flame, coals, and ashes.

II, 469 :   "le" is a direct object referring to "fuego"; the "la" of BM would have to be read as referring back to "llama", line 463.

II, 470 :   "sañudo" modifies "fuego" and therefore cannot be feminine as in BMV.

II, 475–476 :   Again, the line assignation is much more logical than that of BMV.

II, 498 :   Some text may have been cut at this point. Another line is needed somewhere to complete the *romance* in a-a assonance or begin the e-o section. There are also questions regarding the location of the stage direction and the assignment of line 498. See Manuscript Notes and Introduction, Textual Transmission.

II, 517 :   For the change in line assignment in the manuscript, see Manuscript Notes.

II, 522 :   "la" – feminine indirect object pronoun. See Manuscript Notes, I, 292.

II, 536 :   This delightful exchange, with the goddess Palas showing very human irritation at Discordia's interruptions, is a refinement of a similar exchange between two patently diabolical characters, Culpa and Lucero, in the *auto El pintor de su deshonra*. See Aguilar III, 829b–830a.

II, 542: For the use of "u" (or "v") in place of "o", see Keniston, *Syntax of Castilian Prose*, 42.24, p. 666.

II, 545: The addition in B of a syllable to "villages" led to the alteration in V of "rústicos" to "rudos" in order to maintain the proper syllable count. It also breaks the sequence of three geographical designations, "pueblos, villages, desiertos", changing the center one to a class or caste description.

II, 555–6: Calderón has altered the role of Pandora in the Prometheus story. In Hesiod's *Theogony* and *Works and Days*, she is created by the gods as punishment to Prometheus; in Pérez de Moya (see Appendix), Pandora was indeed created from earth and water, and animated by the stolen fire – but as a man, not a woman.

II, 556: Calderón's unconventional translation of "Pandora" as "la probidençia del tiempo" appears to derive from an unorthodox amalgamation of several etymologies given in Pérez de Moya. The standard two renderings are 1) "all gifts" (as the various gods each bestowed a gift on Pandora), or 2) "the all-giver" (viewing her as in origin an earth-goddess). Padre Vitoria gives an academic definition: "la llamaron Pandora, de Pan, que quiere decir todo, y de esta palabra *Doron*, que significa don, y de los dos nombres juntos, que quieren decir don de todos, ó dotada de todos" (I, 446). Pérez de Moya also gives an orthodox rendering of Pandora as "todas las cosas, o cosa ayuntada de muchas partes" (f. 223r) or "todo don" (f. 224r). He mentions "providence" not in connection with Pandora but Prometeo (who is often identified as "forethought", in contrast to Epimeteo as "afterthought"), saying (224r), "Prometheo se dize de vn nombre Griego, que quiere dezir prouidencia". He also says, "Otros entienden por Prometheo el entendimiento, que prouiene lo por venir, Orpheo entendio por Prometheo el tiempo, porque este es inuentor, y maestro de todas artes". (224r). Calderón has apparently arrived at "la providencia del tiempo" by combining these etymologies for Prometeo and Pandora. It is perhaps a possibility, as Prof. Douglass Parker has suggested to me, that he is also seeing a false etymology, derived through Latin, combining "hora" with "pando" – "to spread out, to throw open, to unfold".

II, 565–572: See note I, 631–2.

II, 579–580: i.e., Let me owe to you, what you will owe me . . . That is, Palas will owe her victory to the dissension ("cizañas") sowed by Discordia, while Discordia will owe to Palas the triumph of seeing the whole world at battle.

II, 587–590: "No prosigas . . . del ruego" – This pompous, awkward sentence really means "Don't crawl", or, equally roughly, "It is beneath one's self-respect that a command should take advantage of the humiliation of pleading".

II, 591–2: "su tosco trage" – i.e., that of the peasants.

II, 596: Calderón is true to classical sources in giving Pandora an urn, rather than the now-proverbial "Pandora's box". Hesiod wrote that the evils were contained in a great urn, and pre-Renaissance accounts and illustrations depict some sort of urn or jar. Erasmus apparently was responsible for the transformation of the urn into a box, as he twice calls it a box in his *Adagiorum chiliades tres.* Because of the wide circulation of his work, his "box" replaced the classical urn in many subsequent accounts. See Panofsky, *Caja de Pandora,* pp. 27–41.

II, 602–609: Discordia was pictured in the sixteenth and seventeenth centuries as an infernal demon associated with the political and religious dissension threatening the stability of the monarchy. See Jonathan Brown and J. H. Elliott, *A Palace for a King: The Buen Retiro and the Court of Philip IV* (New Haven: Yale University Press, 1980), pp. 160–161.

II, 605: "le alteren" – that they (Prometeo and Epimeteo) might stir up the people.

II, 610–611: This line and a half could also have been spoken by Discordia, as in BMV. I have respected the line assignment of the manuscript, as expressing Palas' promise that she, too, will "stir up" the mortals.

II, 628ff.:   The ending of the second and beginning of the third act closely parallels two passages in the *auto El pastor Fido* in which the conspiracy of Luzbel and Culpa threatens the celebration being sung in honor of Naturaleza humana:

Música: Que a la hermosa,
             Deidad de los siglos
             aplauden festivos,
             saludan contentos.
Gracia: El aire con plumas,
             la tierra con flores,
             con vidrios el agua
             y con luces el fuego.
Música: El aire con plumas,
             la tierra con flores,
             con vidrios al agua
             y con luces el fuego.
             (Aguilar III, 1588a–b)

Luzbel: . . . a ejecutarle, Culpa,
             que yo aguardo.
Culpa: Pues yo espero.
Luzbel: Que lo que es ahora encanto..
Culpa: Algún día sea lamento.
Los Dos: Por más que repitan
             voces e instrumentos . . .
Ellos y Mús.: Que a la hermosa beldad de los siglos
             festivos aplauden, saludan contentos,
             con rayos el sol, con estrellas la luna,
             los astros con dones . . .
             (Aguilar III, 1590a)

III, 9:   "Pandorga" – Merlín's mispronunciation is a play on words with the two definitions given by (A), the second specifically linked to his irony – whether by usage prior to his work, or resulting from it we cannot tell: 1) "Junta de variedad de instrumentos, de que resulta consonancia de mucho ruido", and 2) "En estilo festivo y familiar se llama la muger mui gorda, pesada, dexada y floxa en sus acciones. Pudo decirse ironicamente de Pandóra, aquella mugér de las fábulas, en quien fingen que depositaron los Dioses todas las gracias, cada uno la suya". Covarrubias includes only the first meaning.

Merlín continues the "musical" imagery of "Pandorga" in lines 19 and 20, saying that he is protecting others from having to "trobar el sonsonete" – another play on words, since "trovar" means either to write or sing verses, or to misconstrue.

III, 13:   This line contains three extra syllables. In order to regularize it, Vera Tassis added "Pandorga" – arbitrarily changed to "Pandorra" – to the following line, and drastically altered that line to accomodate it.

III, 24ff: This entire comic passage revolves around Merlín's mispronunciations. Much of the humor has been lost in the standard line of transmission; e.g., the twisting of Cáucaso into Cacaoso, essential to the word play of being "sobido de preçio" – on the one hand, elevated or dignified, and on the other, expensive, as was cacao, chocolate then being a stylish, luxurious beverage available only to the rich because of its high price. See José Deleito y Piñuela, *La mujer, la casa y la moda (en la España del Rey Poeta)*, 3rd ed. (Madrid: Espasa-Calpe, S.A., 1966), pp. 124–125.

Merlín's twisting of "loor" into "olor" or "oloor" was rejected by Vera Tassis, and thus was lost the full humor of his saying that he is "a sus patas" – not only a vulgarization of the courtly expression "at your feet", but also a suggestion that those "paws" might be unpleasingly fragrant.

Given this general pattern of mispronunciation, and Merlín's use of "enquiboque" in line 18, I have added the extra "n" as suggested in BM in line 15.

III, 41:   The garland is an appropriate ornament for Prometheus' creation. Fragmentary evidence of the lost Aeschylean drama *Prometheus Unbound* links the festive use of garlands with the chains with which Prometheus had been bound. The Graeco-Egyptian scholar Athenaeus said that "Aeschylus in the *Prometheus Unbound* expressly says that it is in honor of Prometheus that we put the garland about our heads, as a recompense for his chains." (*Deipnosophistae*, Book 15, p. 674. Cited by Scully and Herington in their edition of Aeschylus, *Prometheus Bound*, p. 109). Hyginus wrote: "Several people have said that he (Prometheus) wore a garland in order that he could say that he had been the victor, since he had sinned without being punished for it; and for that reason mankind began the custom of wearing garlands in moments of their greatest joy, and in victories." (in *Astronomy in the Poets* 2.15, cited in Aeschylus, *Prometheus Bound*, p. 108.)

III, 43–44: Vera Tassis arbitrarily switches the adjectives "fragrante" and "brillante" to add a *conceptista* note which, however characteristic it may be of Calderón's style, he surely did not intend here.

III, 48–53: This gift would be a string of pearls, produced by oysters from the dew – "the tears of the dawn". As A. A. Parker notes in his edition of Góngora's *El Polifemo* (p. 147): "It was believed in antiquity that at the appropriate time of the year, the oysters opened their shells and were filled with dew which impregnated them; thus pearls were produced".

III, 51: Vera Tassis shows his strength as an editor here, recovering the word "hilos" garbled in BM as "y los".

III, 55: "hechos grabes" - Neither the "hechos grabes" of the manuscript nor the "ojos graves" of BMV have any clear referrant. Either one could refer to her importance or authority.

III, 77–79: It would be consistent with the pattern previously established in this scene to have "Todos" join Discordia at line 78, but not at line 77, as BMV indicate. The BMV variant "essos" for "en sus" en line 77 makes it possible to consider that line the beginning of a new sentence. However, the manuscript form is a more reasonable reading: "this urn, in which you will see enclosed more than in echo, air, water and earth give, in their offerings, the earth with flowers, the water with pearls, the air with feathers, the echo with salvos". "Salvos" can mean the twittering of birds at dawn as well as the militaristic sense of salvo in English.

III, 138:   "oi" = "hoy", not "oí".

III, 143:   This line also could logically be added to Epimeteo's next
            speech, as it is in BMV.

III, 147:   This sort of courtly debate over points of amorous
            etiquette is a standard feature in Calderonian drama. Such
            scenes are often criticized by opponents of the genre as
            empty rhetoric. They were extremely popular in their
            time, however. Furthermore, in Calderón's thoughtful
            usage, an attentive reader generally will find that they
            subtly illustrate some central point of the theme. In this
            case, the point is the egotism espoused by the passionate
            Epimeteo as opposed to the altruism proclaimed (if not
            perfectly embodied) by the "reasonable" Prometeo.

III, 201:   This second "disfrás" is not, as Aubrun suggests, an
            indication that Discordia is a mask, or secondary aspect,
            of Pandora – who is a neutral, not evil creature – nor even
            of Palas. It is a factual foreshadowing of her second,
            disguised appearance. See lines III, 958 ff. Discordia is
            indeed an element in all human personality, but should
            not be confused with the other characters of the play,
            who also, on one level, represent other elements of that
            personality.

III, 215:   The manuscript "ellas" is correct, since it refers back to
            the "pardas nubes" of line 210.

III, 216:   "culebrinas" – (A) "La pieza de artilleria del primer
            género, que aunque tira menor bala que otras, la arroja á
            gran distancia: y por esso se hace para efeto de ofender de
            lejos al enemigo".

III, 220 ff: This sort of scene, of omnious changes in the physical
            universe reflecting human discord, either occurs or is
            referred to in a large number of Calderón's plays. It not
            only heightens the drama of the chaotic or violent scene,
            but also illustrates the philosophical concept of the
            intimate link between man, the microcosm, and the
            universe as macrocosm.

III, 222:   The BMV "desarrugadas", modifying "sombras", ap-
            pears to be preferable to the manuscript masculine form,

unless "desarrugados" were to be read as modifying "rayos" and "truenos".

III, 226– 230: The manuscript line assignment is a decided improvement over that of BMV, which yield:

BM	Merl	El humo de la Discordia.
	Liu.	A todos ciega.
	Merl	No es bueno,
		que.
	Liu.	Que con ser Griegos todos parece con los mas Griegos á quien del rigor . . .

V	Merl.	El humo de la Discordia á todos ciega
	Libia	No es bueno.
	Me.	Qué? *Li* Que cõ ser Griegos todos parece, que somos Griegos: á quien . . .

III, 228– 229: Play on the word "griego" meaning both "Greek nationality" and "speaking Greek" or gibberish. "Griego" can also mean a swindler or card-shark, but the more probable play here is with the meaning of unintelligibility.

III, 317: Aubrun found the correct reading "por don" in Suriá y Burgada, which is surprising, since that *suelta* in general is based on V.

III, 320: Vera Tassis overlooked the garbling of "aber sabido" into "aborrecido", which makes no sense; Apolo obviously does not despise himself.

III, 323: "hajadas" – An interesting use of "ajar"; in context it means that his authority is "delegated" to Palas, yet it retains the normal meaning of tarnished, crumpled, or otherwise debased.

III, 326– 327: A dramatic image for thunder and lightening.

III, 329: "di la primera alborada" – "Alborada" is preferable to the "alboreada" of BMV, as it adds the suggestions of military attack to that of dawn, and Apolo appears here both in militaristic dress, as he points out in line 335, and a bellicose frame of mind.

By the same token, "di" should be preferred to "de". The latter meaning only sets a time frame – i.e., Apolo is arriving at first light; the use of "di" means that he brought the dawn/first attack.

III, 331:   This line has suffered several alterations, not the least of which was Aubrun's arbitrary substitution of "a Faetonte" for "a Flegon (or Pyrois) y Etonte", which is totally misleading. Apolo gave the reins of his chariot to Faetón only once, with disastrous results, as Calderón's audience would know, being familiar with his play on the subject, *El hijo del sol, Faetón*. Furthermore, Aubrun's change breaks the metric structure of the passage, which is constructed of lines of 4, 8, and 12 syllables.

Flegón (Phlegon) and Etonte (Aethon) are two of the four horses traditionally depicted as pulling the chariot of the sun. Ovid, in the *Metamorphoses* (II, 153–160) listed them as Pyrois, Eous, Aethon and Phlegon. As in this play, in *El hijo del sol* and *Apolo y Climene*, Calderón reduces them to two (the number traditionally ascribed to the chariot of the moon) and gives them the same name: "Los dos, Etonte y Flegón/caballos que le conducen", (*El hijo del sol*, Aguilar I, 1946b) and "cuando de Flegón y Etonte/mi voz las coyundas unce". (*Apolo y Climene*, Aguilar I, 1901a)

Vera Tassis's preference for Pyrois over Flegón is an example of his less commendable editorial practices.

For other treatments of the theme in Spanish literature see Antonio Gallego Morrell, *El mito de Faetón en la literatura española* (Madrid: Consejo Superior de Investigaciones Científicas, 1961), pp. 65–68.

III, 375:   "ofir" – used as a synonym for gold. Ophir was a region famous in the Old Testament for its gold. "It cannot be valued with the gold of Ophir". (Job 28:16) See also I Kings 9:28, 10:11 and 22:48. Ophir has been variously identified with several sites in the Arabian peninsula, Somaliland, Zimbabwe or India. See J. Gray, "Ophir", *Dictionary of the Bible*, Rev. ed. by Frederick C. Grant and H. H. Rowley (New York: Charles Scribner's Sons, 1963).

III, 376:   "Si en" – Vera Tassis recognized that "siendo" was grammatically awkward here, but his alteration to "Si es" did not remove the awkwardness. "Si en" is the correct form, the meaning being, "If in just one little ray of yours . . . I gave the greatest blessing to mortals . . ."

III, 388–
391:   "La lumbre material" versus "la [lumbre] elemental" – Calderón makes a distinction between elementary light (or fire) in the Aristotelian sense of an element as qualitatively indivisible, pure "substance" or principle, and its material embodiment. Although men may possess fire as a material fact, they cannot deny that "pure" fire, the source of light and life, belongs to Apolo.

III, 428–
429:   Proverbial expression: "El sol y el hombre engendran al hombre". Martínez Kleiser 58.648.

III, 435:   This line without the "a" as it exists in the manuscript is one syllable short. I have added the "a" in this position rather than adopting the BMV reading because it seems doubtful that this quite careful scribe would have transposed "acción" and "la" without noticing it, as the switch makes a noticeable change in the rhythm of the line. He might well have dropped the "a", however.

III, 441:   "çiuil" – used here as a synonym for "ruin", as in the third definition given in (A): "En su recto significado vale sociable, urbano, cortés, politico y de prendas proprias de Ciudadáno; pero en este sentido no tiene uso: y solamente se dice del que es desestimable, mezquino, ruin, y de baxa condicion y procederes".

III, 455:   "consigue" – The manuscript form is correct rather than the BMV past tense; Palas is not referring to Discordia's first disguise as a *villana*, but to the second "disguise" which she will assume. See III, 938–940.

III, 474,
479, stage
directions: I have added these only for clarity, in agreement with the manuscript stage direction above. In BMV, Minerba and Palas never left the stage.

III, 477:   Aubrun makes a valiant effort to explain the "no huyas" of BMV as Palas telling herself not to flee Epimeteo. In this case, however, the solution is simpler than his guess.

III, 491– BMV omit this second of Discordia's three treacherous
498:     appearances on earth, significant in explaning Prometeo's
         subsequent complaint that no one will follow him in
         sacrificing to Minerba.

III, 506: "diga" – The first person singular form of BMV might
         seem preferable here; however, the same imperative form
         is also used in Line III, 730, an indication that it was
         probably not a scribal error.

III, 519: "vestirte" – Aubrun says Hartzenbusch was wrong in
         correcting the "le" to "te"; actually, Hartzenbusch was
         right and Aubrun wrong. Although Prometeo is speaking
         to Minerba the goddess, he *believes* he is addressing
         Minerba-Pandora, the statue come-to-life, and "te" is
         therefore the correct pronoun.

III, 526: "viril" – (A) "vidrio mui claro, y transparente, que se
         pone delante de algunas cosas, para reservarlas, ú defen-
         derlas, dexandolas patentes á la vista".

III, 529: "gualda" – golden.

III, 562: "siuil" – a small cave or cellar, especially for cold storage
         of food and beverage.

III, 569– That is, he spoke to the statue thinking that he was
570, 574: speaking to Minerba; the situation is now reversed: he
         speaks to her thinking she is the statue come to life.

III, 633– Lines 637–638 of this passage present an editorial puzzle.
638:     The BMV form seems more logical: i.e., "if the rose is
         queen of any garden, why, in order to put her in doubt,
         do you want the rose in this [garden] to be in the shadow
         of the jasmine?" (see III, 590). It continues the idea of her
         hiding mentioned by Epimeteo in line 630. On the other
         hand, the scribe deliberately corrected "en este" to
         "oneste" (see Manuscript Notes), and his version cannot
         therefore be attributed to a casual oversight. I have
         incorporated the BMV version because, while it is
         possible to make sense of the manuscript lines 637–638
         by themselves – "why do you want this marvel of the
         jasmine to honor the rose", it requires too many mental
         gymnastics to incorporate it logically into the rest of the
         passage.

III, 643–
656:   The general sense of this ornate passage is: Now that I am
       more loving and less foolish, I no longer ask you to
       appreciate, but to scorn my love; see how [desperate] he
       must be whose pleasure is to solicit his pain; but you
       would not be surprised at my cruel anguish, since you see
       it in yourself, despised by a faithless lover.

III, 673: "saludadores" - Alonso Hernández defines these "mira-
       cle workers" as "Un tipo de curandero de la rabia y otros
       males que pretende tener poderes terapéuticos que con-
       sisten en oraciones más o menos estrafalarias y en
       aplicaciones de saliva en las partes enfermas o, echando
       aliento en ellas. Según el folklore literario de la época,
       solían ser borrachos". [José Luis Alonso Hernández,
       Léxico del marginalismo del Siglo de Oro (Salamanca:
       Universidad de Salamanca, 1977)]

III, 703–
704:   Because of the danger of the loss of a ship to storms or
       pirates, important correspondence between Spain and the
       Indies was always sent in at least two copies, in separate
       ships.

III, 721–
724:   The *tramoyas* were not without risk, and actors and
       actresses were sometimes paid the seventeenth-century
       equivalent of a stunt man's fee for being airborne.
       Shergold cites an occurrence in the performance of a
       machine-play by Alarcón, *El Anticristo*, in which, "Val-
       lejo, one of the leading actor-managers of the day, when
       playing the part of Antichrist in Madrid in 1623, found
       that at the last moment he dared not make the ascent on
       the *tramoya*, which would presumably have carried him
       up to a Heaven located at second-floor level. Thereupon
       an actress, Luisa de Robles, with more courage and a
       genius for improvisation, snatched his crown and robe
       and made the ascent in his place, an incident which
       caused much amusement and about which Góngora
       wrote a sonnet." [N. D. Shergold, *A History of the
       Spanish Stage from Medieval Times until the End of the
       Seventeenth Century* (Oxford: Oxford University Press,
       1967), p. 229] The sonnet is:

                  Quedando con tal peso en la cabeça,
                  Bien las tramoias rehusó Vallejo,

Que ser venado i no llegar a viejo
Repugna a leies de naturaleça.

Ningun cieruo de Dios, segun se reça,
Pisó jurisdicciones de vencejo;
Volar, a solo vn angel lo acconsejo,
Que aun de Roble suppone ligereça.

Al zephyro no crea mas ocioso
Toro, si ia no fuesse mas alado,
Que el de el Euangelista glorióso.

"No ai elemento como el emperado",
Dixo; i assi el theatro numeroso
Volar no vió esta vez al buei barbado.

[Luis de Góngora, *Obras poéticas* (New York: The Hispanic Society of America, 1921), III, 18–19.]
The actor's fears were not groundless, for on at least one occasion an actor fell off a *tramoya* during a rehearsal and was killed. See Shergold, *History of the Spanish Stage*, p. 314, n. 1.

III, 730:   The BM line was obviously garbled, since no goddess was in discussion; Vera Tassis succeeded in removing that confusion, but could not divine the correct reading of the manuscript, which, with the "otra vez lo diga", refers back to Minerba-Pandora's previous verbal assault on Epimeteo in line 705–709.

III, 760:   "alitem" – The reach of Merlín's malapropisms extends to Latin, as he confuses the stock legal phrases *item* and *ad litem*. A "curador" is a court-appointed guardian named to supervise the legal affairs of a minor or a person incompetent for other reasons to conduct his own affairs. A "curador ad litem" refers specifically to the guardian of a minor. Merlín's legalistic garble caps a miniature mock trial in which he accuses Minerba/Pandora of being a woman not only of two faces but of two bodies (753–754). She pleads not guilty, saying that it is not her fault that Epimeteo's love has made him imagine things. Merlín then asks why he too saw the double, since he is not in love, but is only involved as Epimeteo's "curador ad litem", watching out for his suits.

III, 798–   Prometeo, realizing when she speaks that he is not now
800:    addressing the goddess, but Minerba-Pandora, curses the
difference in voice (as a mortal, she speaks rather than
singing), which is, after all, nothing but wind.

III, 808–   The "al" of manuscript line 810 makes unnecessary the
812:    Vera Tassis modification to retrieve the sense: Prometeo
tells Minerba-Pandora not to come close because he is
afraid his heart will be infected to the point of self-
destruction by the poison of her voice, which reminds
him of the cause of his suffering.

On the other hand, the Vera Tassis correction of the "te"
to "se" is necessary to the sense of the passage. The "te"
is an error common to B and the manuscript, probably
caused by the proximity of "te" and "temo" (the scribe
having written "teme" without a penlift) in line 808.

The reference to the erasing of his heart is a foreshadow-
ing of the punishment normally associated with Prometeo, the daily devouring of his liver – or in Calderón's
version, his heart (III, 962) – by an eagle.

III, 816–   A number of proverbial expressions deal with this
818:    subject. See Martínez Kleiser, 7.308–7.319 and 38.176,
especially 7.319: "El mal crece y permanece; mas el bien
luego fenece", and 7.310: "El bien viene andando, y el
mal, volando".

III, 865:   i.e., in honor of Minerba, his partisan goddess.

III, 875:   "notaren" – changed to the past indicative "notaron" by
Hartzenbusch, and Aubrun has followed this reading. It
is an arbitrary and unnecessary change, as the future
subjunctive form in BMV and the manuscript is satisfactory in the context: i.e., if they should denounce my
withdrawing from persecution before it is a battle, those
few who call upon me shan't criticize me for turning my
back like a coward, now that it has come to battle.

III, 877:   "de corrido" – persecuted.

III, 886 st.d.:   "Bosque" – see Manuscript Notes.

III, 890:   Either "sigas" or "rigas" (i.e., "rijas") is possible here,
since Timantes is "following" Prometeo's faction, but is,

at this particular point, in Prometeo's absence, "leading" the group opposing Epimeteo.

III, 893 :   Although the BMV variant "lides" seems more obviously logical here, "ruinas" is not impossible. According to (A), "batir en ruinas" means "disparar la artillería contra alguna fortaleza, para arruinarla y echarla a tierra". In this military meaning, "ruinas" fits the context; and since it is not the kind of variant likely to occur accidentally, I have respected the manuscript reading.

III, 909– 912:   From a scientific point of view, this comment on meteors roughly follows Aristotle's explanation: that they are atmospheric ("del aire") or meteorological (hence the name "meteor") phenomena, produced like comets from the ignition by motion in the upper atmosphere of vapors rising from the moisture contained in the earth (as opposed to "exhalations", which rise from the dry earth itself). (See note II, 158) According to Aristotle, the vapors can either catch fire from motion in the upper atmosphere, or under different conditions, the air can be condensed by cold, squeezing out the "hot element", which then appears to fall downward to land or sea. (See Aristotle, *Meteorology*, Book I, 4–5).

De Calderón is describing meteors as a combination of the two phenomena, a fire in the atmosphere whose vapors, for reasons not understood, condense and freeze.

For the thematic importance of this phrase, see Introduction, Myths and Texts.

III, 923 :   The "Los dos" here are Prometeo and Timantes.

III, 944 :   "En la ruda política" – Calderón wrote another version of this song, to be sung in similar circumstances by Culpa in the *auto El pastor fido:*

> En la docta República vuestra
> dos leyes tenéis, y tan justas las dos,
> como que viva el que fuere observante,
> como que muera el que fuere agresor.
> Pues, ¿qué más sacrílego insulto,
> qué más aleve e inicuo traidor,
> que el que llevado de humanos afectos,
> a Dios atrevido, conspira a ser Dios?

¿Y el que después, llevado no menos
de afectos humanos a ilícito amor,
adulterando la Ley adultera
también de esperado Esposo el Honor?
En esta funesta espelunca la Humana
Naturaleza, con torpe pasión,
quebrada la Ley, la Obediencia rompida,
en brazos la dejo de indigno Pastor.
Y así a Júpiter, Dios de los Dioses,
Fiscal de mí misma, pidiéndole voy
justicia, pues es justicia que trueque
el tálamo injusto en justa prisión.
Que aunque no puedo llegar yo a su vista,
bien puede llegar a su oído mi voz,
pues para mí cerradas las puertas,
abiertas quedaron a mi acusación.
Y más cuando son tan dos mis querellas,
que a un tiempo capaces de dos muertes son,
pues temporal y eterna apellidan
de un fuego y otro una y otra oblación.
Sino es que la valga la Ley su epiqueya
y usando la glosa, que tiene en favor,
en victima humana, que muera por ella,
por ella dé al cielo la satisfacción.
Más esto no cabe el día que infausto,
criatura no habrá que ofendido el Criador
dé a entender que la Culpa fue suya
habiendo de ser ajeno el perdón.
Y pues pronunciada en rigor de justicia
está la sentencia y dado el pregón,
temed el rigor del Dios de los Rayos
si no la ponéis en ejecución.
Oh el Mundo, volcán, Mongibelo o Vesubio
de más vivo incendio, de más vivo ardor,
hoguera será que lleve en pavesas
de leves cenizas el aire veloz.
(Aguilar III, 1602b–1603a)

The song apparently gained considerable popularity, as
the opening stanza reappears in parodic forms. A collection of *bailes* (Biblioteca Nacional Ms. 14.856) signed by
Mathias Godos [or perhaps Mateo de Godoy, an actor

and author of the entremes *El Desafío* published in
Ramillete de Sainetes escogidas (Zaragoza, 1672)]
includes the "Baile de la Ruda política", a lovers' quarrel
ending with the marriage of Fila y Pasqual; one stanza is
adapted from the play:

> En la ruda politica nuestra
> dos leies tenemos tan justas las dos
> como que muere el que fuere tirano
> como que pene, el que fuere traydor.
> (folio 76)

The same stanza, sung by Diana, forms part of the "Baile
de Júpiter y Calixto" (probably a late eighteenth century
baile, incorporating parodic bits of various *tonadas* in
another collection of dances) (BN Ms. 15.788). Here the
stanza forms part of a petition to Júpiter:

> En la Ruda Politica Nuestra
> Dos leyes tenemos tan Justas las dos
> Como que espere el que traiga ocho escudos
> Como que ver al que pague mexor.

(Louise Stein kindly furnished me with the information
about the two *bailes*.)

III, 957:   "en" – The use of "en", missing in BMV, is important
here, as it makes clearer that Discordia is representing
herself as Júpiter's duly appointed spokeswoman, that he
is announcing his verdict in her words.

III, 969:   "oblazión" – an offering or sacrifice to God – is the
correct form, not "obligación", as Vera Tassis realized.

III, 976:   As Cruickshank notes in his edition of *En la vida* (p.
206–207), Calderón considered "volcán" to be a specific
volcano, active in contrast to Etna, described as snow-
covered. In *La estatua de Prometeo*, Calderón names four
volcanos as symbols of immense fires. He uses Vesubio
and Mongibelo as the same symbol in *Celos aun del aire
matan* (Aguilar I, 2234–2235a). Etna is also a flame-
thrower in *Afectos de odio y amor* (Aguilar II, 1755b) and
in *Para vencer amor, querer vencerle* (Aguilar II, 548a),
although also snow-covered in the latter.

III, 979– i.e., all the Caucausus will become a huge bonfire that the
980:       swift breeze will carry away in embers ("pavesas") and
           ashes.

III, 986: See note I, 363.

III, 1013– This refrain, repeated at lines 1099–1104, and then
1014:   reversed, line 1156-1157, 1196–99 and 1236–38, appears
           in a number of other plays by Calderón: *Peor está que
           estaba, Apolo y Climene,* and *Mejor está que estaba.* They
           are all cited by Wilson and Sage, *Poesías líricas en las
           obras de Calderón,* pp. 131–132, who give as the probable
           source verses 31–35 of "Sôbolos rios que vão . . ." of
           Camoens:

> Vi aquilo que mais val'
> que então se entende melhor,
> quando mais perdido fôr;
> vi ao bem suceder mal,
> e, ao mal, muito pior.

III, 1084: i.e., Minerba's complaint, and Minerba's accusation
           against Discordia, for posing as Jupiter's ambassadress.

III, 1087: See Note II, 542.

III, 1096: Although the scribe has deliberately altered "del" to
           "el", the "d" is needed for a full eight syllable count.

III, 1110– The jealous character Fineo of *Fortunas de Andrómeda y
1116:   Perseo* makes a similar speech:

> Quien me acusa de tirano,
> de ingrato, fiero y aleve,
> vea sus celos: verá
> que el más atento y prudente
> puede callar con desprecios
> pero con celos no puede.

III: 1139– A reference to the traditional fate of Prometeo, of having
1140:   his liver (here his heart) consumed daily by an eagle,
           which Calderón calls a "boreal fiera", the eagle being
           "una de las veinte y dos Constelaciones celestes, que
           llaman boreales". (A)

III, 1146: speaker – Although the manuscript has only "villana",
           not the plural form, I believe it is more likely that

Calderón intended some sort of choral effect here – probably of the "zagalas" mentioned in line 1095 as accompanying Minerba-Pandora. BMV are no help, since they have the abbreviation *Villan.*, which has been rendered as "villanos" by subsequent editors.

III, 1148–
1149:   A reference to Minerba and Pandora, whose simultaneous presence had confused Epimeteo, and whom Merlín had called a "pliego duplicado" in lines III, 703–704.

III, 1174:   "parte" – in the legalistic sense of "party"; that is, they no longer have Apolo as an opponent.

III, 1183–
1185:   i.e., the smoke-born spells of Discordia will flee the rosy glow of my splendor.

MANUSCRIPT NOTES

Title Page   The title appears in the upper right corner, with a second line, "Xornada primera", immediately below it. Both lines are in the same hand, and the same light brown ink. The handwriting is different from that in the body of the manuscript; very probably it was written by Juan Francisco Sáez de la Tejera. The writing is very similar to that of Tejera on the covering page of the second act of *Afectos de odio y amor* (Biblioteca Nacional Ms. 16.835) and his *Mojiganga de las casas de Madrid.* (BN Ms. 16.700) (See handwriting sample in Figure 8 8) The best clues are the special manner in which Tejera wrote "X", "de", and "r", as they appear in the two lines of the *Prometeo* manuscript title.

Immediately below these two lines, in a different hand and a slightly darker ink, appears the name "Mosquera". This may quite possibly have been written by Mosquera himself; except for the capital "M", it is very similar to his signature on the lists of actors in his company made for the Corpus Christi *auto sacramental* performances in 1684 and 1685, if indeed Mosquera personally signed those lists. Both samples are too small, however, to offer any weighty evidence.

The title page also bears a number of *legajo* numbers, most of them crossed out: "Leg. 4.0" (4.0 crossed out); "No. 47" (47 crossed out); "42" (crossed out) with "Legajo 3.0" written around it (3.0 crossed out); "21911" (crossed out; the 9 may be another number); and finally, upside down on the bottom of the page, the Biblioteca Municipal manuscript number 1–110–12.

ACT I

Title   "s" omitted in "Estatua"; Scribe first wrote "fiesta de Zarzuela", then crossed out "zarzuela" and wrote "Años" above.

Personas   Apolo, Minerba, Palas, Discordia and Libia are followed
          by an "=" sign. "Soldados" were entered in the list and
          then crossed out. Merlín omitted.

Act Title   Omitted on this page, but it appeared on the cover sheet
          of the manuscript.

Line	Manuscript Form
12	"tuve"
31	speakers "1a Vna", "2a otra", and "3a otra" all written with an "s" which was then blotted out.
31	St.d. appears in the right margin with a bracket to indicate that these four partial lines are sung. As the st.d. in BMV indicates, the next line was also sung.
32	"Todos y ellas"
45	Punctuation: "afan, dejando"
46–47	St.d. in right margin: "Salen todos y/todas con arcos/y flechas"
65	A double line precedes "Opuestos" in the left margin. Similar marks are commonly used in 17th century manuscripts (including autograph manuscripts of Calderón) to indicate the beginning of new sentences in long speeches. They occur in a number of sections of the manuscript, but will be noted only where the sentence division they indicate differs from that of other editions.
101–102	Punctuation: "que al del hombre, al bruto, ay/del hombre, al hombre, Si junta"
114–115	Sentence mark. Although BMV do not show a sentence break here, the marking in the left margin indicates that a new sentence begins with "La lógica".
134	"empezado" has been corrected, apparently changing the "m" to "n" by scatching out the second loop. It is possible, however, that the change was in the opposite direction, from "n" to "m".
179	Line in left margin, not like other sentence marks. Various editors have vacillated over whether or not "Pues" should begin a new sentence, and the scribe may have encountered the same problem.
227	Punctuation: "amarte, y palas"
231	"C" of "con" advanced into left margin as if to indicate a sentence break.

237 "Y" advanced into left margin.

237–238 Punctuation: "Ydiscurriendo, en que obsequio/podria yo haçerla, que Supla"

246–247 Punctuation: "dela noche, Siempre obscura/(pues hasta aora no, Viõ, Luz"

251 Sentence mark, contrary to BMV punctuation.

301 "Dã"; unnecessary accent deleted. (The scribe consistently reverses the present-day use of tildes and accents.)

304 Punctuation: "Sagrados Ritos, constuia". In general, the scribe prefers commas to the semicolons frequently used in BM.

305 "ãra"

327, 329 "es" written with tilde over the "e"

347 Punctuation: "venera, pero"

355 Punctuation: "Sol, la"

386 The st.d. "Builtas" was added to the manuscript in the upper right corner of folio 9v, probably by a third hand. It is written in a large, spidery hand (see Figure 8-7), and the lines around it cross over the "L" of "La" in the line below. The same hand almost certainly wrote the illegible, deleted notation on the same page, in the right margin by lines 396 and 397.

403 Speaker: "Sale timantes"

406 Scribe apparently wrote "destruian" and then deleted the "n".

451 Punctuation: "tu, Veras"

462 "del Bulla"; "de la" needed to complete 8-syllable line.

472 St.d. in right margin by "No": "Sale minerba de/fiera y canta"; "Sale" by speaker Minerba on next line.

473 The scribe wrote an echo by "Música" of Minerba's lines: "Musi = No/Las dispares". These two lines were then deleted by slashes through the words, a box around them, and a faint "no" in the left margin. Whether the deletion was made by the scribe while writing or by another hand at another time cannot be discerned from the handwriting of the "no" or the ink color. See Introduction, on transmission of the manuscript.

475–476   St.d. in right margin: "quitaselas pieles/yquedacomo la/
          estatua delagruta"

478   tilde over "u" of "monstruo"

500   St.d. "Rezitatibo" in right margin.

554   Punctuation: "ygnoro, llegue"; see Notes.

572   "aRancando"

574   St.d. in right margin: "Suben asidos a/vn arbol". Two
          lines below, there is a cross potent in the right margin
          written in light black, as if by a pencil. This could be an
          indication by an *autor* that the stage direction was to
          apply at this line, the point in which it appears in BMV.
          There is another mark which appears to have been made
          by the same instrument before the speaker name
          "Prome" on line 575.

579   St.d. in left margin, by line 580: "Sale despaborido"

592   "aRojese"

600   The placing of this st.d. is debatable with regard to the
          text (BMV place the corresponding st.d. after line 609);
          however, the manuscript has a line and a cross potent in
          the left margin indicating that the st.d. is to be placed
          after line 600. The st.d. is written in the left margin,
          extending from line 598–602: "entra y Sale/p̄ otra parte/y
          abrese otra/grutaenel/foro mas horro/rosa q La otra".
          The st.d. is boxed into two separate sections, one dealing
          with Epimeteo's exit and entrance, the other with the
          scene change.

614   Punctuation: "estorbe, aque"

616–617   Two lines written as one line in manuscript, with a "+"
          and an underscore between "altibo" and "bien": "al*tibo*-
          +bien". The second of the two lines seems to be an
          addition, as it breaks the rhyme scheme, although
          heightening the emotional effect of the passage. There are
          two plausible explanations for the occurrence: 1) that the
          second half of the line was added in the margin of an
          earlier manuscript, and our scribe (or perhaps another
          copyist who preceded him in the chain of transmission)
          copied not only the added line, but also the marks made
          to indicate where the added line was to be inserted; or 2)
          that it is a dangling line left from a cut made at this point.
          The whole long line is in the principal scribal hand,
          although necessarily in smaller script to fit it on the page.

622 St.d. in right margin: "dentro delacueba/con cajas y trompetas"

629 St.d. "cajas" appears in right margin by line 630.

630 St.d. appears on line 631: in left margin, "Salecantando palas", and in right margin, "armada".

637 Punctuation: "Semblante, quien"

676 The manuscript seems to suggest a sentence break at the end of line 676 (as do BMV), as the next line begins with a capital "M" set in the left margin, the technique used to indicate a sentence break in long monologues, often reinforced with horizontal marginal lines, although not so reinforced at this point. In fact, the sentence continues until line 692.

684 "enziendan" lacks final "n"; the line runs to the page edge.

700 Punctuation: "es, Rabia, es, yra, es, biolençia"

709 Both the manuscript and BM write this line as if assigned to one speaker: Palas, in the manuscript, and "Todos y Música" in the *Parte* texts. I think it quite possible, however, that Palas sang "Contra Prometeo" and then was joined by "Todos y Música" in "Arma, arma, guerra".

709 St.d.: "Desapareçe" in the left margin, and "-SS-" in the right margin, immediately following "guerra".

710 Punctuation: "Oye espera, no"

735 Punctuation: "obedezco, de"

747 Mark ":–" after "fingir"

747 Speaker: "timan" with a mark like a capital "S" above; apparently just marking an abbreviation of the name.

750 St.d. in right margin: "Salen todos Los/villanos"

813 There is a cross potent in the right margin, probably to cue the *mutación*. St.d. occurs in the right margin by line 814: "Aqui puede aber/mutazion deçielo"

815 St.ds.: in left margin by line 816, "dentro/Canta Apolo"; in right margin, from lines 816–819, "a su tiempo/apareçe El Sol q va/pasando de vna a/otra parte y estaran/minerba y prometeo/Sobre vna nube y al/pasar le quita Vn Rayo".

823 The first letter of "transparente" has been corrected from "p" to "t" by overwriting, and the lower loop crossed off with two marks.

827 Punctuation: "quieres, que"

838 The scribe apparently began writing another word and then corrected it to "Planetas" by overwriting, and altered "las" to "los".

862 St.d. "ynstrumentos" in right margin by line 863.

867 St.d. in right margin by line 868: "Va pasando El/Sol poco apoco".

885–886 Manuscript has "que naçe para morir Ettª" and omits following line.

906 St.d. in right margin by lines 908–909: "al enparejar/El carro le qui/ta vna luz"

910 Punctuation: "Rayo, huio"

ACT II

Covering Page   "Xornada Segunda / La estatua de Prometheo"; apparently written by Tejera.

3 "gruta" written in above crossed-out "estançia". Since BMV also have "estancia", the "gruta" correction was probably a scribal alteration made to match the preceding stage direction.

16 The "e" of "repara" has been written over a smudged out letter.

41-42 Tilde over "a" in both lines.

62 The scribe wrote "tampoco"; however, this should probably not be considered a true variant, but merely a different spelling, as he consistently writes "m" rather than "n" before "f", "b" and "p".

88 Punctuation: "vi, marabilla"

105 Tilde over the "e" of "reserbo".

153 St.d. in right margin by the two sections of line 154: "en lo alto prometeo/con La Luz".

180 St.d. in right margin by line 179: "ocultanse y Sale/prometeo".

184 St.d. in right margin.

192 St.d. in right margin by line 193.

197 St.d. in right margin by line 197, "este", and line 198: "ponele La Luz en/la mano derecha".

220 Punctuation: "mano, que"

229 St.d. in right margin by line 228 and first section of line 229: "al llegar Los asusta/hablando minerba".

238   St.d. in right margin by two sections of line 239: "Sale La estatua/dela gruta".

252–253   Punctuation: "ymfluye, mas quien anda/alli, quien vã, quien es"

263   Tildes over "o" of "yo" in both instances.

267   Punctuation: "anima, y"

285   St.d. in right margin, from line 286 to line 289: "azercan-dose/vno Sealeja/El otro y queda/prometheo y Se/va epimeteo/con estas voçes".

287   Scribe wrote "venid q ay Ett^a",

289   Scribe wrote "que admirar en Ett^a"

291   Scribe wrote "Sacudid El Ett^a"

293   Scribe wrote "dejad dejad Ett^a"

302   Speaker: The manuscript has "Sale" by the speaker "Prometeo"; however, this contradicts the previous st.d., line 285, which indicated that Prometeo remained on stage.

312   Punctuation: "mano, vea"

314   Tilde over "o" of "miro"

320   Punctuation: "ymagen, dioses"

331   The scribe wrote "Vajas", which may be the correct reading, if the scene is taking place in an elevated grotto, as the first st.d. of both Act I and Act II might indicate. More likely, however, it is a miswriting of the "vayas" of BMV, perhaps prompted by the proximity of "bajas" in line 323, which did refer to Minerba's theoretical descent from heaven.

340   Punctuation: "conozca, y otra"

346   Punctuation: "Voz, aun"

356   Scribe wrote "desluçe", but the sentence requires the imperative form "desluzga", as in BMV.

358   Punctuation: "pena, q"

374–375   Line division: "minerba = y es don de minerba/Promete = eso admiras"

375   "De" is written over (or perhaps under) the "=" sign which the scribe uses after the speaker's name.

383   There are strange marks rather like an apostrophe over the "u" of "Euro" and "Aura".

405   The scribe has corrected this line, either from "fiel" (as in BMV) to "Si, él" by changing the "f" to "S", or vice-versa. The crossbar on the "f" is heavily written, which

would seem to indicate correction from "ſ" to "f";
however, there is a comma between the "i" and "e", as if
to indicate a deliberate word separation, which would
make sense only if he meant to correct from "f" to "ſ".
There is also a mark like a comma or accent over the "e".
Either reading is grammatically possible, but "Si él" is
preferable, since the sense of the passage requires a
contrast between what Prometeo and Epimeteo are
offering to the crowd they have convoked. See Note on
Act III, line 72, and Introduction, Textual Transmission.

413   St.d. in left margin by line 414.

446   St.d. in left margin by line 447.

498–500   St.d. and speakers: The st.d. comes after line 499 in the
manuscript. The location has been changed in this text in
order to reflect the scribe's second thoughts with regard
to assigning Discordia's first line. The speaker "discordia" has been crossed out on line 500, and "discor"
entered above, on line 499. In the st.d., "La discordia"
has been crossed out and "Palas" written in above. Some
text may well have been cut here, contributing to the
confusion. See Notes and Introduction, Textual Transmission.

517   This line was originally written "*discor* =alto espiritu, de
ambos", then "discor" and "de ambos" crossed out,
leaving "alto espiritu" assigned to Palas. "discord = de
ambos" was then written in below, in small letters, as if
squeezed between existing lines.

575-576   "Yasi pues tu Sediçion/deydad es, Sembrar enellos"

618   St.d. in left margin by line 619: "dentro musica/y gritos"

610–611   The manuscript begins Palas' speech with "Si llego" of
line 610, and BM with line 611. Beginning her speech at
612, as V does, yields a more logical reading.

636   Act ending note written "fin de 2ª X^{da}

ACT III

Covering   "Terçera Jornada de la estatua/deprometheo"; written in
Page   scribal hand.

13   Punctuation: "veras, deuina"

30   St.d.: "quatro Cornet" in left margin, in a different hand
from that of the scribe. Probably added by Tejera.

31–36   Line 31 written "alfestejo al festejo Etta", omitting the rest of the song, which is given as it occurs in lines 1–6 of this act.

36   St.d. in right margin, by lines 31, 37–38: "Con esta Repetizion/Sale de villana La/discordia y Se mez/cla con Ellos".

40   Punctuation: "trono, tuio, y"

69   St.d. inserted in left margin below speaker "con La musica", by line 71. Added by the same hand as that of line 30 st.d., apparently Tejera.

72   The scribe first wrote "de la fieRa", writing the "R" over an "r", and either reinforcing the "f" by going over it again, or perhaps correcting an indistinguishable letter below. He then drew a box around "fieRa" and added "Sierra" after it. See Introduction, Textual Transmission.

78   The "s" is missing from "perlas". The line runs to the page edge.

160   Punctuation: "La Cuestion, dejo, Laqueja"

168   Punctuation: "desi, esta"

198   St.d. in left margin by line 199.

208   St.d. added in right margin, diagonally between lines 209 and 210 in lighter ink, probably by Tejera.

217   St.d. in right margin by line 218.

219   St.d. in right margin by line 220.

222   Manuscript has "dessarrugados", but the BMV form "desarrugadas" is correct, since it modifies "sombras" in the next line.

268   Punctuation: "Ve, tras"

277   St.d. in left margin, together with speaker, line 278: "alo lejos todos/y musc^a"

299–304   A line has been drawn in the left margin as if to box these lines off for omission, and Tejera has added the following lines, writing vertically in the left margin: "pormas quediga el estruendo/ demusicas y derraios/ derrelampagos ytruenos/ fabor zielos Ett^a". See Introduction, Textual Transmission.

306   In right margin, just above "Vase", Tejera has written in "Xornada", writing an "X" over a "J".

308   In the right margin, just below the line below the stage direction, Tejera has added "3^a X^{da}fabor/zielos ett^e. A photocopy of this folio is included as Figure 8–9.

321   For the first letter of "se", the manuscript has a strange letter, which could be either a "t" or an "s".

326–327 The "s" is missing in "cajas" and "trompas". Both lines run to the page edge.

361 St.d. with speaker, line 362: "Sale minerba/cantado"

435 Manuscript has "acciõ La mas Ruin"; the line is short one syllable in this form.

471 In the left margin, the scribe wrote "Selba"; then a cross potent has been written in, either by the scribe or Tejera. The latter has then added "Selbaflorida", squeezing it in between the cross potent, the beginning of line 471, and the line drawn above the following stage direction.

471 St.d.: the scribe wrote "bosque", which was crossed out, and Tejera wrote in below "Selba florida".

483 St.d. in left margin with speaker: "dentro cajayVnos"

490 St.d. in left margin with speaker: "Reptadiscordiaden"

501 St.d. "Sale Prometeo" with speaker on next line.

503 St.d. in right margin: "encuentra con/minerba"

534 "çenid"

540 Punctuation: "animõ, nunca"

564 St.d. in right margin: "vase ayr y canta/Ella y Se detiene"

572 Punctuation: "hablando, a"

607 St.d. in right margin, above and below lines 608: "escondese y salen/epimeteo y merlin"

628 St.d. in right margin between lines 625 and 630: "estos versos Los/ dira detras dela/ estatua q estara/ puestaensulugar/ y endiçiendo los/ Sepasara alaotra/ parte del teatro"

637–638 Manuscript has "oneste LaRosa/este asombro". The "o" of "oneste" has been written in above a smudged-out letter, which appears to be an "e" – as in BMV, which reads "en este". The ink color the scribe was using lightens between lines 638 and 639, and the "o" is written in the lighter ink. Perhaps he paused in his copying, and on resuming, reread and corrected the next-to-last line he had written. The validity of the correction is questionable; see Notes.

656 Punctuation: "amante, mas"

661 Punctuation: "voz, de"

662 Manuscript has "an desdeñado El"

676 Punctuation: "estatuas, y"

677 Punctuation: "es, que"

678 Punctuation: "Robō, pusola"

679 Punctuation: "voca, Ella"

684 Punctuation: "Ronca, aplica"

687 The "d" of "del" (missing in BMV, which read "el") is written slightly in the left margin, and is followed by a space: "d El"

697 St.d. in right margin by lines 697 to 698: "Salep^r la otra/ p.^{te}minerba/Representando/q aorahaçe/Laestatua"

704 Manuscript has "trai"

705 Speaker: "Minerb" has been written over some other name – possibly "Merlin", and a superscript "a" has been written over the "r", perhaps to clarify the correction.

705 Punctuation: "posible, tirano",

717 St.d. in right margin by "pues como"

732 Punctuation: "vandos, puesto"

736 There is a cross after "aliento" – perhaps to mark the position for a stage direction or other addition that was not then made.

741 Manuscript has "Serbian"

748 Punctuation: "Ver, mas"

750 Punctuation: "Serā. telo"

760 Punctuation: "Curador, alitem, puesto"

773 St.d. in left margin with speaker, "Sale Prometeo"

793 Punctuation: "nubes, Logre"

805 Speaker: Manuscript has "Min" without the usual "=" sign between speaker name and line. It is not in the principal scribal hand, and does not resemble that of Tejera either. Possibly it was added by the same hand as "Builtas" Act I, folio 9v.

811 Manuscript has "teme aCuerda"

813 Punctuation: "otro, es"

816 Punctuation: "admires, es"

841 Manuscript has "Ó nó"

849 Manuscript has "yõ"

866 St.d. in right margin by "viua Epimetheo"

870 The scribe first wrote "embuelto", then crossed out the "em".

886 St.ds.: There is a cross potent in the right margin by "despreçio", with "bosque" squeezed in by Tejera above the line separating the text from the following stage direction.

896   Punctuation: "como, mas"

907   Punctuation: "para, en"

918   St.d. in right margin by lines 918 to 910: "Salen prometeo/y minerba y Se/mezclan con Ellos"

918   Speaker: The manuscript has an overwrite, apparently correcting "Todos" to "Los dos", and then reinforcing the correction by adding p^{teo}yminer" to the left of "Los dos".

923   St.d. in right margin by lines 923-924: "van aembestirSe y baja/Ladiscordia Rapida y/Canta Lo Sigte"

928   "que El vencimiento ett^a".

938   Punctuation: "apalas = Soi"

944   Letter "O" crossed out between "politica" and "buestra"

946   "El" deleted between "como" and "que"

973   Punctuation: "decretos; Los"

985   Punctuation: "tanto, por que"

987   Punctuation: "Cuanto, Por que"

1003 Punctuation: "ausente, pero"

1029 St.d. in right margin between lines 1029 and 1034: "– entransecon Ellos/Yal bolber ala/llamada SaCan/otra mug^r vestida/como laestatua/y cubierto El Rostro/Yatrabiesan El/tablado con Ella"

1030 Punctuation: "disponga, pero"

1042 The "S" of "si" has a peculiar shape, perhaps resulting from another case of S-f confusion. It has an unusual subscript downstroke, as in the S-f corrections, and has been written without a penlift between it and the preceding word, whereas the scribe in other instances does separate an "S" from preceding letters.

1048 St.d. in right margin by "al monte": "al entrarse Sale/minerba y canta"

1052 The scribe has first written "Su" and then corrected it to "tu" – or perhaps vice-versa.

1062 St.d. in right margin by lines 1062, "eso no", and 1063: "baja palas/Rapida"; in left margin by same lines, "Sale Palas/Canta"

1068 St.d. in right margin.

1096 Scribe has first written "del", then crossed it out and written in "el" above it.

1097 Scribe first wrote "gruta", then crossed it out and wrote "risco"above. Epimeteo, in his speech beginning with line 1105, mentions both a "gruta" and a "risco".

1098 St.d. in right margin between lines 1098 and 1103: "Sordinas y Cajas/destempladas y las/Caras cubiertas/ Sacanalos dos/aVna p^{te} mugeres/Ya otra hombres/Y Salen todos Los demas"

1104 St.d. in right margin, immediately below preceding st.d., by lines 1104 and 1105: "mesclasecon Ellos/La discordia y/Sale palas"

1107 Punctuation: "Risco, en que"

1115 Punctuation: "çelos, y"

1127 The scribe wrote and then deleted an "y" between "yo" and "mas".

1142 Punctuation: "Siento; (pues"

1146 Speaker: "Villana"

1153 St.d.: in right margin, "ensol/Apolo baja", and in left margin of line 1154, as speaker, "bajaapolocant°"

1186 The scribe apparently first wrote "Cobradon", then realized his mistake and corrected the word by writing a large "o" over the "on" and adding an "n" above the "a".

1198 "El mal Ett^a"

1217 "di" and the "ca" of "casar" have both been partially obscured by an ink blot.

1228 "Bodas" is an overwrite, correcting an indecipherable word beginning with "a".

1229 The same ink blot has seeped through the page, nearly blotting out the "so" of "dichoso". See Introduction, Textual Transmission.

APPENDIX

Libro. IIII., Capitol. XL. De Prometheo.

Prometheo fue hijo de Iapeto, y de Asia Nimpha (segun Marco Barron). (*Libr. de origine linguae latinae.*) Otros le dã por madre a Themis. Deste Prometheo dize Ouidio, donde comiença. *Quam satis iapetus,* &c, (*li. 1 del Meta.*) Quiere dezir, el hijo de Iapeto, que es Prometheo, tomo tierra y mezclola con agua, y hizo imagen y semejança de los Dioses, que todas las cosas rigen. A esta imagen, o hombre viendola la Deesa Minerua, marauillose de cosa tã hermosa, y tan al natural al hombre, y auiendo placer de la tal figura, dixo a Prometheo, que si alguna cosa menester auia delas del Cielo, para cumplimiento de su obra, que ella se la daria. Prometheo respondio, que no sabia q̃ cosa auia en el Cielo, para que supiesse que es lo que aprouecharle pudiesse. Minerua tomo entonces a Prometheo, y leuantole al Cielo, mostrandole las cosas q̃ enel auia. Y el, viendo que todos los cuerpos celestiales tenian animas de fuego, queriendo del dar anima a su hombre, allego secretamente vn instrumento que lleuaua a las ruedas del carro de Pheuo, y hurto fuego que lleuar a la tierra. Assi lo dize Horacio, donde comiença. *Audax Iapeti genus,* &c. (*Libr. I. Odas.*) Y llegando aquel fuego a los pechos del hombre que auia formado de barro, hizo que viuiesse, y pusole por nombre Pandora. Los Dioses conociendo el hurto de Prometheo, mucho por ello enojados, mandaron a Mercurio que lo pusiesse enel monte Caucaso atado a vna peña y cerca del vn Aguila, o Buytre, que le comiesse las entrañas y coraçon, como dize Vergilio, donde comiença. *Caucaseasq; refert,* &c. (*Egloga.6.*) Y que comiendo nunca se acabasse, nasciendole de noche, lo que le comian de dia, porque siẽpre padeciesse pena. Fingẽ assi mesmo que Hercules mato el Aguila q̃ de cõtino comia el higado a Prometheo. Otro si, por pena deste hurto embiarõ ala tierra los Dioses, enflaquecimientos, tristezas, enfermedades, y mugeres.

Declaracion.

El sentido Historico, y Alegorico desta fabula. Es que Iapeto tenia a Prometheo, y a otros dos hijos, y aunque Prometheo era el mayor, y auia de succeder enel mayorazgo de su padre, creciole desseo de saber, y para

esto mejor alcançar fuesse a la prouincia de Asiria, y despues de auer
oydo la doctrina delos sabios Caldeos, fuesse al mõte Caucaso (*Plinio lib.37, proemio*), en donde entendio el mouimiento de las estrellas, y sus naturalezas, y otras cosas de Philosofia natural, y despues de mucho tiempo boluiose a los Asirios, los quales aun no tenian orden de vida politica, mas medio saluage, a los quales trajo con leyes y costumbres a conuersacion ciuil. Por lo qual parece que de nueuo hizo a estos hombres, no siendo ellos antes hombres por su grosedad de entendimiento. Ya por esto, ya porque segun Lactancio, fue el primero que hizo estatuas de hombre de barro, q̃ por si solas se mouiã, por tãto se le atribuye, como la fabula dize auer hecho el hõbre. Este Prometheo inuẽto engastar el anillo, y traerle enel dedo q̃ dizen del coraçõ. (*Plinio libr. 33.c.1.*)

Marauillarse Minerua dela obra de Prometheo. Es que por Minerua se entiende el hombre sabio, y el sabio es el q̃ se marauilla del hombre que no es entendido, y viue como saluage, siendo de tan buena naturaleza, y capaz de todo biẽ, y viẽdole falto de sabiduria, cubdicia, y dessea, q̃ obra tan buena reciua su perfictiõ, y no este falta, y por esta causa promete Minerua ayuda a Prometheo para su obra. Hazer aqui menciõ de Minerua, mas q̃ de otro de los Dioses, ni Deesas. Es por razõ q̃ Minerua fingẽ ser Deesa dela sabiduria, y por tanto esto pertenecia mas a esta, q̃ a otro. Respõder Prometheo q̃ no sabia q̃ auia en el Cielo. Esto pertenece al hazer la fabula creedera. Que Minerua lleuasse a Prometheo al Cielo. Significa la altura dela cõtẽplaciõ, y como el entẽdimiẽto es lleuado del saber, o especulaciõ alo alto, apartandolo delas cosas bajas mediante lo qual se alcança conocimiento dela verdad, y orden para el gouierno dela vida politica. Por las quales cosas lo que primero era de barro, quiere dezir los ignorantes comẽçaron a ser hombres. Esto es a saber vsar d̃ razõ. Ver Prometheo enel Cielo q̃ los cuerpos celestiales erã animas de fuego. Significa que el hombre leuantado en altura de especulaciõ halla las verdades delas cosas manifiestas. Y porque la claridad es principio de manifestar, y al fuego pertenece la claridad. Por esto dize que todas son animadas de fuego, y resplandecientes. Hurto Prometheo fuego de Pheuo. Por que assi como el Sol denotado por Pheuo, es el mas resplãdeciẽte delos cuerpos celestiales: assi delas especulaciones se han de tomar las que parecieren, mas llegadas a la claridad dela verdad. Dize hurtar, porque como el hurto se haze secreto, y sin que le vean: assi la especulaciõ de cosas altas no se alcançan, ni aprenden estando entre muchedumbre de gente. O dizen que hurto fuego, porque segun Plinio, Prometheo fue el primero que enseño sacar fuego del pedernal, o dela cañaheja. (*Li.7.c.56.*)

Poner este fuego, o sciencia que Prometheo hurto, despues enel pecho del hombre de varro. Es porque el saber se recibe enel anima. La qual esta enel pecho, como alli esta el coraçon, que es comienço dela vida, por esto se dize que le dio vida, porque al saber dezimos vida. Dezir que tomo Prometheo este fuego de la rueda de los carros de Pheuo. Es porque assi como la rueda, o cosa circular, no tiene principio ni fin: assi la sabiduria eternal de Dios, dela qual desciende, y se deriua todo nuestro saber, no tiene principio ni fin. Que los Dioses enojados mandassen a Mercurio atar a Prometheo enel monte Caucaso en vna peña. Mandar esto a Mercurio mas que a otro. Es porque fingen los poetas ser Mercurio mensajero delos Dioses. O porque Mercurio que es el desseo de saber, lleuo a Prometheo (como dize Lactancio) al monte Caucaso, en donde en especulaciõ estuuo mucho tiempo, como si atado estuuiera, consider-ando los secretos de Astrologia, y dela Philosofia Metheorica. Y porque estaua en continuo trabajo desu especulacion, y los vulgares piensan que quãdo vno esta en trabaxo que esta ayrado Dios con el, por esto dezian que los Dioses enojados le pusieron en aquella pena y trabajo. Y cierto es trabajo procurar saber, como se lee enel sagrado volumen. *Qui addit scientiam. addit labore*, &c. [*Ecclesi. cap. I.*] Dezir que le ataron a vna peña. Denota la firmeza y perseuerãcia que Prometheo alli tuuo en sus estudios, en que estuuo tan firme, y quedo como si con cuerdas estuuiera atado. Que el Buytre, o Aguila le este comiendo el coraçõ, sin jamas acauarle de comer. Denota dos cosas. El Aguila que es aue que buela muy alto, y vee mucho. Significa las subtiles y altas consideraciones que con la especulacion, y cuydado, los estudiosos siempre descubren. Por el Buytre que es aue que ama la obscuridad y tinieblas, son entendidas las obscuras dudas, o difficultades que en los estudios delas sciencias se offrecen, que lo vno y lo otro: assi lo que denota el Aguila, como lo que significa el Buytre cuesta fatiga, y mata al estudioso. Y esto es comerle las entrañas. Denota que cõ el mucho estudio, el gusto delo que de nueuo se descubre, haze crecer las fuerças, y animarse siempre para mas trabajar, y mas saber, que es cosa que no se acaua: porque mientras el estudioso viuiere, nunca dexara de ser fatigado con pensamientos de especulacion. Llamar Prometheo Pãdora al hombre que hizo de barro, q̃ en Griego, quiere dezir todas las cosas, o cosa ayuntada de muchas partes. Es porque el hombre sabio tiene en si todas las virtudes jũtas de las cosas del mundo. Enesta fabula de Prometheo, mudaron los poetas el orden. Porque primero estuuo estudiando enel monte Caucaso, y en otras partes, que hiziesse, o instruyese con doctrina al hombre, y esto porque assi pertenecia a la fabula.

Lo que dize que de noche solia crecer a Prometheo tanto el higado,

quanto el Aguila le auia comido de dia. Es declarar que la naturaleza
determino, tiempos alternados para al descanso, y para los cuydados, y
pensamientos del coraçon.

En lo que dize que Hercules mato el Aguila que de continuo comia a
Prometheo el higado, segun sentido Historico. Es que algunas vezes el
rio Nilo de Egypto, al tiempo de los caniculares, quando por los vientos
punientes, y del deshazerse de las nieues suele crecer mucho, rompia las
presas, y anegaua a Egypto, principalmente aquella parte donde señore-
aua Prometheo, y eran tantas las auenidas, que casi todos los hombres se
vehian muchas vezes en peligro de perecer. Por lo qual Prometheo estaua
afligidissimo, y cuydoso, desseando remedio. Y por el presuroso
mouimiento, y furia deste rio, fue llamado Aguila, y porque segun fama.
Hercules con su industria quito el impetu, y reduxo el rio a su corriente,
por esto los Griegos fingieron, que Hercules vuiesse muerto el Aguila
que de contino comia el higado a Prometheo que le tornaua a nacer.

Los enflaquecimientos y tristezas, enfermedades, y mugeres que por el
hurto de Prometheo los Dioses embiaron al mundo. Denotan que estos
trabajos vnos son causados de la vida especulatiua, y otros son contrarios
a ella, y la impiden.

El enflaquecimiento se causa del especular, segun dixo Aristoteles,
porque del mucho especular se enjuga y seca el cuerpo del animalia,
corrompiendosse algo dentro. Por las tristezas se entienden las afictio-
nes, y congojas corporales que del pecado original contraemos.

Las enfermedades y fiebres se ponen assi como impedimentos, porque
estas cosas quitan la fuerça dela cabeça, y enflaquecen los instrumentos
de la especulacion.

Las mugeres. Otrosi, son estoruo a la especulacion, porq̃ como en
muchas otras obras buenas la conuersacion de las hẽbras empide al varõ,
muy mayormẽte se haze cerca dela especulacion, porque el estudio
requiere leuantamiento del entendimiento y apartamiento dela carne, y la
conuersacion delas mugeres torna al ingenio todo carnal, y le embuelue
en las hezes solas dela tierra. O dize que fueron dadas mugeres, por la
natural necessidad, porque el hombre no puede perseuerar mucho
tiempo sin generacion. La qual no se haze sin muger, como no la vuiesse
formado Prometheo, mas solo varon llamado Pandora, fue necessario,
que en alguna manera pusiesse la fabula auer mugeres y no fue otra
manera mejor que dezir, que vinieron de la yra delos Dioses, assi como
las fiebres, y eufermedades [sic].

Theophrasto, dize, (*En los comẽtarios.*) que traer Prometheo fuego a los
hombres del Cielo. Es porque fue el primero delos mortales, que dio
noticia delas cosas diuinas, y de la Philosophia, y el primero que alço los

ojos a especular las cosas de los cuerpos celestiales. Prometheo se dize de
vn nombre Griego, que quiere dezir prouidencia, y fue el mayor hijo
delos tres, que con Noe entraron enel arca. El fuego que truxo del Cielo,
con que dio ser a su estatua que auia formado. Es el diuino fuego, o
anima que Dios inspiro enel hombre. Y assi por Prometheo se entiende el
poderoso Dios que crio el mundo, y el hombre de nada. Dezir que forma
a Pandora, que quiere dezir todo don. Es que el anima es vn don general
de todos los dones. Otros entienden por Prometheo el entendimiento,
que prouiene lo por venir, Orpheo entendio por Prometheo el tiempo,
porque este es inuentor, y maestro de todas artes.
Los sabios Griegos quisieron por esta fabula dela formacion del hombre,
declarar el principio de la humana vida. Darle a Prometheo por padre
Iapeto, no es otra cosa sino el mouimiento rapto del Cielo, porq̃ en
Griego a este mouimiento llaman Iapeto. Danle por madre a Themis,
porq̃ por Themis se entienden los effectos, y buenas propiedades de
nuestros animos, q̃ del mouimiento delos Cielos cõ nosotros nacẽ. O
Themis denota la justicia, y equidad de que nacen los buenos consejos, y
la prudencia de administrar y gouernar en las cosas priuadas, y publicas,
y las inuenciones, y artes necessarias a la vida humana.

Libro.VI., Capitulo. II. De Epimetheo.

Epimetheo fue hijo de Iapeto, y de Asia. Este segun Leoncio, fue el
primero que hizo vna estatua de hombre de barro como su hermano
Prometheo, por lo qual, segun Theodoncio, enojado Iupiter lo conuirtio
en mona, y lo desterro a la Isla Pitagusa.

Declaracion.

El entendimiento desta fiction, es. Que porque la mona es animal que
por naturaleza tiene, q̃ lo q̃ vee hazer al hombre lo dessea hazer, y lo
pone por obra. Y porque Epimetheo (que era estatuario) quiso por arte
hazer semejança delo que naturaleza: dize la fabula, que Iupiter lo
conuirtio en mona: porque tomo condicion de mona, en querer remedar
a la naturaleza, como este animal al hombre. En lo q̃ dize q̃ Iupiter
enojado: pertenece a la fabula, porque para auerle de conuertir, y
desterrar algun enojo auia de auer recebido Iupiter. En lo que dize que lo
hecho, despues de ser mona a la Isla de Pitagusa (que algunos dizen
Buxia). Es que en aquellas tierras auia gran copia de monas. O que eran
hombres ingeniosos, que en sus obras imitauan a la naturaleza. Este
Epimetheo dizen que fue Chan hijo de Noe. Quisieron por el significar
el apetito sensual, y porque este apetito le puso en execucion haziendo lo
que se le antojo, dixeron ser mona animal que imita a quanto vee.

TEATRO DEL SIGLO DE ORO
Ediciones críticas

Dirigidas por KURT Y ROSWITHA REICHENBERGER
En colaboración con DON W. CRUICKSHANK/ALBERTO PORQUERAS

1 Pedro Calderón de la Barca: Cada uno para sí. A critical edition with introduction, including a study of the transmission of the text, and notes by José M. Ruano de la Haza. 1982. X, 404 pp.

2 Gabriel Lobo Lasso de la Vega: Tragedia de la destruyción de Constantinopla. Introducción, edición y notas de Alfredo Hermenegildo. 193. X, 134 pp.

3 Pedro Calderón de la Barca: Fieras afemina Amor. A critical edition by Edward M. Wilson. 1984, X, 256 pp.

4 Álvaro Cubillo de Aragón: Auto sacramental de la muerte de Frislán. Introduction, texte et notes de Marie-France Schmidt. 1984. XII, 210 pp.

5 Andrés de Claramonte: Deste agua no beberé. Edición crítica por Alfredo Rodríguez López-Vázquez. 1984. X, 178 pp.

6 Lope de Vega Carpio: La fábula de Perseo o La bella Andrómeda. A critical edition by Michael D. McGaha. 1985. 178 pp.

7 Pedro Calderón de la Barca: La estatua de Prometeo. A critical edition by Margaret Rich Greer. 1986. VIII, 409 pp.

8 Andrés de Claramonte: Púsoseme el sol, salióme la luna. Edición crítica por Alfredo Rodríguez López-Vázquez. 1985. 208 pp.

9 Pedro Calderón de la Barca / Tomás de Torrejón y Velasco: La púrpura de la rosa. Edición del texto de Calderón y de la música de Torrejón, comentados y anotados por Ángeles Cardona, Don Cruickshank y Martin Cunningham. En prensa.

10 Gabriel Lobo Lasso de la Vega: Tragedia de la honra de Dido restaurada. Introducción, edición y notas de Alfredo Hermenegildo. En prensa.

11 Juan de Zabaleta: La honra vive en los muertos. Edición crítica por Ana Elejabeitia. En prensa.

12 Andrés de Claramonte: El Burlador de Sevilla. Edición crítica por Alfredo Rodríguez López-Vázquez. En prensa.

13 Pedro Calderón de la Barca: El laurel de Apolo. Edición crítica por Ángeles Cardona y Francisco Mundi Pedret. En preparación.

14 Pedro Calderón de la Barca: El agua mansa / Guárdate del agua mansa. Edición crítica de las dos versiones del texto por Ignacio Arellano Ayuso. En preparación.

15 Tres églogas sacramentales inéditas. Edición crítica por Ricardo Arias. En prensa.

Bibliografías y catálogos

Collección dirigida por KURT Y ROSWITHA REICHENBERGER
En colaboración con THEO BERCHEM / HENRY W. SULLIVAN

1 José Simón Díaz: El libro español antiguo. Análisis de su estructura. 1983. X, 182 pp.

2 Kurt y Roswitha Reichenberger: Dramaturgia en el Siglo de Oro. Inventario de bibliografías. 1986. ca 210 pp.

3 Valeriano Soave: Il fondo antico spagnolo della Biblioteca Estense di Modena. 1985, X, 296 pp.

4 Margarita Vázquez Estévez: Fondo de la Biblioteca del Museo del Teatro de Barcelona. Respuesta al Anexo A "Comedias sueltas impresas en Valencia según Faxardo" del RIEPI, T.I. En prensa.

5 Kurt y Roswitha Reichenberger: La vida es sueño. Materiales críticos y bibliográficos. 1986. ca. 180 pp.

6 Maria Grazia Profeti: La collezione "Diferentes Autores". En preparación.

Estudios de literatura

Dirigidos por KURT Y ROSWITHA REICHENBERGER
En colaboración con EVANGELINA RODRÍGUEZ / ANTONIO TORDERA.

1 Alberto Navarro González: Calderón de la Barca: de lo trágico a lo grotesco. 1984. VII, 176 pp. PREMIO FASTENRATH 1984 de la Real Academia Española.

2 Wit of the Golden Age. A homage to Terence E. May edited by P. Bacarisse. J. Cummins and I. R. Macdonald. 1986. XIV, 290 pp.

3 Ansgar Hillach, Sebastian Neumeister: Calderón: alegorías y antinomías del Barroco. En preparación.

También en nuestra casa editorial:

PROBLEMATA SEMIOTICA

PROBLEMATA IBEROAMERICANA

EDITION REICHENBERGER
Pfannkuchstraße 4, D-3500 Kassel